Serials to Graphic Novels

UNIVERSITY PRESS OF FLORIDA

Florida A&M University, Tallahassee
Florida Atlantic University, Boca Raton
Florida Gulf Coast University, Ft. Myers
Florida International University, Miami
Florida State University, Tallahassee
New College of Florida, Sarasota
University of Central Florida, Orlando
University of Florida, Gainesville
University of North Florida, Jacksonville
University of South Florida, Tampa
University of West Florida, Pensacola

Serials to Graphic Novels

The Evolution of the Victorian Illustrated Book

∽

Catherine J. Golden

UNIVERSITY PRESS OF FLORIDA

Gainesville Tallahassee Tampa Boca Raton
Pensacola Orlando Miami Jacksonville Ft. Myers Sarasota

First cloth printing, 2017
First paperback printing, 2018

23 22 21 20 19 18   6 5 4 3 2 1

Library of Congress Cataloging-in-Publication Data
Names: Golden, Catherine, author.
Title: Serials to graphic novels : the evolution of the Victorian illustrated
book / Catherine J. Golden.
Description: Gainesville : University Press of Florida, 2017. | Includes
bibliographical references and index.
Identifiers: LCCN 2016035951 | ISBN 9780813062297 (cloth)
ISBN 9780813064987 (pbk.)
Subjects: LCSH: Illustration of books, Victorian—Great Britain—History. |
Serial publications—History. | Caricatures and cartoons—History. |
Graphic novels—History. | Illustration of books—History.
Classification: LCC NC978 .G64 2017 | DDC 741.6/4094109034—dc23
LC record available at https://lccn.loc.gov/2016035951

The University Press of Florida is the scholarly publishing agency for the State University
System of Florida, comprising Florida A&M University, Florida Atlantic University, Florida
Gulf Coast University, Florida International University, Florida State University, New
College of Florida, University of Central Florida, University of Florida, University of North
Florida, University of South Florida, and University of West Florida.

University Press of Florida
15 Northwest 15th Street
Gainesville, FL 32611-2079
http://upress.ufl.edu

For my sons,
Emmet and Jesse,
and foremost my husband, Michael

〜〜

Contents

Illustrations

Abbreviations for Books Commonly Referred to for Parenthetical Citations

Alice's Adventures in Wonderland from *The Annotated Alice*: AA
Alice's Adventures Under Ground: UG
A Christmas Carol: CC
Charles Dickens and His Publishers: CDP
David Copperfield: DC
Dispossession: D
Dombey and Son: DS
Fagin the Jew: FTJ
Jack Sheppard: JS
John Caldigate: JC
The Journal of Beatrix Potter from 1881–1897: JBP
The Martian: M
Official Descriptive and Illustrated Catalogue of the Great Exhibition of 1851:
    ODIC
Oliver Twist: OT
Our Mutual Friend: OMF
Peter Ibbetson: PI
Pickwick and *The Pickwick Papers*: P
Trilby: T
Vanity Fair: VF
Wuthering Heights: WH

Preface and Acknowledgments

On the bookshelves of my home and office sit nineteenth- and early twentieth-century illustrated editions of the complete works of Charles Dickens and William Makepeace Thackeray. Alongside them are illustrated versions of books by Jane Austen, Anthony Trollope, Elizabeth Gaskell, and George Du Maurier and treasured books of my childhood—the complete *Peter Rabbit* series, *Alice's Adventures in Wonderland*, *The Wizard of Oz*, and *Winnie-the-Pooh*. Some volumes came from the library of my mother, who read them aloud to me when I was a child, and others are gifts from my husband, sons, and friends.

Illustrated books sparked my desire to become a Victorianist. During my senior year at Brown University, I enrolled in a course entitled "The History of the Printed Book," which met at the John Carter Brown Library. Each week, my professor, Roger Sherman, showed us the riches of Brown University's Special Collections. I became hooked by the look, smell, and feel of rare books and periodicals with their elaborate bindings, marbleized papers, gilded edges, pictorial capital letters, and full-page engravings. For my senior project at Brown, I created an exhibition on *Oliver Twist* at the John D. Rockefeller, Jr. Library entitled "The Impact of George Cruikshank on the Social Novel of Charles Dickens." I still list this library display on my CV, and, after all these years, I have kept the captions and introduction I wrote for the exhibition.

In graduate school at the University of Michigan, I studied a wide range of literary works. When it came time to choose a dissertation topic, I gravitated to the Victorian illustrated book. I designed a course entitled "The Victorian Illustrated Book: A Marriage of Image and Word" at Skidmore College to offer my students the kind of archival experience that convinced me to become an English professor. I have partnered with Special Collections to design library exhibitions based on the Norman M. Fox Collection, an extensive holding of nineteenth-century illustrated books in the College's Pohndorff Room. Part of the pleasure in taking students to the rare book room lies in its mystique; even graduating English majors are often surprised to learn of the Pohndorff Room's existence and awed by its treasures. Some students who took this course or my Victorian literature classes have followed in my footsteps to become English professors or high school English teachers.

Like Lewis Carroll's Alice, I often ask myself, "What is the use of a book without pictures"? This book aims to answer that very question. It is my hope that *Serials to Graphic Novels* will encourage readers to put aside their Nooks and Kindles, collect rare books and periodicals with their original illustrations, read illustrations as the Victorians once did, and grow "curiouser and curiouser" about graphic novel adaptations of Victorian classics.

Acknowledgments

I am grateful to the many research institutions far and near that opened their collections of hard-to-find and out-of-print materials to facilitate my research. This project led me to London to the British Library Reading Room and the National Art Library at the Victoria and Albert Museum. I conducted much of my research at the Lucy Scribner Library at my home institution. I am indebted to the Fox family who first loaned and then donated the Norman M. Fox Collection to the library's Special Collections. Some of the books in the Fox Collection are like old friends; I know just where *Bentley's Miscellany* (with the complete installments of "Oliver Twist") and a first edition of *The Pickwick Papers* sit on the shelves.

Wendy Anthony, Special Collections Curator, and Jane Kjaer, Public Access Assistant, have made the Fox Collection readily available to me as I researched and wrote this book. They gave me a designated library cart to facilitate my research and arranged for me to use materials from the Pohndorff Room and the Hoge Building when the library was closed for renovations.

I am particularly grateful to Wendy for teaching me how to handle rare books with love and care. I also appreciate the assistance of other Scribner Library staff members, foremost John Cosgrove, humanities librarian; Sandy Brown, interlibrary loan coordinator; Doris Pettit, Circulation Department; and Andy Krzystyniak, interlibrary loan/science librarian. John graciously helped me to locate and access hard-to-find period reviews of nineteenth-century novels. John and Wendy were also invaluable resources for questions large and small as I wrote and copyedited this book.

I am grateful to Skidmore College for granting me a sabbatical leave for the 2014–15 academic year and awarding me a sabbatical enhancement, stipend, and faculty development grants to cover the reproduction rights for the pictures included in this book. I appreciate the expert assistance of David Seiler, Visual Resources and Digitization Director of the Scribner Library, who scanned and photographed books from the Fox Collection. I am greatly indebted to Hunt Conard, Director of Media Services, who kindly assisted me in scanning book illustrations from my personal library in January 2015 and January 2016. I extend my thanks to Jerome McGann of the University of Virginia and the University of Virginia Library for granting me permission to reproduce material for this book.

I have deep appreciation for my longtime publisher, University Press of Florida. This is the third book I have published with UPF. Amy Gorelick, former Acquisitions Editor, showed great enthusiasm for this book and my two previous books, *Posting It: The Victorian Revolution in Letter Writing* (UPF 2009) and *Images of the Woman Reader in Victorian British and American Fiction* (UPF 2003), and she oversaw my advance contract. I am grateful to Dennis Lloyd, former Deputy Director for Sales, Marketing, and Acquisitions, for transitioning me smoothly to my new Acquisitions Editor, Shannon McCarthy. I am thankful for Shannon's guidance as I wrote and revised the manuscript, secured permissions for illustrations, responded to readers' reports, and finalized details for publication. I am grateful to Peter Betjemann, Paul Goldman, and a third anonymous reviewer who read my manuscript and offered helpful suggestions to strengthen this book. I benefited, too, from the talent and guidance of Eleanor Deumens, Assistant Editor and project manager; Beth Detwiler, copy editor; Robyn Taylor, designer; Ali Sundook, Acquisitions Assistant; and Valerie Melina, Editorial Assistant.

I greatly appreciate the insights and support of my Skidmore colleagues. Two distinguish themselves. Linda Simon, professor emeritus of English, is an insightful literary critic who has written biographies on William James, Alice B. Toklas, and Coco Chanel and books on topics ranging from the history of electricity to the circus. Linda encouraged me to pursue this project, read the prospectus for my book, offered very helpful suggestions, and cheered me on as I revised *Serials to Graphic Novels*. Tillman Nechtman, a specialist in British Imperial history at Skidmore, was an invaluable sounding board for my project. During our many conversations, some over lemonade and cookies in Tillman's backyard, we discussed methodological approaches, terminology, and possible titles. I, in turn, learned about his current book project on Britain's Empire at Pitcairn Island in the South Pacific entitled *The Pretender of Pitcairn Island*.

I am grateful for the many excellent students in my courses at Skidmore College on "The Victorian Illustrated Book," "The Nineteenth-Century British Novel," "Jane Austen," "Children's Literature," and "Victorian Literature and Culture." Some stand out. Melissa Rampelli '06 is among the strongest thesis students in my career at Skidmore College; she earned an award for her dissertation on nineteenth-century British and American literature that she completed under my guidance. Teaching high school English after her graduation, Melissa returned to academia and earned a PhD in 2016 in English Literature at St. John's University with a dissertation on hysteria in eighteenth- and nineteenth-century British literature. Melissa has taught summer school at Skidmore for the past several summers, and I have relished our discussions about her research and my own. I am grateful to Melissa for her insights into nineteenth-century literature and culture.

Douglas Pilawa '12 fell in love with rare books when he took my course on "The Victorian Illustrated Book." An excellent reader of images and texts and a strong researcher and writer, Douglas, who began law school at Case Western Reserve University in 2016, has attended the Fox-Adler Lecture series even after his graduation. Through the years, I have benefited from Douglas's insights into the Victorian illustrated book and Jane Austen. Like Douglas, Mae Capozzi '15 is wise beyond her years. In my course on "The Nineteenth-Century British Novel" and in conversations in my office, Mae asked me smart and insightful questions that shaped my thinking and informed, in particular, chapter 4 and the conclusion. Finally, Aimee Hall '19, the top student in my first-year seminar on the history of children's literature, served as my research assistant for the final stages of this book. I am grateful to Aimee for her invaluable assistance in proofing and indexing. Her enthusiasm for Victorian literature and skill in copyediting brought enjoyment to these important tasks as I brought *Serials to Graphic Novels* to completion.

Many dear friends and supporters have enriched my life. I thank Pam Golden (my sister whom I count as my friend), Lollie Abramson, Peri Allen, Elaine Alfert, Jeannie O'Farrell Eddy, Jo-Ellen Unger, Diana Fenton, Robyn Silverman, Barbara Black (my fellow Victorianist at Skidmore), Lisa Morey, Aurora Lamperetta, Kathryn Hefter, Selma Nemer, Maureen Cormier, and the late Norman M. Fox. They listened to me as I conceptualized this book and revised it over a period of several years. They asked me questions about my research, showed great interest in the topic, and cheered me on when I was feeling overwhelmed writing a book on an enormous topic. Some of these individuals gave me invaluable suggestions on how to keep fit, injury-free, and active as I wrote and revised this book. I am particularly grateful to Lisa for her advice on co-pyediting queries and to Elaine for helping me to type a portion of my bibliography. Lollie and Peri encouraged me throughout every stage of the writing and copyediting processes. I deeply miss Norman, who took great interest in this entire project; without him, I would not have had a collection of Victorian illustrated books at my fingertips.

Foremost, I thank my family for their support, encouragement, and belief in this book. I have spent countless hours visiting archives, reading, writing, revising, copyediting, proofreading, and indexing. During the first part of my sabbatical while I was drafting this book, my beloved mother grew ill and passed away, and my book—which I discussed with my Mom during her illness—ironically sustained me. My mother was a wonderful listener and an intelligent thinker; I reflect fondly on the many conversations we had about literature and art over the years, particularly in the months before her passing. I wish my mother, Nancy Posmantur Golden, and my father, Dr. Lawrence H. Golden, were alive to read this book. I am grateful to my big brother, Dr. Grant Golden, and my sister, Pam Golden, who took a keen interest in my work and offered feedback on possible book titles. My sister-in-laws, Deborah Goldman and Judy Marx, my Aunt Esther Posmantur, and my cousins Halli Glina and Caren Golden also regularly asked about my progress and were very supportive of me as I wrote and revised this book.

I am most grateful to my sons, Jesse and Emmet Golden-Marx, avid comic book readers who sparked my interest in the graphic novel. Emmet read a draft of the conclusion and offered excellent feedback. I have both of my sons to thank for an extensive library of graphic novel adaptations of my favorite nine-teenth-century novels by Jane Austen, Charles Dickens, Charlotte and Emily Brontë, and Lewis Carroll. Will Eisner's *Fagin the Jew*, a gift from Emmet and Jesse, has been invaluable to my understanding of how graphic novel adaptation can inform a canonical novel like *Oliver Twist*. I dedicate the concluding chapter of this book on the Victorian graphic classics to my two astronomical sons.

Among all those who helped me to bring this book to fruition, I thank my husband, Michael Marx. When I was immersed in the Victorian era, Michael—my academic partner since our graduate school days at the University of Michigan—recalled me to the twenty-first century. Whether reminding me to stop writing and come eat dinner when the clock struck 8:00 p.m., reading yet an-other draft of a chapter, telling me to take breaks and not to work past midnight, consulting with me while I was copyediting, or offering input on which illustrations to choose, Michael was an invaluable supporter and guide. I love Michael with all my heart. And I dedicate this book to him.

And where would I be without my beloved cats? Writing a book is a solitary venture. No matter what time of the day I chose to write, at least one of our cats was usually curled up on a cat bed close to my computer. My late cat Lee purred by me at the very beginning of this project; his photo on the wall above my writing desk remains a great comfort. Rose has always provided a calming and heartening presence that I cherish as a writer. Jules, like Lee, frequently typed extraneous page breaks and letters into my book manuscript as he pranced across the keyboard and blocked the computer screen, but he often sat on my lap as I wrote. Jules, Rose, and the late Lee are my feline muses.

Introduction

The Arc of the Victorian Illustrated Book

One's self—for other people—is one's expression of one's self;
and one's house, one's furniture, one's garments, the books one reads,
the company one keeps—all these things are expressive.[1]

Henry James, *The Portrait of a Lady*, 1881

The Victorians, as Henry James wrote, expressed themselves through the clothes they wore, the furniture they purchased, the things they collected, the ornaments they placed on their mantels, and the illustrated books they arranged on their drawing room tables. Victorian society was indeed a material culture. The fully furnished drawing room of the High Victorian era was a public space within a private domestic sphere where the middle-class family put values, personal tastes, and their selves on display.[2] "If the drawing room was the center of the middle-class home, the center of the drawing room was the circular table with its display of books" (5), as Lorraine Kooistra reminds us in *Poetry, Pictures, and Popular Publishing*.[3] One need only turn to *North and South* (1855) by Elizabeth Gaskell or *Drawn from Memory* (1957), a recollection of Victorian childhood by Ernest Shepard (famed illustrator of A. A. Milne's *Winnie-the-Pooh* [1926]), to find descriptions of prized books read by the fire or put on view in the Victorian drawing room.[4] The claw-footed circular table with its books positioned like spokes on a wheel might include a nicely bound copy of *Pilgrim's Progress* (1678, 1684); next to the Bible, John Bunyan's classic was the most common book within the library of a middle-class Victorian home. Perhaps next to *Pilgrim's Progress* is a quarto-sized, gilt-edged gift book of poems by Poet Laureate Alfred Lord Tennyson. The gift book, a mark of gentility and taste, was made expressly for table display. The circular table in the Victorian drawing room I have imagined also includes an illustrated volume of the era's most popular novelist, Charles Dickens.

How did Dickens's novels, first published with caricature-style illustrations in serial form—considered a second-rate form of publication—evolve into gold-stamped hardbound editions that found their way into well-appointed middle-class drawing rooms of the High Victorian era? The serial publication of Dickens's *The Posthumous Papers of the Pickwick Club* (1836–37)—a sequence of comic adventures—generated an unprecedented publishing boom and established a formula for publishing new fiction: an installment accompanied by illustrations came out independently in a part issue or as a feature in a monthly or weekly periodical; upon the serial's completion, publishers bound the parts along with the illustrations into a single printed edition. Caricature-style illustration created a lively market for illustrated serials, and, in turn, stimulated production of theatrical adaptations of popular serials like Charles Dickens's *Oliver Twist* (1838) and William Harrison Ainsworth's *Jack Sheppard* (1839).

As the century progressed, the public began to favor naturalism in book illustration. The works of Dickens—a champion of the illustrated book whose works were originally designed with caricature-style illustrations in demand in the 1830s and 1840s—were reillustrated in a representational style by Royal Academy-trained artists for the Household Edition that Chapman and Hall published after the author's death in 1870. The Household Edition (1871–79) came out in weekly numbers, monthly parts, and large-volume editions marketed to a middle-class reader, who could buy the entire set of Dickens's novels to read by the family hearth.[5] Dickens's fiction thus straddles two periods of illustration, which critics often define as "opposing styles" (Jackson 12) and associate with specific illustrators; Thomas Hardy scholar Arlene Jackson calls the caricature school of illustration the "Cruikshank-Phiz era (1830–55)" and names the school of representational realism "the Millais era (1855–70)" (12).

The Victorian illustrated book came into being, flourished, and evolved during the long nineteenth century. *Serials to Graphic Novels* focuses on fluidity in styles of illustration across the arc of the Victorian illustrated book to foreground how illustrative styles are perpetuated and revised and a canon of illustrated books is refashioned for new generations of readers. Schools of illustration, if viewed as discrete segments with abrupt shifts in emphasis, hide or obscure the Victorian illustrated book's evolution and mask the complexities of a given style of illustration. For example, caricature, often linked with broad humor and grotesque exaggeration, is foremost a theatrical style that can stage social commentary and reveal psychological insight. Even as the Victorian illustrated book evolved, the caricature school of illustration popular in the 1830s and 1840s was not a transient first period in the history of the Victorian illustrated book. Well after its heyday, caricature retained its prominence in *Punch*, and publishers reissued books with caricature-style illustration into the late decades of the Victorian era.

In the 1870s, Academy-trained artists for the Household Edition of Dickens refined characters created by the caricaturists for a public that desired naturalism in book illustration, but their illustrations carry the imprint of the caricaturists. At the fin de siècle—which some critics consider a third period of the illustrated book and others call the Victorian illustrated book's decline[6]—book illustration thrived in areas where we again witness a reengagement with the caricature tradition as well as a continuation of the realistic school. The representation of a minority group, such as a persistent racialized assumption of the Jew, resonates and is reimagined in George Du Maurier's *Trilby* (1894), published serially in *Harper's New Monthly Magazine* and in volume form. This stereotype comes again in *Oliver Twist*'s reimagining as a graphic novel, a modern form of material culture that is an heir of the Victorian illustrated book. Across this chronological sweep from the serial to the graphic novel, illustrative styles of caricature and realism are applauded, scorned, refashioned, revaluated, maintained, and revised.

Serials to Graphic Novels provides a record of a genre diverse enough to include serial installments, British and American periodicals, adult and children's literature, and—most recently—graphic novels. Scholarship on the Victorian illustrated book has often taken the form of an essay collection. Richard Maxwell cautions in *The Victorian Illustrated Book*: "It is unlikely that any one person, at present, knows enough to write a comprehensive history of Victorian illustrated books; perhaps for this reason, much of the best work in the field has taken the form of essay collections" (xxvi), and this assumption justifies his use of the format of a collection of essays for his study.[7] Although this book does not claim to be a "comprehensive history," it takes up Maxwell's challenge by providing a single-authored, sustained record of the illustrated book from the vantage point of the genre's evolving aesthetics. Not unlike a biographer, I am examining artistic developments in a genre that spans a Victorian lifetime and finds new expression in our time.

Serials to Graphic Novels is intended for the general reader and the undergraduate and graduate student interested in the evolution of the Victorian illustrated book, a visual form that peaked in Victorian times and finds new expression in present-day graphic novel adaptations of nineteenth-century novels. This book revisits seminal critics and illustrated texts well known to book historians or specialists of the illustrated book. Engagement with such information brings readers entering the field of illustration studies into an understanding of how critics have previously examined the Victorian illustrated book through its separate periods as well as how those invested in the "Sixties," a rich period of the genre's history, have minimized or mocked the contributions of the caricaturists. Simultaneously, in its methodological approach to connect illustrative styles across decades, genres, and national borders, this book aims to offer those well versed in illustration studies a new framework for viewing the arc of a vibrant genre.

Scholarship on the Victorian Illustrated Book, 1895–2016

This study complements broad histories of the illustrated book, such as Franz Weitenkampf's *The Illustrated Book* (1938), David Bland's *A History of Book Illustration* (1958), Jonathan Harthan's *The History of the Illustrated Book: The Western Tradition* (1981), and more recently John Buchanan-Brown's *Early Victorian Illustrated Books: Britain, France and Germany* (2005). These works, tailored to antiquarians and book historians, cover illustrative traditions in numerous countries and foreground design history. Bland, for instance, discusses developments in the East and the West with attention, respectively, to Japanese, Chinese, Islamic, Persian, and Hebrew traditions as well as French, German, Italian, Dutch, Spanish, and English. Buchanan-Brown, in contrast, limits his scope to illustrated books produced in England, France, and Germany between 1820–60. My study centers specifically on Victorian England with attention to related developments in late nineteenth-century America and modern developments in England and the US market.

This book acknowledges pioneering scholarship that privileges the Sixties—principally *English Illustration, 'The Sixties': 1855–70* by Gleeson White (1897), *Illustrators of the Eighteen Sixties* by Forrest Reid (1928), and *Modern Illustration* by Joseph Pennell (1895). For example, in his zeal to praise the work of artists turned illustrators including Ford Madox Brown, George Du Maurier, John Everett Millais, and Dante Gabriel Rossetti, White queries, "is there a single illustration by Cruikshank, 'Phiz,' Thackeray, or even John Leech, which tempts us to linger and return again and again purely for its art?" (18). To White, caricature-style illustration is "broad farce" that is "slipshod" and "ridiculously feeble" (18). White and Reid, who were foremost collectors, gained a new generation of readers when publishers reissued their works, respectively, in 1970 and 1975, and their contributions remain influential.[8] These critics championed the artistic merit of Sixties illustrators because they believed that illustrations in leading periodicals of their day were collectible art. Regrettably, however, these same collectors removed illustrations from the serials "they were designed to accompany, and separating them from the publications they were intended to promote, the collector changed their value along with their meaning" (Meyrick 179). Similarly disapproving in his assessment of the caricaturists, Pennell declares in *Modern Illustration*: "among artists and people of any artistic appreciation, it is generally admitted by this time that the greatest bulk of the works of 'Phiz,' Cruickshank [sic], Doyle, and even many of Leech's designs are simply rubbish" (83).

Privileging the large-scale compositions of William Hogarth over the smaller-scale work of his heirs, David Kunzle carries this line of criticism into the present day in *The History of the Comic Strip, Vol. II: The Nineteenth Century* (1990). Small vignettes "arranged on a single page like an artist's sketch book, and sold in a set" (20) are, to Kunzle, a jumble of "graphic bric-a-brac," a "hodgepodge of inchoate miscellanies and whimsical ephemera" (20). Philip Allingham more kindly calls Phiz's illustrations "quaint caricatures" (176) but similarly undervalues "the small-scale, humorous and melodramatic etchings of Phiz, Cruikshank, Doyle and Leech" (178) in an essay for *Reading Victorian Illustration, 1855–1875* (2012).[9] In "Defining Illustration Studies: Towards a New Academic Discipline" (2012), Paul Goldman also underestimates the caricature school in generalizing that "[g]estures were grandiose, facial expressions generalized, printing was usually light and there was little psychological depth or true interaction with text" (28).

Caricature-style illustration, after a period of scholarly neglect, became the subject of serious critical inquiry post 1970. In 1971, John Harvey published *Victorian Novelists and Their Illustrators*, which establishes *The Pickwick Papers*'s importance and privileges the contributions of George Cruikshank, Hablot Knight Browne (often known by his pseudonym, Phiz), Charles Dickens, and William Makepeace Thackeray. Harvey's incisive final chapter, "Illustration and the Mind's Eye," suggests that some modern novels might have benefited from "the strength, suppleness, and sensitivity of [an illustrator's] hand" (181); it provides the impetus for my conclusion, which explores how today's graphic novelists and artists have revived a canon of great books. The 1970s and 1980s also witnessed Richard Frederick Kaufman's unpublished dissertation entitled "The Relationship Between Text and Illustration in the Novels of Dickens,

Thackeray, Trollope, and Hardy" (NYU 1979). Kaufman focused his study on the connections between the verbal and the visual at a time when the field of "Word and Image" studies was just emerging.

Much scholarship on the illustrated book dating to the 1970s and 1980s centers on Charles Dickens. I include in this list Jane R. Cohen's *Charles Dickens and His Original Illustrators* (1980), Michael Steig's *Dickens and Phiz* (1978), and Robert L. Patten's *Charles Dickens and His Publishers* (1978). Cohen approaches the illustrated book through the eighteen illustrators who span Dickens's literary career. Her introduction, "Dickens and the Rise of the English Illustrated Novel after 1836," and conclusion, "Dickens and the Decline of the English Illustrated Novel After 1870," situate the genre of the Victorian illustrated book within the arc of Dickens's publishing career. Cohen thus recasts the Victorian illustrated book as a Dickensian phenomenon as opposed to a cultural phenomenon. Likewise, Steig illuminates the genre from the vantage point of Dickens and his main illustrator, Browne, and explores how *Pickwick*'s success, in turn, encouraged many authors and publishers to choose the format of monthly, one-shilling installments with two engravings per episode. In *Charles Dickens and His Publishers*, Patten argues that Dickens—who experimented with part issues, periodical installments, and publishing in book form before a serial's conclusion—legitimized and democratized serial publication. N. N. Feltes's *Modes of Production of Victorian Novels*, published in 1986, focuses on Victorian publishing trends. These studies have been influential to my own research on the illustrated book that began with my 1986 unpublished dissertation entitled "The Victorian Illustrated Book: Authors Who Composed with Graphic Images and Words." In examining the arc of the Victorian illustrated book, *Serials to Graphic Novels* analyzes author and illustrator pairs alongside the work of author-illustrators and contextualizes Dickens's contributions within the larger history of the Victorian illustrated book.

Essay collections have appeared foremost in recent examinations of the Victorian illustrated book. These include *Book Illustrated: Text, Image, and Culture 1770–1930* (Golden 2000), *The Victorian Illustrated Book* (Maxwell 2002), and, most recently, *Reading Victorian Illustration, 1855–75* (Goldman and Cooke 2012). *Book Illustrated* includes eight essays by leading scholars who examine the work of Cruikshank and Rossetti, Romantic and Victorian era illustrated editions of Shakespeare's works, Aubrey Beardsley's fin-de-siècle illustrations, and the rise of American women illustrators from 1880 to 1920. The introduction to *Book Illustrated* raises ideas about the decline of the illustrated book as a form of adult fiction that I develop in this book. The ten chronologically arranged essays in Maxwell's collection are by some of the same noted scholars; for example, Patten, who contributed an essay on Cruikshank for *Book Illustrated*, wrote a chapter on *David Copperfield* for *The Victorian Illustrated Book*, and Elizabeth Helsinger, who wrote on Rossetti for *Book Illustrated*, provided a chapter on William Morris for *The Victorian Illustrated Book*. In his introduction, Maxwell addresses some of the reasons motivating the rise of the Victorian illustrated book. His afterword entitled "The Destruction, Rebirth, and Apotheosis of the Victorian Illustrated Book" considers the illustrated book's influence on modernist and postmodernist forms of the book (for example, collage books by Max Ernst and boxes by Joseph Cornell).

Whereas Maxwell's 2002 collection begins with the historical fiction of Sir Walter Scott and covers the long nineteenth century, Goldman and Cooke's 2012 collection gives shape and depth to the most distinguished period of the Victorian illustrated book. Its nine essays by a range of distinguished international scholars deepen our understanding of the Sixties by considering illustration in diverse publications—serial novels, gift books, the Bible, scientific works, and German illustrated books. Other important critical examinations of Victorian illustration were published in the early twenty-first century. Kooistra's *Poetry, Pictures, and Popular Publishing: The Illustrated Gift Book and Victorian Visual Culture, 1855–1875* (2011) places the illustrated gift book at the heart of book production and consumer culture. Mary Elizabeth Leighton and Lisa Surridge's "The Plot Thickens: Toward a Narratological Analysis of Illustrated Serial Fiction in the 1860s" (2008) examines the role of illustration in the plot of the serial novel that was "intrinsic to the first reading experience of the mass Victorian public" (66).[10]

Some recent works focus on a single productive illustrator, such as John Everett Millais and George Du Maurier. In *Beyond Decoration: The Illustrations of John Everett Millais* (2005), Goldman foregrounds this leading British painter's range as an illustrator and treats Millais's book illustrations in context of the literature they accompanied. Goldman and Simon Cooke co-edited a collection entitled *George Du Maurier: Illustrator, Author, Critic Beyond Svengali* (2016); the fifteen essays by leading international specialists demonstrate the multifaceted career of this important nineteenth-century illustrator, critic, and author-illustrator.

Two recent works on caricature—Victor Navasky's *The Art of Controversy* (2014) and Brian Maidment's *Comedy, Caricature and the Social Order, 1820–50* (2013)—have also been influential to my scholarship on the Victorian illustrated book.[11] Beginning with William Hogarth and James Gillray and concluding with Jonathan Shapiro and David Levine, Navasky examines the political cartoon across three centuries. Of consequence to my own revaluation of caricature, Navasky's work challenges "the many art critics, art historians, and artists who themselves have, over the years, dismissed cartoons and caricatures as fundamentally 'not serious,' 'inconsequential,' 'irrelevant,' 'marginal,' 'harmless,' 'frivolous,' 'a benign—even childish—indulgence,' 'immoral,' and 'silly'" (xiv). Taking a narrower historical approach in *Comedy, Caricature and the Social Order, 1820–50*, Maidment convincingly argues that "the cultural importance and the aesthetic appeal of Regency and early Victorian caricature and visual comedy, when not discussed with outright scorn or disdain, have at least been undervalued in recent scholarly discussions" (3). Committed to a revaluation of comedy and caricature, Maidment tackles contempt for comic art to demonstrate how inventive repackaging, reimagining, and adaptation sustained a form of print culture for a new generation of consumers. Maidment follows the comic print from its decline in the production of large single-plate caricatures popular in the Regency period into new forms of Victorian publication (for example, periodicals and fiction) with the rise of wood engraving and lithography. In making a successful case for fluidity in visual culture across two literary periods, Maidment's book informs my examination of the evolution of the Victorian illustrated book over the long nineteenth century and beyond.

The emerging discipline of illustration studies still needs "to be recognized within the scholarly community and beyond" (15), as Goldman advocates in "Defining Illustration Studies." Art history, book history, bibliographic studies, and literary studies have traditionally slighted book and periodical illustration. Nonliterary texts including travel narratives, natural histories, religious texts, and anatomy books invite examination as illustrated material. Reprints of Victorian texts in the forms their first audiences read and viewed them, now available through databases such as *The Database of Mid-Victorian Illustration* at Cardiff University, may also promote more scholarship on the Victorian illustrated book and hopefully establish, in Goldman's words, "a proper master's course, devoted exclusively to the subject of Illustration Studies" (32).

Chapter Summaries

In the opening chapter of *Victorian Novelists and Their Illustrators*, John Harvey presents "the large first question the monthly parts provoke: how was it the illustrations came to be there at all?" (7).[12] The success of *The Posthumous Pa-*

pers of the Pickwick Club made serialization a popular vehicle for new adult fiction that publishers and authors readily adopted, hoping to bank on *Pickwick's* success. *Pickwick* generated *Pickwick* mania,[13] a term that speaks to *Pickwick's* huge fan base and the rise of commercial products related to it. Past and recent critics have acknowledged *Pickwick's* importance and factors that impacted its success,[14] but chapter 1 offers a synthetic reading of this material to help explain how pictures "came to be" in an illustrated serial and how the serial, in turn, generated a mass consumer market for the illustrated book. This chapter emphasizes how intertwining factors including commodity culture, a growth in literacy, innovations in printing, and the popularity of comic illustrations accelerated *Pickwick's* popularity.

Chapter 2 studies the theatrical quality of caricature-style illustration produced in the 1830s and 1840s for the Victorian illustrated serial, a thriving form of mass-market literature. Caricature-style book illustration by George Cruikshank, Phiz, Richard Doyle, John Leech, and (Isaac) Robert Cruikshank approximates the tableau style popular in the early nineteenth century. The caricaturists used lighting, props, and detail-laden backdrops to capture dramatic and sentimental scenes in works by Dickens, Ainsworth, and Thackeray as well as to stage psychological episodes and broadly comic moments. This chapter adds two Victorian author-illustrators to the above list of recognized caricaturists. Better known as a writer than an artist, Thackeray designed illustrations for *Vanity Fair* (1848) that cast his heroine Becky Sharp in various stage roles. To dramatize Alice's bodily transformations, Lewis Carroll recalled popular caricature techniques in *Alice's Adventures Under Ground* (1864), his author-illustrated version of *Alice's Adventures in Wonderland* (1865) published at a time when consumers preferred naturalistic illustration. This chapter also examines artistic limitations and scandals, leading to a depreciation of the caricaturists and a favoring of Academy-trained artists who, beginning in the 1850s, entered the lucrative field of book illustration.

By the mid-nineteenth century, the public desired artistic book illustration with the lifelike quality of photography. Chapter 3 examines two styles of illustration—realism and caricature—during what critics commonly label the "Golden Age" of British illustration, a period that emphasizes academic standards. This chapter frames the realistic school of illustration, commonly referred to as the Sixties, with the Great Exhibition of 1851: this first ever world's fair of culture and industry stimulated production of beautiful objects including books with decorative bindings, culminating in a richly illustrated exhibition catalogue in a representational style (also referred to as realism or naturalism) in vogue from the 1850s to the 1870s. The *Official Descriptive Illustrated Catalogue* from the Great Exhibition is a material artifact from a period when Victorians valued books for their bindings, talented painters entered the field of illustration (for example, John Everett Millais, Dante Gabriel Rossetti, George Du Maurier, and Marcus Stone), and illustrations within books and periodicals came to be viewed as collectible art worth framing.

Of importance to my overarching argument on the fluidity of aesthetics across illustrative periods, chapter 3 features the work of Fred Barnard, James Mahoney, and John Tenniel, who refashioned caricature-style illustrations for popular consumption. Barnard's and Mahoney's illustrations for the Household Edition of, respectively, *David Copperfield* and *Oliver Twist* (among the first works adapted in this 22-volume series) demonstrate how Sixties artists fleshed out inventive caricature designs from the 1830s and 1840s to suit popular taste of the 1870s. This same kind of revision of the caricature tradition appears in *Alice in Wonderland*; John Tenniel recreated Carroll's caricature-style illustrations with realism, adding domestic interiors and nature settings to suit the taste of middle-class readers.

At the end of the nineteenth century, the Victorian illustrated book entered what some critics view as a time of decline and others consider a third period of development. Chapter 4 examines both viewpoints. Publishing trends and intertwining economic and aesthetic factors led to a drop in newly released, large-circulation illustrated adult fiction in volume form in England. These reasons include the waning of serial fiction, cost and quality factors, a growth in literacy, the evolution of the novel, advances in illustration, and the rise of competing media. The Victorian illustrated book prospered in some serial formats, artists' books, children's literature, and the US market. Chapter 4 provides a survey of late Victorian illustrated fiction that targeted audiences according to age, gender, social class, and nation. It features two fin-de-siècle author-illustrators—Beatrix Potter and George Du Maurier—and demonstrates continuity across the arc of the Victorian illustrated book. Beatrix Potter illustrates *Peter Rabbit* (1902) and successive children's tales with near photographic realism, following the realistic school of illustration associated with Millais. George Du Maurier, a recognized Sixties artist, brings theatricality in illustration and a persistent racialized depiction of the Jew from the caricature tradition to his self-illustrated fiction published in the US market in *Harper's*; his best-known *Trilby* instigated a media frenzy of Pickwickian magnitude referred to as Trilby-mania.[15]

The conclusion looks forward from the Victorian illustrated book to the "graphic classics."[16] Canonical texts adapted into graphic novel format are inheritors of the illustrative schools of caricature and realism, adapted in a hyper-modern form to appeal to twenty–first-century reader-viewers. This chapter explores parallels between the serial and the comic book. It surveys graphic novel adaptations of nineteenth-century novels by Jane Austen, Charlotte and Emily Brontë, Charles Dickens, and Anthony Trollope as well as Neo-Victorian graphic novels (for example, *The League of Extraordinary Gentlemen* [1999]) and original Victorian-themed graphic novels (for example, *Batman: Noël* [2011]). The conclusion features adaptations of two Victorian illustrated books—Dickens's *Oliver Twist* and Carroll's *Alice in Wonderland*—to demonstrate how the graphic classics is reviving a genre that a century before recognized pictures play a central role in the development of plot and characterization. This chapter foregrounds Will Eisner, the father of the graphic novel and author-illustrator of *Fagin the Jew* (2003), for his direct challenge to a religious and ethnic stereotype of the Jew that Dickens and Cruikshank develop in *Oliver Twist* and Du Maurier carries into *Trilby*. Looking beyond Eisner, this chapter also considers how graphic novelists and artists have developed aspects of the Victorian source texts too unseemly for the tastes of the illustrated book's original middle-class readership.

Forerunners of the Victorian Illustrated Book

Serials to Graphic Novels centers on the Victorian period, which Percy Muir dubs "the heyday of book illustration" (1). But the Victorian illustrated book has important antecedents—including the classical concept of *ut pictura poesis*, medieval manuscripts, and eighteenth-century graphic satire and caricature—all of which created an audience for the Victorian illustrated book, which, in turn reimagines techniques that resurface from these earlier dual art forms.

The Horatian concept of *ut pictura poesis* fascinated the Victorians and has bearing on why—long before *Pickwick*—pictures in word and image collaborations "came to be there at all" (Harvey 7). Horace's now famous phrase—which literally means, "As with the painter's work, so with the poet's" (358)—comes from *Ars Poetica* (*The Art of Poetry*) composed circa 19 BC. Horace advances that poetry—and by extension imaginative texts—deserves the same kind of critical attention that painting received in his day. Horace compares poetry to the more established art of painting, noting: "one piece will take you more if you stand close to it, another at a greater distance. This loves a dark corner, that will desire to be seen in a strong light, for it fears not the critic's keenest taste. This pleased but once; that will be asked for ten times and always please" (358). In this famous passage, Horace advises that some poems, like paintings, delight those with a critical eye and endure while others, in contrast, please only for the moment or when viewed under favorable circumstances.

Horace's comparison of poetry and painting primed a visually literate Victorian audience schooled in classical languages to appreciate the relations between word and image in the nineteenth century, an age that increasingly produced illustrated material in a range of forms and for different audiences. However, the impulse to compare pictures and words predates Horace by many centuries. In one section of the *Phaedrus* (ca. 370 BC), Plato elevates spoken discourse over written discourse by comparing writing—a new invention in ancient Greece—to painting. Socrates, Plato's mouthpiece, declares to Phaedrus:

> I cannot help feeling, Phaedrus, that writing is unfortunately like painting; for the creations of the painter have the attitude of life, and yet if you ask them a question they preserve a solemn silence. And the same may be said of speeches. You would imagine that they had intelligence, but if you want to know anything and put a question to one of them, the speaker always gives one unvarying answer. And when they have been once written down they are tumbled about anywhere among those who may or may not understand them, and know not to whom they should reply, to whom not: and, if they are maltreated or abused, they have no parent to protect them; and they cannot protect or defend themselves. (485)

Socrates warns his pupil against the new art of rhetoric, prone to sophistry. Writing, like painting, cannot speak, answer questions, or defend itself against misinterpretation. Spoken discourse is the only true form of communication. Plato criticizes the value of written and visual forms of communication in comparison to spoken discourse, but this oft-quoted passage remains important in aligning painting and writing as sister arts.

The concept of painting and writing as sister arts helped bring about a cultural climate in Victorian England that was receptive to pictorial illustration. In the first part of his still influential book *The Sister Arts* (1958), Jean Hagstrum explores *ut pictura poesis*, tracing the interrelationship of written and visual forms of expression from the classical period through the early Christian era, the Renaissance, the Baroque period, and onto the Age of Enlightenment. Of particular relevance to the Victorian illustrated book is the work of Gotthold Ephraim Lessing, the German Enlightenment poet, philosopher, dramatist, and critic. In "Laocoön: An Essay on the Limits of Painting and Poetry," Lessing challenges what he considered to be a too literal application of Horace's famous expression "as is painting, so is poetry" (another common translation of the phrase). Lessing's famous treatise takes its name from the ancient Greek statue *Laocoön and His Sons*, which depicts the Trojan priest of Poseidon and his two sons being destroyed by two serpents.[17] Although Lessing published his treatise in German in 1766, the first English translation, which Royal Academicians took seriously, did not appear until 1836, the year Charles Dickens launched *The Pickwick Papers* and the year before Queen Victoria took the throne.

In *Laocoön*, Lessing describes the distinct strengths and limitations of painting and poetry by introducing two terms, "bodies" and "actions": "Objects which co-exist, or the parts of which co-exist, are termed bodies"; "It follows that bodies, with their visible properties, are the proper objects of painting" (131). In other words, "bodies" are forms, colors, figures, and shapes that coexist on one picture plane. In contrast, "Objects which succeed, or the parts of which succeed to each other, are called generally actions. It follows that actions are the proper object of Poetry" (131); moreover, objects arranged in succession indicate time. To Lessing, painting and poetry have opposite strengths: materiality (through "bodies") is painting's strength while narrative (through "actions") is poetry's forte. Lessing qualifies that poets can indicate "bodies" by creating word pictures to describe people and scenes. Although painting "can only avail itself of one moment of action," a canvas, in turn, can indicate time ("actions") if the artist wisely chooses a moment "which is the most pregnant, and by which what has gone before and what is to follow will be the most intelligible" (132). Such a "pregnant moment" provides "intelligible" glimpses into past and future time through the scene depicted on canvas. The Victorian illustrated book is filled with narrative illustrations that function as pregnant moments, conveying the past and future through rich symbolism and telling details.[18]

Techniques used in the creation of the earliest forms of illustrated material resurface over time, establishing the illustrated book as a recursive genre. As Percy Muir notes in *Victorian Illustrated Books* (1971), "Pictures came before letterpress. In a very real sense, they were originally letterpress. Our alphabet derives, through the Phoenicians and the Greeks, from the picture-writing of the ancient Egyptians—hieroglyphics" (1). The phrase "picture-writing" dates to ancient hieroglyphics, but it also aptly describes mechanically reproduced illustrated books dating to the fifteenth century. Johannes Gutenberg's revolutionary invention of letterpress printing in 1439 made it possible to produce multiple copies of a work with speed and precision. William Caxton's *The Mirror of the World* (1481), a popular one-volume digest that records the feats of ancient times, is generally recognized as the first illustrated book printed in England although some critics believe that Caxton's *Cato*, published around the same time, may have been the first.[19] Caxton, who published at a time when paper was very expensive, was a shrewd businessman who printed titles that would sell. Caxton remains an important figure in the history of printing because he brought to public awareness major works of medieval literature including Sir Thomas Malory's *Le Morte d'Arthur* (1485) and Geoffrey Chaucer's *The Canterbury Tales* (ca. 1387–1400).

In addition to printed books, the fifteenth century witnessed short block books, typically of a religious nature and aimed at a popular audience. The block book, also called xylographica, was a cheap alternative to books composed with movable type. The block book is composed entirely of wood engravings that incorporate text into their artistic designs. In illuminated manuscripts of the thirteenth to sixteenth centuries, "words are recorded on a page in a way that results in a work of art," as James Bettley notes in *The Art of the Book: From Medieval Manuscript to Graphic Novel* (2001, 14). Illumination was initially reserved for sacred subjects: "With the advent of printing, however, ... illumination and calligraphy became a much more deliberate and self-conscious activity, reserved for only the most special occasions" (Bettley 14), such as the production of deeds and coats of arms.

The Victorians reimagined many of these illustrative practices. Dante Gabriel Rossetti reinvented the medieval practice of pictorial inscription in his poem-painting pairs, which inscribe a poem written expressly for that painting onto a canvas or frame, as demonstrated in *Proserpine* (1874) and *Astarte Syriaca* (1877). Thackeray, among others, recalled the illuminated letter from medieval manuscripts in his pictorial capital letters to preview the plot of a chapter or deepen theme and characterization.

The nineteenth century also witnessed a revival of calligraphy and medieval illumination in William Blake's turn-of-the-nineteenth-century wood blocks that blend poetic lines and illustrations into single, hand-printed, hand-colored plates. *Songs of Innocence* (1789) and *Songs of Experience* (1794) present an unparalleled creative vision of pastoral England at the brink of industrialization, emphasizing the loss that accompanies an increasingly urban world. In writing, drawing, designing, and coloring his illuminated manuscripts, Blake not only recalled the tradition of medieval illumination but also charted a way of composing through two art forms followed by many Victorians, including Thackeray and Du Maurier. A century after Blake, William Morris foregrounded illumination and calligraphy in publications for his Kelmscott Press (founded in 1891) that kept alive medieval book arts practices that were becoming obsolete.[20] Two centuries after Blake, Will Eisner and other graphic novelists similarly have composed through two art forms to present a creative vision.

Fifteenth-century block books of wood engravings illustrated with minimal text also anticipate the early nineteenth-century works of Pierce Egan and William Combe, who provided "letterpress" for artists' pictures in, respectively, *Life in London* (1821) with pictures by George and Robert Cruikshank and *The Tour of Doctor Syntax* (1812) with plates by Thomas Rowlandson. Most influential to Rowlandson and the history of the illustrated book is the work of William Hogarth, a painter who specialized in a series of sequential paintings that tell a story, called a "progress." Akin to block books and progresses, wordless novels composed entirely of woodcuts surfaced in the early twentieth century in Frans Masereel's *Passionate Journey* (1919) and Lynd Ward's *God's Man* (1929). These latter examples of "picture-writing" have been influential to modern material forms of word and picture storytelling including the graphic novel.

The eighteenth-century tradition of graphic satire and caricature closely associated with Hogarth commanded a market for illustrated material in eighteenth-century England and the continent. Hogarth's progresses appealed across the social classes and "graced the walls of the humblest shops and hovels as well as prosperous homes like those of Mrs. Thrale, Lord Byron, and, much later, Dickens's own at Gad's Hill" (J. R. Cohen 4). Two well-known Hogarthian progresses, *The Rake's Progress* (ca. 1733–35) and *Marriage à la Mode* (ca. 1743–45), use eight and six plates, respectively, to narrate a story about a dandy's misfortune and the foibles of an imprudent marriage. *The Rake's Progress*, for example, depicts the rise and fall of Tom Rakewell, who comes to London and wastes his inheritance on high living. Gambling and engaging prostitutes, Rakewell first lands in the notorious Fleet Prison and then meets a worse fate, incarceration in Bethlehem Hospital, an insane asylum better known as Bedlam. Expressive gestures, settings, clothing, and props in Hogarth's progresses resurface in the Victorian illustrated book and the graphic novel.

There was vibrancy in English book illustration in the late eighteenth and early nineteenth centuries. Thomas Bewick's *History of British Birds* (1797, 1804), which fascinates young Jane Eyre ensconced in the window seat at the opening of Charlotte Brontë's *Jane Eyre* (1847), is one such popular illustrated natural history that stimulated the literary imaginations of the Brontë sisters and William Wordsworth. Bewick was both an engraver and an artist. James Gillray and Thomas Rowlandson as well as George Cruikshank—who became a household name—were all printmakers and Hogarth's heirs. Cruikshank began his career by finishing etchings that Gillray could not complete due to his madness. Of note, Cruikshank gained fame for producing comic prints before entering the field of book illustration. When he began to work with Dickens, Cruikshank guaranteed the young author a large audience. Cruikshank's satirical prints and progresses regularly hung in the shops of popular print sellers like William Hone, G. Humphrey, and Thomas Tegg (Patten, *CDP* 53). Moreover, the satirical works of Hogarth, and to some extent the caricatures of Gillray and Rowlandson, influenced the creative imaginings of Dickens and Thackeray and the illustrations of Seymour, Browne, and Cruikshank, who, in turn, trained Thackeray as an etcher. As Harvey notes, "The imaginations of author and artist naturally had recourse to the same pictorial idiom" (3). This common inheritance in pictorial narrative and graphic satire and caricature distinguished the Victorian illustrated book from its earlier incarnations and led to its growth during an age of production and consumption that witnessed a sharp rise in literacy.

It is difficult to determine how many people across the social classes could read and write in the nineteenth century. Social class factored into literacy rates since "few people in the working class had more than two or three years of full-time schooling" (Mitchell, *Daily* 166). According to the 1841 census (produced just four years into Victoria's reign), 51 percent of females and 67 percent of males were literate although literacy was often determined by the ability to sign one's name in the marriage register rather than simply make an "X" (166). With the growth in literacy, there was an explosion of different types of illustrated material—crude broadsides and chapbooks as well as literary annuals and gift books—designed for readers ranging from the barely educated to the privileged, sophisticated consumer.

In early nineteenth-century England, inexpensive parts publication, broadsides, and chapbooks proliferated and catered to the barely literate and the working class. A century before *The Pickwick Papers*, piecemeal publishing was well established in England and took numerous forms, ranging from fascicle publication of lengthy and expensive works to cheap parts printed separately or in installments within newspapers and magazines.[21] A purchaser of the fascicle issues of, for example, Dr. Johnson's *Dictionary* (1755), could take the part issues to a bookseller to be bound in a style appropriate for his or her own personal library. In contrast, broadsides and chapbooks, cheap forms of piecemeal publishing, made the buying and reading of books possible for those of the working class.

A broadside, also called a broadsheet and a street ballad, was a large single sheet printed on one side of a page; it sold for a penny and was, in essence, the poor people's press. Hundreds of London printers published broadsides with stock woodcuts and short lines and verses that were understandable even to those who were barely literate. Broadsides included advertisements, ballads, fabricated feuds among members of the Royal Family, romances, and news stories, particularly sensational crimes. In the eighteenth and nineteenth centuries, printers prepared broadsides for sale at public executions; these typically included a picture of the criminal or the crime scene along with the prisoner's declaration of guilt, "last dying words," and a cautionary verse. While both broadsides and chapbooks printed crude woodcuts along with text on a single sheet, chapbooks were made out of a single page folded into either 16 or 32 small pages to form a small book that sold for one or two pennies. In the nineteenth century, typically English fairy tales such as "Jack and the Giant Killer" appeared in chapbook form, and the main audience was children. However, as Sally Mitchell notes, "Ballads and broadsides were both newspaper and entertainment for poor people until the rise of the cheap press in the 1850s" ("Broadsides" 94).

The 1820s witnessed the growth of illustrated literary annuals and keepsake books that became popular Christmas items. Different from the broadside and the chapbook, the annual, also called a keepsake, and the illustrated gift book targeted middle-class readers and were lavishly illustrated. Lloyd Siemens notes that annuals

> reflect conventional views on hearth and homeland, morality and mortality . . . and nearly all feature the same spectrum of sentimental literary stereotypes: the deepening of married love, the wages of sin, the virtues of the country life, and the blessings of poverty. The diction and imagery are as formulaic as the sentiments. It is little wonder that the annuals became favorite gifts at birthdays and weddings as well as at Christmastime. (27)

With the growth of the publishing industry, Christmas became a commercial holiday. Illustrated Christmas books, most famously Charles Dickens's *A Christmas Carol* (1843) and subsequent titles following its success, found their place alongside annuals and gift books produced inexpensively enough to attract middle-class consumers.

The gift book is a hybrid art form that grew out of the literary annual and gained popularity by the 1840s. In *Poetry, Pictures, and Popular Publishing*, Kooistra elevates this oft-neglected cultural artifact of Victorian material culture. "Encased in ornamental covers and advertised as Christmas presents," notes Kooistra, "these gift books united poetry and pictures in one tasteful package for middlebrow consumption and cultivation" (79–80). Gift books, which moved poetry into the popular consciousness, featured steel engravings, rich interior decoration, and lavish covers. Printers, who played a key role in the creation and packaging of the gift book, commissioned skilled artists and engravers to illustrate the works of noted poets, such as William Wordsworth, Samuel Taylor Coleridge, Robert Southey, and Alfred Lord Tennyson, although some gift-book poets were considered second-rate (for example, Eliza Cook, Adelaide Anne Proctor, and Jean Ingelow).

The production of illustrated books in the nineteenth century—whether in the gift book, the part issue, or the periodical—also depended upon the related processes of etching, engraving, printing, publishing, and binding. In most cases—with George Cruikshank a notable exception—the illustrator relied on an etcher or engraver to transfer a drawing onto a metal or wooden plate for reproduction. Prior to the 1830s, an etcher applied an acid-resistant layer of wax to metal plates and used a needle to create the design before dipping the plate in acid, which bit into the exposed lines and deepened them. An engraver, however, used a tool called a graver, stylus, or burin to cut the design directly into the steel or copper plate to form deeper, narrower, and more precise lines. By the 1840s, wood engraving gained preeminence. Notorious in this "age of mechanical reproduction," to recall Walter Benjamin's phrasing, are the complaints of illustrators like Dante Gabriel Rossetti, who blamed the Dalziel brothers, among the finest engravers of the Victorian age, for poorly transferring his drawings onto wood. Etchers and engravers, in turn, complained that the fault of reproduction lay with the artist, who could not create drawings suitable for transfer, respectively, onto metal or increasingly onto wood.

Even from this brief historical sketch of the illustrated book's antecedents, we can glean that the Victorian illustrated book is not bound in time; it transcends the nineteenth century in both directions and was an important literary and artistic genre in its own time. To apply Kooistra's insight about the Victorian gift book more generally, the illustrated book provides a fundamental "way of seeing and understanding for generations of Victorians" (*Poetry* 86). The phenomenal success of *The Pickwick Papers* led to the rise of the Victorian illustrated serial and, in turn, illustrated volumes that adorned the circular tables of Victorian drawing rooms and still delight readers today. How serendipitous that publisher Chapman and Hall commissioned Charles Dickens to "write up" pictures by Robert Seymour, and Dickens agreed, but subverted his assignment.

1

The Pickwick Papers and the Rise of the Serial

The illustrations are, as usual, full of excellent character. The ease and skill with
which they are drawn are among the least of their merits; they have an artistical
feeling and arrangement, most rare in things of this kind. But it is enough to say
of them that they are scarcely unequal to the subjects they illustrate—we feel
this to be extraordinary praise.

Unsigned review of *The Pickwick Papers, Examiner,* 1837

Beginning in April 1836 and concluding with a double number in November
1837, *The Posthumous Papers of the Pickwick Club* (P) came out in nineteen illustrated part issues in decorative green wrappers for the cost of a shilling each.[1]
An unprecedented publishing phenomenon, *Pickwick* attracted fans across the
social classes, generated a host of *Pickwick*-related products, and earned glowing reviews. In his above (unsigned) *Examiner* review, Dickens's first biographer, John Forster, devotes a full paragraph to the illustrations "full of excellent
character." Four decades later in his biography of Dickens, Forster describes a
snowball effect in the admiration of this illustrated Victorian blockbuster far
better appreciated in its time than today. *Pickwick*

> sprang into a popularity that each part carried higher and higher, until
> people at this time talked of nothing else, tradesmen recommended their
> goods by using its name, and its sale, outstripping at a bound that of all
> the most famous books of the century, had reached to an almost fabulous
> number. (*The Life* 1: 129)

To Forster, "Judges on the bench and boys in the street, gravity and folly, the
young and the old, those who were entering life and those who were quitting
it, alike found [*Pickwick*] to be irresistible" (130). As the author of *The Life*

of Charles Dickens (1872–74) and Dickens's close friend, Forster had a vested interest in promoting Dickens and his reputation for posterity. But William Makepeace Thackeray, who was never a fan of Dickens, likewise singled out *Pickwick*'s importance to Victorian publishing, noting: "I am sure that a man who, a hundred years hence, should sit down and write the history of our time, would do wrong to put that great contemporary history of 'Pickwick' aside as a frivolous work" (*Paris Sketch Book* 119).

I place *The Pickwick Papers* at the beginning of the arc of the Victorian illustrated book because this quintessential Victorian "commodity-text . . . could reach, as it produced, a mass audience" (Feltes 13). This chapter examines interwoven factors that contributed to *Pickwick*'s popularity, including the growth of commodity culture, a rise in literacy, new printing technologies, serialization, and the appeal of reading pictures, particularly humorous ones. *Pickwick*'s blend of comedy, theatricality, and social commentary led to the serial's success and, in the process, created a mass market for new fiction with illustrations.

Pickwick was not the first popular illustrated serial in nineteenth-century England. Pierce Egan's *Life in London* (1821), illustrated by George and Robert Cruikshank, first appeared in monthly parts at a shilling per issue and had a large Regency fan base. *Life in London* follows Tom, a fashionable London rake, and Jerry, his country cousin, as they experience the high and low pleasures of London life. Some Victorians including Thackeray found *Life in London* vulgar, and present-day scholars have lamented how "the plates and the text proper often have absolutely nothing to do with each other" (Meisel 54). *Life in London* entered the Regency marketplace through an array of material forms, merchandise, and productions—broadsides, chapbooks, pottery, souvenir programs, and performances—and its commodification could be seen as an anticipation of *Pickwick* mania. In *Picturing Scotland Through the Waverley Novels* (2010), Richard Hill alternately argues that Sir Walter Scott's early nineteenth-century novels impacted the market for illustrated books well before "the more celebrated Victorian illustrated novels of Dickens and Thackeray" (4). To Hill, "The illustration of novels by a living author was an innovation in publishing at the beginning of the nineteenth century. Constable, Cadell, and Scott together created something new for a developing middle-class readership: the affordable, popular, illustrated novel" (2).[2]

Alternately, critics including Richard Maxwell claim that Scott was indifferent to illustration or only interested in book illustration for commercial reasons.[3] The illustrated editions of Scott's Waverley novels do not follow the definition of the Victorian illustrated book that guides this examination:

"The novelist wrote in collaboration with an artist he had worked with often before; he wrote knowing he must have illustrations" and often determined which scenes should be illustrated while writing the monthly parts (Harvey 180). Whereas the first illustrations for the Waverley novels came out in 1820 in a separate supplement to accompany preexisting editions of Scott, Dickens's *Pickwick Papers* came out in monthly parts with illustrations that were integral to the serial's success.

Serendipity

In the early to mid-1830s, Charles Dickens was an energetic but relatively unknown author. Working as a journalist, Dickens covered election campaigns for the *Morning Chronicle* and, between 1833–36, published dozens of literary "sketches" of London life in periodicals and newspapers, such as the *Evening Chronicle*, the *Monthly Magazine*, *Bell's Life in London*, and the *Morning Chronicle*. Publisher John Macrone collected fifty-six of Dickens's nonfiction sketches and printed them in two volumes under the title *Sketches by Boz* (1836) with illustrations by George Cruikshank. Already well established as a caricaturist and satirist, Cruikshank drew an audience to Dickens's vignettes of character types that Dickens developed into memorable characters in his best-known novels: a parish beadle from *Sketches by Boz* forms the basis for Mr. Bumble in *Oliver Twist* (*OT*, 1838); a schoolmaster from *Sketches* reappears first in *Hard Times* (1854) as the exacting Mr. Thomas Gradgrind and later in *Our Mutual Friend* (*OMF*, 1865) as the mentally unbalanced Bradley Headstone; a pickpocket from *Sketches* transforms into the Artful Dodger in Fagin's merry band in *Oliver Twist*.

The positive reception of *Sketches by Boz* led Edward Chapman and William Hall to approach Dickens with the idea of providing letterpress for a series of engravings by Robert Seymour to be published in monthly parts. Chapman and Hall specifically hired Dickens in "the secondary role of script-writer" (Kinsley vii) to enhance Seymour's pictures. This contractual arrangement recalls a pre-1820s definition of illustration, which meant verbal explanation, enrichment, or annotation (Meisel 30–31),[4] not an "illustrative picture; a drawing, plate, engraving, cut, or the like, illustrating or embellishing a literary article, a book, etc." (*OED*) as we take for granted today; the insertion of a well-known artist's name or a term like "engraved" in the book's title was essential to convey that a picture illustrated the text and not vice versa. Only after the 1820s, when technological innovations expanded the production of illustrated books, did the meaning of illustration begin to shift from verbal enrichment or annotation to a Victorian conception of illustration meaning pictorial re-creation and/or enhancement, an image shedding light on a written text.[5]

There are Regency precedents for Chapman and Hall's proposed arrangement of contracting an author, in this case Dickens, to illustrate by writing up an artist's pictures. William Combe provided comical verse to accompany Thomas Rowlandson's caricatures for *The Tour of Doctor Syntax, in Search of the Picturesque: A Poem* (1812) and its two sequels published in 1820 and 1821.[6] These parodies of the popular picturesque movement, particularly books by William Gilpin, follow Dr. Syntax, a comical clergyman and schoolmaster, who sets out on his horse to make a tour with the intention of writing about his rambles, which are filled with silly misfortunes. Rowlandson's enormously popular hand-colored caricature-style illustrations grant the hapless character a decidedly long chin that did not escape the attention of Jane Austen, who told her beloved sister, Cassandra, in a letter dated 2–3 March 1814: "I have seen nobody in London yet with such a long chin as Dr Syntax."[7]

Dr. Syntax—a genteel and good-natured figure of folly who visually anticipates the character of Samuel Pickwick in inviting viewers to laugh at him—has an excessively long jaw in Rowlandson's "Doctor Syntax & The Bees" (see fig. 1) for *The Second Tour of Doctor Syntax, in Search of Consolation: A Poem* (1820). Combe's comic verse magnifies the plate's broad humor:

> Talk'd o'er in terms of frolic ease
> His curious battle with the bees,
> And made his tumble in the water
> A source of fun and gen'ral laughter. (221)

At war with a swarm of bees attacking his white wig, Dr. Syntax in this plate rises out of his chair and "tumbles" toward a large sarcophagus of water to escape the bees' stings.[8] The pointed configuration of insects above Syntax's head exaggerates the conical shape of his wig and his exquisitely pointed nose and chin, which juts out far beyond his nose. Combe's verse narrative also draws the reader-viewer's attention to the crowd of amused onlookers, who view Dr. Syntax's mishap as a "source of fun and gen'ral laughter." One woman to the left of the picture plane leans over a parapet to get a better look at the humorous spectacle of bees pursuing Dr. Syntax, whose hat is literally tipping off his head; six additional onlookers armed with pots and pans to scare away the insects reveal in their facial expressions that they are enjoying watching Dr. Syntax's battle with the bees.[9]

Figure 1. "Doctor Syntax & The Bees." Illustration by Thomas Rowlandson for William Combe's *The Second Tour of Dr Syntax, in Search of Consolation: A Poem*, 1820. From the Norman M. Fox Collection, Scribner Library, Skidmore College.

Pierce Egan also provided letterpress to annotate illustrations by George and Robert Cruikshank for *Life in London; or, The Day and Night Scenes of Jerry Hawthorn, Esq. and his elegant friend Corinthian Tom, accompanied by Bob Logic, The Oxonian, in their Rambles and Sprees through the Metropolis.* In serial and volume form, *Life in London* captured a large audience because of George and Robert Cruikshank's illustrations. In the first chapter, which Egan calls a "preface, or a prelude to the work" (1), the author pays lavish tribute to the Cruikshanks for their lead role in this picture-word collaboration:

> In all thy varied portraiture of the interesting scenes of Life, let me invoke thy superior talents, BOB AND GEORGE CRUICKSHANK [sic] (thou *Gilray* of the day, and of *Don Saltero* greatness), to my anxious aid. Indeed, I have need of all thy illustrative touches; and may we be hand and glove together in depicting the richness of nature, which so wantonly, at times, plays off her freaks upon the half-finished bone-rakers and cinder-sifters round the dust-hill. (11–12) [10]

Egan places "Bob and George" in the illustrious tradition of eighteenth-century graphic satire and caricature associated with William Hogarth and James Gillray, the latter named in the above tribute. Egan also ranks the Cruikshank brothers with Don Saltero's Coffee House and Curiosity Museum, a Chelsea establishment founded by James Salter in 1695 that drew Londoners and noted overseas visitors including Benjamin Franklin. Most telling, however, is Egan's description of the artist and author relationship as "hand and glove together."

The Cruikshank brothers' illustrations are clearly the "hand" in this collaboration and Egan's annotations the "glove" that adorns them. For example, in chapter 2 of book 2, Egan both directs the reader to and describes the full-page hand-colored engraving entitled "Midnight. Tom & Jerry, at a Coffee Shop near the Olympic" (see fig. 2): "This group (which the plate so correctly delineates, and in the point of *character*, equal to any of HOGARTH'S celebrated productions) displays a complete picture of what is termed 'LOW LIFE' in the Metropolis; drunkenness, beggary, lewdness, and carelessness, being its

Figure 2. "Midnight. Tom & Jerry at a Coffee Shop near the Olympic." Illustration by George and Robert Cruikshank for Pierce Egan's *Life in London*, 1821. From the Norman M. Fox Collection, Scribner Library, Skidmore College.

prominent features" (181). Here Egan praises the Cruikshanks' depiction of respectable and lowlife characters by comparing the plate to work by the great Hogarth, well known for mixing gamblers, prostitutes, and prosperous gentlemen in serial paintings like *The Rake's Progress* (ca. 1733–35). "Midnight" brings the viewer into a crowded room with drinkers, looters, prostitutes, and fighters of mixed races. For example, one woman with grotesque features is in the act of climbing over a booth to fight another similarly grotesque woman, who raises both her fists and also opens her mouth wide, seemingly to shout obscenities back at her. Front and center, amidst the "drunkenness, beggary, lewdness, and carelessness," a scantily dressed prostitute—baring her arms, breasts, and ankles—tugs on the coat of Jerry Hawthorn, who seems oblivious to her enticements. In a setting conspicuous for its cracked windows, bare furnishings, and dirt, Corinthian Tom and Jerry Hawthorn, dressed like gentlemen with fashionable coats and top hats, stand out amidst the "LOW LIFE" that Egan here calls to the reader-viewer's attention.[11]

Chapman and Hall designed *Pickwick* to follow in this tradition of an author writing up a popular artist's pictures. "The Adventures of the Nimrod Club" was the title Chapman and Hall intended for the series of Seymour's engravings about amateur Cockney sportsmen on holiday to be accompanied by Dickens's letterpress. Although he is relatively unknown today, Seymour was the senior partner in this original production. "By the time [Seymour] started *Pickwick* in 1836," notes Jane R. Cohen in *Charles Dickens and His Original Illustrators*, "Seymour was fully established with the public as a prolific, influential, and popular caricaturist. His fame even crossed the Channel" (40). Seymour's acclaim as a political caricaturist and humorist came from his weekly front-page caricatures for *Figaro in London* (the precursor of *Punch*) and his own published *Sketches by Seymour* (1835) where overdressed and bumbling working-class Londoners on holiday and Sunday outings, masquerading as sportsmen, chase stray cats and pigs. Seymour initially used the nom de plume of "Short-shanks" for his illustrations until Cruikshank protested. Seymour did not have the reputation of George Cruikshank, whose style and name he emulated, but Cruikshank clearly recognized Seymour as a competitor.

"Mr. Pickwick in Chase of His Hat" demonstrates Robert Seymour's skill as a humorist and reminds us how "Seymour's plates had called *Pickwick* into existence" (J. R. Cohen 46). In this plate (see fig. 3), a stout, out-of-breath, Mr. Pickwick races after his hat "gambolling playfully away" (*P*, Oxf. 45). Pickwick loses his hat when he and three companions chance upon troops in full uniform performing regimental maneuvers, including the firing of muskets with blank

Figure 3. "Mr. Pickwick in Chase of His Hat." Illustration by Robert Seymour from an 1836 serial installment of Charles Dickens's *The Posthumous Papers of the Pickwick Club*. From an 1837 edition in the Norman
M. Fox Collection, Scribner Library, Skidmore College.

cartridges. Like Combe and Egan, Dickens provides script for a picture that
in this case shows the embarrassing moment when Pickwick, "an enthusiastic
admirer of the army" (42), runs after his hat that has blown off his head. Even
in this second *Pickwick* installment, we see Dickens creating a word picture rich
in metaphor and onomatopoeia that is concomitantly earnest and comical and
in no way derivative of the picture:

There are very few moments in a man's existence, when he experiences so much ludicrous distress, or meets with so little charitable commiseration, as when he is in pursuit of his own hat. A vast deal of coolness, and a peculiar degree of judgment, are requisite in catching a hat. . . . The best way is, to keep gently up with the object of pursuit, to be wary and cautious, to watch your opportunity well, get gradually before it, then make a rapid dive, seize it by the crown, and stick it firmly on your head: smiling pleasantly all the time, as if you thought it as good a joke as anybody else. (45–46)

The hat continues to roll away "as merrily as a lively porpoise in a strong tide" (46). A "completely exhausted" (46) Samuel Pickwick prepares to give up the chase just when his hat rubs against the wheel of an open carriage, and the "porpoise" stops moving.

This is the pregnant moment Seymour stages. Samuel Pickwick's respectable black hat, placed brim down in the cloud of dust, serves as an essential prop on Seymour's illustrative stage. Although hats are not commonplace today, to the Victorians, a misplaced hat in public was more than a major wardrobe malfunction; losing one's hat meant losing one's dignity. Seymour hints at the future restoration of the hat by showing a flustered Pickwick, extending both of his arms to "seize [the hat] by the crown, and stick it firmly on your head: smiling pleasantly all the time, as if you thought it as good a joke as anybody else" (P, Oxf. 46). An onlooker gingerly sticks out his foot as if to stop the hat's approach before it is flattened by the oncoming open barouche; this choice of Regency vehicle affords the artist the opportunity to show mirth on the faces of all the passengers, who—akin to Rowlandson's onlookers in "Doctor Syntax & The Bees"—consider Mr. Pickwick's hat chase a very good joke indeed. Two jeering members of the crowd waive their own hats at Mr. Pickwick as if to magnify that they have what he has lost (but happily will soon regain). One onlooker even climbs high up a tree to get a better view of Pickwick's distressed spectacled face and his rounded butt. "Dickens himself made the most of Mr. Pickwick as a butt" (9) of a practical joke, notes John Harvey, and Seymour literally exposes portly Pickwick's "butt" in "Mr. Pickwick in Chase of His Hat."

Dickens was one of four authors Chapman and Hall considered as potential scriptwriters for Seymour's comical engravings in the fashion of "Mr. Pickwick in Chase of His Hat." The other three contenders—Thomas Hood, Theodore Hook, and Leigh Hunt—had already proven themselves as authors. Why did

Chapman and Hall choose Dickens, who had only a book of collected sketches to his name? Percy Muir speculates in *Victorian Illustrated Books*:

> One imagines that the publishers had encountered reluctance on the part of established authors to subject themselves to the artist's whims and William Hall, who interviewed Dickens on the subject, may have thought that youth and inexperience would make him more subservient. (89)

"Subservient" is an unlikely adjective to describe Dickens at any age—he was never submissive or a secondary player. But Dickens took on the job of providing letterpress for Seymour's engravings in 1836 for a practical reason: he was poor and needed money to be able to marry his intended, Catherine Hogarth. Dickens could not resist the steady income of £14. 3s. 6d. per monthly part to be paid on the date of publication (typically the last day of the month). In a letter to Catherine Hogarth dated 10 February 1836, he confides: "The work will be no joke, but the emolument is too tempting to resist" (House and Storey 1: 129). This regular income could amply provide for a wife. Receiving a slight advance after completing the first two *Pickwick* installments, Dickens, who was newly married, went on a honeymoon.[12]

Although Seymour's pictures were foremost in the genesis of *Pickwick*, the up-and-coming Dickens, immediately upon accepting Chapman and Hall's offer, shaped not only *Pickwick* but also the arc of the Victorian illustrated book. Perhaps Dickens simply interpreted to his own advantage Chapman and Hall's request to provide a monthly script "for a book illustrative of manners and life in the Country to be published monthly" (House and Storey 1: 648). To Catherine Hogarth, Dickens discloses that Chapman and Hall "have made me an offer of £14 a month to write and edit a new publication they contemplate, entirely by myself" (House and Storey 1: 128–29). We can assume that Dickens, daydreaming of fame, may never have considered his text secondary to Seymour's drawings. At twenty-four, Dickens was strong-willed and ambitious enough to turn to his own advantage what became *The Posthumous Papers of the Pickwick Club*, better known as *The Pickwick Papers* or just *Pickwick* for short. Neither a sportsman nor a countryman, Dickens considered Seymour's pet topic of amateur Cockney sportsmen on country escapades to be narrow, stale, and decidedly not suited to his interest in urban London or his creative imagination. To Seymour, Dickens conceded the idea of a club, but he revised the assignment to his liking and quickly determined that illustrations should light up the text, not vice versa. *Pickwick* combines urban and rural settings as backdrops for the comic adventures of Samuel Pickwick (named after a "jobmaster"[13] Dickens knew in Bath) and his fellow members of the Pickwick Club—Tracy Tupman, Augustus Snodgrass, and Nathaniel Winkle.

Much as chance favored Dickens when Chapman and Hall serendipitously chose him to provide letterpress for Seymour's pictures, chance again favored Dickens after Seymour tragically ended his life.[14] Seymour's death freed an ambitious author from the unpleasant yoke of writing up an artist's pictures as he was hired to do. The contractual format for the first two monthly numbers that Seymour illustrated gave the artist top billing in the picture-word collaboration: Dickens provided twenty-four pages of text to write up four illustrations by Seymour.[15] Following Seymour's decease, Dickens hit on what became a popular formula for serial publication that was advantageous to the writer: for each monthly number, the author provided thirty-two pages of text while the artist contributed two illustrations. Different from his Regency predecessors, Combe and Egan, who acquiesced to the task of writing up an artist's pictures, Dickens quickly elevated the authority of the author over the artist and essentially reversed the dynamic for future author and artist collaborations: to recall Egan's own analogy of the relationship between author and artist, Dickens turned the illustrator into a "glove," molded to fit the author's "hand." Increasing the allotment of text and decreasing the number of plates expanded the author's role, granting Dickens greater room for plot and character development.[16] With this improved plan, Dickens earned more money (£21 a part); however, by cutting the number of plates in half and hiring artists less established than Robert Seymour, Chapman and Hall offset the total cost.

Many artists applied for Seymour's position: John Leech, who gained fame as an illustrator and later provided engravings for Dickens's *A Christmas Carol* (1843); Thackeray, whose growing acclaim as a writer enabled him to illustrate his own fiction, most notably *Vanity Fair* (1848); Robert Buss, who become a painter of humorous and historical subjects and memorialized Dickens in *Dickens's Dream* (ca. 1875), an unfinished painting that now hangs in the Dickens House Museum; and Hablot Knight Browne, a young aspiring illustrator known by the pseudonym Phiz. Buss provided two illustrations for the third number of *Pickwick Papers*, but Chapman and Hall quickly dismissed him. Dickens took a lead role in selecting Browne, who, not yet twenty-one, was impressionable, self-effacing, and inexperienced. Phiz, who illustrated Parts 4–20 of *Pickwick*, helped launch Dickens to literary stardom and went on to become Dickens's major illustrator.

A "Desultory" Format Made Profitable and More Respectable

William Harrison Ainsworth—who had aspirations to be a three-volume novelist of Sir Walter Scott's stature—believed Dickens "was making a grave mistake in writing fiction in this popular form, the loose-covered serial; a form hitherto reserved only for low trash" (A. N. Wilson 19). Jane R. Cohen concurs that in the 1830s, "The only respectable method of publication, as Dickens's friends were quick to remind him, was the traditional three-volume novel" (42). When Dickens wrote *The Pickwick Papers*, serialization, also known as piecemeal publishing, was a cheap form of publication designed for the middle and working classes.[17] Installments came out independently or as parts published within leading monthly and weekly periodicals. Prior to Dickens's success with *Pickwick*, serialization was not exclusively a vehicle for "low trash" (A. N. Wilson 19). Late eighteenth- and early nineteenth-century publishers used part issues to print ballad sheets, the Bible, and previously published popular books like John Bunyan's *Pilgrim's Progress* (1678, 1684). However, newly released fiction published serially was generally thought to have little literary merit.

In his preface to the first edition of *The Pickwick Papers* (1837) published by Chapman and Hall, Dickens recognizes serialization's low reputation, admitting: "while the different incidents were linked together by a chain of interest strong enough to prevent their appearing unconnected or impossible, the general design should be so simple as to sustain no injury from this detached and desultory form of publication, extending over no fewer than twenty months" (*P*, Oxf. xxxiv). In the preface to the 1847 Cheap Edition of *Pickwick*, Dickens offers an even harsher assessment of *Pickwick*'s structure: "experience and study afterward taught me something, and I could perhaps wish now that these chapters were strung together on a stronger thread of general interest, still, what they are they were designed to be" (*P*, Books, Inc. xvi).

Dickens made this comment at the peak of his career. Two years after he wrote the preface to the Cheap Edition of *Pickwick*, Dickens launched *David Copperfield* (1850), the work he referred to as his "favourite child."[18] Critic Harry Stone carries this same term, "desultory," into his analysis of *Pickwick*, noting in the opening line of *Dickens' Working Notes for His Novels* (1987): "Very early in his career, soon after launching his novel writing with the desultory *Pickwick Papers*, Dickens demonstrated that he was profoundly concerned with the overall design of his books" (xi). Stone goes on to contrast the improvised nature of *Pickwick* to the superior structure of *David Copperfield* and *Our Mutual Friend*, works that show Dickens to be "the story-weaver at his loom" (*OMF*, Penguin

893), as Dickens refers to himself in the postscript to *Our Mutual Friend*. Nonetheless, even the harshest critics recognize that *Pickwick* became a novel even if it was not "designed to be." In *The Victorians*, A. N. Wilson contends that "Few famous novels can have had more desultory origins" (18), but he acknowledges that *Pickwick* is a "famous novel" even if it is a "rambling picaresque" (19).

When Dickens changed the format to thirty-two pages of letterpress with two illustrations per month, "At a single stroke something permanent and novel-like (Chesterton called *Pickwick* 'something nobler than a novel') was created out of something ephemeral and episodic" (Patten, *CDP* 65). Robert Patten's simile "novel-like" captures *Pickwick's* quasi status as a serial *cum* novel that reached readers all across England and abroad. Although it is easy to excerpt chapters from *Pickwick*, the episodes are not entirely disconnected despite Dickens's avowal in his preface to the first edition that he "gradually abandoned" the idea of the Pickwick Club as a structuring principle (*P*, Oxf. xxxiv). While the adventures are diverse, the book has a sustained "chain of interest" (xxxiv) since we can read it as a written record of the various proceedings of the club that Pickwick himself is editing. Dickens does not declare the club's disbanding until the final chapter of the novel when Pickwick retires to Dulwich and tells his fellow Pickwickians: "'The Pickwick Club exists no longer'" (714). In the novel's final paragraph, we learn that Mr. Pickwick is "employing his leisure hours in arranging the memoranda which he afterwards presented to the secretary of the once famous club" (718). "By the end of *Pickwick's* run," Patten observes, "people in Edinburgh or Glasgow, or even in a remote hamlet like the one where Mary Russell Mitford was virtually imprisoned, were reading *Pickwick* at the same time as people in London. The lag between the city and the country was eliminated, and *Pickwick* parts—more, I suspect, even than Scott's or Byron's new works—achieved an instant island-wide circulation" (*CDP* 66–67). "The reputations of both author and artist were made by *Pickwick*" (Muir 91) owing to its quick rise to fame and "island-wide" distribution. "It became topical matter," notes Patten, "almost like news; people asked themselves, 'What were the Pickwickians doing last month?' and hastened to their booksellers to find out" (*CDP* 67).

A Confluence of Factors

How did Pickwick assume the status of daily news? Its success grew out of Victorian commodity culture, new printing technologies, growth of the middle class, serialization, a climbing literacy rate, an increase in population (especially in urban areas), self-improvement movements, increased wages that augmented buying power, the growth of leisure time accompanying the Industrial Revolution, and the appeal of reading pictures. The confluence of these factors in the late 1830s shaped *Pickwick* and the arc of the Victorian illustrated book.

Pickwick became a highly marketable commodity even though it originally seemed destined to be "a ready-made, copper-bottomed recipe for failure" (Muir 89). Chapman and Hall produced 1,000 copies of the first print run; only 400 copies sold, despite detailed and well-placed advertisements. After barely surviving a recession in the book trade, Chapman and Hall boldly continued the serial despite Seymour's death and *Pickwick*'s initially poor sales. However, Chapman and Hall dramatically reduced the print run for part 2 from 1,000 to 500 copies. Surprisingly, sales quickly skyrocketed. By the tenth installment, so many Victorians were clamoring to know what the Pickwickians were doing that Browne had to make duplicate copies of the steel-faced copper plates to allow for the massive print runs: one set of plates could not withstand deterioration caused by so many reprintings. In February 1837, 14,000 copies sold, followed by 20,000 copies in May 1837, 29,000 copies in October 1837, and almost 40,000 copies by the publication of the final double number, issued in November 1837. From serial sales alone, Chapman and Hall made a profit of £14,000 (Patten, *CDP* 68), huge by Victorian standards. "Profitablity," as Jane R. Cohen advances, "made the once despised form respectable" (5) as a means for publishing newly released adult fiction. Eager to capitalize on and repeat *Pickwick*'s financial success, savvy publishers and editors determined to recreate the formula exactly.[19]

The Pickwick Papers took off in the 1830s, a decade of burgeoning production and consumption. *Pickwick* appealed to a mass audience ranging from the barely literate, who could "read" the pictures and listen to friends recite the adventures to them, to highly educated ladies and gentlemen of the upper reaches.[20] Often quoted is authoress Mary Mitford's recognition of *Pickwick*'s wide appeal in a letter dated 30 June 1837 to a Miss Jephson in Castle Martyr, Ireland:

> So you never heard of the "Pickwick Papers!" Well! They publish a number once a month and print 25,000.... All the boys and girls talk his fun—the boys in the streets; and yet those who are of the highest taste like it the most. Sir Benjamin Brodie takes it to read in his carriage between patient and patient; and Lord Denman studies "Pickwick" on the bench whilst the jury are deliberating. Do take some means to borrow the "Pickwick Papers." (L'Estrange 3: 78)

Mr. Samuel Pickwick likely endeared himself to Mitford's described audience—ranging from boys in the London streets, a prominent surgeon, and the Lord Chief Justice—because he is a very human character. Pickwick engages in activities of daily Victorian life—playing cards, attending a gentleman's club, dining with friends, making social calls, drinking too much on occasion, and getting into scrapes. Despite having a generous heart, Mr. Pickwick is fallible and not above the law—Pickwick lands in London's Fleet Prison when he refuses to pay damages to his landlady, Mrs. Bardell, who wins a breach of promise suit.[21] Samuel Pickwick, nonetheless, succeeds as a small-time merchant and retires comfortably. Realizing the Victorian middle-class dream of financial independence, Samuel Pickwick, in essence, validates the entrepreneurial myth of the self-made man central to "the Victorian frame of mind."[22]

Pickwick, as Dickens conceived it, is both nostalgic and modern, a combination that likely stimulated the unbridled success of the serial and products related to it. This was an age of transportation, increasing mobility, and industrialization. People were traveling for job advancement (for example, to India in service of the East India Company), to settle in new homelands (most commonly in the United States, Canada, New Zealand, and Australia), and increasingly for pleasure. The popularity of travel literature alone drew countless fans eager to follow the Pickwickians on their city and country adventures.[23] Dickens produced *The Pickwick Papers* between 1836 and 1837, but he set the serial in 1827. By about the time publication of the serial ended, steam engines had replaced stagecoaches for transportation of people and the post (in 1838), and London had a bustling railway terminal, Euston Station.

With sentimentality, Dickens looks back upon a sleepier decade prior to the advent of the railway and its associated railway mania, which was growing in England during the years Dickens was producing this very serial. In *Pickwick*, Dickens takes his readers along the coaching routes that John Palmer established when he became Comptroller General of the Mails in 1786. Monthly installments carry us from London's massive General Post Office, St. Martin's-le-Grand, to old London coaching inns across the English countryside to visit, for example, Georgian Bath where Nathaniel Winkle courts Arabella Alam and the country towns of Eatanwell, Dingley Dell, and Dulwich, where Mr. Pickwick takes a house in the final number. Reflecting on the charms that *Pickwick* offered its original readers, Arthur Locker notes in an 1870 article entitled "Charles Dickens" published in *The Graphic*: "to us oldsters *Pickwick*, quite independent of its fun, recalls the England and the London of our youth, and thus conjures up a host of delightful recollections" (452). In the illustrations, we also glimpse the rapidly disappearing provincial landscapes of an England from Dickens's youth. For example, Browne's "Mr. Pickwick Among the Ruins of the Chaise" is a comical example of Victorian drag racing—Mr. Pickwick climbs out of an overturned chaise, having failed to overtake his friends in another chaise—but the plate offers its urban viewers a verdant country landscape with a secluded lane, gnarly trees, postboys, and horses.

Dickens was sentimental about England's rural past, but Samuel Pickwick settles into a home in Dulwich filled with the advantages of Victorian commodity culture. Dickens devotes a paragraph to:

> The lawn in front, the garden behind, the miniature conservatory, the dining-room, the drawing-room, the bed-rooms, the smoking-room, and above all the study with its pictures and easy chairs, and odd cabinets, and queer tables, and books out of number, . . . and then the curtains, and the carpets, and the chairs, and the sofas! Everything was so beautiful. (*P*, Oxf. 716)

In "Archives of the Interior: Exhibitions of Domesticity in *The Pickwick Papers*," Leslie Simon describes this final setting as Pickwick's move into the "frontiers of his own domestic space" (33) and a "deliberate retreat into bourgeois domesticity" (33). How fitting that Samuel Pickwick comes to express himself through the purchase of material things since *The Pickwick Papers* found its way into middle-class Victorian homes resembling the very one Mr. Pickwick inhabits.

The monthly numbers themselves promoted commodity culture. Each installment included an ample advertising supplement. "The Pickwick Advertiser," which Andy Williams describes as "a paratextual supplement that consisted of page upon page of advertisements for all manner of commodities" (319), anticipates the catalogue of the Great Exhibition. In "Advertising and Fiction in *The Pickwick Papers*," Williams correlates the material objects included in each month's advertiser (for example, reclining chairs, Macassar oil, and a wide range of optical products) with the contents of each monthly number and concludes, "the Dickensian serial is thoroughly entangled with the commodity culture of Victorian Britain" (332).[24] The manufacture of *Pickwick*-inspired merchandise further stimulated *Pickwick*'s popularity. Victorians who bought *The Pickwick Papers* in serial and volume form also purchased a host of products inspired by it or bearing the imprint of its illustrations. *Pickwick*-inspired household items, clothing, and confections sprang up everywhere. Popular Toby Jugs called Philpots[25] bore the faces of Tracy Tupman, Nathaniel Winkle, Augustus Snodgrass, and Samuel Pickwick as Browne drew them, and manufacturers cast these same characters as salt and pepper shakers. Browne's illustrations also adorned china plates showing Mr. Pickwick in his various antics. Drapers produced curtains called Pickwick chintzes for middle-class Victorian homes. Tailors fashioned gentlemen's breeches as described by Dickens and given life by Browne to imitate the style of Sam Weller, Mr. Pickwick's Cockney servant, often dubbed his Sancho Panza.[26] Pickwick pastries and sugar candies in the shape of Joe the fat boy lined the shelves of London bakeries and confectionaries.[27]

In a preglobal age, *Pickwick* went viral. A German translation appeared in 1837, and in Germany, *The Pickwick Papers* was the most popular Dickens novel throughout the nineteenth century. French and Danish translations of *Pickwick* appeared in 1838, and Polish and Italian versions in 1840.[28] *Pickwick* joke books, bootleg copies of the book, and parodies appeared in England and other countries (for example, *Deutsche Pickwickier* and *Berliner Pickwickier* are two popular nineteenth-century German imitations). The effects of *Pickwick* on trade lasted well into the twentieth century. In 1899, Joseph Grego published "extra plates" and numerous paraphernalia from stage adaptations of *Pickwick* in a volume entitled *Pictorial Pickwickiana*. Adams and Ridgways created a *Pickwick* line of fine bone English china that was popular at the turn of the twentieth century. In their line of Dickens figurines, Royal Doulton produced character jugs and miniature figures of Alfred Jingle, Sam Weller, Joe the fat boy, Mrs. Bardell, and Mr. Pickwick from 1922 into the 1980s[29]—further testimony to the sustaining force of *Pickwick* mania.

The caricature-style illustrations for *Pickwick* are foremost theatrical, paving the way for stage adaptations that appeared even before the serial's conclusion. In his 1837 production entitled *The Pickwick Club; or, The Age We Live In!* (City of London), Edward Stirling[30] relied heavily on the original book illustrations to determine costume and setting; for certain scenes, he even evoked specific plates—for example, the script directs the reader to Phiz's "The Middle-Aged Lady in the Double-Bedded Room" for the bedroom farce scene where Pickwick peeps through the curtains to find himself in a strange woman's bedroom. Two other popular adaptations, William Thomas Moncrieff's *Sam Weller; or the Pickwickians* that appeared at the Strand in 1837 and W. L. Rede's *Peregrinations of Pickwick* staged at the Adelphi in 1837, likewise drew upon the illustrations, though less directly. *Pickwick* mania, unlike today's profitable merchandizing by Pixar and Disney, "was spontaneous, and the market tapped by Chapman and Hall—a new market, a new class of people altogether—had partially defined itself by its response to Dickens" (A. N. Wilson 19). This new class of buyers who attended play versions of *Pickwick* also bought popular prints called "extra plates" designed by various artists, often without the approval of Dickens or Chapman and Hall; one such artist named Thomas Onwhyn sometimes signed his plates Samuel Weller, bringing a fictional character to life.

The commodity culture that supported *Pickwick* in the 1830s depended upon a series of major innovations in printing[31] that helped the serial's popularity to spiral.[32] In 1800, Lord Stanhope's iron printing press came into use. In 1803, the manufacturing firm of Gamble and Donkin created a prototype for a paper-making machine, which allowed for continuous production of paper; paper size increased with this new papermaking process, a move which, in turn, decreased taxes on paper since the government charged according to the number of sheets and not the exact number of printed pages generated by each sheet. Friedrich Koenig's steam-powered cylindrical printing press, patented in 1811, revolution-ized printing; it yielded six times as many copies per hour as a hand press (900 versus 150 copies).[33] By 1816, Koenig's double cylinder steam-operated printing press made it possible to manufacture great amounts of paper inexpensively. In turn, cheaper and faster production enabled publishers to print longer works.[34]

Other new inventions in papermaking and printing carried *Pickwick* into the lives and homes of countless Victorians. These include the facing of cop-per plates with steel and duplicate plates to ensure quality printing for major print runs and the newer printing processes of electrotyping, lithography, and glyphography.[35] Although photographic methods became part of the illustra-tive process as early as 1826, techniques used in halftone and photogravure did not widely come into use until the second half of the nineteenth century be-cause they were too costly. Nonetheless, in the first half of the nineteenth cen-tury, alternatives arose to woodblock engraving, itself a variation on traditional woodcutting used in the fifteenth and sixteenth centuries by, most famously, Albrecht Dürer. Thomas Bewick excelled in woodblock engraving, a technique that integrated illustration into commercial printing. Copperplate engraving became common in the late eighteenth and early nineteenth centuries; how-ever, with this technique, the quality of reproduction suffered with mass pro-duction. Steel engraving came into commercial use in the 1820s; compared to copper, steel improved the quality of printing for a far larger print run, but even steel plates required duplication to keep up with growing demand for Dickens's works (Patten, *CDP* 68).

In this age of information and industrialization, printers were reproducing better and cheaper images. The market for illustrated fiction, particularly il-lustrated serials, was steadily growing, attaining previously impossible heights. The publishing industry was also becoming specialized—there were printers, binders, advertisers, and booksellers, et cetera. Specialization stimulated the growth of the publishing industry since it cut the financial risk for any one party. This move toward specialization eroded the art of the handmade book, which the Arts and Crafts movement revived at the fin de siècle. At the time of *Pickwick*'s creation, however, expensive handcrafted books were giving way to machine-made books and serials, a development Walter Benjamin famously laments in "The Work of Art in the Age of Mechanical Reproduction."[36]

Pickwick was selling record numbers and attracting a mass audience in an age of mechanical reproduction. England was shifting from a two-tiered agrarian society to a three-tiered, industrial new class society, and literacy was rising.[37] In 1837, about 15 percent of the population was middle class, but in 1901, approximately 25 percent of the population was middle class (Mitchell, *Daily* 20). In 1841, four years after the final installment of *The Pickwick Papers* appeared, the number of inhabitants in England and Wales was 15,914,148. By 1901, the year of Queen Victoria's death, the population of England and Wales had more than doubled, reaching a figure of 32,527,843.[38] Of equal importance is the distribution of the British population. *Pickwick* took off with the growth of urbanism. In the early years of the nineteenth century, approximately 75 percent of the populace lived in small rural villages and towns. This percentage essentially reversed by the end of the nineteenth century; historians estimate that by 1901, 75 to 80 percent of the population lived in large cities mainly in the north of England.[39] The serial appealed to this growing and increasingly literate urban middle-class population and the enterprising working class eager for self-improvement.

Literacy was steadily on the rise in Victorian England (even if all factions did not endorse universal literacy). *Pickwick* appeared three decades after King George III's 1803 pronouncement that all the members of his kingdom should be able to read the Bible. When Queen Victoria took the throne, about half the population could read and write although children under ten labored over ten hours a day in coalmines and factories. "By the time Queen Victoria died in 1901," notes Sally Mitchell in *Daily Life in Victorian England*, public education was compulsory, 97 percent of the population of England and Wales was literate,[40] and "the modern world had taken shape" (xiv). In *The English Common Reader*, Richard Altick aligns the rise of literacy to the production of attractive and affordable reading material following the coming of the Penny Post in 1840. The Society for the Diffusion of Useful Knowledge and Mechanics Institutes, which also impacted the growth of literacy, predate this 1840 measure. The Society for the Diffusion of Useful Knowledge, founded in 1826 and associated with the publisher Charles Knight, printed the popular *The Penny Magazine* and *The Penny Cyclopaedia* to promote literacy and provide cheap reading material to members of the working class and lower middle class who were eager to improve themselves but did not have ready access to education.[41] Mechanics Institutes with an emphasis on technical subjects geared for working-class men also sprang up in England in the 1820s, offering adult education to members of the working class.

In this new industrialized society, Dickens's fiction readily appealed across the social classes, and serialization lowered the cost of book production. Savvy publishers could increase or decrease the number of copies in a print run according to the popularity of a given work.[42] For serials published within monthly and weekly periodicals, publishers commonly featured a new serial alongside a popular one to persuade audiences to continue buying that same periodical.[43] A successful serial published either independently in parts or within periodical publication kept Victorian consumers in a stream of continuous buying over a period of years and "put the ownership of novels within the means of the middle class" (Patten, *CDP* 60). Moreover, *Pickwick* appeared in an era when members of the middle and working classes had time for leisure. With England's shift from an agrarian to an urban society and the growth of industry, Sunday, the Sabbath day, allowed some time for relaxation—including reading. Dickens's serial numbers found their way into pubs, a common leisure pastime for the working class. Most Victorians who were illiterate knew at least one person in a circle of friends who could read; "You did not need to be literate to enjoy literature" (43), as Simon Eliot reminds us in "The Business of Victorian Publishing."[44]

"Dickens was the first English novelist really to *belong* to the people of England," Patten notes, "and they loved him all the more because he was, so to speak, a resident in their homes" (*CDP* 60). Dickens was not a resident in the homes of all his admirers, however. One could pay one shilling a month for an installment of *Pickwick* or use that same shilling to buy a family of seven at least one week's supply of candles and soap (Mitchell, *Daily* 38).[45] A shilling was still a considerable sum in 1837, especially for entertainment, and hardback books were luxury items in the economic reality of early Victorian times. A three-volume novel produced at the time of *Pickwick* cost £1. 11s. and 6d. (A. N. Wilson 19); for the same price as a novel, one could purchase a used bicycle or a low-cost women's dress (Mitchell, *Daily* 32). When *Pickwick* was completed, it cost a total of 20 shillings, which was approximately two-thirds of a hardback book and nearly the price of a yearly subscription to a lending library. However, the payments were spread over one-and-a-half to two years or longer since the consumer bought the serial as it was being produced.[46] In this economic climate, savvy publishers produced multiple editions of a particular work, including cheap editions with roughly cut edges and bindings made of boards (as opposed to cloth or leather), and also pitched serial publications for an increasingly literate urban population with augmented buying power and leisure time to read.

The Appeal of Illustration: Social Commentary and, Quintessentially, Humor

Today it may seem surprising that Seymour's black-and-white illustrations "had called *Pickwick* into existence" (J. R. Cohen 46). Illustrations captivated early nineteenth-century viewers and provided a peak form of entertainment. Today, we easily succumb to media overstimulation, but the early Victorians lived in an age that was, in comparison, visually sparse. In 1837, there were no computers, movies, television, radio, public art museums, or even free circulating libraries. Following the reduction of the Stamp Tax on newspapers in 1836 and postal reform enacted in 1840, newspapers and letters could, respectively, travel anywhere in the United Kingdom for only a penny.[47] These measures led to an increase in pictorial material passing through the post. The Victorians savored pictures in broadsides, valentines, seed catalogues, pattern books, fashion magazines, and newspapers. Inaugurated in 1842, *The Illustrated London News* was the first illustrated weekly newspaper in the world. The first issue has only sixteen pages of text, but thirty-two wood engravings. Circulation of *The Illustrated London News* soared in England after the magazine published designs for the Crystal Palace, the crowning landmark of the Great Exhibition of 1851, and tintypes of the Crimean War (1853–56). The inauguration of *The Illustrated London News* and its unprecedented popularity demonstrate the importance of the picture in a range of material forms valued by the early Victorian consumer.

By the mid-nineteenth century, works not originally published with illustrations, such as Shakespeare's plays and many of Scott's Waverley novels, were reissued with illustrations alongside newly published illustrated fiction in serial form. By then, there was a financial advantage for publishers to bring forth new fiction serially with illustration: advertisers, savvy to the marketing incentive of illustrated periodicals, paid publishers to include their advertisements, which guaranteed a large audience if the serial became as popular as *Pickwick*. Also, *Pickwick* and successive serials had "extra illustrations," additional scenes not included in the serial that had prime market value. The front window of a print seller's shop was a powerful marketing tool. Shrewd publishers and print sellers recognized that with a month lapsing between parts, illustrations refreshed readers about a serial's plot, characters, and themes, bringing them up to date before they resumed reading the latest installment. Pictures often enticed a new reader to purchase a serial or reminded potential buyers that it was time to buy the latest part issue. Bystanders gathered to read prints and book illustrations displayed in shop windows. Illustrations engaged marginally literate readers in an unfolding storyline; if the words eluded this population of readers, the barely literate could read the pictures while they listened to the text. Simultaneously, a cultured and sophisticated audience read beyond the lines of the text; illustrative cues both delineated and foreshadowed developments in plot, theme, and characterization and in some cases introduced material not present in the text. In this climate, illustrations, integral to Dickens's serials, brought him popular acclaim and commercial success.

Critics align the illustrations for *The Pickwick Papers* with the eighteenth-century tradition of graphic satire and caricature associated with William Hogarth.[48] A multifaceted artist, Hogarth was a portrait painter, political satirist, printmaker, and social critic who could paint with realism as well as exaggeration. Robert Seymour and Phiz produced comic prints and illustrations that use caricature techniques of exaggeration and distortion, theatricality, and Hogarthian realism to make a point and alternately to amuse—to present social commentary as well as to entertain with broad farce. Seymour and, in turn, Phiz drew Samuel Pickwick as a big-hearted, comical character in full motion. Pickwick has misadventures with horses, drinks too much, falls asleep and awakes in an animal pound, plays "peeping tom," finds himself the unwelcome object of his landlady's affection, and falls through the ice. "Character and situation had to be seen to be funny," notes Harvey in *Victorian Novelists and Their Illustrators*, "and it is evident that for some readers they had to be drawn to be seen" (8). Visual humor as witnessed in plates like "Mr. Pickwick in Chase of His Hat" helped to make *Pickwick* a resounding international success. The serial's comic appeal has overshadowed its ability to make piercing pleas for philanthropy and to promote Christian charity, traits that did not go undetected by Dickens's contemporaries. An 1838 reviewer named T. H. Lister comments in *Edinburgh Review*:

> One of the qualities we most admire in [Dickens] is his comprehensive spirit of humanity. The tendency of his writings is to make us practically benevolent—to excite our sympathy in behalf of the aggrieved and the suffering in all classes; and especially in those who are most removed from observation. (139)

Samuel Pickwick acts with moral responsibility and, as early as the second number, shows empathy for those less fortunate in the oft-criticized "The Stroller's Tale."

"The Dying Clown," which accompanies the "The Stroller's Tale," is one of the most contentious plates that Seymour created for *Pickwick* before his untimely death. Dickens harshly criticized Seymour's first sketch and demanded another drawing of "The Dying Clown," which Seymour completed just hours before he took his own life. Dickens later asked Phiz to re-etch the drawing, but Browne did not substantially alter Seymour's design. The scene as Seymour created it—and Browne essentially redrew to make it more aesthetically pleasing to Dickens—is melodrama with a humanitarian purpose. This plate drips with melodrama, but it also turns the Victorian viewer's attention to "those who are most removed from observation" to recall the words of the 1838 *Edinburgh* reviewer. Seymour resented the inclusion of Dickens's lengthy episode in a comedy allegedly about sporting gentleman. Dickens admits that this tale tells of "'Want and sickness . . . too common in many stations of life'" (*P*, Oxf. 32). It is a story within a story: a struggling "strolling actor" named Jem Hutley (40), known as "Dismal Jemmy," tells Samuel Pickwick and Augustus Snodgrass about a dying clown, a "'low pantomime actor; and, like many people of his class, an habitual drunkard'" (33). The clown and his wife and child live in poverty and experience slow starvation. "The Dying Clown" as conceived by Seymour and redrawn by Browne (see fig. 4) pictures the actor just before his death: wandering in his mad delirium to happier days in the theater, the dying clown raises himself up and melodramatically extends one arm toward his wife and child, who look on with horror.[49] With the other hand, the dying man grabs hold of Hutley's shoulder, attempting to speak, just before he "'fell back—dead!'" (38).

Perhaps in an attempt to provide letterpress for Seymour's original illustration as he was contracted to do, Dickens prepares us for the death scene, poignantly commenting on the clown's "bloated body and shrunken legs," "glassy eyes," "grotesquely-ornamented head, trembling with paralysis," and "hollow and tremulous" voice (*P*, Oxf. 34). Earlier in the scene, Hutley takes pity upon the dying clown, who, Dickens tells us, looks more "ghastly" than the figures in the late medieval allegory *Dance of Death* (34). Hutley gives the stroller a few shillings and twice comes to the dying man's lodging in a "comfortless" (35) wind-riddled coal shed. The emaciated actor in Browne's version is still "frightful to behold," for "the dry hard skin glowed with a burning heat, and there was an almost unearthly air of wild anxiety in the man's face, indicating even more strongly the ravages of the disease" (36). The stroller's large wild eyes and

Figure 4. "The Dying Clown." Illustration by Hablot Knight Browne (based on Robert Seymour's 1836 illustration) for Charles Dickens's *The Posthumous Papers of the Pickwick Club*, 1837. From the Norman M. Fox Collection, Scribner Library, Skidmore College.

ribs, visible through his partially open nightshirt, illustrate starvation. We can almost hear the death rattle in the poverty-stricken clown's gaunt throat as he takes his last breath. The gaunt-cheeked, hollow-eyed wife looks miserable, no doubt fearing the uncertain future awaiting herself and the babe she desperately clutches to her chest. The starving family in such cramped quarters expresses dire poverty to move the viewer to pity and charity.

This philanthropically minded *Pickwick* plate is not an isolated case. Likewise, in "The Discovery of Jingle in the Fleet" (see fig. 23B, ch. 2, 89), one of four prison plates, Browne ushers us into Fleet Prison to witness the miserable poverty of those forced to live in the poor area of debtors' prison. In "Discovery," Pickwick encounters the now impoverished Alfred Jingle, a strolling actor and trickster reduced to the common side of the Fleet. In the plate, Pickwick and Jingle are posed melodramatically, although the staging directions seemingly come from Dickens's "hand," adorned by Phiz's "glove." Pickwick has his arms aloft to indicate his "amazement" (*P*, Oxf. 535) at discovering Jingle, "his head resting upon his hand, his eyes fixed upon the fire, and his whole appearance denoting misery and dejection!" (534). The exclamation mark invites pictorial exaggeration. Indeed, upon seeing Pickwick, Jingle as Browne pictures him covers his face with his hands and "sobbed like a child" (537). Mr. Pickwick can afford a private apartment in the Fleet, but here he enters the poor side of Fleet Prison to find someone to run his errands. Jingle's servant, Job Trotter, who is free to leave the prison, is just returning with food for the starving Jingle, who has pawned his clothes for a meal. Goodhearted Pickwick will eventually bail Jingle out of prison, helping him to settle in the West Indies and begin life anew.[50]

Like "The Dying Clown," this plate, which closely matches Dickens's text, presents caricature for a social purpose.[51] The poorest inmates of the Fleet—young and old, male and female, human and canine—are locked up because they cannot pay their debts. In "The Discovery of Jingle in the Fleet," Browne fills this small dreary prison stage with eleven figures, objects scattered on the floor, clothing hanging to dry, and a few crude pieces of furniture. We see a crazed countryman holding a worn-out whip that he flicks against his boot since he is "riding, in imagination" (*P*, Oxf. 534); a diminutive fireplace; men conversing by a window; a prisoner's "haggard" (534) wife tending a dying plant; and an elderly, diseased grandfather unaware of his granddaughter's "voice that had been music to him" (534).[52]

But Browne also adds details not mentioned in the text—posters, an alcoholic woman, and a dog. The poster on the left wall spells out the rules of the prison, an ironic feature given the unruliness of the place; Cruikshank likewise uses this caricature technique in *The Drunkard's Children* (1848), posting rules that the inhabitants of the gin room blatantly ignore. Browne's antislavery poster on the right wall, not mentioned in the text, comments on the inmates' situation at the Fleet. Attributing this stage prop to Browne's ingenuity, Michael Steig suggests the poster is a famous antislavery design entitled "Am I Not a Man and a Brother?" that "has made the imprisoned hero suddenly conscious of his common humanity with [Jingle and Trotter]" (*Dickens and Phiz* 14). An alcoholic hag, rendered as a grotesque caricature, looms ominously behind and above Trotter. The old woman raises her wrists in fury because Trotter is blocking the doorway, but the cramped common area makes ironic her mad urgency to enter the small closed prison space. Also in a fury, the small dog, skillfully rendered, barks at the huntsman, who is so engaged in his imaginative steeplechase that he does not notice the canine at all.[53] The woman, dog, and granddaughter project rage, frustration, and sadness, respectively, vibrant emotions trapped in the immobility of prison.

These *Pickwick* illustrations could move the reader with their social commentary, but comic fancy undeniably commanded the attention of the original reader-viewers and made *Pickwick* a commercial triumph. Phiz stages humor to dramatic effect in "The Middle-Aged Lady in the Double-Bedded Room." The scene occurs when Pickwick arrives in Ipswich in pursuit of the rascally Alfred Jingle (before he lands in the Fleet). At the Great White Horse Inn in Ipswich, Pickwick dines with a Mr. Peter Magnus, who has come to propose to a middle-aged lady named Miss Witherfield. Given the lateness of the hour and the many rows of doors at the inn, Pickwick mistakenly enters a double-bedded room, the very chamber prepared for Miss Witherfield, who quietly enters the room after Mr. Pickwick has retired to his bed. In this illustration set as a dramatic stage, Pickwick, with a pointed nightcap, peeps out from the bed curtains to discover a mysterious lady (aka Miss Witherfield) in a nightgown combing out her hair. The scene anticipates the next moment where Miss Witherfield shrieks, "'A strange man!'" (*P*, Oxf. 278) and "thrust him into the passage, and locked and bolted the door behind him" (279). This is a quintessential example of "'English bedroom farce,' that is, a situational comedy with mistaken identity but without genuine sexual impropriety" (P. Allingham, "Standing"),[54] and the illustration prompts us to laugh at the absurdity of the situation.

Two chapters later, after Magnus proposes to and is accepted by Miss Witherfield, Magnus introduces his fiancée to Mr. Pickwick, and pandemonium breaks out. The two immediately recognize each other, but decency forbids them telling Mr. Magnus how they previously met. Magnus and Pickwick quarrel, and, fearing a duel has taken place and that Magnus is shot, Miss Witherfield tells her tale to a Magistrate named Mr. Nupkins, who promptly arrests Pickwick and Tupman, believed to be the second in the duel. Of course, no duel has taken place, and eventually, Pickwick secures his own release and Tupman's by informing Mr. Nupkins of Alfred Jingle's designs on the Magistrate's own daughter.

The accompanying plate is a pregnant moment: it anticipates Miss Wither-field's indignation, which, in turn, sets in motion a series of events that lead to Pickwick's mistaken guilt, temporary incarceration, and pardon. The dramatic expression of "horror and dismay" (*P*, Oxf. 277) on the bespectacled, night-capped Mr. Pickwick intimates he is worried what will come of a man being found in a woman's bedroom, a most unbecoming situation in the early Victorian age even if it is a simple misunderstanding. To ensure that there is no actual impropriety in this English bedroom farce, Browne draws bed curtains around Mr. Pickwick (although the drapes reveal the silhouette of his wide shoulders) and depicts Miss Witherfield in a full-length nightgown. Nonetheless, Miss Witherfield has already removed her dressing gown and nightcap to comb her hair, and Pickwick looks as if he knows full well he should not be peering at a lady who is clearly unaware of his presence (her back is turned toward him). Broad-faced Mr. Pickwick peeps anyway, elevating the comedy.[55]

Pickwick's plumpness and the inclusion of a chorus of laughing onlook-ers in two particular plates—"Mr. Pickwick in the Pound" and "Mr. Pickwick Slides"—make "the comic fancy a reality one could laugh at" (Harvey 8). To be funny, Mr. Pickwick had to be fat.[56] We can trace the well-established connec-tion between plumpness and jollity from Shakespeare's fleshy, jovial Falstaff to today's portly, jovial Santa Claus with his trademark "ho, ho ho." Readers today may be surprised to learn that Seymour in his original sketches drew Pickwick as a tall, thin sporting enthusiast.[57] Chapman, in particular, urged Seymour to fatten up Pickwick even though Seymour, in drawing him as slim, was not actu-ally contradicting Dickens's text. In the monthly numbers, Dickens stipulates baldness, glasses, and genteel dress, but makes no mention of Pickwick's physi-cal size. Chapman, however, had peeked at Dickens's script and knew that Pick-wick remains good-humored throughout all his scrapes. Chapman insisted that Mr. Pickwick be plump and allegedly took Seymour with him to Richmond to see "'a fat old beau who would wear, in spite of the ladies' protests, drab tights and black gaiters'" (qtd. in Muir 89).

Whether or not Seymour based Pickwick on this fat Richmond beau,[58] Pickwick wears fitted tights and gaiters in the initial plates by Seymour, who sealed Pickwick's appearance in the early Victorian consciousness. Indeed, Pickwick's look changed surprisingly little from the pencil of Seymour to Buss to Browne, who perfected Pickwick's image.[59] Another stage technique, the inclusion of amused bystanders, like plumpness, invites viewers to laugh at Pickwick in an embarrassing moment. The tickled onlookers encourage laughter—not by holding up cue cards, as we still witness in live television programming today—but by giggling at Pickwick and encouraging the audience to laugh along with them. In "Mr. Pickwick in the Pound" and "Mr. Pickwick Slides," the onlookers, far slimmer than Pickwick, magnify Pickwick's roundness. And in both scenes, Pickwick wears a beaming expression and looks "as if [he] thought [his current misadventure] as good a joke as anybody else" (*P*, Oxf. 46).

"Mr. Pickwick in the Pound" (see fig. 5) is a visual climax of a gaming outing where Pickwick joins three members of the Pickwick Club (Wardle, Winkle, and Trundle) when they go hunting in an open carriage and boldly trespass upon Captain Boldwig's land. Mr. Pickwick—eager to observe the sport of hunting—accompanies the shooting party in a wheelbarrow, pushed by his faithful servant, Sam Weller. During a picnic lunch, Pickwick consumes too much punch, and his drunkenness along with the heat leads him to fall into a stupor. The shooting party, now including Weller, heads off to hunt some more, so the group leaves Pickwick asleep, snoring in a wheelbarrow in the shade. According to Dickens, "a gentleman in a barrow" is "a gross violation of all established rules and precedents" (*P*, Oxf. 225) of a shooting-party. When Boldwig, a "little fierce man in a stiff black neckerchief" (232), discovers a snoring gentleman in a wheelbarrow trespassing on his land, he takes action. This plate features the adventure's climax: Pickwick awakens in an animal pound where he is being pelted with "a turnip, and then a potato, and then an egg, with a few other little tokens of the playful disposition of the many-headed" (235).

A theatrical illustration, "Mr. Pickwick in the Pound" places an undignified, portly Samuel Pickwick center stage, sitting in a wheelbarrow in an animal pound next to a fat sleeping sow and two young pigs who sniff the turnip positioned close to Pickwick's black-gaitered feet. A donkey turns away from its baby to bray directly into Pickwick's right ear, exposed because his hat—though on his head—is askew. Pickwick's slim legs sticking straight out of the wheelbarrow call attention to Pickwick's huge belly. Browne also exaggerates the gestures and facial features of the young and old villagers chuckling at the spectacle, tipping—but not losing—their hats, some jeering at Pickwick, embarrassed by his predicament. Happily, Pickwick's friends discover him in the pound, and he escapes intact with his good-humored smile on his face.

"Mr. Pickwick Slides" (see fig. 6) also incorporates a crowd of amused onlookers as well as exaggerated expressions and gestures, caricature techniques

Figure 5. "Mr. Pickwick in the Pound." Illustration by Hablot Knight Browne from an 1836 serial installment of Charles Dickens's *The Posthumous Papers of the Pickwick Club*. From an 1837 edition in the Norman M. Fox Collection, Scribner Library, Skidmore College.

Figure 6. "Mr. Pickwick Slides." Illustration by Hablot Knight Browne from an 1837 serial installment of Charles Dickens's *The Posthumous Papers of the Pickwick Club*. From an 1837 edition in the Norman M. Fox Collection, Scribner Library, Skidmore College.

that liken this plate to slapstick comedy. Pickwick is attempting the sport of ice skating, also called "sliding." Dickens describes sliding as "skimming over the ice on one foot, and occasionally giving a two-penny postman's knock upon it, with the other" (*P, Oxf.* 369). Pickwick is envious of the "fancy slide" of his fellow Pickwickian, Mr. Weller, whose fancy footwork on ice resembles a common sound in the days before affordable prepaid postage.[60] Though Pickwick admits he has not skated since he was a boy, at the urging of the ladies pictured here, Pickwick amiably agrees to join Weller, Wardle, and Winkle and slide in his black gaiters.[61]

Browne elects not to show the climax of the scene where Pickwick falls through the ice, "and Mr. Pickwick's hat, gloves, and handkerchief were floating on the surface; and this was all of Mr. Pickwick that anybody could see" (P, Oxf. 372). Nonetheless, Browne chooses a "pregnant moment" that might have even pleased Gotthold Ephraim Lessing (originator of that term in *Laocöon*) in foreshadowing Pickwick's ice escapade. Staged for comic effect, the illustration shows Pickwick just before he plunges into the water and surfaces with his clothes covered with water and clay. In this illustrated moment, Pickwick, complete with his trademark circular spectacles and black hat and gaiters, stands erect in the center of the ice with his legs very wide apart. Pickwick is approaching a split "with his feet about a yard and a quarter apart" (370), and he looks as if he may just split his breeches or be knocked down, "which happened [to him] upon the average every third round" (370). The woman to the right of the picture plane looks straight at the audience, covering her mouth to hide her laughter. A cute canine positioned in the front of the plate also looks amused and wags its tail. Other onlookers gaze at each other and Pickwick, a figure of folly. In this plate, we glimpse the future amusement Mr. Pickwick will afford the crowd when he actually falls through the ice. Friends quickly rush in to drape Pickwick in shawls and carry him to his friend Tupman's farm. Tucked in bed, Pickwick, essentially unharmed, presides as President of the Pickwick Club and readies himself for his next adventure.

Packed with comedy, theatricality, and some social commentary, *The Pickwick Papers* generated a broad readership for illustrated fiction in the 1830s and quickly became a model for publication of newly released, illustrated serial fiction for adult readers. Browne stands among the first generation of caricature-style illustrators who visually interpreted texts by Dickens and other early Victorian authors for a mass public, as I explore in the next chapter. Clearly something magical and momentous was happening in 1836–37 in England, and *Pickwick* was at the heart of this confluence of events.

2

⌒⌒⌒

Caricature

A Theatrical Development

And, indeed, what does not the great Dickens himself owe
to Cruikshank and Hablôt Browne, those two delightful etchers
who understood and interpreted him so well!

George Du Maurier, "The Illustrating of Books
from the Serious Artist's Point of View—1," 1890

When George Du Maurier published "The Illustrating of Books" at the fin de
siècle, Charles Dickens's works had already been re-illustrated for the Household Edition. Du Maurier, a Sixties artist and a fan of the caricaturists, returns
his late Victorian readers' gaze to the aesthetics of two of Dickens's original
caricature-style illustrators, George Cruikshank and Hablot Knight Browne
(Phiz), whose *Pickwick* illustrations gave Dickens celebrity status.

Caricature-style illustration of the 1830s and 1840s evolved from sixteenth-
century mock portraits by Annibale Carracci, satiric eighteenth-century progresses by William Hogarth, and individual comic prints by Hogarth's heirs:
James Gillray; Thomas Rowlandson; and George Cruikshank, who earned a
reputation for his early nineteenth-century satiric plates before he entered the
field of book illustration. The term "caricature" derives from the Italian "*caricare*," which means "to overload" or "surcharge." In the sixteenth and seven-
teenth centuries, *caricare* applied only to mock portraiture. Beginning with
Gillray and Rowlandson, Cruikshank's direct forebears, comic "prints and similar products began to be called 'caricatures,'" note E. H. Gombrich and E. Kris
in *Caricature* (19); "Aims and means were the same in both types—to ridicule
and castigate by means of light-hearted playful distortion" (19). Distortion and
exaggeration have come to stereotype the achievement of the caricaturists and

diminish their contribution to the Victorian illustrated book, but even those invested in Sixties illustration recognize that the caricature school of illustration is "above all, theatrical" (Goldman and Cooke 28).[1]

In its theatricality, caricature-style book illustration approximates the dramatic tableau, a style of performance that predates the nineteenth century but is closely associated with early nineteenth-century drama. Defined inclusively, "*tableau vivant*, or 'living picture,' refers to the representation of some well-known person, scene, or incident, whether taken from a verbal or visual source, by a performer or performers who, appropriately attired and positioned, hold their poses silently and motionlessly" (J. E. Hill 438). In the nineteenth century, charades, private theatricals, and *tableaux vivants* were enormously popular forms of entertainment in private homes among members of the upper middle class and the gentry. As Martin Meisel notes in *Realizations*, "The *tableau vivant* apparently took hold as a widespread genteel social entertainment on the order of charades after Goethe published *Die Wahlverwandtschaften* (1809)" (47). In England, James Robinson Planché and Douglas Jerrold established the *tableau vivant* on the London stage with, respectively, *The Brigand* (1829), based on three paintings by Charles Eastlake, and *Rent Day* (1832), after two paintings by David Wilkie.[2] Painting, drama, and fiction were interdependent genres, as Meisel reminds us: "In the nineteenth century all three forms are narrative and pictorial" (3). Moreover, at the time Cruikshank was designing plates for serials by Charles Dickens and William Harrison Ainsworth, the middle class was beginning to attend the theater (although this group once considered the theater disreputable), and Dickens's and Ainsworth's popular serials were quickly being translated into plays.[3] The success of such dramatizations drew more potential reader-viewers to these very serials with illustrations that reflect the style of the dramatic tableau.

As Jonathan Hill posits in "Cruikshank, Ainsworth, and Tableau Illustration," Ainsworth's works were well suited to the stage because Cruikshank's illustrations "were never really designed to be viewed buried within the pages of an Ainsworth novel but rather to be resurrected on the stage and 'mysteriously made to breathe'" (459). To apply this insight more broadly, popular serials illustrated by Cruikshank and Phiz were easily adapted into plays because the illustrations often present the illusion of a stage. Indeed, one anonymous 1838 reviewer of *Oliver Twist* in the *Spectator* points to the appropriateness of theatrical illustration for Dickens's early novels by calling the literary characters "actors": "[Dickens] has the great art of bringing his actors and incidents before the reader by a few effective strokes" ("Boz's Oliver Twist" 1115).

This chapter examines book illustrations by George Cruikshank, Hablot Knight Browne, Richard Doyle, John Leech, and Robert Cruikshank that, like tableaux, capture a theatrical moment in works by, among others, Dickens, Ainsworth, and William Makepeace Thackeray. Using theatrical techniques including lighting, props, clever casting, and detail-laden backdrops, the caricaturists staged scenes ranging from the sensational to the sentimental, from the deeply psychological to the broadly comic. I include two Victorian author-illustrators on this list of recognized caricaturists: Thackeray, Cruikshank's most fervent fan, and Lewis Carroll. Better known as an author than an illustrator, Thackeray designed pictorial capital letters, vignettes, tailpieces, and full-page engravings for his best-known *Vanity Fair* (*VF*, 1848). In his casting of Becky Sharp in various stage roles, Thackeray arouses our suspicions without ever condemning his heroine. Carroll designed amateur caricature-style illustrations for *Alice's Adventures Under Ground* (*UG*, 1864), the first version of *Alice's Adventures in Wonderland* (1865). Looking across the arc of the Victorian illustrated book, we see how at a time when realistic illustration held sway, Carroll in the 1860s recalled popular caricature techniques of the 1830s and 1840s to dramatize Alice's frequent bodily transformations. This chapter concludes with a discussion of the caricaturists' artistic limitations and scandals (for example, Robert Seymour's suicide and Cruikshank's claim of authoring Dickens's works) that led to a devaluation of the caricaturists and a privileging of Royal Academy-trained artists who became book illustrators in the 1850s.

Theatricality in Early Illustrated Blockbusters

Charles Dickens's *Oliver Twist* (1837–39) and William Harrison Ainsworth's *Jack Sheppard* (1839–40)—both illustrated by George Cruikshank[4]—made their appearance in *Bentley's Miscellany*, reminding us of the fluid relationship between nineteenth-century book publication and the periodical press. From the vantage point of the twenty-first century, we might be surprised that *Jack Sheppard* (*JS*), a largely forgotten "book of the hour," surpassed *Oliver Twist* (*OT*) in sales; today, it is hard to find a copy of *Jack Sheppard* in print while *Oliver Twist* is a "book of all time."[5] Reviews compared *Oliver Twist* and *Jack Sheppard*, which overlapped in *Bentley's Miscellany*, a journal associated with Newgate fiction. "The two novels were naturally linked in the eyes of the reading public," as Diana Archibald argues in "'Of All the Horrors . . . the Foulest and Most Cruel': Sensation and Dickens's *Oliver Twist*" (54).[6]

The Newgate novel is a popular subgenre in the literature of crime that drew upon the lives of real criminals.[7] A second-generation thief, Jack Sheppard (1702–24)[8] became a lower-class hero and gained more acclaim as an escape artist (he broke out of prison four times) than for his crimes of fencing, shoplifting, pickpocketing, and burglary.[9] The association of *Oliver Twist* with *Jack Sheppard* riled Dickens,[10] who vented his frustration in a letter to R. H. Horne dated February 1840: "I am by some jolter-headed enemies most unjustly and untruly charged with having written a book after Mr Ainsworth's fashion. Unto these jolter-heads and their intensely concentrated humbug, I shall take an early opportunity of temperately replying" (House and Storey 2: 20–21).

Dickens's humbug aside, both serials were publishing sensations, quickly adapted into dramatic productions that generated performance paraphernalia—for example, play bills, posters, press releases, and cheap imitations.[11] Productions of *Oliver Twist* began in the spring of 1838 when the serial was only half complete. Translations of *Twist* into numerous languages swiftly followed including Danish and Italian in 1840, French in 1841, Czech and Hungarian in 1843, and Swedish in 1844 (Hollington xxvi). George Almar's adaptation of *Oliver Twist*, produced at the Surrey Theatre ten days after the serial's completion, unmistakably evokes and animates Cruikshank's plates, sometimes reversing the orientation of an illustration or expanding an illustrative frame by adding interior developments to an exterior scene. Dickens's *Nicholas Nickleby* (1838–39) came out in tableaux based on Browne's sketches when only a third of the twenty parts had appeared serially.[12] This same formula of dramatization continued for Ainsworth's popular serials. "A scant two years after the first stage versions of *Pickwick*," as Martin Meisel observes in *Realizations*, "the pictorial novel dramatized pictorially reached an exemplary climax in the *Jack Sheppard* craze" (265). *Jack Sheppard* generated a commodity craze: its pamphlets, prints, cartoons, piracies, and plays eclipsed *Pickwick* mania.[13]

Cruikshank's illustrations drew a mass readership to *Jack Sheppard* and *Oliver Twist*, and the sensational elements in both serials electrified theatergoers. Scenes such as "Nancy's murder," notes Sue Zemka, "always belonged to the art of the theater more than the art of the novel—so much so that Dickens finally performed it himself in his farewell reading tours of 1868–69" (30–31). Although Cruikshank did not illustrate this scene, the Household Edition of *Oliver Twist* and graphic novel adaptations of *Oliver Twist*, which I examine, respectively, in chapter 3 and the conclusion, depict Nancy's graphic end.

The "dramatic versions of *Jack Sheppard* that survive are faithful to the pictures, and rather free with the text. They rely on the pictures for effect" (Meisel

271). Cruikshank's scenes on the stormy Thames and Jack's prison escapes were well suited for the theater since these illustrations were already staged for effect.[14] In *An Essay on the Genius of George Cruikshank*, a lengthy laudatory essay first published in the *Westminster Review* in 1840, Thackeray proposes "that Mr Cruikshank really created the tale, and that Mr Ainsworth, as it were, only put words to it" (53).[15] To Thackeray, the Victorian reader-viewer long remembers *Jack Sheppard* not because of Ainsworth's descriptions, but for "George Cruikshank's pictures—always George Cruikshank's pictures" (*An Essay* 53).[16] One memorable theatrical illustration entitled "Jack Sheppard in Company with Edgeworth Bess Escaping from Clerkenwell Prison" (see fig. 7) features Jack with Elizabeth Lyon; known as Edgeworth Bess, Lyon was the prostitute who led the real Jack Sheppard to a life of crime and was instrumental in his third prison break.[17] In the serial, Ainsworth glamorizes the hurdles that Jack must surmount to escape incarceration as well as Jack's bravado: "'It's almost worth while being sent to prison to have the pleasure of escaping,'" Jack declares boldly; "'I shall now be able to test my skill'" (*JS* 284).[18] In Cruikshank's dramatic illustration, Lyon is escaping from New Prison along with Jack.[19] Indeed, Ainsworth explains how Sheppard rips part of Bess's gown and petticoat, forms a running noose, and descends from the high prison window. In the illustration, the night sky, streaked with dramatically rendered clouds and a pastoral landscape, provides a romantic backdrop that contrasts to the brick prison; the natural world offers freedom from the built world of legal conventions that cannot contain Jack Sheppard, escape artist extraordinaire.

In the escape scene, Cruikshank spotlights the upper half of Jack's slender but muscular physique; his strength and small stature—Sheppard was only 5 foot 4 inches tall—were a perfect combination for slipping through prison bars. Framed by an arched window, Jack holds the makeshift rope and guides his lover/prostitute to safety. The chosen moment of illustration depicts Jack Sheppard in a gallant gesture that refined him for a middle-class audience who read Ainsworth's work as eagerly as those of the lower reaches. There is also sensuality to this plate. Cruikshank's drawings of women were never his strongpoint, but in this plate, full-figured Bess has definite appeal. Bess is not "bulky" as Ainsworth describes her (*JS* 284). Partially disrobed of gown and petticoat, Bess bares her sensual curves—an ample bosom, shapely thighs, flowing hair (that is not covered as would be the custom), and delicate ankles (revealed by her now torn petticoat). These features to a Victorian viewer marked Bess a fallen woman, but Cruikshank recognized that such sensuality made the illustration soft pornography for the male viewers drawn to Newgate fiction. Note-

Figure 7. "Jack Sheppard in Company with Edgeworth Bess Escaping from Clerkenwell Prison." Illustration by George Cruikshank for William Harrison Ainsworth's "Jack Sheppard" in *Bentley's Miscellany*, July 1839. From the Norman M. Fox Collection, Scribner Library, Skidmore College.

worthy, too, is Bess's vulnerability: we see the fear in her eyes, directing our attention to the next hurdle—the high wall of Clerkenwell that surrounds New Prison with its formidable *chevaux-de-frise* (spikes), dramatically lit.

Theatricality similarly resonates in Cruikshank's plates for *Oliver Twist*.[20] In "Oliver Asking for More" (see fig. 8), George Cruikshank sets a dramatic stage for Dickens's attack on the abuse of the newly amended 1834 Poor Law, exacerbated by the government's decentralization and laissez-faire principles. Dickens, writing for a class-conscious readership, presents Oliver's now famous request for more in perfect, polite English: "'Please, sir, I want some more'" (*OT*, Oxf. 1982 10). Engaging the Romantic conception of the child of innocence, Dickens makes his parish orphan, who is unaware of his middle-class parentage, a victim of social injustice. The cruel workhouse system grants a starving child only a legally predetermined dietary allotment of "one porringer, and no more—except on occasions of great public rejoicing, when he had two ounces and a quarter of bread besides" (*OT*, Oxf. 1982 9–10). Oliver is temporarily rotated downward in class affiliation as Dickens himself was as a child "in an age when social slippage was so common that societies were often formed against it"; as Mark Spilka comments, Dickens "seduced his original class-conscious readers into putting their own children, if not themselves, in Oliver's place" (169).

Readers of *Oliver Twist* easily get caught up in the commotion that follows this climactic moment—the master strikes a blow at Oliver, pinions his arms, and calls for Mr. Bumble, the parish beadle, who rushes into the boardroom where the gentleman in the white waistcoat proclaims Oliver will be hanged. The plate freezes the theatrical moment of Oliver asking for more—a scene that caught the attention of Queen Victoria, who in 1839 wrote in her diary about the starving workhouse children (Victoria 44). Alternately, one anonymous 1838 *Spectator* reviewer criticizes Dickens for combining "the severity of the new system with the individual tyranny of the old,—forgetting that responsibility amongst subordinate parish-officers and regularity of management came in with the Commissioners" ("Boz's Oliver Twist" 1115).

Cruikshank stages "Oliver Asking for More" as a *tableau vivant*. The hollow-eyed, sunken-cheeked, thin-ankled workhouse children form an exaggerated backdrop that strengthens Dickens's commitment to social reform. In Cruikshank's illustration, we can actually see why

> The bowls never wanted washing. The boys polished them with their spoons till they shone again; and when they had performed this operation, (which never took very long, the spoons being nearly as large as the bowls,) they would sit staring at the copper, with such eager eyes, as if they could have devoured the bricks of which it was composed; employing themselves, meanwhile, in sucking their fingers most assiduously, with the view of catching up any stray splashes of gruel that might have been cast thereon. (*OT*, Oxf. 1982 10)

Figure 8. "Oliver Asking for More." Illustration by George Cruikshank for Charles Dickens's "Oliver Twist" in *Bentley's Miscellany*, February 1837. From the Norman M. Fox Collection, Scribner Library, Skidmore College.

The little bowls and large spoons serve as stage props to accentuate the theme of starvation. Oliver holds a spoon much larger than his bowl, and the spoon makes the bowl appear even smaller. Another orphan appears to be licking every stray bit of gruel from his dish. All the boys have "eager eyes"; many have the "wild with hunger" (*OT,* Oxf. 1982 10) look of the orphan who fears he just may eat one of the other children to sate his immense hunger.

Cruikshank's illustrative stage also includes details not mentioned in Dickens's text. Cruikshank allegedly directed Dickens's attention to a pamphlet by Dr. T. J. Pettigrew, a physician friend who recommended shaving children's heads as a measure to prevent ringworm (Vogler 149).[21] In Cruikshank's illustration, the heads of Oliver and the other boys look recently shaved, strengthening the authenticity of the plate. Dickens informs us that the master has donned his cook's uniform. Cruikshank stretches the white apron tightly across the master's belly to accentuate his girth in contrast to Oliver's gaunt form that looks even thinner and leaner positioned alongside the big-bellied master. Cruikshank also shines a spotlight on Oliver to validate his middle-class origins and inherited goodness that miraculously survive as Oliver journeys into the criminal world of urban London.

Stage Effects: Lighting and Visual Cuing

Shadows, moonlight, filtered sunlight, firelight, candlelight, and torchlight are all dramatic forms of lighting that the caricaturists incorporated into their illustrations to magnify hope or despair and, often times, to foreshadow developments of the plot. We witness foreshadowing through shadow play in Cruikshank's "Oliver Amazed at the Dodger's Mode of 'Going to Work'" (see fig. 23A). In the backdrop, Cruikshank positions the bookstall keeper in a shaded area where, undetected, he can observe the Artful Dodger reach into the pocket of the unsuspecting Mr. Brownlow, who has his nose in a book. An innocent bystander of the theft, Oliver stands in the foreground with his arms raised, a gesture indicating that he suddenly comprehends "the whole mystery of the handkerchief, and the watches, and the jewels, and the Jew, rushed upon the boy's mind" (*OT,* Oxf. 1982 60). The real thieves escape, leaving Oliver to be chased and captured, but not convicted of pickpocketing. Shadow play allows reader-viewers to anticipate the bookstall keeper's arrival in court in the following chapter, just in time to provide Oliver with a reliable witness and clear his name.

In Dickens's *A Christmas Carol* (1843), John Leech skillfully uses moonlight in a part-realistic, part-theatrical illustration entitled "Ignorance and Want" to

Figure 9. "Ignorance and Want." Illustration by John Leech for Charles Dickens's *A Christmas Carol*, 1843.

advance a humanitarian message about the consequences of unchecked indus-trialism during a period of rising manufacturing in England. Leech spotlights two ragged children symbolically named "Ignorance and Want" (see fig. 9). They are "a boy and girl. Yellow, meagre, ragged, scowling, wolfish; but pros-trate, too, in their humility" (118). As Phillip Allingham notes in his description of this Leech plate:

The street urchins, although symbols of the forces unleashed by the factory system and the new capitalistic applications of Malthusian population theories, are shockingly real, while the desiccated trees and smoking factory chimneys in the backdrop constitute a heightened realism amounting to visual commentary on Dickens's scene to reveal Scrooge as the exemplar of the entire upper-middle class. ("Ignorance")

The branches of two barren, stark trees frame Scrooge, positioned in profile. Factory chimneys billowing black smoke and the façade of the workhouse strengthen the social realism of this scene, even though these two architectural structures would not have realistically been next-door neighbors in urban London.

Leech uses moonlight to illuminate the urchins' starved forms and tattered, ill-fitting clothes. Using a caricature technique evident in Cruikshank's "Oliver Asking for More" (see fig. 8), Leech juxtaposes thin and ample figures. The bones of the urchins' bodies seem even more angular and their haggard faces more dark and pinched in contrast to the looming full figure of the Spirit of Christmas Present, dressed in a flowing robe. Seeing these ragged children, Scrooge queries, "'Have they no refuge or resource?'" (120). The Spirit replies to a now anguished Scrooge by returning the very hardened words Scrooge once speaks when asked to provide charitable relief for the poor: "'Are there no prisons?' . . . 'Are there no workhouses?'" (120). Scrooge's once greedy face now registers concern. Gone in "Ignorance and Want" is the outrage in Scrooge's features previously evident in "Marley's Ghost," an earlier plate where Leech lights up Scrooge's face by candlelight and firelight when his former partner's ghost comes to warn him of his probable fate. "Ignorance and Want" projects an urgent message: Scrooge must reform, and Dickens's readers must be charitable to those unable to ask "for more."

In his plates for *Dombey and Son* (*DS*, 1848),[22] Phiz likewise uses light and shadow play to theatrical effect. "The Shadow in the Little Parlour" and "Let Him Remember It in That Room, Years to Come" stage, respectively, a reunion between two separated lovers and a reconciliation between an erring father and a wronged daughter. Both of these plates feature Florence Dombey, a Dickensian angel in the house, who is submissive to a fault; she remains devoted to her father after he spurns her for being loyal to his unfaithful second wife, Edith Dombey. "The Shadow in the Little Parlour" (see fig. 10) features Florence, now residing in the working-class home of her kindly friend Captain Cuttle, just before she discovers that her childhood sweetheart and future husband,

Figure 10. "The Shadow in the Little Parlour." Illustration by Hablot Knight Browne for Charles Dickens's *Dombey and Son*, 1848.

Walter Gay, is miraculously not drowned, but has returned from sea unharmed and is standing at their very door.

To prepare Florence for the news that Walter is alive, Cuttle tells her a yarn about a spirited lad, who, along with another seaman and the second mate, miraculously survive a shipwreck by being "'lashed to a fragment of the wreck, and driftin' on the stormy sea. . . . Days and nights they drifted on them endless waters'" (*DS*, Oxf. 1982 578). Riveted by the tale, Florence lays aside the book she has been reading, a prop that marks her intellect, and looks intently at Captain Cuttle, who tells Florence one of these seamen was spared. Cuttle, in turn, looks intently at the shadow on the wall, which is the silhouette of Walter Gay. Phiz illustrates the pregnant moment just before Florence "started up, looked round, and, with a piercing cry, saw Walter Gay behind her!" (581). In this illustration, we foresee this happy reunion through Walter's silhouette in shadow, which the audience sees before Florence does. Through light and shadow, we anticipate the joy Florence will experience when she beholds her long lost lover and "held him in her pure embrace" (581).

Equally dramatic is Phiz's use of filtered sunlight to foreshadow an imminent reconciliation in "Let Him Remember It in That Room, Years to Come" (see fig. 11) from a later chapter aptly entitled "Retribution." Browne lights up the despondent face of old Paul Dombey, now a "ruined man" (*DS*, Oxf. 1982 701) but once a prominent owner of a shipping company. Dombey passes the days alone in his once lavish, but now dusty, neglected, decrepit house where he contemplates all of his losses—his first wife, who dies soon after giving birth to Florence's brother; little Paul Dombey, his beloved son, now dead; his proud second wife, Edith Dombey, who betrays him; and his neglected, spurned daughter, Florence, who "had never changed to him—nor had he ever changed to her—and she was lost" (702). Browne shines a filtered light on Old Dombey, who "was proud yet" (702) even though he sits immobile in a heavy armchair. His eyes, staring blankly ahead, are partially reflected in an oval mirror. In tableau-like fashion, Dombey appears to be literally frozen in time. Dickens repeats the phrase "'Let him remember it in that room, years to come!'" and variations of this phrase, such as "He did remember it" (701), as Old Dombey recalls "what he had done . . . now, when every loving blossom he had withered in his innocent daughter's heart was snowing down, in ashes, on him" (702).

Florence's innocent heart is not "withered," however. Reconciliation will take place in this dusty room with haphazardly arranged books and writing implements and letters strewn across the table and on the floor. Phiz positions a

Figure 11. "Let Him Remember It in That Room, Years to Come." Illustration by Hablot Knight Browne for Charles Dickens's *Dombey and Son*, 1848.

decorative screen that partially blocks our view of a key stage prop—Florence's portrait on the wall—but the portrait's eyes remain visible and lead the viewer's gaze to the figure of Florence stealing into the room at this very moment. A "gleam of light; a ray of sun" (*DS*, Oxf. 1982 705) dramatically lights up Florence just before she beseeches her father for forgiveness and insists that old Dombey come to live with her. Foreshadowing this reunion, the glimmer of sunlight catches on the ribbons of Florence's hat and illuminates her gentle face. Angelic Florence has come to save the erring, broken old man, who, shortly after this illustrative moment, cries aloud to his dear neglected daughter: "'Oh my God, forgive me, for I need it very much'" (706).

Visual cuing or prompting is another stage effect in the caricaturists' dramatic repertoire, as evidenced in Phiz's "Mr. Pickwick Slides" (see fig. 6, ch. 1, 48) and "Mr. Pickwick in the Pound" (see fig. 5, ch. 1, 47). George Cruikshank uses cuing in "The Short Courtship" for *Points of Humour* (1823), a Regency publication that was very popular with the Victorians. This picture accompanies a tale about two strangers discovered drunk in a kennel in the London streets and assumed to be man and wife. Taken to a public house by a "charitable" (9) gentleman, the two "whom the laws of God had not made one" (10) awake from their stupor to discover they are sharing one bed. Cruikshank illustrates the climax of this humorous vignette just as the old woman "set up a scream, and roused the old gentleman, whose astonishment was not a jot less than the lady's" (10). Clothes are strewn on the surrounding furniture, offering ocular proof that the lady and gent are in a state of relative undress.[23] To the amusement of the peeping Toms, who peer through the cracks to see what the ruckus is all about, the old lady proclaims her virginity and shouts at the old man: "'make me an honest woman, thou wretch, ... villain that you are,—make an honest woman of me, or I'll be the death of thee;'" (10–11). Although the owner of the public house vouches for the old lady's honor, the old man agrees to "make an honest woman of" his odd bedfellow, much to the amusement of the peepers, who cue the audience to chuckle along with them.

Richard Doyle skillfully uses visual cuing to stage a funny spectacle in the ballroom in "The Marquis 'en Montagnard'" for Thackeray's *The Newcomes* (1855) (see fig. 12). Thackeray makes fun of the Marquis in the text:[24]

> His English conversation was not brilliant as yet, although his French was
> eccentric; but at the court balls, whether he appeared in his uniform of
> the Scotch Archers, or in his native Glenlivat tartan, there certainly was

Figure 12. "The Marquis 'en Montagnard.'" Illustration by Richard Doyle for William Makepeace Thackeray's *The Newcomes*, 1855 (vol. 2). From the Norman M. Fox Collection, Scribner Library, Skidmore College.

not in his own or the public estimation a handsomer young nobleman in Paris that season. It has been said that he was greatly improved in dancing; and, for a young man of his age, his whiskers were really extraordinarily large and curly. (2: 78)

Building upon Thackeray's mockery, Doyle positions the partygoers in an enclosed small space—not of a bedroom, as in "The Short Courtship"; or a skating rink, as in "Mr. Pickwick Slides"—but of a dance floor. All the gentlemen but the Marquis are dressed in formal attire. The Marquis (whom Ethel Newcome's grandmother favors over the protagonist Clive Newcome) looks ridiculous in his Highland costume complete with a flamboyant tartan skirt and laced up stockings. The finely dressed ladies visually prompt us to laugh at the Marquis, who steps clumsily toward Ethel, indicating his inability to dance even though "it has been said that he was greatly improved in dancing" (2: 78). So "extraordinarily" bushy are his sideburns that they extend into his shirt collar. One of the partygoers hides her amused smile with a fan, a stage prop that she twirls in a gesture that, according to Victorian fan language, means, "I wish to get rid of you."

Expressive Gestures and Stage Props

Clichéd gestures, meaning-laden fruits and flowers, allegorical paintings on a parlor wall, and figurines on a mantel were "standard practice of early English graphic artists" (Steig, "Dickens" 227). A recognizable visual vocabulary of gesture, expression, and interior decoration, drawn from the Hogarthian tradition of graphic satire and caricature, advances the theatricality of book illustrations by caricaturists who use gestures and props to comment on plot developments and characterization. For example, gesturing to the nose, as a Victorian viewer would recognize, means being "in the know." Cruikshank incorporates this gesture into *Oliver Twist* and deepens our understanding of the corruption transpiring between Morris Bolter (aka Noah Claypole) and Fagin in "The Jew and Morris Bolter Begin to Understand Each Other" (see fig. 45B, ch. 4, 181). Spying on Nancy for Fagin, Bolter puts into motion a series of events that culminate in Sikes's murder of Nancy.

Backdrops contain props to advance the drama of a scene. In "Mr. Bumble and Mrs. Corney Taking Tea," Cruikshank plants a small porcelain figurine of Paul Pry on the far left side of the mantel. This detail—easily overlooked today, but readily identified by a Victorian viewer—foreshadows the parish beadle's corrupt motivation for marriage well before Dickens reveals it in the text. Paul Pry—a popular dramatic character from John Poole's 1825 comedy *Paul Pry*—was known to appear at inopportune moments with umbrella in hand, saying: "I hope I don't intrude." The figurine, never mentioned in the text,[25] foreshadows a development at the end of chapter 23: Mrs. Corney is called away to witness Old Sally the pauper's death, and Mr. Bumble begins to poke his nose into her drawers, counting her silver. Later in the novel, an unhappily wed Bumble confirms he has taken the part of Paul Pry: "'I sold myself, . . . for six tea-spoons, a pair of sugar-tongs, and a milk-pot; with a small quantity of second-hand furniter, and twenty pound in money'" (*OT*, Oxf. 1982 226).

In "Traddles and I, in Conference with the Misses Spenlow" (see fig. 13) for Dickens's *David Copperfield* (*DC*, 1850), Browne draws Clarissa and Lavinia Spenlow, Dora's spinster aunts, as bird-like figures, much as Dickens describes

Figure 13. "Traddles and I, in Conference with the Misses Spenlow." Illustration by Hablot Knight Browne for Charles Dickens's *David Copperfield*, 1850.

them: "They were not unlike birds, altogether; having a sharp, brisk, sudden manner, and a little short, spruce way of adjusting themselves, like canaries" (*DC*, Norton 503). Stage props abound in this illustration. A pair of lovebirds in a birdcage positioned directly behind Lavinia magnifies both sisters' resemblance to the feathered species and David's love for Dora, which he only later realizes is "'the first mistaken impulse of [an] undisciplined heart'" (558). Paintings on the wall and books on the mantelpiece, not explicitly mentioned in the text, comment powerfully on plot and characterization.

Phiz's inventive use of allegorical paintings here anticipates the work of Victorian narrative painters. For example, in his triptych *Past and Present* (1858), Augustus Egg incorporates *The Fall*, an iconic scene of Adam and Eve's expulsion from the Garden of Eden, in the first of the three canvases. Egg places the painting above a small portrait of the fallen wife, who is peeling an apple just as her husband opens the letter disclosing her treachery.[26] In "Traddles and I, in Conference with the Misses Spenlow," Phiz likewise includes books and paintings to stage David's hopes and fears as he seeks Dora Spenlow's hand in marriage following the propitious death of Dora's father, who forbids the match. Titles of some of the books on the mantelpiece—*Paradise Regained* and *The Loves of the Angels*—announce David's great expectations for marriage. A trio of paintings—*The Momentous Question* on the left, *The Last Appeal* on the right, and *Arcadia* in the center—proclaim, respectively, David's love for Dora, his fear of rejection, and his hope for married bliss.

The Good Samaritan (see fig. 29, ch. 3, 113) was a popular interior prop to comment on character. In *Vanity Fair*'s most dramatic illustration entitled "Becky's Second Appearance in the 'Character of Clytemnestra'" (see fig. 14),[27] Thackeray includes the picture of this parable, not mentioned in his text, on the wall directly above a dying Jos Sedley when Dobbin visits Jos and pleads with his brother-in-law to leave Becky Sharp and return to England with him. The left half of this illustration functions as a well-lit open stage. *The Good Samaritan* painting seemingly becomes a *tableau vivant*: Jos assumes the role of the wayfarer in need of tending, and honest Dobbin takes on the role of the Good Samaritan, who tries to persuade Jos not to take artful Becky's bait. Gesture and expression are also telling in this plate. Jos's sagging flesh and pronounced facial lines suggest recent weight loss and sickness. Fear exudes from Jos's quivering knees to his raised eyebrows and his nightcap. Thackeray poses Jos melodramatically; sitting in an armchair, Jos clasps his hands in supplication, as if he is begging Dobbin to save him from Becky: "'they mustn't say anything to Mrs. Crawley:—she'd—she'd kill me if she knew it. You don't know what a terrible

Figure 14. "Becky's Second Appearance in the 'Character of Clytemnestra.'" Illustration by William Makepeace Thackeray for his *Vanity Fair*, 1848.

woman she is'" (*VF* 874). But even the Good Samaritan cannot save Jos, who is "'destined to be a prey to [one] woman'"—Becky Sharp (36).

The Good Samaritan painting also makes a moral comment in an illustration that Thackeray's artistic mentor, George Cruikshank, designed for *Oliver Twist*. In "Oliver Recovering from a Fever," Cruikshank places this painting above the hearth on the wall of Mr. Brownlow's parlor. The visual allusion to this parable, which Dickens does not mention in the text, reflects how Mr. Brownlow's heart is "large enough for any six ordinary old gentlemen of humane disposition" (*OT*, Oxf. 1982 72). Oliver, cast as the wayfarer in this plate, has just narrowly escaped from Fagin's den. Mr. Brownlow, playing the Good Samaritan, ministers to orphan Oliver, who appears thin, poorly, and in need of tending. Stage props and costuming—for example, medicine bottles on the mantelpiece and the wide skirt of Mr. Brownlow's dressing gown that rivals Mrs. Bedwin's in girth—magnify Brownlow's kindly disposition. *The Good Samaritan* painting foreshadows Oliver's happy fate—Brownlow will adopt Oliver and tend to him as his own son. Moreover, a second painting on the wall above Oliver—a portrait of Oliver's real mother, Agnes Fleming, of which Oliver is the "living copy" (72)—is visual proof of Oliver's rightful middle-class heritage likewise revealed at the novel's end.

Casting, Recasting, and In-depth Character Studies

As author and illustrator of the highly theatrical *Vanity Fair*,[28] Thackeray casts Becky Sharp in various roles that compromise her character. A consummate actress, Becky begins her dramatic career in chapter 2 when, as a child, she mimics the Miss Pinkertons to the delight of her Bohemian father's friends. Becky's triumph comes in a production of Clytemnestra staged at Lord Steyne's Gaunt House in chapter 51, a scene which incorporates a *tableau vivant*. In between these chapters, Thackeray casts Becky as a Napoleon in petticoats in the pictorial capital to chapter 64, "A Vagabond Chapter," making an implicit association between the "Corsican upstart" (*VF* 211) and manipulative Becky, so proud of her French ancestry. Here Becky is in exile: "She felt she was alone, quite alone: and the far-off shining cliffs of England were impassable to her" (816). Positioned in profile, Becky has a distinctively sharp nose that identifies her as Thackeray's "heroine." The tri-corner hat and uniform partially covering her petticoats and her placement alone on a cliff make a visual allusion to B. R. Haydon's popular paintings of Napoleon in exile. This series begun in 1829 shows Napoleon alone facing the "impassable" cliffs of the remote South Atlantic island, St. Helena.

In pictorial capitals to chapter 44 and chapter 63, Thackeray recasts his brilliant military strategist as a siren figure who is, respectively, alluring to men and capable of their destruction. In chapter 44, Thackeray draws Becky in profile as an enchanting mermaid strumming on a lute by moonlight. The capital *O* stands for the moon. Becky's long hair flutters behind her, nearly touching her mermaid tail, but she is easily identifiable by her sharp nose, again accentuated in profile. The pointed rocks below the waterline signal the darkness that lurks beneath Becky's charm: in this very chapter, Becky sings enchantingly to wealthy Lord Steyne, who lavishes her with jewels and bank notes, but she boxes her son's ears when young Rawdon sneaks into the room to hear her sing. In the design for chapter 63, Becky becomes a diabolical siren. With wild and loose hair, she assumes the role of Circe and holds in her hand a crucial prop—a trademark staff that extends into the capital letter S that begins the paragraph. Becky's nose is particularly sharp, her eyes decidedly evil, her eyebrows dark and arched, and her expression completely wicked. Thackeray never condemns Becky of adultery or murder, enabling her to remain the "heroine" in his novel "without a Hero," but he adds jagged rocks and sculls of past victims to the illustrative stage. While a pictorial capital letter typically introduces the theme of its accompanying chapter, it is not until the following chapter that Thackeray calls Becky a "siren" and a "monster" "writhing and twirling, diabolically hideous and slimy, flapping amongst bones, or curling round corpses" (VF, Oxf. 812).

Even more than her role as a siren, Becky's casting as the mythical Clytemnestra puts her dubious character on stage. The right half of the illustration of "Becky's Second Appearance in the 'Character of Clytemnestra'" comes close to confirming Becky's part in Jos's death, although Thackeray never convicts Becky of a legal crime. Daughter of Leda and Tyndareus, Clytemnestra in Greek mythology kills her husband, Agamemnon, when he returns from the Trojan War to seek revenge for Agamemnon's murder of their daughter Iphigenia. Becky twice plays the part of Clytemnestra. The first is in the charades[29] episode accompanied by Thackeray's illustration "The Triumph of Clytemnestra." At Gaunt House, Becky performs in the last act of the second charade composed of two words of two syllables each. The first syllable is "Aga," staged as an Eastern scene to recall the black eunuch who guarded the Imperial Harem of the Ottoman Empire, and the second syllable is a tableau of "Memnon," the Egyptian god. Costumed to play the role of Agamemnon's wife, Clytemnestra, Becky makes her appearance in the last act of this charade. She performs in the scene where Clytemnestra murders Agamemnon, played by Rawdon Crawley. In the text, Becky is performing in a *tableau vivant* in which she seizes a dagger from her accomplice, Aegisthus, and thrusts it at Agamemnon as the stage suddenly goes dark in a theatrical blackout. Lord Steyne intuits Becky's capacity to kill when he reviews her acting and exclaims: "'Mrs. Rawdon Crawley was quite killing in the part'" (VF, Oxf. 646). Of course, "to kill" is a clever figurative reference, but in the accompanying full-page engraving entitled "The Triumph of Clytemnestra," a smiling Becky holds the dagger, a damning theatrical prop, as she bows gracefully to her admiring audience.

More incriminating is "Becky's Second Appearance in the 'Character of Clytemnestra,'" which led Elizabeth Rigby to "advise our readers to cut out that picture of our heroine's 'Second Appearance as Clytemnestra,' which casts so uncomfortable a glare over the latter part of the volume" (161); believing Becky innocent of a capital crime, Rigby also confides in her 1848 *Quarterly Review* article, "Who can, with any face, liken a dear friend to a murderess?" (161). Becky looks like a murderess in this plate. However, a stage curtain separates Becky from Jos and Dobbin, creating the kind of ambiguity about Becky's guilt for which Thackeray was renowned; when asked whether or not Becky actually murders Jos, Thackeray declined to answer.[30] His novel instead leaves a trail of gossip, speculation, and visual and verbal clues (for example, Becky's solicitors, Burke, Thurtell, and Hayes, are named after notorious murderers).[31] Jos urges Dobbin to visit him that particular night because "Mrs. Crawley would be at a *soirée*, . . . they could meet *alone*" (*VF*, Oxf. 873). If we believe that Becky is at a party and not actually in the room, then the ambiguity of the text is preserved, and the plate moves us deep into Jos's fragile psyche where Becky becomes an ominous realization of Jos's fear of her. But if we read Becky as actually present in the room, then Becky in her loose robe with her wild hair and "killing" smile looks unmistakably like the murderess Clytemnestra as she appears in Pierre-Narcisse Guérin's *Clytemnestra* (1817), a painting well known to Thackeray's Victorian viewers. If we believe Becky is in the room, then this illustration is a *tableau vivant* of the Gaunt House charade. Becky, who appears to be holding a dagger, glares at her Agamemnon through the curtain in a manner reminiscent of Guérin's painting. In this staged picture of Clytemnestra, Becky is poised to kill.

In-depth character study is another important dimension of the caricaturists' theatricality. George Cruikshank skillfully leads us into the psyche of two of Dickens's darkest character-actors, the robber-murderer Bill Sikes and the thieving Fagin, in, respectively, "The Last Chance" and "Fagin in the Condemned Cell." Cruikshank's contemporaries compared him to Rembrandt for his skill in dramatic lighting.[32] The plate of Sikes haunted by his brutal murder of Nancy is as notable for its stage lighting as it is for its psychological terror, which also exudes from the illustration of Fagin alone in the prison cell. "The Last Chance" and "Fagin in the Condemned Cell" theatrically light up the extreme anxiety of a criminal who is confronting his demise.

In "The Last Chance" (see fig. 15), Sikes is standing precariously on the edge of a rooftop, holding onto a rope tied to the chimney in an attempt to lower himself into Folly Ditch and escape capture by the mob that hotly pursues him. Dickens sets the scene at darkest night with "lights gleaming below" (*OT*, Oxf. 1982 325). In this dramatic plate, which Dickens did not think his illustrator should attempt,[33] Cruikshank simulates torchlight and

Figure 15. "The Last Chance." Illustration by George Cruikshank for Charles Dickens's "Oliver Twist" in *Bentley's Miscellany*, February 1839. From the Norman M. Fox Collection, Scribner Library, Skidmore College.

the intensity of the mob by spotlighting the onlookers in neighboring buildings who lean out their windows to stare at the criminal; one woman even
raises her outstretched arm to point directly at Sikes. In the text leading up
to this moment, the mob is shouting for ladders and sledge-hammers "with
the ecstasy of madmen" (326). Sikes is wanted not only by this "infuriated
throng" (326) but also by Oliver's protector, Mr. Brownlow (319), who offers
an ample reward to capture Sikes.

Well-lit are the ominous noose at the end of the rope (dangling along the
wall of the tenement building), Sikes's muscular front leg (trying to steady his
wavering balance), his scarf whipping in a strong wind (inferred from the angle
of the cloth), and his eyes (emanating terror of what likely awaits him). The
diagonal clouds in the sky magnify the one onlooker's outstretched arm as well
as the angle of Sikes's downward-turning eyes and his muscular arms that strain
against the pull of the rope and the violent wind.[34] Cruikshank stages a pregnant moment that teeters between the present and the future. Sikes's desperate
eyes and the noose foreshadow his impending death and how he will die by
hanging. In contrast to Jack in "Jack Sheppard in Company with Edgeworth
Bess" (see fig. 7), Sikes is not romanticized in this plate, nor will he escape to
safety. The "murderer," as Dickens now refers to Bill Sikes,

> uttered a yell of terror. "The eyes again!" he cried, in an unearthly screech.
> Staggering as if struck by lightning, he lost his balance and tumbled
> over the parapet. The noose was at his neck. It ran up with his weight,
> tight as a bow-string, and swift as the arrow it speeds. He fell for five-and-
> thirty feet. There was a sudden jerk, a terrific convulsion of the limbs; and
> there he hung. (*OT*, Oxf. 1982 328)

Rather than render Sikes's graphic end—all jerking motion and convulsed
limb—Cruikshank dramatizes the moment before Sikes dies in a noose of his
own making. In Sikes's haunted eyes, which project his "yell of terror," we see
Sikes's psychological undoing. Cruikshank also spotlights Sikes's abused but
loyal canine, Bull's-eye, concealed from Sikes's view but visible to the reader-
viewer. We anticipate Bull's-eye's frantic leap after his cruel master:

> A dog, which had lain concealed till now, ran backwards and forwards
> on the parapet with a dismal howl, and, collecting himself for a spring,
> jumped for the dead man's shoulders. Missing his aim, he fell into the
> ditch, turning completely over as he went; and striking his head against a
> stone, dashed out his brains. (328–29)

Bull's-eye's end becomes a gruesome coda to his master's death, but "The Last Chance," which arrests the moment before dying, captures canine and human desperation.

"Fagin in the Condemned Cell" (see fig. 16), one of Cruikshank's most famous etchings and among the most powerful examples of Victorian book illustration,[35] delineates psychic terror, demonstrating how the caricaturists were

Figure 16. "Fagin in the Condemned Cell." Illustration by George Cruikshank for Charles Dickens's "Oliver Twist" in *Bentley's Miscellany*, March 1839. From the Norman M. Fox Collection, Scribner Library, Skidmore College.

capable of capturing psychological depth.[36] Dickens's Fagin is strange and ugly in appearance with matted hair and a large nose, and he is deceitful, greedy, miserly, smarmy, and cowardly.[37] As critics have previously noted, the characterization of Fagin subscribes to conventions of the archetypal "stage Jew" from Elizabethan drama and is second in notoriety only to Shylock. Popular cartoonists of the late eighteenth and early nineteenth centuries including Isaac Cruikshank and Thomas Rowlandson characterize Jews as having a different physical appearance than gentiles; Isaac Cruikshank's "A Jew and a Bishop" (1796) and Thomas Rowlandson's "Money Lenders" (1784), for example, present this stereotype of the hook-nosed Jew, but it was Dickens's Fagin that "embedded itself in popular culture and prejudice. . . . Over the years, *Oliver Twist* became a staple of juvenile literature, and the stereotype was perpetuated" (Eisner, *FTJ* 123).

Just as the eyes of martyred Nancy haunt Sikes until his final hour delineated in "The Last Chance," the swinging rope terrorizes "the Jew" as he contemplates his death by hanging in "Fagin in the Condemned Cell." Dickens presents the judge's pronouncement of a guilty verdict and Fagin's punishment through indirect discourse. Cruikshank pictures the scene where Fagin "began to remember a few disjointed fragments of what the judge had said . . . To be hanged by the neck, till he was dead—that was the end. To be hanged by the neck till he was dead" (*OT*, Oxf. 1982 343). In this pregnant moment where Fagin is envisioning his death at the gallows, Cruikshank moves us into Fagin's now deranged mind. Fagin crouches on a stark pallet bed and endlessly repeats the judge's death sentence. The stippled effect on the dungeon walls—a pattern of circles about the size of Fagin's widened pupils—magnifies his crazed eyes that project Fagin's intense fear of the rope and the scaffold.

Well known is Thackeray's comment on this plate—"the Jew,—the dreadful Jew—that Cruikshank drew!" (57); less well known is a line in this very same paragraph of *An Essay on the Genius of George Cruikshank* where Thackeray declares this illustration rendered him near speechless: "As for the Jew in the dungeon, let us say nothing of it—what can we say to describe it?" (57–58). Nonetheless, G. K. Chesterton aptly describes Fagin's psychological terror: "it is not drawn with the free lines of a free man; it has the half-witted secrecies of a hunted thief. It does not look merely like a picture of Fagin; it looks like a picture by Fagin" (112). While this picture looks as if it could be a self-portrait of a "hunted thief," Cruikshank allegedly based it on his own image in a cheval glass when he was acting the part of the desperate thief in an attempt to capture the pose just right.[38]

Even if Cruikshank incorporated his own likeness into this character study of Fagin, the illustration engages a stereotype of the villainous Jew perpetuated from the Elizabethan stage. Spotlighted are pronounced features of a Sephardic Jew—large nose, jutting chin, shifty eye—that carry into Du Maurier's depiction of Svengali as I explore in chapter 4. These are the very repugnant Semitic features that Will Eisner revises in his graphic novel adaptation of *Oliver Twist* as I demonstrate in the conclusion. In "Fagin in the Condemned Cell," Fagin may not be grinning like a devil as he appears, for example, in "Oliver Introduced to the Respectable Old Gentleman," but in this plate Fagin embodies the repugnant anti-Semitic traits of Dickens's typecasting, and he appears appropriately subhuman: "the hideous old man seemed like some loathsome reptile, engendered in the slime and darkness through which he moved: crawling forth, by night, in search of some rich offal for a meal" (*OT*, Oxf. 1982 116). Cruikshank's Fagin looks like some slimy, coldblooded "loathsome reptile," a Jew "as if Jews were a species of which he was a representative example," notes Jeet Heer; "Fagin's Jewishness is not an incidental feature of his character but rather is the term that is used to sum up what he is" (130) and what he looks like—an anti-Semitic character type.

Different from earlier representations of Fagin in *Oliver Twist*, in "Fagin in the Condemned Cell" he is completely alone in a bare setting. The only light in this plate comes from a thick double-barred Newgate Prison window that illuminates the shackles on Fagin's legs, the hand he is biting, his terrified eyes, and two sheriff's notices, possibly referring to his looming execution. The book against the wall, presumably a Bible, lies in shadow. There is no redemption for Fagin, whose death takes place off stage.[39] His dark hat on the bed lies brim up and ominously empty. The confident Fagin from his earlier appearances—grinning at Oliver as he toasts sausages at his hearth in "Oliver Introduced to the Respectable Old Gentleman" and gesturing he is "in the know" to Noah Claypole/Morris Bolter in "The Jew and Morris Bolter Begin to Understand Each Other" (see fig. 45B, ch. 4, 181)—has simply vanished. What remains of "the Jew" is raw terror, lit up by a stream of filtered light.[40]

Caricature, Comedy, and Bodily Distortion

Distortion, exaggeration, and comparison are standard caricature techniques to stage comedy. No facial feature or body shape escaped the attention of the caricaturists, particularly George Cruikshank, who specialized in nose play. Cruikshank twists and distorts noses into a range of humorous and, at times, grotesque forms in "A Chapter of Noses" for *My Sketch Book* (1834): the top vignette features two dozen gentlemen drawn in profile with noses that vary in length, width, shape, and species. Some curve into beaks, some extend outward like Pinocchio's, and others—in the manner of Rowlandson's Dr. Syntax and Cruikshank's Fagin—nearly touch their chins.

Thackeray's caricatures of Jos Sedley for *Vanity Fair* recall to comic effect the tradition of fatness and folly associated with Samuel Pickwick. In the pictorial capital to chapter 2, Jos's ample form nearly fills the entire capital letter *A*. The design realizes Thackeray's own description of Jos as "[a] very stout, puffy man, in buckskins and hessian boots, with several immense neckcloths, that rose almost to his nose, with a red striped waistcoat and an apple-green coat with steel buttons almost as large as crown pieces (it was the morning costume of a dandy or blood of those days)" (24). Jos's small head, swathed in neck cloths, sits upon an enormous torso. Jos's fatness makes him funny especially because, like a true dandy, he is very vain.

Jos takes the form of a fat fish in the comical pictorial capital to chapter 4 (see fig. 17). Becky Sharp, like the Widow Bardell in *The Pickwick Papers* (1837), is fishing for a husband. In this design, sharp-nosed Becky daintily holds a fishing rod as she sits on a capital P that resembles a tree. The fish shares Jos's girth and appetite—he is ogling the bait. The design gives concrete form to a figurative reference that Old Mr. Sedley makes later in this chapter: "'Here is Emmy's little friend making love to him as hard as she can; that's quite clear; and if she does not catch him some other will. That man is destined to be a prey to woman . . . mark my words, the first woman who fishes for him, hooks him'" (36). The *Oxford English Dictionary* uses this very line from *Vanity Fair* to define the figurative meaning of hook, "to catch, secure as a husband." This picture also directs us to earlier scenes where orphan Becky, daughter of a Bohemian artist and a French opera dancer, meets Jos Sedley, brother of her school chum Amelia Sedley, and determines, "'If Jos Sedley is rich and unmarried, why should I not marry him?'" (23). Within this first installment, Becky attempts to hook Jos with a feigned rapture for India (where he served in the East India Company as the Collector of Boggley Wallah), keen interest in his tiresome elephant stories, eagerness to sample a "chili" that does not taste as coolly delightful as it sounds, and display of her "*byoo-ootiful*" singing, as Jos calls it. The pictorial capital design predicts that Jos, the dandy caricatured as a fat fish, is "destined to be a prey to woman."

Lewis Carroll's illustrations of Alice's bodily distortions in *Alice's Adventures Under Ground* turn the first version of *Alice* into a dark comedy, a quality that

CHAPTER IV

THE GREEN SILK PURSE

OOR Joe's panic lasted for two or three days; during which he did not visit the house, nor during that period did Miss Rebecca ever mention his name. She was all respectful gratitude to Mrs. Sedley; delighted beyond measure at the Bazaars; and in a whirl of wonder at the theatre, whither the good-natured lady took her. One day, Amelia had a headache, and could not go

Figure 17. Pictorial capital to chapter 4. Illustration by William Makepeace Thackeray for his *Vanity Fair*, 1848.

subsequent illustrators like Barry Moser have likewise accentuated. Carroll elongates, truncates, twists, distorts, shrinks, and expands Alice's form. Her head reaches above the treetops when she is taken for a serpent, and then her head bangs into her feet when she nibbles on a mushroom stalk. Only after nearly drowning in her own tears and outgrowing a house does Alice learn to regulate her own growth. In "'Alice' in Time," Gillian Beer sees the disruption of "the time the body takes to grow" as "the most profound disturbance of the [*Alice*] books" (xxxvi). Carroll dramatizes Alice's fast paced growing and shrinking through the technique of comic comparison. Placing Alice next to smaller and larger creatures and objects, Carroll makes Alice appear, in turn, taller and bigger or smaller and narrower.

Alice's neck truly looks like a telescope in the illustration for chapter 1 that accompanies the scene where Alice nibbles on a cake marked "EAT ME" and exclaims, "'Curiouser and curiouser! . . . now I'm opening up like the largest telescope that ever was! Goodbye, feet!'" (*UG* 11). While Alice stands 5 ¼ inches tall on the hand-written page, her neck alone is 1 ⅛ inches long. In this scene, Alice's hair, which reaches her shoulders in the other illustrations, falls midway down her giraffe-like neck. Carroll positions Alice next to a column of handwritten text comprised of twenty-five lines; the lines of text per page, which remain relatively constant throughout the handwritten manuscript, function as a ruler, a prop to measure Alice's growth. In this illustration, Alice's feet reach just below the text, and her head extends just above it, giving the allusion that she is outgrowing the page.

In chapter 2, Alice nearly outgrows the White Rabbit's house, which Carroll delineates as a simple stage set, a rectangular box (see fig. 18). Alice's imposing head (*UG* 37) crowds into the upper-right corner of this full-page illustration, and her elbow rubs against a door that is not pictured. Michael Hancher calls this setting a "'naïve' substitution of the picture frame for the physical structure of the room" (31), but he applauds Carroll "for more powerfully evoking fetal claustrophobia" (31) than John Tenniel, who redeploys this very scene for *Alice in Wonderland* (see fig. 39B, ch. 3, 145). In Carroll's original, Alice's head is growing faster than the rest of her body, so the illustration looks like a caricature of Alice, who curls into a fetal position to fit into the confining box/room. Carroll leaves only a very small margin of space in the far right corner of the illustrative box; Alice's head strains against the top of the picture frame, suggesting her head will soon burst through the ceiling.

Figure 18. "Alice Outgrowing the White Rabbit's House." Illustration by Lewis Carroll for his *Alice's Adventures Under Ground*, 1864.

The White Rabbit's house cannot contain Alice, who "went on growing, and as a last resource she put one arm out of the window, and one foot up the chimney" (UG 36). The next illustration (UG 40) shows Alice's outstretched arm reaching toward the frightened White Rabbit, who is falling into a cucumber frame. Alice's gigantic arm is a visual synecdoche for her enormous size that Carroll implies but does not stage. Just before the White Rabbit and Bill the Lizard attempt to burn down the house, Alice luckily shrinks. In a vignette introducing chapter 3 of Under Ground, Alice is smaller than a puppy with fluffy fur, who looks "down at her with large, round eyes" (46).

The darkest comedy occurs when Alice eats a mushroom stalk, and her body shrinks so quickly that "the next moment she felt a violent blow on her chin: it had struck her foot!" (UG 61; see fig. 19). Carroll draws Alice with a dreamy-like acceptance of this extremely destructive breakdown of her body and identity. Alice's large head balances precariously on her disproportionately small feet and hands. She literally has no body in this curious caricature that anticipates how the Cheshire Cat (a character Carroll added for the Wonderland version of Alice) appears without its body and fades into a grin. This illustration fills a 2½ inch square space in the left-hand corner of the

Figure 19. "She Felt a Violent Blow on Her Chin." Illustration by Lewis Carroll for his Alice's Adventures Under Ground, 1864.

handwritten page. Alice's hair, which falls mid-neck in the "telescope" illustration, now drapes the ground. The accompanying text facilitates Alice's distortion—twelve lines of text form a column alongside her that boxes her in while sixteen lines of text above her graze the top of her head and function as a wide, horizontal ceiling, seemingly pushing her head even closer to her chin. When *Alice in Wonderland* made its public debut in 1865 with Tenniel's illustrations,[41] Tenniel elected not to illustrate this disturbing scene or that of Alice's head rising well above the trees.

Stage Sets

The backdrops of caricature-style illustrations approximate stage sets, moving the reader-viewer from the filth of Jacob's Island and Newgate Prison in *Oliver Twist*, to a graveyard in *A Christmas Carol*, genteel drawing rooms in *Vanity Fair*, and the stormy Thames in *Jack Sheppard*. The natural world features keenly in the backdrops of John Leech's illustrations for Robert Smith Surtees's hunting novels about country life and provincial towns.[42] Surtees's series features Mr. John Jorrocks, a good-natured Cockney grocer turned master of the hounds, who—like Jos Sedley and Samuel Pickwick—is fat and funny. Jorrocks experiences Pickwick-like indignities, like getting lost, losing his hounds, and being bitten in the seat of his pants by one of his own hunting dogs. However, in Leech's illustrations, comedy unfolds within beautifully rendered stage sets.[43] For example, in Surtees's *Handley Cross; or, Mr. Jorrocks's Hunt* (1843), one full-page illustration entitled "Mr. Jorrocks (loq)—'Come hup! I say—You ugly Beast'" (see fig. 20) combines humor and naturalism. Jorrocks, much too plump for his sprightly horse but eager to keep apace with the other riders and hounds, has dismounted to avoid leaping over a ditch on horseback. Leech pictures Jorrocks as he pulls on the horse's reins "much in the style of a school-boy who catches a log of wood in fishing" (106). The horse, Arterxerxes, will not listen to this grown up "school-boy"; Arterxerxes flatly refuses to leap over the ditch to continue the hunt. Leech illustrates a pregnant moment—just before the horse "flew back, pulling Jorrocks downwards in the muddy ditch. Arterxerxes then threw up his heels and ran away, whip and all" (106). As the narrative continues, Jorrocks, who finally retrieves his horse and hounds, becomes the "object of unmerited ridicule by the fair but rather unfeeling portion of the populace" (107), including the barber's pretty wife, who exclaims loudly, "'old Fatty's had a fall!'" (107).

This plate anticipates "old Fatty's" fall. Jorrocks stands perilously close to

Figure 20. "Mr. Jorrocks (loq)—'Come hup! I say—You ugly Beast.'" Illustration by John Leech for Robert Smith Surtees's *Handley Cross; or, Mr. Jorrocks's Hunt*, 1854. From the Norman M. Fox Collection, Scribner Library, Skidmore College.

the muddy ditch. His black boots and plump belly, bursting from his ill-fitting bright red riding jacket, lead the viewer's gaze toward the mud that will soon splatter all over him. Jorrocks locks eyes with Arterxerxes as the horse digs in its powerful legs and refuses to jump the ditch. Comically, the horse is in command of the Master of Hounds. Leech lingers over the powerful haunches and strong neck of a beast that pulls Jorrocks toward the ditch, anticipating a comic climax. But Leech stages humor amid the beauty of the countryside and the thrill of the hunt. Verdant grass on either side of the ditch and bare trees and bushes suggest it is a clear, crisp fall day. In the backdrop, horses and canines with powerful legs are dashing across the ditch and after a fox, beyond the frame of the picture.

Well rendered stage sets even surface in broadly comic caricature plates, such as Robert Cruikshank's "A Piece of China" for Matthew H. Barker's *The Old Sailor's Jolly Boat* (1844). In this particular yarn, which is politically incorrect today (for example, Barker refers to all the natives as "John Chinaman" [343]), a native has attempted to steal iron from the invading British seamen. Barker directs the reader-viewer to a visual climax—"the contortions of [the native's] face and body, that he was suffering great agony from the burning, and which our friend Robert Cruikshank has so well depictured" (344). In the accompanying plate entitled "Hot Work in China" (see fig. 21), Cruikshank stereotypes the natives in their

Figure 21. "Hot Work in China." Illustration by Robert Cruikshank for Matthew H. Barker's *The Old Sailor's Jolly Boat, Laden with Tales, Yarns, Scraps, Fragments, etc., to Please All Hands*, 1844. From the Norman M. Fox Collection, Scribner Library, Skidmore College.

appearance and dress: the local inhabitants wear coolie hats and have Fu Manchu moustaches, and the queues of some of the natives are visible.[44] The setting is decidedly exotic with Pagoda-style structures, flying birds, rice fields, and trees strikingly different than those Leech pictures in the English landscape (for example, some have dripping fronds, and others appear to be in the shape of Chinese pine trees). The plate preserves the repugnance of British imperialism distasteful to readers today, but to the Victorians, Robert Cruikshank guided his audience to a distant land by creating a convincing stage set.

Limitations, Problems, and Scandals

Even the most enthusiastic fans recognize the limitations of the caricaturists, who, unlike Sixties artists (for example, John Everett Millais, Marcus Stone, and Du Maurier), were largely unschooled. "Cruikshank's pretty woman leaves no very delightful impression on the mind" (2: 371–72), observes Du Maurier in "The Illustrating of Books." In *An Essay on the Genius of George Cruikshank*, Thackeray, for example, concedes that the eyes of Jack Sheppard's mother are "much caricatured" in "Mr. Wood Offers to Adopt Little Jack Sheppard" and admits further that this is "not an uncommon fault with our artist" (55). Thackeray also pinpoints Cruikshank's difficulty drawing women—noting, for example, how the plate "'May I be cursed,' muttered Jack Sheppard, 'if ever I try to be honest again'" is marred by the "disagreeable and unrefined" (56) depiction of Mrs. Wood, wife of the gentleman who apprentices Jack Sheppard. In *The Dickens Picture-Book*, J. A. Hammerton likewise calls attention to the "atrocious features of Nancy, as delineated by Cruikshank" (4). George Cruikshank simply could not draw an attractive woman, and this fault, as I have argued elsewhere, often compromised the accompanying text.[45]

In *Oliver Twist*, Cruikshank could not satisfactorily depict the saintly prostitute who assuages Dickens's middle-class readers with her love for and loyalty to Oliver Twist. Dickens describes Nancy as "not exactly pretty, perhaps" but "hearty" and "agreeable" (*OT*, Oxf. 1982 57); Cruikshank pictures her not exactly ugly, perhaps, but slovenly and unattractive, which was of consequence in an era that aligned external appearance with inner worth. Although Nancy initially helps Sikes to kidnap Oliver, she risks her life to return him to his rightful class station by seeking out Rose Maylie and Mr. Brownlow and disclosing information about Oliver's rightful parentage. Nancy, through Dickens's pen, exhibits morality and goodness, qualities that reassured Dickens's middle-class readers that Nancy is a character worth caring about. Dickens conceived of

Nancy and Rose as a pair; "Two Sister-Women" is the first descriptive headline for chapter 40.[46] Cruikshank's illustrations compromise the text's capacity to show Nancy to be like her angelic sister, Rose Maylie.

In "The Meeting" (see fig. 22), a well-staged illustration, Nancy stands across from Rose Maylie and Mr. Brownlow while Morris Bolter (aka Noah Claypole) hides in the shadows and overhears Nancy's plan to help Oliver. Passably pleasant, Rose has a slender build and refined features that match Oliver's own, but squat Nancy, in contrast, has a coarse face and looks prematurely old. Rose's bonnet is trimmed, her shawl appears neat, and her gown is full-length and respectable; in contrast, Nancy's bonnet seems frumpy, her shawl looks ragged, and her dress is too short—it exposes her ankles and suggests her dubious profession. In this plate and in "Oliver Claimed by His Affectionate Friends," Nancy does not look the sympathetic, conscientious character who risks her life for Oliver, but rather like a low-class London type.

Much debated, too, is the artistic merit of illustrations by Thackeray and Carroll. Often cited is Dickens's rejection of Thackeray as a possible illustrator for *The Pickwick Papers* following Seymour's suicide. On the other hand, Thackeray earned the praise of Charlotte Brontë and Du Maurier[47] and received glowing reviews well after *Vanity Fair*'s serial publication; one 1865 commentator in the *North American Review* proclaims: "The designs with which Thackeray illustrated his works, which are, so to speak, his own commentary upon them, and without which the story loses half its point,—which illustrate Thackeray's character scarcely less than his pages,—are admirably reproduced" (626). Other reviews are mixed. For example, John Harvey recognizes Thackeray's "art of versatile visual irony, learnt from the caricatures, that he carried into his novels as illustration" (76), but he laments that "[t]he inadequacy of Thackeray's draughtsmanship frequently poses problems at just those places where an illustration is most appropriate" (79).[48]

Harvey's critique of Thackeray's draughtsmanship easily applies to Carroll's amateur, caricature-style illustrations.[49] Carroll skillfully stages Alice's bodily distortions, but at times it appears as if a different character is growing and shrinking. Alice is presumably seven in this story, but she looks like a dreamy-eyed teenager when she first meets the White Rabbit (*UG* 13); a few scenes later when Alice is talking to the Caterpillar, she looks about six years old (49). Many of Carroll's talking beasts, such as the Caterpillar, are riddled with anatomical inaccuracy. As I explore in the next chapter, Tenniel, a recognized Sixties artist, redrew Carroll's caricature sketches with naturalism and ensured the success of *Alice* for an 1860s audience and successive generations.

Figure 22. "The Meeting." Illustration by George Cruikshank for Charles Dickens's "Oliver Twist" in *Bentley's Miscellany*, December 1838. From the Norman M. Fox Collection, Scribner Library, Skidmore College.

Browne's artistry,[50] too, came under attack by, for instance, Sacheverell Sitwell, who insists that "If [Phiz's] engravings are compared with those by Cruikshank for *Oliver Twist* the inferiority of 'Phiz' is to be seen at the first glance" (21–22). Anthony Trollope was displeased with Browne's mundane illustrations for the first half of *Can You Forgive Her?* (1864); he replaced Browne with E. Taylor as illustrator for the second half of the novel. Attuned to the changing taste in book illustration, Dickens did not employ Browne after 1859. Rather, Dickens chose Stone, a Royal Academy-trained artist, to illustrate *Our*

Mutual Friend (1865) and Luke Fildes, another Academy-trained painter, to illustrate his final unfinished novel, *The Mystery of Edwin Drood* (1870).

Undeniably, visual clichés from melodrama and theater manuals of the day recur throughout caricature-style illustrations.[51] Browne uses a stock pose of raised arms to indicate Pickwick's surprise in stumbling upon Alfred Jingle in "The Discovery of Jingle in the Fleet" (see fig. 23B). Likewise, in *Oliver*

Twist, Cruikshank positions Oliver with both arms raised and his mouth open wide in "Oliver Amazed at the Dodger's Mode of 'Going to Work'" (see fig. 23A) to show Oliver's alarm upon realizing the Artful Dodger is actually a pickpocket. Thackeray, too, uses this same stock pose in *Vanity Fair* to depict Jemima Pinkerton's astonishment when Becky Sharp flings the parting gift of Dr. Johnson's *Dictionary* out the carriage window in "Rebecca's Farewell."

Figure 23. A (*opposite*): "Oliver Amazed at the Dodger's Mode of 'Going to Work.'" Illustration by George Cruikshank for Charles Dickens's "Oliver Twist" in *Bentley's Miscellany,* July 1837; B (*above*): "The Discovery of Jingle in the Fleet." Illustration by Hablot Knight Browne for Charles Dickens's *The Posthumous Papers of the Pickwick Club,* 1837. Both plates come from the Norman M. Fox Collection, Scribner Library, Skidmore College.

These predictable expressions, poses, and gestures made illustrations under-standable and popular with their Victorian reader-viewers, but they may well have readied the public for a fresher style of illustration by Academy-trained artists beginning in the 1850s.

Scandal, disagreement, and tension between authors and illustrators also riddle the legacy of the caricaturists. Was Dickens to blame that Robert Seymour went into his garden on Liverpool Road in Islington late at night on 20 April 1836 and shot himself with a fowling piece? An exacting author, Dickens did not like the figures in the initial sketch of "The Dying Clown"; the strolling actor's anguished wife looked too old and the clown too despondent to be sympathetic. Seymour and Dickens met at Furnival's Inn just days prior to Seymour's suicide. Dickens ultimately approved the revised sketch (see fig. 4, ch. 1, 42), but the incident rattled Seymour, who was working on revisions of "The Dying Clown" to accommodate Dickens's instructions late into the very night that Seymour committed self-murder, as the Victorians called suicide.[52] Dickens was never an easy collaborator; he had a total of eighteen illustrators over his prolific literary career. But to some critics like A. N. Wilson, Seymour was "an unhappy man, of illegitimate birth and depressive temperament" (18). Two years before Seymour shot himself, Gilbert à Beckett, who had lavished praise on Seymour's front-page caricatures for *Figaro in London* (a forerunner of *Punch*), publicly smeared Seymour in a November 1834 issue of *Figaro* after the illustrator quit. Seymour left because the *Figaro* editor could not pay him; Beckett had squandered his money on poor theatrical speculations. In turn, Beckett hired Robert Cruikshank to replace Seymour and insulted and libeled Seymour in *Figaro* in a column entitled "To Correspondents": "It is not true that Seymour has gone out of his mind because he never had any to go out of" (184), notes Beckett. Worse, Beckett insists, "the *ideas* for the caricatures in *Figaro* were always supplied to him by the Editor, [Seymour] being a perfect *dolt*, except in the mechanical use of his pencil" (184). Even Seymour's wife believed that her husband's public humiliation in *Figaro* contributed to the suicide.[53]

For a time, the public deeply mourned Seymour; *The Satirist* proclaimed his death a "public loss" and remarked that with "the exception of Cruikshank, he had no rival 'near his throne'" ("Posthumous" 138). But Seymour's fans soon for-got him, and sales of *The Pickwick Papers* soared without him. From Seymour's widow's vantage point, her husband was the true originator of *Pickwick*. In 1840, Seymour's widow and son appealed to Dickens, well known for his philan-thropy, to help their family as their resources diminished, but Dickens refused.

Again in 1849, Jane Seymour appealed to Dickens as debt and illness plagued her family, but Dickens rebuffed her appeals for money and asserted her claim of her husband's authorship was false. The controversy flared again in 1866, four years before Dickens's death.

Shortly after Dickens died, a new controversy arose with a different illustrator. George Cruikshank claimed to be the creator of *Oliver Twist*. Cruikshank took many Londoners by surprise when more than three decades after the publication of *Oliver Twist*, and two years after Dickens's death, he published a pamphlet entitled *The Artist and the Author* (1872) in which he claimed to be the "originator" of Dickens's *Twist* and several of Ainsworth's novels, including *The Miser's Daughter* (1842) and *The Tower of London* (1840). The controversy found its way into the periodical press and "potboiler" biographies of Dickens.[54] Critics variously view Cruikshank's statements as "absurd" (Ainsworth), "deserving of sympathy" (Harvey), or "not without some basis" (J. R. Cohen).[55] "One thing . . . these foolish claims of Cruikshank's and of Seymour's widow do emphasise," observes Hammerton in *The Dickens Picture-Book*, "is the importance of the illustrator in book-production at the time when Dickens first came before the public" (4). To Martin Meisel, the importance of Cruikshank's illustrations for dramatizing Dickens's and Ainsworth's works "did reinforce the practices and attitudes that led Cruikshank to think of himself in some of his collaborations as more *auteur* than illustrator" (279).

When Cruikshank made these claims in 1872, there was a new aesthetic in Victorian illustration. Nonetheless, for many Victorians, the caricaturists left a lasting impression of characters and iconic scenes that they staged in their book illustrations. Robert Surtees declares in his preface to *Handley Cross*: "Mr. Jorrocks, having for many years maintained his popularity, it is hoped that, with the aid of the illustrations, he is now destined for longevity" (n. pag.). Oft-quoted is Henry James's admission in *A Small Boy and Others* (1914) that *Oliver Twist* "perhaps even seemed to me more Cruikshank's than Dickens's" (120). Cruikshank immortalized Fagin, Leech "maintained [Jorrocks's] popularity," and Phiz brought to life countless Dickensian characters. The evolution of the Victorian illustrated book demonstrates how the indelible designs of the caricaturists set the stage for subsequent professional artists who returned to these very illustrations and revised them.

3

꧁꧂

Realism, Victorian Material Culture, and the Enduring Caricature Tradition

The many drawings [Fred Barnard] made for the Household Edition,
as well as some larger pictures, illustrating the works of the great author
[Dickens], all possess a certain peculiarity: while the drawings are strictly
in his own style, there is just enough resemblance to the figures created
by H. K. Browne to save you a shock.

George and Edward Dalziel, *The Brothers Dalziel*, 1901

By the mid-nineteenth century, the aesthetics of the Victorian illustrated book were changing. The new style of illustration did not simply replace the popular designs of the 1820s–1840s. Caricature-style illustration remained in circulation through *Punch* and reprints of George Cruikshank's and Robert Seymour's publications; Cruikshank's *Illustrations of Time* (1827) and *My Sketch Book* (1834) were reprinted, respectively, into the 1870s and 1880s, and reprints of Robert Seymour's *Sketches by Seymour* (1835) were reproduced into the 1880s.[1] Publishing houses on both sides of the Atlantic—Chapman and Hall, and Macmillan in England; Lippincott and Company, and Scribner's in America—reissued editions of Charles Dickens's novels with the original illustrations,[2] even as Chapman and Hall produced the Household Edition (1871–79) with Fred Barnard as lead illustrator.

In the 1850s came the new art of photography, the Great Exhibition, and a different style of book illustration. Sixties illustration arose during a decade where pioneering photographers were capturing the horrors of war (for example, the Crimean War [1855] and the Indian Mutinies [1857–60]), and famous personages were sitting for photographic portraits (such as Napoleon III in 1859 and Queen Victoria in 1860). Lewis Carroll, the well-known author of the *Alice* books, gained acclaim in the 1860s as an amateur photographer using his real name, Charles Lutwidge Dodgson; the author-illustrated hand-written *Alice's Adventures Under Ground* (*UG*, 1864)—the original manuscript version of *Alice's Adventures in Wonderland* (*AA*, 1865) with Carroll's own caricature-style illustrations—includes a photograph Dodgson took of the real Alice Liddell to signal the end of the heroine's curious dream.[3] Realistic illustration simulates the lifelike quality of photography. This style, commonly referred to as "Sixties" illustration, began in the mid-1850s and extended into the 1870s.[4] In its commitment to observation and its aim to render figures, domestic interiors, and landscape with accuracy, Sixties illustration—also referred to as naturalism, representational realism, or simply realism—is foremost a representational style.[5]

Whereas the first generation of caricature-style illustrators was relatively unschooled, the second generation of accomplished painters turned illustrators was Royal Academy–trained. As Paul Goldman and Simon Cooke note in *Reading Victorian Illustration*, the "'new art'" emphasized "academic standards, importing the conventions of painting into the small domain of the printed page" (1). While an eminent caricaturist like Cruikshank could engrave his own work, Sixties illustrators relied on engravers (foremost the Dalziel Brothers) to transform a tasteful drawing into a reproducible illustration to be marketed on a vast, industrial scale for a growing middle-class audience. The Pre-Raphaelites and eminent genre, portrait, and landscape painters increasingly entered the field of magazine and book illustration because they were "attracted to the idea of reaching a wider audience and eager to supplement their income while working on their submissions for the annual Royal Academy summer shows" (Meyrick 180).[6]

This chapter demonstrates that the Sixties style is multifaceted, "By turns lyrical and dramatic, journalistic and psychologically penetrating," but always "a means of representing deep feeling which was still rooted in observation of the 'real' world" (Goldman and Cooke 2, 1). Representative illustrations by Dante Gabriel Rossetti, John Everett Millais, George Du Maurier, Helen Paterson, and Marcus Stone for the literature of William Allingham, Christina Rossetti, Anthony Trollope, William Makepeace Thackeray, Thomas Hardy, and Charles Dickens demonstrate a commitment to naturalism and feeling, a privileging of close-ups over panoramic views, and an attention to figures over backgrounds. This chapter frames the changing aesthetics in book illustration with a major development in Victorian material culture—the Great Exhibition of 1851. This unprecedented exhibition stimulated production of beautiful objects, including books with decorative bindings, and culminated in a richly illustrated exhibition catalogue in the representational style that came into vogue in the Sixties. D. G. Rossetti, featured in this chapter, viewed bookmaking as part of a Pre-Raphaelite commitment to design artful objects for the Victorian home.

Foremost, this chapter looks across illustrative periods within the arc of the Victorian illustrated book to examine how the creative vision of the caricaturists underpins the achievement of some Sixties artists who fleshed out inventive caricature designs to suit popular taste. In Barnard's drawings for *David Copperfield* (*DC*, 1850) in the Household Edition of Dickens's work, there is "just enough resemblance to the figures created by H. K. Browne to save you a shock" (337), according to the Dalziel Brothers (who helped select illustrators for the Household Edition). Re-illustrating *Oliver Twist* (*OT*, 1838) for the Household Edition, James Mahoney recalls Cruikshank's theatrical staging and the look of many characters, particularly Oliver and Fagin. We witness this same kind of revision of the caricature tradition in *Alice in Wonderland*: to appeal to middle-class consumers of the 1860s, John Tenniel refashioned Carroll's caricature-style illustrations in *Alice's Adventures Under Ground* by adding domestic interiors and landscape details and realistically recreating Carroll's social caricatures.

"Paper, Printing, and Bookbinding": Books on Display at the Great Exhibition

The Sixties style of illustration arose in a decade that witnessed an unprecedented international exhibition of innovation and commodity culture at which England was at the fore.[7] The Great Exhibition held in London from 1 May to 15 October 1851 put on display a Victorian aesthetic that frames the contributions of Sixties illustrators, who carried artistic standards into book illustration. Illustrated books with choice bindings were exhibited along with technological, military, economic, and aesthetic wonders of culture and industry. Over 14,000 exhibiters from around the globe showcased innovation in a glass-and-iron building in Hyde Park—dubbed a "Crystal Palace"—an edifice that itself stood for modernization, owing to the invention of cast plate glass as recently as 1848.[8] Over six million visitors from England and other nations came to see fancy goods, geological displays, industrial machinery, new inventions like an envelope-folding machine, fine jewels, agricultural specimens, military artillery, furniture, carriages, and books from England, Europe, and colonial holdings.[9]

The catalogue for the Great Exhibition is a massive three volumes entitled *Official Descriptive and Illustrated Catalogue* of the Great Exhibition of 1851

(*ODIC*). Section 3, class 17, of the second volume is devoted to "Paper, Printing, and Bookbinding,"[10] which includes books. Introducing this section, Robert Ellis privileges the Holy Scriptures, "exhibited in one hundred and fifty different languages—a noble evidence of the highest application of industry to the enlightenment and welfare of mankind" (*ODIC* 2: 538); however, in the following sentence, Ellis acknowledges, "Beautiful specimens of the bookbinder's art are likewise shown" (538).[11] Decoration infused the entire exhibition including the displays of books. Manufacturers entered books "mainly for their bindings, not for their contents" (64), as Asa Briggs notes in *Victorian Things*. With the exception of the entry by the Religious Tract Society (entry 154), the manufacturers' narratives in "Paper, Printing, and Bookbinding" focus on aesthetics, even for ecclesiastical literature. William Jones Cleaver, a London manufacturer, describes the material beauty of the Bible in the following narrative: "Oak and glass case, containing an assortment of Bibles and books of Common Prayer, and a selection of other books in ancient and modern bindings. Exhibited for the colours of the leather, general design, and workmanship" (2: 552).

Bibles are foremost among the "[b]eautiful specimens" (*ODIC* 2: 538) on display for their design and workmanship. J. & J. Leighton, a London manufacturer, highlights one of its most "splendid" (539) editions, the late King William IV's Royal Bible, which the manufacturer bound for His Highness in Morocco leather from a design by Luke Limner (see fig. 24). The accompanying full-page illustration in the catalogue (opposite 539) shows the cover and sides embossed with royal emblems and nautical imagery "in honour of the sailor king" (539); the book clasps take the shape of anchors and ships' cables. Manufacturer J. & J. Leighton presents the Bible to advantage: "reflectors" (mirrors) show the back, end, and fore-edge of the magnificent binding. From this manufacturer's narrative and the illustration of King William IV's Bible, we learn about the life of the book's royal owner, social class, and aesthetic taste. A Scottish designer, W. Clark, likewise features exquisite bindings of Bibles and other books including "Chalmers' *History of Dunfermline*, 8vo, full-bound in red Turkey Morocco, hand-tooled in gold and silver on back and sides, and with silver and satin linings" (546). The eight volumes have rich leather bindings adorned with precious metals and expensive fabric trim. These books manufactured by J. & J. Leighton, W. Clark, and other bookmakers were affordable only to the upper reaches—or in J. & J. Leighton's case to royalty—but the bindings garnered appreciation from all social classes. Members of the working class regularly frequented the Great Exhibition, buying less expensive tickets for off-peak entrance times.

44. ROYAL BIBLE. MESSRS. LEIGHTON THE TOP, BACK, AND FRONT ARE SEEN AS REFLECTED IN A MIRROR.

Figure 24. "The Late King William IV's Royal Bible." Illustration in the *Official Descriptive and Illustrated Catalogue* of the Great Exhibition, 1851.

Many books on display were illustrated, and manufacturers' narratives make pointed references to illustrations. James Wild, a London bookmaker, exhibited atlases with as many as sixty-seven full-colored maps (2: 549). Clark & Davidson, a Scottish manufacturer, references a "Pictorial Bible, bound in wood boards, ornamented with arabesques" (546). This is one of many pictorial Bibles extravagantly illustrated with vignettes, pictorial capitals, tailpieces, and full-page engravings.[12] Robert Neil, an Edinburgh publisher, directs attention to "the etchings of three churches—top, St. John's, Edinburgh; bottom, St. Giles', Edinburgh; front, St. Mungo's, Glasgow" (544) that are printed on the satin flyleaves of an imperial quarto Bible. Moreover, this manufacturer describes a Morocco display case "so designed that the Bible may be fully seen, without handling or removing it from the cushion at the bottom of the case" (544). In context of the Great Exhibition, a finely bound book was a material object to be appreciated from every vantage point.

Books from other nations also were on exhibit. Egypt submitted a prize-winning collection of 165 volumes in Turkish, Arabic, and Persian published at Bulaq, the first Egyptian printing press.[13] The Bulaq Press, established in 1822 in the port of Cairo, arose in response to ruler Muhammed Ali Pashi's aim for military expansion and education; as Peter Colvin notes, Ali Pashi's "reign had turned Cairo into the publishing and intellectual center of the Arab World" (259). This collection of leather-bound works ranging from literature and history to military techniques won Egypt an honorable mention in the Great Exhibition. Significant is Colvin's observation: "it would appear that they were exhibited primarily for their bindings, which may be what gained them their honorable mention" (257). By 1851, books were artful objects.

Other prize-winning book collections came from Saxony and Austria. F. A. Brockhaus of Saxony received a medal for "'his collection of 356 volumes, the whole printed at his own establishment in the year 1850'" (qtd. in Briggs 65). The Austrian section features a grand Gothic bookcase from carved oak designed to house a collection of books as a gift from the Emperor of Austria to Queen Victoria (Briggs 64–65). The Viennese manufacturer Carl Leistler & Son notes that "The design for the Queen's bookcase was made by Bernardo di Bernardis, architect, assisted by Mr. Joseph Kramer, of Prague" (*ODIC* 3: 1039). The full-page illustration of the bookcase with its Gothic arches, fretwork, and inlaid design reveals an awareness that beautiful books needed high quality bookcases to display them.

The *Official Descriptive and Illustrated Catalogue* itself merits observation for its lavish number of representational-style illustrations; it is a picture gallery of decorative objects and innovations of Victorian England and foreign lands.[14] Compilers of the catalogue call it an "illustrated book of this kind" (1: vi). As the title indicates, the catalogue is both a "descriptive" and an "illustrated" book, and the illustrations, particularly those of items from other countries, align this publication with travel literature, a genre that was growing in popularity in the mid-nineteenth century. Aware that "these pages will be read in many lands long after the Exhibition shall have become a matter of history" (viii), Ellis, author of the preface, notes that the compilers designed it "to serve as a lasting memorial of the splendid collection to which it professes to be the exponent" (vi). The word "memorial" indicates the significance of this illustrated book to future generations as does Ellis's remark that this three-volume catalogue provides a "record of the most varied and wonderful collection of objects ever beheld" (viii) to be cherished long after "the great spectacle it illustrates will pass away" (vii).

The plentiful black-and-white and occasional color illustrations in the *Official Descriptive and Illustrated Catalogue* display an unprecedented collection of material objects. The title-page design, an encircled crown and shield, is by John Tenniel, a recognized Sixties illustrator. The three volumes of the catalogue include over thirty views of the Crystal Palace's construction and interior and hundreds of illustrations of the wondrous objects and inventions on exhibition. The manufacturers' narratives transmit details of the fancy goods trade and technological and industrial innovation. The pictures in the catalogue, if read along with the narratives, allow us to glimpse why a noted visitor like Charlotte Brontë describes the Great Exhibition as "such a Bazaar or Fair as eastern Genii might have created. It seems as if magic only could have gathered this mass of wealth from all the ends of the Earth . . . with such a blaze and contrast of colours and marvelous power of effect" (J. R. V. Barker, *Letters* 324).

The Coalbrook Dale Company of Shropshire includes a full-page drawing entitled "Fountain and Park Gates in Cast Iron" (see fig. 25) that is a spectacle to behold. The narrative includes intricate design details that the picture, in turn, realizes with near photographic precision. According to the manufacturer, the bronzed cast-iron entrance consists "of a pair of principal gates, and two side gates, hung on iron pillars of new construction, combining lightness and strength, having finials, emblematic of Peace, supporting an insular crown; also on either side an ogee fencing, terminating in stag's-head vases, suggestive of a park" (2: 659). "[A]s if [by] magic," reader-viewers of the *Official Descriptive and Illustrated Catalogue* are transported into this charming illustration. Inside the crowned gates sits an enormous ornamental cast-iron fountain after "Cupid and the Swan" (2: 659). The waters rise high from the fountain, nearly touching the trees just outside the gates. The frontage of this scene anticipates a theme park. Posed, too, in the illustration is an exhibition goer, a genteel Victorian lady dressed in a bonnet and full ruffled cape and gown admiring this spectacle of technical innovation and beauty. Moreover, the display is sixty feet long, giving a sense of the enormity of the Great Exhibition as well as this particular exhibit.

Small representational illustrations in the catalogue are equally fascinating. In class 22, "General Hardware, Including Locks and Grates," manufacturer Chubb & Son provides several small pictures including a drawing of a fireproof safe (sketched to show the "form and interior" [2: 663]); a specimen of an ornamental Gothic lock, showcasing new technology crafted with an historical

Figure 25. "Fountain and Park Gates in Cast Iron." From the Coalbrook Dale Company. Illustration in the *Official Descriptive and Illustrated Catalogue* of the Great Exhibition, 1851.

design; and the Koh-i-Noor diamond case with Queen Victoria's precious diamond inside it. The case, a curious looking object that resembles a birdcage, "contains an arrangement for elevating and depressing the diamond without unlocking"; moreover, the manufacturer maintains, "It is considered to be impossible to pick the lock or obtain an entrance into this receptacle" (663).

Perhaps most compelling are the illustrations of objects from foreign countries—Sèvres china from France, water jugs from Egypt, an elaborate leather saddle from Tunis, a carved table from China, and Grecian Palicar attire for men. A carefully executed illustration accompanying an entry by Saris & Rengos of Athens pictures a man wearing the local costume, which includes a tunic embroidered in gold, a fez with a gold tassel, a fermeli (an upper jacket), a pair of gaiters, silk garters, a silk sash, shirt, trousers, and Morocco leather shoes (3: 1406). Saris & Rengos uses the narrative to describe improvements in embroidering (for example, "The art of embroidering, both in silk and gold, has of late been considerably improved in Greece"); the narrative also points to the higher quality of the leather used for the manufacturing of shoes. The accompanying picture of the richly clad male figure set against a Grecian landscape seemingly transports the viewer to Athens (3: 1406); we can even see the Acropolis and the hills in the background as well as the details of stitching and ornamentation on the costume. By 1851, trains and steamships made distances more surmountable, but only for those of means. This picture is but one of hundreds in the *Official Descriptive and Illustrated Catalogue* that provided Victorian middle-class viewers a voyeuristic opportunity to travel to foreign and exotic lands and to see the wonders of all nations.

The Artful Book in the Victorian Drawing Room

"The crowds at the Crystal Palace . . . spurred consumption, even if the objects on display were not for sale" (154), as Elizabeth Helsinger advances in "Rossetti and the Art of the Book." The Great Exhibition stimulated an appetite for material objects that resembled the spectacular items on display. In addition, periodicals such as *The Art Journal*—produced in 1851 to bring fine art into the Victorian home through wood engravings[15]—show that by the very start of the decade, bookbinding and wood engraving were considered forms of fine art. "For middle-class Victorians in the 1850s and 60s," notes Helsinger, "the object forms of art and literature were a focus of consuming interest. New technologies and materials helped make decorative covers and illustrated books widely available and much less expensive" (149). As more middle-class Victorians could afford to buy books with attractive bindings and quality illustrations to adorn their libraries and parlors, purchasing a book for its binding—not for its contents—became a source of humor.

In *Library Jokes and Jottings* (1914), Henry Coutts includes the following epigraph in his chapter entitled "Books as Furniture": "'No furniture so charming as books, even if you never open them or read a single word'" (118). Coutts recalls a trick played on a millionaire with "literary pretensions" who viewed books simply as a means of furnishing his estate; the foolish man falls prey to a savvy bookseller, who rebinds a large stock of remainders of one single third-rate novel "in gorgeous bindings, lettered with the names of authors and titles of classical and modern standard works and duly despatched. The millionaire is exceedingly proud of his library, and it is very unlikely that he will ever discover the trick that was played upon him" (121–22). In a later chapter, Coutts tells of a visitor at a seaside resort who complains to a librarian that she cannot read a particular book because its binding does not match her outfit: "'It may be a very nice book, but look what an atrocious cover it has; haven't you one bound in saxe-blue to match my costume? I really couldn't take a scarlet-covered book on to the promenade'" (147).[16]

Consumers often bought whole collections of books bound in saxe blue or another handsome color to decorate their libraries and drawing rooms. George Eliot's Mr. Tulliver of *The Mill on the Floss* (1860) likewise purchases a collection of books for its covers, not its contents. The set includes Daniel Defoe's *The Political History of the Devil* (1726)—not suitable reading for his daughter, Maggie—but Tulliver buys it because "'They was all bound alike—it's a good binding, you see—and I thought they'd be all good books'" (18). Tulliver thinks he can judge a book's worth by its cover "in an age where more volumes entered into circulation (or gathered dust on more shelves) than ever before" (Price 2). Elizabeth Gaskell describes such a costly book gathering dust on a library shelf in the home of a prosperous mill owner, Mr. Carson, in *Mary Barton* (1848). The Carsons rarely open "the great large handsome Bible, all grand and golden, with its leaves adhering together from the bookbinder's press, so little had it been used" (435).[17] The Carson family Bible with its gold binding and fully gilt edges recalls the illustrated Bibles on display for their sumptuous covers at the Great Exhibition of 1851.[18]

At the same time as books with beautiful bindings became art objects to decorate one's home, illustrations within books became collectible art worth framing. Many nineteenth-century prints on the market today are the handicraft of collectors who cut them out of illustrated books and periodicals.[19] Publishers and collectors often separated illustrations from the books that they were designed to accompany to show them "to their best advantage," as Robert Meyrick notes; "If a painting demanded a canvas, an engraving should at least warrant a folio. . . . Publishers of the 1860s were quick to respond to this perception and to produce vehicles showcasing the exquisite works of art they had commissioned" (180). One prime example of this kind of artistic elevation of illustration is folio publication, such as *The Cornhill Gallery*, first published in 1864 and then reprinted in 1865.[20] This volume of 100 engravings includes 28 illustrations by Sir John Everett Millais for Anthony Trollope's *Framley Parsonage* (1861) and *The Small House at Allington* (1864) and other illustrations by, among others, Fred Walker, Frederick Leighton, and George Du Maurier. Smith, Elder and Co. worked closely with the Dalziels to produce fine woodblock engravings of works previously printed from electrotype casts, resulting, as noted in the preface, "'in a style which will place them in their proper rank of Works of Art'" (qtd. in Reid 12).[21] Akin to a book of paintings, the folio printed on fine paper included little to no textual accompaniment, even though the engravings were actually illustrations to serials and stories published in *The Cornhill Magazine*. Smith, Elder and Co.'s capitalization of "Works" and "Art" in the preface also speaks to the publisher's motive: to convince potential buyers that quality illustrations by recognized artists be appreciated and bought as fine art. Priced at just one guinea, *The Cornhill Gallery* was affordable art for burgeoning middle-class consumers, and its republication just one year after its original printing attests to the volume's success.

In an age of growing literacy and consumerism, savvy publishers produced multiple versions of a popular title, varying the material and color of the binding: boards for a cheap edition, and cloth and primarily leather for a collector's edition. A "cheap edition" was affordable to members of the rising middle class. An ornate edition, like those displayed at the Great Exhibition or arranged on drawing-room tables of prosperous homes, was an aesthetic object to buy, enjoy, collect, catalogue, and exhibit, and it was often richly illustrated.

Publishers variously packaged Richard Harris Barham's *The Ingoldsby Legends*; this collection of myths, legends, and ghost stories with plates by George Cruikshank, John Leech, and John Tenniel first appeared in *Bentley's Miscellany* in 1837 and remained popular in volume form throughout the nineteenth century. The book's frequent reprinting kept caricature-style illustration by Cruikshank and Leech in circulation alongside plates by Tenniel. Publisher Richard Bentley brought out many editions of *The Ingoldsby Legends* including a three-volume set in 1855 with a cloth binding and minimal decoration and an 1864 edition with a richly-gilt, full-calf binding (see figs. 26A and 26B). While the spine of the 1855 edition is gold stamped, the front and back covers have a blind impress design. The fore and bottom edges of the 1855 edition are trimmed, but the top edge is roughly cut. Not a "cheap" book—the 1855 version contains a bit of gold stamping—this edition caters to a middle-class consumer with some pocket money to spend. In contrast, Bentley's 1864 edition, marketed to the book collector, has fully gilt edges and is bound in brown Morocco leather with elaborate gold tooling on the spine as well as the back and front covers. This 1864 edition is a prime example of the kind of "artful objects suited to domestic consumption: art to live with" (Helsinger 154). Such richly illustrated leather and gilt volumes found a market among "consumers [who] expected books to be not only attractive objects in their own right but also potential elements in the decoration of their homes" (Helsinger 169). The gift book, designed explicitly for display, also brought foreign lands, popular science, religion, art, and poetry into the Victorian parlor. The popularity of such gift books lies as much

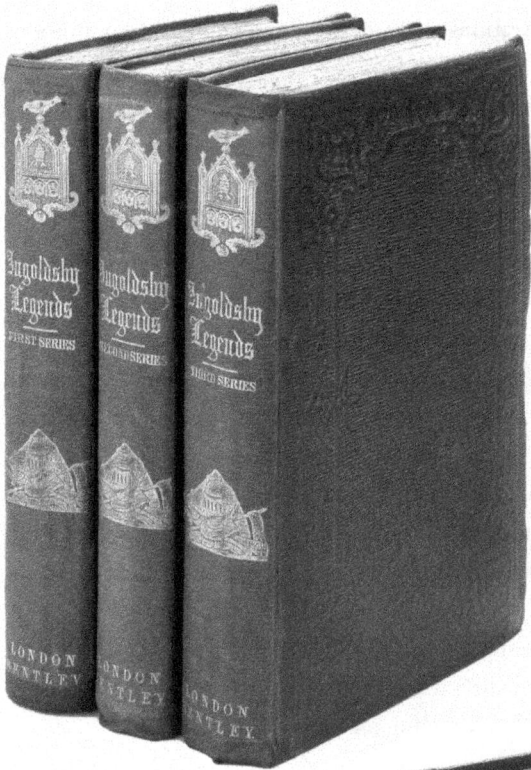

Figure 26. A (*left*): Cover for *The Ingoldsby Legends, or Mirth and Marvels* by Richard Harris Barham, published by Richard Bentley, 1855; B (*below*): Cover for *The Ingoldsby Legends, or Mirth and Marvels* by Richard Harris Barham, published by Richard Bentley, 1864. Both editions come from the Norman M. Fox Collection, Scribner Library, Skidmore College.

in their wood-engraved illustrations, brilliant bindings, and gilt decorations as in their contents.

The binding was as important as a book's illustrations to an artist-turned-illustrator like Dante Gabriel Rossetti. Innovative in his approach to book-binding, Rossetti conceived of the book's front and back covers and spine as a unified design. For example, Rossetti's cloth binding for his sister Christina's *Goblin Market and Other Poems* (1862)—though far simpler than the bindings displayed at the Great Exhibition or of *Mary Barton*'s "grand and golden" Bible in the Carson home—includes interlacing vertical and horizontal gold lines with triangular groupings of small circles in a balanced asymmetrical pattern evocative of 1860s' Japanese design.[22] Rossetti, who also designed frames for his own paintings, was involved in every stage of bookmaking: layout, illustration, printing, and binding. Rossetti worked with commercial publishers to create what Helsinger calls a "work of many hands" (172). In overseeing the handi-craft of other "hands"—checking and correcting the work of binder, printer, and engraver, and notoriously complaining about the Dalziels for not following his instructions—Rossetti sustained the feel of a handcrafted book for works produced by commercial publishers for middle-class consumers with money to spend on books to decorate their drawing rooms and libraries.

The Sixties

Rossetti was a Sixties illustrator as well as an artist and a bookmaker. Critics from Rossetti's time and our time have singled out Rossetti's first book illustra-tion, "The Maids of Elfen-Mere," as a premier example of Sixties book illus-tration. Rossetti designed it to accompany William Allingham's supernatural ballad called "The Maids of Elfin-Mere" included in *The Music Master* (1855). This edition of Allingham's poems has seven plates by Arthur Hughes, a second gen-eration Pre-Raphaelite painter, and one engraving each by John Everett Millais and D. G. Rossetti, founding members of the Pre-Raphaelite Brotherhood (cu-riously, Rossetti changed the spelling of Allingham's poem, substituting an "e" for the "i" in "Elfin" when he titled his illustration).[23] Young Edward Burne-Jones decided to give up Holy Orders and pursue a career as an artist upon seeing Rossetti's "The Maids of Elfen-Mere."[24] Often quoted is Burne-Jones's description of the "marvellous beauty" of this illustration in his unsigned "Es-say on *The Newcomes*" published in 1856 in the *Oxford and Cambridge Magazine*: "it is I think the most beautiful drawing for an illustration I have ever seen, the weird faces of the maids of Elfin-mere, the musical timed movement of their arms together as they sing, the face of the man, above all, are such as only a great artist could conceive" (60). Echoing Burne-Jones's praise of Rossetti's illustration a century and a half later, Helsigner calls it a "single, stunning engraving" (157), noting that this illustration along with the five plates that Rossetti contributed to Edward Moxon's 1857 edition of Tennyson's *Poems* "suggested to artists wholly new conceptual and visual possibilities for book illustration" (157).

This illustration (see fig. 27)—which Rossetti believed the Dalziels ruined in the process of engraving it onto wood[25]—is stunning in its depiction of two worlds cohabiting a close, shared space.[26] Rossetti privileges figure over background. Four large figures fill the page: three ethereal maids, who look as if they are from a distant world, and the Pastor's son, who belongs to the human world but exhibits a self-absorption that disengages him from it. Rossetti moves the viewer closest to the face of the Pastor's son, who captivated Burne-Jones. The Pastor's son looks away from the otherworldly inhabitants, who are

> Spinning to a pulsing cadence,
> Singing songs of Elfin-Mere;
> Till the eleventh hour was toll'd,
> Then departed through the wold.
> Years ago, and years ago; (lines 5–9)

The "Three white Lilies, calm and clear" (line 11)—with near identical faces hauntingly similar to that of Rossetti's wife, Elizabeth Siddal—are arrested in the acts of spinning and singing; their fingers clasp the threads they are twirling, and their mouths are open as if captured mid-song.

The town, "Düreresque . . . with its pointed roofs and the fateful clock tower" (Reid 35), appears through a narrow window on the top of the picture plane. The setting cues the viewer to the "fateful" passing of what turns out to be a false eleventh hour. The Pastor's son, who loves the maids, does not want them to leave at this appointed time, so he has changed the hour on the village clock. Does the Pastor's son look away fully knowing that he is tricking the maids into staying on earth beyond the true eleventh hour, sealing their destruction and his own? After this night, the maids never return, and "The Pastor's Son did pine and die" (line 37). Rossetti's book illustration also allows for the possibility that the Pastor's son, locked in a moment of intense psychological introspection, looks away from the maids because they are not truly there—they are apparitions, symbols of lost love and the lost innocence of the Pastor's son.

Arguably no artist has illustrated Christina Rossetti's long narrative poem *Goblin Market* more perceptively than Dante Gabriel Rossetti,[27] who produced

Figure 27. "The Maids of Elfen-Mere, engraved by the Dalziel Brothers." Illustration by Dante Gabriel Rossetti for William Allingham's *The Music Master*, 1855, ©Tate, London 2014.

two illustrations for the 1862 Macmillan edition of *Goblin Market and Other Poems* (see figs. 28A and 28B): a frontispiece and a title page.[28] Dante Gabriel and Christina Rossetti worked together intimately on these projects, recalling how in the 1830s and 1840s authors and illustrators collaborated to publish novels serially.[29] *Goblin Market* is a coming of age fairy tale about two sisters enticed by goblin men with seasonal fruits that forebodingly ripen at the same time of year:

> Apples and quinces,
> Lemons and oranges,
> Plump unpecked cherries,
> Melons and raspberries,
> Bloom-down-cheeked peaches,
> Swart-headed mulberries,
> Wild free-born cranberries,
> Crab-apples, dewberries,
> Pine-apples, blackberries,
> Apricots, strawberries;—
> All ripe together
> In summer weather,—(lines 5–16)

Saintly Lizzie withstands such temptation, but erring Laura succumbs to the forbidden earthly delights.

The opening of the book offered Victorian reader-viewers two interpretations of the poem through Rossetti's designs: a frontispiece with a moral allegory privileging the saintly Lizzie over her erring sister Laura (see fig. 28A), and an adjoining title page showing two radiant golden-haired sisters with the fallen Laura looking as pure as her sinless sister (see fig. 28B). These opposing readings troubled the poem's initial Victorian readers, who were eager to determine whether the poem warned against sin or promoted it.[30] Rossetti placed these images directly opposite, putting them in conversation with each other.[31]

The frontispiece foregrounds "the primordial struggle between the sensuous and the spiritual," notes Kooistra, who views "Lizzie and Laura as types for the archetypal sisters, Flesh and Spirit" (*Rossetti* 70). This connection, Kooistra argues, recalls a woodcut of two sisters from Francis Quarles's "Emblem 14" in book 3 of *Emblems* (1635), a didactic text we can assume was well known to Christina Rossetti and her audience. In this seventeenth-century woodcut, "Flesh," naked with flowing hair, tries to hand a prism to her sister, "Spirit," dressed and coiffed conservatively, to prevent "Spirit" from looking toward the

"Buy from us with a golden curl"

Figure 28. A (*above*): "Frontispiece," and B (*opposite*): "Title-Page Illustration." Illustrations by Dante Gabriel Rossetti for Christina Rossetti's *Goblin Market and Other Poems*. PR5237 .G62 1862. Albert and Shirley Small Special Collections Library, University of Virginia, Charlottesville, VA.

heavens with the telescope she holds in her hand. In the frontispiece for *Goblin Market* (see fig. 28A), Lizzie (placed in the upper far-left corner of the picture) in her dark conservative dress and coiffure visually alludes to "Spirit" and suggests a moral superiority to Laura, but Laura assumes center stage in this design that illustrates the poetic line, "'Buy from us with a golden curl'" (line 125). Rossetti positions the erring sister close to the viewer. Laura, who appears disproportionately larger than pictorial scale would allow,[32] oozes fleshly sensuality. She has long flowing golden locks, which she is pictured in the act of cutting to pay the goblin men for her indulgence. Rossetti also positions the goblins startlingly close to the viewer, who can observe their realistically rendered animal features—beaks, feathers, fangs, and whiskers—as well as their

GOBLIN MARKET
and other poems
by Chriſtina Roſſetti

"Golden head by golden head"

London and Cambridge
Macmillan and Co. 1862

human hands and dress. One goblin resembling a cat clutches Laura's lock that snakes around his neck and onto the plate of tantalizing fruits. If we read this plate as a Christian allegory, which some Victorian readers did, either Laura's lock of hair or the lengthy tail of the goblin-cat (whose whiskers seemingly touch Laura's golden tresses) symbolizes the serpent of Genesis, and Laura is fallible Eve.

D. G. Rossetti's title-page design (see fig. 28B) illustrates the lines that read:

Golden head by golden head,
Like two pigeons in one nest
Folded in each other's wings,
They lay down in their curtained bed: (lines 184–87)

In contrast to the frontispiece, the title-page design visualizes a connection between the fallen sister and the virtuous one. Rossetti provides a close-up of the two sisters with gleaming locks "nesting" in each other's arms on an open bed. Christina Rossetti, who regularly visited fallen women at the Penitentiary of St. Mary Magdalene well before she wrote this poem, permits Laura to return to innocence with her sister's intervention: "Life out of death. / . . . Laura awoke as from a dream, / Laughed in the innocent old way," (lines 524, 537–38).

In his own poetic meditation on a prostitute entitled "Jenny" (1870), D. G. Rossetti does not imagine such a possibility for a fallen woman, insisting: "So pure,—so fall'n! How dare to think / Of the first common kindred link?" (lines 207–08). However, Rossetti does not illustrate Laura growing gray and nearly dying, the fate of the sisters' fallen friend, Jeanie. Rather, in the title-page design, Rossetti pictures Laura recovered: "Her gleaming locks showed not one thread of grey, / Her breath was sweet as May" (lines 540–41). The title-page design does not fully expunge Laura's temptation by the goblin men. Laura clutches her virginal sister's golden lock, and a dream circle above Laura's head shows the goblin men carrying the tempting fruits that ripen altogether. Readers today might more readily comment on the homoeroticism of this illustration of two sisters nestled in each other's arms than on their twin pureness. But for a Victorian audience, the frontispiece with its clear indication of Lizzie's virtue and Laura's fallibility softens the title-page design's radical message of equal purity of "Golden head by golden head" (line 184).[33]

Rossetti dabbled in book illustration and bookmaking, but he was foremost a painter. His fellow Pre-Raphaelites William Holman Hunt and John Everett Millais also became illustrators. Millais produced more book illustrations than the other members of the Pre-Raphaelite triumvirate and is notable for the range of subjects he illustrated with artistry as well as his skill and productivity. In "The Illustrating of Books from the Serious Artist's Point of View," Du Maurier calls attention to the importance of Millais's contribution of eighteen illustrations to Moxon's edition of Tennyson's *Poems* (1857): "a new impulse was given to the art of illustrating books" (1: 351).[34] Millais worked closely with his engravers, particularly the Dalziel Brothers, and illustrated far longer than the other Pre-Raphaelites. He also provided stunning representational-style illustrations for a greater variety of new and reprinted books and periodicals. Millais illustrated poetry by Alfred Lord Tennyson and William Allingham, tales such as *Dalziels' Illustrated Arabian Nights' Entertainments* (1865), religious texts including *Dalziels' Bible Gallery* (1881) and *The Parables of Our Lord and Saviour Jesus Christ* (1864), Harriet Martineau's four historiettes (published in *Once a*

Week in 1862 and 1863), children's books by Henry Leslie and Jean Ingelow, and fiction by Wilkie Collins, Victor Hugo, and, in particular, Anthony Trollope. Millais illustrated Trollope's *Framley Parsonage* (1861), *Orley Farm* (1862), *The Small House at Allington* (1864), *Rachel Ray* (1864), and *Kept in the Dark* (1882). Critics including Judith Fisher and Arlene Jackson refer to the illustrations produced during 1855–70 as "the Millais era" and characterize the Sixties as "the representational style of illustration given to Trollope's works" (Jackson 12).[35]

For his book illustrations, Millais chose pregnant moments. He foregrounded one or two expertly rendered figures within the Victorian domestic sphere—the drawing room, library, bedchamber, and balcony window—as well as in the natural world of pasture, countryside, seascape, and forest. "While it cannot be said with truthfulness that Millais is greatly interested in landscape in illustration," notes Paul Goldman in *Beyond Decoration*, "there are instances where he takes particular care to render a setting to strengthen the dramatic sense" (19). Millais takes "particular care" in rendering landscape to dramatic effect in his illustrations for *The Parables of Our Lord and Saviour Jesus Christ*. The setting of "The Lost Sheep" includes an occasional shrub and tree in an otherwise rocky, barren landscape. The accurately rendered ewe has a sloping forehead, rich wooly coat, and rounded rump. The sheep, now slung over the shepherd's shoulders, forms the focus of the plate, but its striking placement—perilously close to the edge of the cliff and to the broad-winged eagle staring directly at the sheep as if anticipating its next meal—intensifies the drama of the parable. The shepherd is rejoicing over finding what the setting shows to be so nearly lost forever. In the foreground of "The Prodigal Son," the wayward son and his elderly father lock in an embrace that holds the viewer's attention. Millais adds to the background two similarly well-executed wooly sheep sitting contentedly on the grass next to a pond, some trees, and a conical barn to make the setting a welcome respite for the son who finally returns home. To Goldman, "The earth-shattering moment of the Parable itself contrasts profoundly with the everyday nature of Millais's landscape. It is this very 'matter-of-factness' which strengthens and clarifies the meaning of the Parable itself by making it immediate and crystal clear to the reader and to the viewer" (*Beyond* 19).

Millais likewise fills the foreground of "The Good Samaritan" with two figures—the wounded man robbed of his possessions and the kindly wayfarer (see fig. 29). Small versions of this iconic image appear on the walls of abodes in caricature-style illustrations. For *Vanity Fair* (1848), Thackeray places the painting in "Becky's Second Appearance in the 'Character of Clytemnestra'" (see fig. 14, ch. 2, 69) on the wall behind Jos Sedley, who begs Dobbin to be his Good Samaritan. Cruikshank incorporates it into "Oliver Recovering from a Fever" to reinforce that Mr. Brownlow is orphan Oliver's own Good Samaritan in *Oliver Twist*.

In contrast to Thackeray and Cruikshank who offer simple renderings of this iconic parable as paintings, Millais makes the biblical tale the subject of an entire plate. The Good Samaritan kneels on the ground and cradles the partially dressed, bony-chested wayfarer, who extends one arm around the Good Samaritan, creating a circular bond of caring and kindness. The partially visible face of the wayfarer registers pain. In contrast, the face of the Good Samaritan is fixed entirely on the man he tends, thus obscuring his face from the viewer. Next to the Samaritan, Millais places the front half of the donkey whose ears and legs point straight along the path the wayfarer is traveling, suggesting the kindly traveler has just dismounted from his beast to tend the man in need with provisions from the donkey's pack. In turn, this is the beast that will carry the wounded man to an inn for much needed rest. Another traveler just ahead, who has presumably ignored the wounded man, is a foil for the kindly Samaritan, who cannot pass by another in distress. The near photographic accuracy of the illustration seems most vivid in the anatomical rendering of the donkey; the small hairs on its hide, a mane palpable to the touch, its large right eye set on the side of its skull, pointed ears, and a realistic muzzle with a well-proportioned chin, nose, and mouth show Millais's skill in observation. Along with the donkey, the setting of this plate also includes details of "everyday nature"—rolling hills, sparse ground vegetation, and trees—to bring the ancient parable into the immediate world of the Victorian reader-viewer.

Singling out Millais as an illustrator of women in *Beyond Decoration*, Goldman argues: "Millais shows a mastery not merely of costume but also of pose and emotion"; Millais is capable of making "a motionless character at the same time intent, concentrating and alive" (15). Du Maurier paid Millais a similar compliment over a century earlier in "The Illustrating of Books": "The crown, or 'cake,' must be given, I think, to Sir John Millais' pretty woman, who is alive at every point, and the most modern of all. She is also a most aristocratic person, even if she be but a dressmaker, or a poor widow with her mite" (2: 372). The frontispiece to *Orley Farm* is of a well-executed landscape filled with trees, a farmhouse on a hill, and a maiden milking a realistically rendered cow in a fertile pasture in the foreground. However, many of the forty illustrations that Millais provides for *Orley Farm* feature pretty women of various social classes—the aristocratic Madeline Staveley, the widowed Lady Mason, and the penniless Mary Snow.

Figure 29. "The Good Samaritan." Illustration by John Everett Millais for *The Parables of Our Lord and Saviour Jesus Christ*, 1864.

"The Angel of Light," also called "Mary's Letter" (see fig. 30), singly features Mary Snow and demonstrates Millais's consummate artistic skill in drawing a convincingly real woman. Mary looks refined even if she is impoverished and dependent upon Felix Graham, a young rising barrister who educates and supports Mary and molds her to be his wife. The plate captures gentility in her modest coiffure (a low bun) and her high-necked, long-sleeved, full-length dress—the billowing skirt was a Millais specialty. The illustration also reveals the realistic school's deep capacity for psychological penetration. Candlelight illuminates the intense look on the face of Mary Snow, furtively reading a letter not from Felix Graham, her fiancé, but a new admirer.

Millais is illustrating a scene in Trollope's novel where Mary finds "Stolen pleasures always are sweet" but simultaneously feels guilty that her "pleasures" do not come from the pen of "her own betrothed lord," which she could read in broad daylight (1: 264). Here Mary reads in the darkness late at night, alone, and by candlelight, which intensifies the illicitness of this act. The setting is relatively uncluttered with only a few domestic items. Her hat hung on the wall to her left and the mirror attached to the dressing table behind her, for example, in no way distract from the single figure of Mary as she finds private pleasure in transgressing social decorum. The single candle in its simple brass holder provides the lone light source in the room. Mary, leaning her body close to the candle and the viewer, seems very much alive.

Like Millais and Rossetti, George Du Maurier began his artistic career as a painter, but Du Maurier left painting altogether to become a book illustrator when, in 1860, he lost vision in his left eye;[36] believing his compromised vision prohibited a career in easel painting and fearing total blindness, Du Maurier made a decision that was not displeasing to him. In his regular correspondence with his mother during this period, he happily describes his first commissions including a Christmas book for the Dalziels and drawings for *Punch* and *Once a Week*. In an April 1861 letter, Du Maurier tells his mother he is "very anxious to be kept on at O.A.W. [*Once a Week*] as it is the swellest thing out, and gets one known, and the more carefully I draw the better it will be for me in the end" (D. Du Maurier 36). *Once a Week* (1859–80) was a literary magazine produced by Bradbury and Evans to showcase the work of innovative Sixties artists and to provide competition for *All the Year Round* (1859–95), Dickens's own weekly.

Du Maurier's illustrations appear in *Once a Week* alongside plates by William Holman Hunt, Millais, Burne-Jones, Arthur Hughes, Frederick Leighton, and Frederick Sandys, artists whose paintings came to grace the walls of the Royal Academy shows. Charles Keene and Tenniel also regularly published illustrations in *Once a Week*. Du Maurier was delighted to publish alongside these artistic illustrators but keenly aware of his competition. In a letter dated January 1861, he asks his mother to compare his illustration of a bedside scene to one that Millais drew—"When it comes out I will send it with Millais and you shall compare" (D. Du Maurier 29). And in April 1861, he laments to his mother that to *Once a Week*, "My name hasn't yet sufficient weight to force on them

Figure 30. "Mary's Letter." Illustration by John Everett Millais for Anthony Trollope's *Orley Farm*, 1862.

drawings which they don't like, like Keene or Tenniel, and I cannot illustrate all subjects with equal facility" (D. Du Maurier 38).

Du Maurier is known for his drawings of tall, statuesque women—a type of illustration that pleased Henry James but bored Forrest Reid, who complains of Du Maurier: "he is content to draw the same face over and over again, so that we find the well-known lady of *Punch* figuring as the heroine of all the novels he illustrates, from *The Hand of Ethelberta* to *The Martian*" (176). In *Punch*—Victorian London's equivalent of *The New Yorker*—Du Maurier published what amounted to thousands of cartoons that satirize the pretentions of the rising middle class as well as the Pre-Raphaelite movement;[37] how ironic that Du Maurier reports in a letter to his mother dated January 1861 that "George Cruickshank [sic] I hear has been abusing me at the Once a Week office, saying I am a damned proeraphaelite [sic]. This can only do me good and him harm" (D. Du Maurier 29).

As the primary illustrator for *The Cornhill Magazine*, founded by George Murray Smith in 1859,[38] Du Maurier illustrated Elizabeth Gaskell's *Wives and Daughters* (1866) as well as Thomas Hardy's *The Hand of Ethelberta* (1876), George Meredith's *The Adventures of Harry Richmond* (1871), Margaret Oliphant's *A Rose in June* (1874), and Thackeray's *The History of Henry Esmond* (1852). Even if his work became somewhat formulaic, Du Maurier's artistic training from Gleyre's atelier in Paris and later at the Antwerp Academy carries into his book illustrations for Gaskell and Thackeray. In "Oh, Molly, Molly, Come and Judge Between Us" (see fig. 31) for *Wives and Daughters* (serialized in *Cornhill* between 1864–66), Du Maurier demonstrates the realistic school's predilection for foregrounding figure over background in a picture plane. Central to this illustration are Molly Gibson and Cynthia Kirkpatrick, stepsisters who both have affection for Roger Hamley (a budding naturalist who is Squire Hamley's second son). In this scene set among "holly-bushes shining out dark green in the midst of the amber and scarlet foliage" (132), Du Maurier reveals that Cynthia, whom Roger loves, has a previous tie to a Mr. Preston, here pictured alongside Cynthia.[39]

As is characteristic of Du Maurier's drawing, the two women in this illustration are tall and dressed in genteel Victorian era clothing: hats, shawls, gloves, and long-sleeved full-length gowns that rustle against the tall grasses. Du Maurier aligns the reader-viewer's sympathies with Molly, who stands in profile and who has journeyed into the lonely wooded path when she hears Cynthia in distress. Mr. Preston is "holding [Cynthia's] hands tight, each looking as if just silenced in some vehement talk by the rustle of Molly's footsteps" (2: 132). In the plate, Cynthia's eyes beseech her stepsister for help while Preston's glare seems to speak the words Preston actually utters: "'The subject of our conversa-

Figure 31. "Oh, Molly, Molly, Come and Judge Between Us." Illustration by George Du Maurier for Elizabeth Gaskell's *Wives and Daughters*, 1866.

tion does not well admit of a third person's presence'" (2: 132). The viewer can nearly feel the pressure of Preston's grip on Cynthia's hands and the palpable tension of "'a third person's presence'" in this emotional encounter.

Du Maurier demonstrates his range as an illustrator in his plates for *The History of Henry Esmond*, which moves readers from a country estate in England during the Restoration to a colonial settlement in Virginia, from an intimate drawing room to a distant battlefield when Henry Esmond joins the British army and prepares for battle in the unsuccessful attempt to restore the Stuarts to the English throne. A war scene entitled "The Chevalier de St. George" shows Du Maurier's skill in rendering equine anatomy.[40] From the flare of the horses' nostrils to the tilt of their heads, from their windswept manes to their strong, muscled legs, from the swish of their tails to the tilt of their bridles—the horses that move across the page look alive, a testimony to Du Maurier's skill in lifelike artistic representation.

For her illustrations for Hardy's *Far from the Madding Crowd* (1874), Helen Paterson, one of few female Sixties artists and the only woman artist to illustrate Hardy, likewise foregrounds figure over background and brings the viewer close to the illustrative page. The plot revolves around various sexual triangles with Bathsheba Everdene and her three lovers: Gabriel Oak, Sergeant Frank Troy, and Farmer Boldwood.[41] One memorable full-page illustration for the eighth installment, "There's Not a Soul in My House but Me To-night," leads the viewer into a dark wood straight out of Hardy's Dorset. Paterson lights up the faces and figures of Troy and Bathsheba, framed by a backdrop of exquisitely rendered trees; twisted branches surround the two figures but hide Farmer Boldwood, whose face registers his jealousy of Troy. The bark, the branches, and the figures that fill the illustrative page appear close enough for the viewer to touch.

New Approaches to Dickens's Novels

Dickens began his literary career in the 1830s working with caricature-style illustrators, but he chose Sixties artists for his last two novels: Marcus Stone for *Our Mutual Friend* (*OMF*, 1865), and Luke Fildes for his unfinished *The Mystery of Edwin Drood* (1870).[42] Dickens's decision to drop Browne, his longtime collaborator, was a strategic move to appeal to "the vast new audience of middle-class viewers who wanted to view high-quality pictures in the comfort of the fireside, and craved an art that would reflect their tastes and values while not costing a fortune" (Goldman and Cooke 2). The era's most prominent author recognized that if he wanted to maintain his popularity, his novels needed naturalistic illustrations.

Dickens chose Marcus Stone to honor a promise to help the Stone family after his friend and fellow artist, Frank Stone, died in 1859. Marcus was a gifted young artist: at age nineteen, he had a painting accepted for exhibition at the Royal Academy; in 1877 at the age of thirty-seven, he became a member of the prestigious Academy. In 1865, however, he was just twenty-five years old and eager to make a name for himself, which an association with Dickens would secure, so he agreed to be an illustrator—a field he abandoned after the 1860s. Stone brings to this psychologically dark Dickens novel his considerable talents as an artist; he guides viewers from the grit of inner city London to domestic interiors, the English countryside, and the Thames that runs through and weaves together the characters' lives.

Lizzie Hexam, the novel's heroine, departs from the Dickensian angel in the house in her physical strength as well as her lower social class status. Stone renders Lizzie's physical prowess and emotional intensity in a compelling opening illustration entitled "The Bird of Prey." Stone focuses on two characters, Lizzie and her father, Jesse "Gaffer" Hexam, a waterman who makes a living by dredging the Thames for dead bodies and stealing their valuables before turning the corpses over to the police. In the plate, a rough-looking Gaffer Hexam has a wild head of hair and a full grizzly beard. His rolled-back workman's shirtsleeves reveal strong arms that grip the sides of the boat as he leans over the edge in search of corpses. The short sleeves of Lizzie's simple work dress show her strong arms to advantage, but her open cape and wavy hair, tousled slightly in the wind, give her a feminine air. An authentic looking industrial setting frames the two figures: cargo boats sail along a shoreline dotted with factories, one billowing industrial smoke.

The illustration entitled "Forming the Domestic Virtues" (see fig. 32) strikingly conveys social class tension. Four characters appear in this plate—Lizzie's working-class brother, Charley; Charley's psychologically unstable schoolmaster, Bradley Headstone, who has risen to the lower middle class; Mortimer

Figure 32. "Forming the Domestic Virtues." Illustration by Marcus Stone for Charles Dickens's *Our Mutual Friend*, 1865.

Lightwood, an upper middle-class attorney with a conscience; and Eugene Wrayburn, a careless, rich, and insolent barrister. Stone realistically depicts the bachelors' comfortable lodgings. There are two easy chairs, a table, fireplace furnishings, and a mantel and wall filled with decorative objects: books, figurines, an elaborate clock, and paintings on either side of the fireplace. Whereas the caricaturists incorporate specific paintings to advance plot and characterization, Stone includes paintings merely to show that both gentlemen live in well-furnished surroundings with material comforts fitting those of their social class. Clouds, a full moon, and the Thames, visible through a window, frame Charley Hexam and recall his rustic roots—Charley is the son of a man who dredges this very river to profit from dead bodies.

Charley's coat and pants are respectable but ill fitting, a combination that speaks to his working-class background but also points to his aspirations to get an education and improve himself. Headstone, an outsider of this milieu despite his social betterment, is holding his top hat behind his back; this detail informs the reader-viewer that he and Charley have just entered the room. The tense rigidity in Headstone's stance intimates his future psychological instability. Headstone's coat is of cruder cloth than that of Wrayburn and Lightwood, who wear well-fitting clothes of fine fabric. Hexam's and Headstone's eyes lead us to Wrayburn, dressed in a light colored, form-fitting three-piece suit; Wrayburn smokes as he nonchalantly rests his elbow on the mantel. Ready to defend his sister's honor, Charley Hexam stands in the center of the room, his left arm raised in a partial fist.

Hexam and Headstone have crossed class lines to confront Wrayburn about his dishonorable intentions toward Lizzie. Mortimer Lightwood hangs his head as if ashamed of his friend while Eugene Wrayburn, the object of Hexam's anger and Headstone's defiance, looks at his confronters with amused annoyance.[43] This illustration primes the reader for a future confrontation between the two rivals for Lizzie's affection in the novel's prime sexual triangle—Lizzie, Headstone, and Wrayburn—and hints at the dramatic scene where a crazed, self-destructive Headstone nearly murders Wrayburn, leaving him to die in the river.

Not all Stone's illustrations are as successful as these two. "Eugene's Bedside" takes place after Headstone's attempt to murder Wrayburn. Lizzie miraculously rescues Wrayburn from the river "as if possessed by supernatural spirit and strength" (*OMF*, Penguin 769). Regrettably, Stone illustrates neither of those two dramatic scenes. The Lizzie that Stone pictures in "Eugene's Bedside" does not look as if she could actually lift Eugene Wrayburn from the river although we have glimpsed the strength in her muscular arms as she rows the boat in "The Bird of Prey." Lizzie Hexam now resembles Agnes Wickfield, a quintessential Victorian angel in the house. Her hair is pinned up neatly; her hands are folded in prayer, and her gaze lovingly rests on Wrayburn, lying lifelessly on the bed.

Wrayburn's wan appearance, too, offers a stark contrast to his self-contented smirk in "Forming the Domestic Virtues." Stone renders every detail of the domestic interior of the sickroom: fabric folds on a bed and bed curtains; a table laden with medicine bottles and vials to confirm the seriousness of Wrayburn's condition; and visitors with concerned expressions—Mortimer Lightwood, Bella Wilfer, and Mr. Milvey. Although Stone includes more figures here than usual for Sixties style illustration, all the figures direct the viewer's attention to Wrayburn, who flutters between life and death. The presence of Mr. Milvey, a clergyman, intimates that a quiet wedding between Wrayburn and Lizzie will soon take place.

The Household Edition: Refashioning Caricature with Realism

Dickens may well have switched his illustrators to please a new generation of reader-viewers eager for photographic realism in book illustration, but the caricature tradition left a visible mark on his fiction even as it was repackaged and reimagined for the Household Edition. In "'Reading the Pictures, Visualizing the Text,'" Philip Allingham presents the two schools of illustration as adversarial (for example, "Phiz to Walker: Caricature *Versus* Realism" [16; my emphasis])[44] and privileges "the 'New Men of the Sixties' [who] . . . shaped the popular taste for sober, three-dimensional realism and character study, and thereby eclipsed the public's appetite for the small-scale, humorous and melodramatic etchings of Phiz, Cruikshank, Doyle and Leech" (178). A century earlier, J. A. Hammerton makes a similar claim about Sixties artists in *The Dickens Picture-Book*, noting:

> The old order of illustrators had passed away, so far as the works of Dickens were concerned, when young Marcus Stone essayed the task of giving pictorial effect to what was to prove the last complete work of the great novelist. In looking over Mr. Stone's illustrations to *Our Mutual Friend*, we are at once conscious of an enormous advance in their artistic quality and the disappearance of the old hearty humour of Phiz and Cruikshank. (19)

Dickens's caricaturists were not fully "eclipsed" by Sixties artists, nor did their achievements "disappear" or "pass away." Rather, when we look across illustrative periods in the evolution of the Victorian illustrated book, we see how the caricaturists provided an illustrative foundation that the realists built upon with the same artistry evident in paintings exhibited at the Royal Academy.

Sixties artists who refashioned Dickens's beloved characters with lifelike artistic representation could focus on figure over background detail and change the scale of a drawing, but they were not totally free to illustrate Dickens anew since the caricaturists' designs were fixed in the public's imagination.[45] Even critic Philip Allingham, deeply invested in Sixties illustration and Fred Barnard's champion, recognizes that Barnard "could flesh out but could not fundamentally alter the timid Tom Pinch or the hypocritical Pecksniff, their balding pates and spiked hair respectively still being the *sine qua non* of these Dickens originals" ("Reading" 176).[46] These "Dickens originals" brought the characters to life on the illustrative page. Barnard's illustrations for the Household Edition of *David Copperfield* expressly won the praise of the Dalziels because "there is just enough resemblance to the figures created by H. K. Browne to save you a shock" (337).

The Household Edition, published between 1871–79, came out in weekly numbers, monthly parts, and volumes. The twenty-two–volume, large-format Household Edition had green cloth covers—recalling the color of the paper wrappers of the original serial numbers—and black and gold stamping on the front cover with decorative sketches of Dickens's most famous characters (for example, Samuel Pickwick). Barnard, the main illustrator for the series, provided more plates than any other artist: 60 illustrations for *David Copperfield* (1872), 59 for *Martin Chuzzlewit* (1872), 61 for *Bleak House* (1873), 46 for *Barnaby Rudge* (1874), 25 for *A Tale of Two Cities* (1874), 59 for *Nicholas Nickleby* (1875), 34 for *Sketches by Boz* (1876), and 28 for *Christmas Books* (1878).[47] The other illustrators for the project were Charles Green, James Mahoney, F. A. Fraser, Harry French, Harry Furniss, and Browne (who re-illustrated *Pickwick* only). The series title is reminiscent of Dickens's illustrated weekly *Household Words* and simultaneously projects assuring middle-class values: a "household" edition is for a middle-class reader, who, over time, could buy the entire set to read by the family hearth.[48]

Barnard, like Du Maurier, received art training in Paris and was an illustrator for *Once a Week* and *Punch,* although his first venture into illustration was for *The Illustrated London News.* Barnard is best known for his re-illustration of Dickens, but he was a realist painter who created large canvases, such as *Sat-*

urday *Night in the East End* (1876) that captures the lowlife of East London with its grime, gin shops, and seedy inhabitants. Barnard also collaborated with G. R. Sims for a series called *How the Poor Live* for *The Pictorial World* (1883), which helped establish him as an artist who brought the urban poor into the consciousness of his middle-class viewers. Barnard's refashioning of *David Copperfield*'s eccentric characters such as Wilkins Micawber and Uriah Heep shows the strongest resemblance to Phiz's originals; however, Barnard's drawing style is not sketchy as that of Phiz, and he made the figures look lifelike.

In chapter 11, Dickens introduces Micawber as a

> stoutish, middle-aged person, in a brown surtout[49] and black tights and shoes, with no more hair upon his head (which was a large one, and very shining) than there is upon an egg, and with a very extensive face, which he turned full upon me. His clothes were shabby, but he had an imposing shirt-collar on. He carried a jaunty sort of a stick, with a large pair of rusty tassels to it; and a quizzing-glass hung outside his coat,—for ornament. (*DC*, Norton 138)

Phiz, who first pictures Micawber in the plate "Somebody Turns Up" (see fig. 33A), visualizes Dickens's description of Micawber's egg-shaped pate and apparel down to the last tassel. Micawber's trademark top hat magnifies his height and his larger-than-life personality. Cocked at an angle, the hat reveals a good bit of Micawber's shiny oval head. Micawber's frock coat strains at the waist to indicate his "stoutness," and the "imposing shirt-collar" frames a face with a most congenial expression.

Phiz's original plate also includes Mrs. Heep serving David and Uriah, who are sitting at a table covered with tea things in the Heeps' "umble" abode. Numerous props—books untidily arranged on a sideboard, letters in a bundle, writing implements, pictures on the wall, and knickknacks on the mantel—fill the illustration, as is characteristic of the caricature school. Micawber enters into this crowded page: the text tells us that when Micawber is walking down a street in Canterbury, he spies David Copperfield (whom he last saw in London) through an open doorway and exclaims "loudly, 'Copperfield! Is it possible!'" (*DC*, Norton 222). Micawber's placement in a doorway is symbolic: one foot rests on the threshold, but the other, beyond the picture plane, is presumably still in the street. In placing Micawber neither in the house nor in the street, Phiz captures the essence of a character who occupies a transitional place from the moment he enters the novel. Micawber changes jobs, moves his family into and out of a debtor's prison, relocates to Plymouth and then to Canterbury until, at the end of the novel, he immigrates to Australia and becomes the Port Middlebay District Magistrate. At this point in the novel, Micawber has not yet ascended, and he is—just as he appears—in between homes, jobs, and places.

Barnard's first depiction of Micawber for the Household Edition (see fig. 33B) appears immediately after Dickens's introduction of him in chapter 11. It is a full-page engraving with a lengthy title, "Mr. Micawber, Impressing the Names of Streets and the Shapes of Corner Houses Upon Me as We Went Along, That I Might Find My Way Back Easily in the Morning." Phiz's Micawber standing in the doorway, looking hopeful that something will turn up, is a model for

Figure 33. A (*above*): "Somebody Turns Up." Illustration by Hablot Knight Browne for Charles Dickens's *David Copperfield*, 1850; B (*opposite*): "Mr. Micawber, Impressing the Names of Streets and the Shapes of Corner Houses Upon Me as We Went Along." Illustration by Fred Barnard for Charles Dickens's *David Copperfield,* Household Edition, 1872.

this plate; Barnard's Micawber is immediately recognizable to those familiar with Phiz's original, even though the setting is urban London. The still loveable but more realistically rendered Micawber holds his arms akimbo, extends his "jaunty sort of a stick" (138) high up in the air, and occupies a great deal of space. Barnard's Micawber has the same trademark top hat, again cocked at an angle to reveal his baldness; a large white-starched collar; and a brown surtout that fits too snugly over his large belly. Different from the original, Micawber in

Barnard's re-creation wears pants rather than hose and is a three-dimensional, lifelike figure. Barnard foregrounds figure over background in his plates, and here he positions Micawber front and center to command the reader-viewer's attention. Micawber stands on a curb in the very bottom front of the plate, and it looks as if he could easily step off the pavement and into the world of the reader-viewer.

The authentic background draws its inspiration from contemporary life and recalls, for example, George Elgar Hicks's depiction of Londoners from different walks of life in his narrative painting *The General Post Office, One Minute to Six* (1860). Barnard pictures a similar intermingling of Londoners of different ages, social classes, occupations, and life situations on a public street. He includes a soldier confronting a rough-looking lad, who is presumably a pickpocket—an all too common criminal that Hicks also incorporates into his painting of the public space of the Victorian post office. The soldier may be working a prospect as we do not actually see the boy pick a pocket; however, his expression on being apprehended reveals he is guilty of some petty crime. The pathetic look on the shabbily dressed chimney sweep carrying a load of coal (positioned behind Micawber to his left) recalls the daguerreotype of the boy crossing-sweeper by Richard Beard accompanying Henry Mayhew's *London Labour and the London Poor* (1851), an early sociological text that gave voice to the street people of London. On Barnard's London street, there are also respectable, well-dressed people. Behind Micawber and between the pickpocket and the sweep, Barnard positions a nicely dressed middle-class couple whispering together as they lean toward a public park. In this urban space, row houses are visible behind the greenery as well as a prominently placed street sign, Finsbury Square—all details that provide a believable 1870s London street scene as a background for Barnard's very human Dickensian characters.

Other *Copperfield* characters bear the imprint of Phiz's designs, such as Barnard's re-embodiments of young David in this very plate (see fig. 33B) and Uriah Heep. Barnard sustains David's near feminine beauty, his slight physique, and naïve wonder, trademarks of Phiz's illustrations that we see in "Somebody Turns Up" (see fig. 33A). Granted, Barnard makes David a tad taller—likely due to the well-rendered top hat he wears in "Mr. Micawber, Impressing the Names of Streets"—and he looks more lifelike than Phiz's David. Barnard's David has an earnest expression as he gazes up at and listens closely to Mr. Micawber, who is giving him directions. Barnard's Heep also unmistakably carries the imprint of Phiz's original. Dickens describes Uriah Heep as a hideous-looking character with an equally slimy personality. In chapter 15, we spy a "cadaverous" face: "It belonged to a red-haired person—a youth of fifteen, as I take it now, but looking much older—whose hair was cropped as close as the closest stubble; who had hardly any eyebrows, and no eyelashes" (*DC*, Norton 191); a few pages later, Dickens again lingers over Uriah's eyes, suggesting they are "like two red suns and stealthily stare at me" (193). Large nostrils, pointed chin, "clammy hand" (196), and false humbleness complete Uriah's verbal portrait.

Phiz's "Somebody Turns Up" (see fig. 33A) depicts the scene where the Heeps invite David to their "umble" abode "and wormed things out of [him] that [he] had no desire to tell" (*DC*, Norton 221). Phiz captures the eyelash-less eyes, "closest stubble" (191), jutting chin, large nostrils, "clammy hand" (196), and cloyingly "umble" (221) demeanor of Heep, who seems to "writhe" over the table—a verb Dickens often uses to describe Uriah (for example, 204)—in an attempt to wheedle information out of David. Barnard renders an unmistakably similar Uriah Heep in the plate "'Oh, Thank You, Master Copperfield,' Said Uriah Heep, 'For That Remark! It is So True! Umble as I Am, I Know it is So True! Oh, Thank You, Master Copperfield.'" Once again, David appears across the picture plane from Heep, who is positioned in three-quarter view. Barnard realistically re-embodies Phiz's depiction of Heep complete with close-cropped hair, thin pointed nose, jutting chin, and "clammy hand" (196)—the touch of which David tries to rub away.[50]

Barnard produced sixty-one illustrations to Phiz's forty-two, and he chose many scenes that Phiz did not illustrate. Some similar choices emerge, such as Peggotty and David saving Martha from drowning in the Thames and Mr. Peggotty's return from Australia to visit David and Agnes. These plates reveal traces of Phiz's original designs and incorporate Barnard's interest in drawing contemporary London life. Barnard's "'Oh, The River!' She Cried Passionately. 'Oh, the River!'" carries the imprint of Phiz's "The River" in its renderings of the three characters as well as the setting of the polluted Thames, although Barnard reverses the orientation of the plate. Whereas Phiz foregrounds Martha as she is about to take her life and draws David and Mr. Peggotty on a smaller scale, positioning them to her right on a dark shoreline well behind her, Barnard provides a close-up of all three figures on the polluted riverbank. Positioned to the left of Martha, David bends solicitously over the fallen woman. Martha, in Barnard's version, bends over melodramatically in grief and covers her face with her hands while Peggotty, to Martha's right, gazes down sympathetically at Martha. The sewage-filled shore, murky water, and smoky sky in Browne's illustration reappear in Barnard's plate, but Barnard pictures the setting in greater detail and with less theatricality. In doing so, Barnard recalls the third panel in Augustus Egg's triptych *Past and Present* (1858), which features a fallen wife clutching her dying illegitimate child along the shoreline of the dirty Thames. Augmenting Phiz's original design, Barnard draws more sewage, debris, and darkness surrounding Martha. His refashioning of Phiz's original plate strengthens the Victorian view of the fallen woman as polluted, which Egg likewise captures in his triptych of marital infidelity.

Peggotty's return from Australia to visit "Mas'r Davy," now a grown man married to Agnes, forms the subject of Phiz's "A Stranger Calls to See Me" (see fig. 34A) and Barnard's "If a Ship's Cook That Was Turning Settler, Mas'r Davy, Didn't Make Offer Fur to Marry Mrs. Gummidge, I'm Gormed—And I Can't Say No Fairer Than That!" (see fig. 34B). In both Phiz's and Barnard's versions of this scene, we see an aged Peggotty and a mature David and Agnes, now married, but there the resemblance stops. Phiz fills "A Stranger Calls to See Me" with a detailed background of props that garner as much attention as the three figures. The paintings in the parlor show settings and characters significant to David in his formative years: Blunderstone Rookery on the left, where he lived a serene childhood with his mother (a prototype for Dora) before she married Mr. Murdstone; Yarmouth, where David spent happy times with his nurse Peggotty's family and, as a child, fell in love with Little Em'ly (here pictured in front of her nautical home); and a portrait of David's first wife, Dora, looking down and seemingly blessing David, Agnes, and their children. Dora's portrait placed above the mantelpiece declares her importance to the plot: Dora is the one who, on her deathbed, makes a final request to Agnes that only she "'would occupy this vacant place'" (*DC*, Norton 726). Agnes holds an open book, a prop that marks her intelligence. A child buries her face in Agnes's lap, symbolizing her role as ideal mother and wife. On the mantel, two symmetrically placed figurines of angels bless this idyllic domestic family circle. These twin angels symbolize Agnes, the quintessential angel in the house, ever guiding David "upward!" (737).

In contrast, Barnard's reunion scene is a close-up of three characters and is absolutely free of setting and symbols. Its illustrative power lies in its lifelike rendering of the characters themselves. Daniel Peggotty with an animated smile on his face sits in the middle of the grouping, recounting a story that serves as the title for this plate. Barnard pictures Peggotty just as he is about to slap his knee to emphasize how truthful his seemingly fantastical tale is. Barnard's David leans forward toward Peggotty and looks more fondly attached to Peggotty than Phiz's David does in the original. While Agnes in both renditions

Figure 34. A (*above*): "A Stranger Calls to See Me." Illustration by Hablot Knight Browne for Charles Dickens's *David Copperfield*, 1850; B (*below*): "If a Ship's Cook That Was Turning Settler, Mas'r Davy, Didn't Make Offer Fur to Marry Mrs. Gummidge, I'm Gormed—And I Can't Say No Fairer Than That!" Illustration by Fred Barnard for Charles Dickens's *David Copperfield*, Household Edition, 1872.

beams angelic grace, Barnard makes Agnes look more serious as she attends to Peggotty's humorous tale of the marital prospects in Australia for all the settlers including old Mrs. Gummidge. Crosshatching and lighting frame the trio in this handsome portrait-style illustration of three Dickens characters who, by the 1870s, had assumed lifelike stature outside the pages of Dickens's novels.

Those familiar with *David Copperfield* will delight in many of Barnard's selections for illustrations that reshaped a beloved author to suit popular taste and extended Dickens's popularity to a new generation of reader-viewers. One such artistic illustration is a close-up of Ham Peggotty for chapter 55 entitled "Tempest." With "determination in his face, and his look, out to sea"—(*DC*, Norton 667), Ham resolutely determines to save the shipwrecked man, who turns out to be Steerforth, the villain who has already robbed him of a happy future with his beloved Emily Peggotty. In the Barnard illustration entitled "The Storm," Ham fills the center of the plate while the other seamen are clustered together in the left side of the picture plane. Seafoam emanating from the tempest splashes against Ham, who wades barefoot into the water. Pictured in profile, Ham gazes with determination at the wreck positioned in the far upper right in the background. The rope that Ham ties to his body in an attempt to lasso and save the lone shipwrecked man anticipates the heroic act that will lead to his death and Steerforth's. But in this realistically rendered illustration, heroic Ham, framed by the raging sea and spray, singly holds the viewer's full attention.

Beautiful, silly Dora becomes the focus of several illustrations, none more touching than "Holding the Pens." Dora holds David's writing implements and looks adoringly upon the budding writer, who sits at his writing desk, pen in hand, composing the novel we are presumably reading. The background of the room contains untidily arranged bookshelves and a large writing desk on a carved wooden table, but the two figures positioned close to the viewer dominate the plate. Lamplight illuminates Dora's upturned face, betraying her awareness of her many limitations as a "child-wife" (*DC*, Norton 644). David, gazing upon Dora lovingly, shows an awareness of a gap widening between him, the aspiring author, and his wife contented to hold his pens.

While Phiz does not depict these two scenes at all, in other cases, Barnard chooses a related, more pregnant moment in an episode Phiz does depict, such as Dora's deathbed scene. For example, Phiz features Agnes coming downstairs to tell David that Dora has died in "My Child-Wife's Old Companion" whereas Barnard in "It is Much Better as It Is!" moves us into the bedchamber just before David's "child-wife" departs from this world. Background details almost overwhelm Phiz's plate: a guitar and sheet music, Jip and his Pagoda house, a mantel filled with ornaments, and a large portrait of Dora (which later hangs on the wall of David and Agnes's home in "A Stranger Calls to See Me") (see fig. 34A). In contrast, David's grief takes center stage in Barnard's tender deathbed scene that foregrounds two figures—David and Dora. A despondent David covers his face to hide his tears as he grasps the hands of "the first mistaken impulse of [his] undisciplined heart" (*DC*, Norton 558). Barnard invites us to linger over Dora's beautiful curls fanning behind her on the pillow—curls that once attracted a boyish David who exclaims upon meeting Dora, "I never saw such curls—how could I, for there never were such curls!" (336). Barnard expertly renders the bed curtains and sheets, as Stone does in "Eugene's Bedside," but Barnard's two realistically rendered figures—one distraught and the other dying—command the reader-viewer's attention.

Whereas Phiz depicts Daniel Peggotty holding his fallen niece after Rosa Dartle berates her in "Mr. Peggotty's Dream Come True," Barnard illustrates a prior moment when an enraged, jealous Rosa lashes out at Emily in "Rosa Dartle Sprang up from her Seat; Recoiled; and in Recoiling Struck at Her, with a Face of Such Malignity, So Darkened and Discolored by Passion, that I Had Almost Thrown Myself Between Them." Barnard realistically renders the cheap lodging house with its few pieces of furniture and scattered clothes and a mirror, but the setting does not take attention away from the two figures divided by social class and virtue. Fallen Emily is on her knees reaching her arms toward imperious Rosa, who glares down at Emily and raises her left hand as if to strike her.

Barnard's illustrations for The Household Edition of *Copperfield* move us from Finsbury Square to this run-down darkened room in gritty London where fallen Emily temporarily takes shelter to the wet and wild storm scape in Yarmouth and into Dora's bedchamber where we glimpse her before she dies. The background of the final illustration resembles Robert Buss's painting *Dickens's Dream* (ca. 1875),[51] which shows Dickens dozing in his study surrounded by a dream cloud of Dickens's most memorable characters. In this final Barnard plate, David and Agnes gaze at a cloud that includes all the memorable *Copperfield* characters; clearly recognizable are Micawber, young David, and Heep, all rendered with just a few brush strokes from the hands of an artist who embodies Dickens's characters with a naturalism desired by the mid-to-late Victorian public.

One year prior to the re-illustration of *David Copperfield*, James Mahoney, an Irish painter sometimes referred to as J. Mahoney, re-illustrated *Oliver Twist*, published in 1871 as the first title in the Household Edition series. Mahoney, who moved to London in 1859, exhibited watercolors at the Royal Academy and, like Barnard, worked for the *Illustrated London News* where he earned acclaim for his illustrations of the Irish famine based on firsthand observation. As part of the team of illustrators for the Household Edition, Mahoney also illustrated *Little Dorrit* (1873) and *Our Mutual Friend* (1875). Whereas Cruikshank provided twenty-four illustrations for the original version of *Twist*, Mahoney in this reillustration provided twenty-eight illustrations including many scenes that Cruikshank did not illustrate. However, Mahoney refashioned the most important Cruikshank plates—for example "Oliver Asking for More" and "Fagin in the Condemned Cell"—and his imitative reworking reveals the indelible mark of the caricaturist.

Mahoney's plates carry Cruikshank's theatrical staging and the look of many of the original characters, particularly of Oliver and Fagin, whose appearance still resembles that of the stage Jew. Cruikshank's "Oliver Asking for More" is foremost a theatrical moment where Dickens makes a social statement about the starvation of the workhouse children. As discussed in chapter 2, this scene is also one that the text quickly moves beyond—the master strikes a blow at Oliver, restrains him, and calls for Mr. Bumble, the parish beadle, who, in turn, rushes into the board room where the gentleman in the white waistcoat declares: "'That boy will be hung,' . . . 'I know that boy will be hung'" (*OT*, Oxf. 1982 13). Mahoney's untitled illustration (see fig. 35B), which serves as the headpiece to chapter 1, approximates Cruikshank's tableau-style illustration (see fig. 35A). Mahoney likewise freezes the climactic moment where an underfed Oliver asks for an additional helping from the well-fed master, dressed in an apron to dispense the daily dietary allotment of "one porringer, and no more" (9). Mahoney keeps Cruikshank's dramatic staging but reverses the orientation of the plate—the cook is positioned at the right side as opposed to the left side of the plate as in Cruikshank's original, and the workhouse children, who look more pathetic than emaciated, appear to the left of Oliver as opposed to his right. Mahoney's realistically rendered boys look thin and ravenous, but they do not have the dripping eyes and shaved heads as in Cruikshank's original caricature. Mahoney positions Oliver in three-quarter view and dresses him in clothes that are too large for his form while in the original Cruikshank places Oliver in profile in skimpy clothes, magnifying his thinness.

As is characteristic of Sixties illustrators, Mahoney zeroes in on the interaction between the master and Oliver. Of note, the master looks even more directly at Oliver in Mahoney's version—the viewer can barely see the eyes of the master, positioned in profile, that seem to bore into Oliver's head. The pauper assistant, now appearing in the far back middle of the picture plane in

Figure 35. A (*left*): "Oliver Asking for More." Illustration by George Cruikshank for Charles Dickens's "Oliver Twist" in *Bentley's Miscellany*, February 1837. From the Norman M. Fox Collection, Scribner Library, Skidmore College; B (*below*): headpiece to ch. 1. Illustration by James Mahoney for Charles Dickens's *Oliver Twist*, Household Edition, 1871.

Mahoney's version, looks less famished and shocked by Oliver's request than in the original, and a small grated window in the background likens the workhouse to a prison cell. Nonetheless, the plate overall "is derivative rather than original," as Philip Allingham notes, "relying for its full meaning not merely on a textual passage in the next chapter, but on the reader's knowledge of the original illustration" ("Illustrations by James Mahoney").

Cruikshank's "Oliver Plucks Up a Spirit" also provides a working model for Mahoney's "Oliver Rather Astonishes Noah." In this scene, orphan Oliver rises up against the abuse of charity-boy Noah Claypole, who insults Oliver's dead mother's honor. Mahoney makes some changes, but the staging of Oliver and Noah imitates the original. Mahoney turns this plate into a close-up of three of the original four figures—Oliver, Noah, and Charlotte. In Cruikshank's original, Mrs. Sowerberry, the undertaker's wife, stands open-jawed and outraged in the open doorway while Charlotte, the Sowerberry's maid, grabs Oliver with one hand and raises her fist to restrain Noah. The backdrop, important to Cruikshank's plate, is filled with props—an overturned table, broken crockery, a sideboard Noah hides under—that confirm a confrontation has just transpired between Oliver and Noah, positioned on the floor in defeat. Cruikshank stages the fight somewhat comically: Oliver's fist is so disproportionately large in relation to the rest of his slight body that Charlotte may not be able to stop Oliver from punching Noah again.

In refashioning this plate, Mahoney retains some props, planting an overturned chair as opposed to a table in the original and broken crockery to convey a physical struggle, but the Sixties artist privileges figure over background and makes the characters more lifelike. In contrast to Cruikshank, Mahoney shows Oliver to be simply victorious over Noah as Oliver glares down upon his much larger tormenter and shakes a clenched fist that matches the proportions of Oliver's frame. In Mahoney's re-illustration, Charlotte is just entering through the doorway, but Oliver remains out of her arm's reach. Oliver stands upright with a tall sideboard behind him, giving him the illusion of strength. With the new orientation of this illustration, there is no sideboard available for Noah to crawl under. Noah cowers at Oliver's feet and raises his left arm protectively to cover his face in a posture of fear and defeat.

Mahoney's final plate in the Household Edition, "He Sat Down on a Stone Bench Opposite the Door" (see fig. 36B), also carries the indelible imprint of Cruikshank's iconic "Fagin in the Condemned Cell" (see fig. 36A). Mahoney illustrates a slightly earlier moment in the text where Fagin has just received his death sentence. Mahoney's focus on Fagin is immediate and close up,

Figure 36. A (*left*): "Fagin in the Condemned Cell." Illustration by George Cruikshank for Charles Dickens's "Oliver Twist" in *Bentley's Miscellany*, March 1839. From the Norman M. Fox Collection, Scribner Library, Skidmore College; B (*below*): "He Sat Down on a Stone Bench Opposite the Door." Illustration by James Mahoney for Charles Dickens's *Oliver Twist*, Household Edition, 1871.

which matches the approach that Cruikshank takes in depicting Fagin in his final hours. In his artistically rendered depiction of the thief contemplating his deserved demise, Mahoney makes Fagin less caricatured, although the artist retains his large nose and chin, features that liken Fagin to a stage Jew and make him immediately recognizable to the viewer familiar with the original *Oliver Twist* plates.[52] However, in accentuating naturalism over theatricality, "He Sat Down on a Stone Bench Opposite the Door" regrettably loses the psychological intensity that distinguishes Cruikshank's original.

Fagin now hangs his head and hunches over his shackled hands—he is not biting them as in the original. Fagin looks sad and defeated in Mahoney's version more than crazed and terrified. Whereas Cruikshank exaggerates the terror in Fagin's eyes through a stippled effect on the prison cell walls, Mahoney uses crosshatching to make the room look more lifelike and impenetrable. The room Fagin sits in is even barer in Mahoney's version since Mahoney removes the few background details that Cruikshank offers. Gone are the Bible, the upturned hat, the two handwritten notices (presumably from the sheriff), and the barred prison window that allows some light into the cell. Mahoney places Fagin on a bench, as opposed to a cot in Cruikshank's rendition, but retains the manacles and the linen bandage. The walls in Mahoney's version are bare with the exception of one chilling detail: initials of previous inmates on death row scratched into the wall (at Fagin's upper left) point to Fagin's own fate that he anticipates as he sits alone on a cold stone bench.

In his rendition of "The Last Chance" entitled "And Creeping over the Tiles, Looked over the Low Parapet," Mahoney better captures Sikes's state of mind in his final hours than he does Fagin's. Mahoney places Sikes alone on a rooftop that is eerily out of focus and, as a result, leads the viewer's eye to concentrate on Sikes, rendered in a close-up.[53] Cruikshank's version is foremost theatrical as described in chapter 2. Despite his powerful frame, Cruikshank's Sikes strains against the harsh diagonal streaks of cloud and wind in a violent skyscape that lights up the terror in his eyes and the noose foreshadowing his doom. Mahoney strips away much of Cruikshank's theatrical staging—the onlookers, the loyal canine hidden in the shadows, the howling wind, and the streaks of lightning. Rather, Mahoney looks deep into Sikes's psyche at the moment the murderer realizes he cannot escape the mob. There is anger on the fugitive's face, which Mahoney lights up from below. However, perhaps as a nod to the original, Mahoney retains one crucial prop from Cruikshank's "The Last Chance"—the rope that hangs ominously like a noose and foreshadows Sikes's accidental death by hanging.

Mahoney consistently uses this Sixties close-up style in *Oliver Twist*. His backdrops do not offer as much attention to authentic Victorian life as Barnard's do for *Copperfield*. Most suggestive of contemporary life is the plate that shows the aftermath of the actual pickpocketing scene that Cruikshank depicts in "Oliver Amazed at the Dodger's Mode of 'Going to Work.'"[54] In its intermingling of Londoners of different social classes and a canine added to the mix, "Stop Thief!" recalls *The General Post Office, One Minute to Six*, Hicks's painting of contemporary life, which also includes a dog in the varied crowd. Oliver is mistaken as a pickpocket, but the actual pickpockets form part of the crowd in Mahoney's plate: Dodger with his trademark top hat accusingly points his finger at Oliver while Charley Bates, also shabbily dressed, holds onto his cap in pursuit of Oliver. Next to Fagin's boys are respectable shopkeepers who have come out to watch and join in the chase. One woman in the background, presumably a shopkeeper, places her arm protectively around her young daughter as if to shield her from the alleged criminal. Into the mix, Mahoney draws a bourgeois gentleman. It is Mr. Brownlow, dressed in a well-fitted jacket and top hat. Brownlow raises his cane and joins Londoners of different social classes, closing in on Oliver and making palpable the danger he is facing. Mahoney offers the viewer no bookstall keeper in the shadows to assure an alibi for Oliver as Cruikshank does in "Oliver Amazed" (see fig. 23A, ch. 2, 88), and Oliver is running from the crowd, suggesting his guilt. Moreover, Brownlow in Mahoney's plate is not Oliver's protector, but his pursuer, and Oliver appears frantic in this illustration and out of breath.

Of note, too, Mahoney illustrates murdered Nancy (see fig. 37), a scene that Cruikshank did not attempt but that Dickens acted out in his dramatic readings. This plate entitled "He Moved, Backwards, Towards the Door: Dragging the Dog with Him" is a close-up of the aftermath of Nancy's murder, chosen perhaps so as not to offend the intended readership of the Household Edition, a family reading Dickens by the hearth. In its attention to one figure, this plate is consistent with the style of Mahoney's other plates. However, Mahoney has staged and lit this scene theatrically in a manner that Cruikshank might have approved. Morning light filters through the window to illuminate the "worst" outcome of "all the bad deeds that, under cover of the darkness, had been committed within wide London's bounds since night hung over it" (*OT*, Oxf. 1982 304). Nancy lies on the floor, her right arm cradling her head as if she were attempting to protect herself from Sikes's fatal blow. Nancy's left hand holds Rose's white handkerchief, a symbolic textual detail that moves the viewer to pity the fallen Nancy and aligns her with her saintly sister-woman,[55] Rose

Maylie. The handkerchief looks stained, and Mahoney includes other signs of a struggle that allow the viewer to imagine the grisly murder that takes place in the previous chapter entitled "Fatal Consequences": a toppled plant on the window ledge, blood pooling from Nancy's head, and what appears to be a broken part of the club that Sikes uses to strike Nancy down.[56]

At the far left of the plate appears Sikes, darkly shrouded, dragging his dog Bull's-eye by the neck out of the room through the barely opened doorway. Sikes is stealthily retreating from the murder scene. Mahoney does not picture the terror of Sikes, who, according to Dickens, looks in horror on the murdered form of Nancy, who is "flesh and blood, no more—but such flesh and so much blood!" (*OT*, Oxf. 1982 304). Indeed, Sikes's head is already out the doorway. Rather, Mahoney fixes our eyes on Nancy, still half covered with a rug that Dickens tells

Figure 37. "He Moved, Backwards, Towards the Door: Dragging the Dog with Him." Illustration by James Mahoney for Charles Dickens's *Oliver Twist*, Household Edition, 1871.

us Sikes places over Nancy's body because "it was worse to fancy the eyes, and imagine them moving towards him, than to see them glaring upward, as if watching the reflection of the pool of gore that quivered and danced in the sunlight on the ceiling" (304). Mahoney does not picture Nancy's haunting eyes—her hand covers her face—or "the pool of gore" that might have offended his Victorian viewers, but he includes just enough detail to condemn Sikes of a crime, which, as Dickens preaches, is "the foulest and most cruel" (304).

In this plate of murdered Nancy, the chase scene, and the close-up of Sikes in his final moment alive, Mahoney situates *Twist* in an urban environment and does not shy away from gritty aspects of London lowlife. But Mahoney's illustrations are foremost re-illustrations of plates Cruikshank drew, particularly the characterizations of Oliver and Fagin. To the viewer familiar with the caricature-style illustrations that first brought Dickens's characters to life, the imprint of Cruikshank's original illustrations is more visible in Mahoney's plates for *Oliver Twist* than Phiz's imprint is in Barnard's plates for *David Copperfield*.

Tenniel's Refashioning of Carroll's Caricature-Style Illustrations

A decade before the publication of the Household Edition of Dickens, John Tenniel used shading, crosshatching, and outlining to lend to *Alice* photographic realism found in natural history illustration. For *Alice's Adventures in Wonderland*, Tenniel redrew many of Lewis Carroll's caricature-style drawings from *Alice's Adventures Under Ground*.[57] Like the Sixties artists who re-illustrated Dickens, Tenniel specialized in close-ups of human, animal, and mythical characters set in naturalistic landscapes that make Wonderland look believable. Tenniel's illustrations of Alice's dream world thus convey "the sensation that the ground beneath our feet has imperceptibly shifted" (189), notes Frankie Morris in *Artist of Wonderland*. The ground beneath Tenniel's feet also seems to have imperceptibly shifted according to an 1866 reviewer for the *London Review*, who notes, "All these things are illustrated by Mr. Tenniel as if he had gone down the rabbit hole with Alice" (n. pag.). Carroll, who wrote and drew the story of Alice's adventures down the rabbit hole, did not publish his original drawings until 1886 at which time the *Under Ground* illustrations were not well received. A comparison of Tenniel's and Carroll's *Alice* illustrations that have been revaluated today[58] reveals the vision of an amateur caricaturist repackaged with realism, demonstrating fluidity between two illustrative styles in the arc of the Victorian illustrated book.

Publisher John Murray brought Tenniel fame as a book illustrator with a publication of *Aesop's Fables* in 1848. Tenniel was largely untutored, a point that aligns him with first-generation caricaturists like George Cruikshank and John Leech with whom he collaborated to illustrate *The Ingoldsby Legends*.[59] A *Punch* cartoonist, Tenniel began his career in oils and exhibited regularly at the Royal Academy from 1837 to 1842 and again in 1851 (Sarzano 9–10). In *Art of Old England*, John Ruskin likens Tenniel to Tintoretto, noting: "Tenniel has much of the largeness and symbolic mastery of imagination which belong to the great leaders of classic art: in the shadowy masses and sweeping lines of his great compositions, there are tendencies which might have won his adoption into the school of Tintoret" (86). Forrest Reid disliked the stiffness of Tenniel's human figures and his partiality to draw from photographs, not from life (likely owing to his loss of vision in his right eye due to a fencing accident),[60] but even he recognized Tenniel's giftedness in drawing animals.[61]

In a letter dated 20 December 1863, Carroll, an avid *Punch* reader, wrote to Tom Taylor, dramatist and editor of *Punch*, asking to be introduced to Tenniel. Admitting dissatisfaction with his own drawing, Carroll indicates, "of all artists on wood, I should prefer Mr. Tenniel. If he should be willing to undertake [the illustrations], I would send him the book to look over, not that he should at all follow my pictures, but simply to give him an idea of the sort of thing I want" (M. Cohen 1: 62). While some early biographers question whether Tenniel actually saw Carroll's illustrations, others like Frankie Morris and Michael Hancher posit, "it is very likely that Tenniel did indeed see the Carroll illustrations, and, furthermore, that they helped shape his drawings for the book" (Hancher 27).[62] Alice Liddell Hargreaves, the real-life model for Alice, goes so far as to say in a letter to her son Caryl Hargreaves published in *Cornhill* in 1932: "As a rule Tenniel used Mr. Dodgson's drawings as the basis for his own illustrations and they held frequent consultations about them" (9).

Tenniel's contribution is all the more considerable because the text of *Alice*, written in the age of the richly descriptive Victorian novel, is relatively bare in its description of characters and settings; as Morris observes, "Carroll's texts are practically all conversation (Alice's with others and those she has with herself), with just sufficient narration to carry the story line and little to no description" (149). In many instances, the illustrations, which Carroll famously directs the reader to view in the case of the Gryphon, define character and place. Different from readers of the Household Dickens who were familiar with Dickens's characters through the caricaturists who brought them to life, *Alice*'s first readers were not privy to the original illustrations and thus not aware of the resemblance of Tenniel's designs to Carroll's originals that Tenniel refashioned. In *Sir John Tenniel*, Rodney Engen notes that

Tenniel realized he had been hired not as an imaginative illustrator but as a drawing machine: someone to polish and perfect Dodgson's own ideas and prepare them for the engraver.... Although Dodgson's original drawings are crude, the compositions are often exactly as Tenniel's final versions, or at best with slight variations. It was clearly Dodgson's book, and he rarely gave in to Tenniel's more imaginative expertise. (74)

Tenniel understood Carroll's imagination, but in redrawing Carroll's illustrations, Tenniel also added domestic interiors and landscapes that appealed to middle-class consumers of the 1860s. This Sixties artist excelled in drawing Carroll's animal characters and literally drew out elements of pantomime in Carroll's text as well as his social caricatures.

Carroll was a fan of pantomime, an avid cardplayer, and an inventor of games. Pantomime was at its peak of popularity as a theatrical form when Carroll published *Wonderland*. Carroll chose a common plot device from early to mid-nineteenth-century pantomime familiar to his Victorian readers when Alice encounters a pack of personified cards in *Under Ground* and *Wonderland*.[63] Carroll draws the card gardeners that paint the white roses red as actual playing cards without heads, but Tenniel turns them into costumed figures by adding human heads to the playing cards of various suits, making the Red Queen's threat of beheading eerily possible. The pantomime connection in *Wonderland* and its sequel, *Through the Looking-Glass*,[64] "was not lost on Tenniel," notes Morris, "who cleverly drew the habitants of Alice's dreams as actors in big-head and other masks, contrivances, and skins" (169). The entire "Pig and Pepper" chapter that Carroll added for *Wonderland* is a pantomime complete with a howling baby, flying objects, an ill-natured cook, and a Duchess with a head too large for her body. Likewise, Tenniel drew the Fish-Footman and the Frog-Footman with human-looking bodies but large animal heads that look like fish and frog masks; in this manner, the artist evokes the style of pantomime wherein actors often wore masks that covered their entire heads. Another illustrative feature of Tenniel's pantomime is the oversized object the Fish-Footman delivers to the Frog-Footman, which appears in this very scene in the form of an enormous letter with a Royal seal, which turns out to be an invitation from the Queen to the Duchess to play croquet. No doubt the element of pantomime in Tenniel's illustrations facilitated *Alice*'s adaptation to the London stage in 1876.

Tenniel had a fuller cast of characters and scenes to illustrate than Carroll since Carroll essentially doubled the length of the tale when he revised it for *Wonderland*; the 18,000 word *Under Ground* text with thirty-seven illustrations became, in *Wonderland,* a 35,000 word text with forty-two illustrations. However, the artist of *Wonderland* refashioned a striking number of Carroll's designs form the original *Alice's Adventures Under Ground.* Tenniel's illustration of Alice conversing with the surly-speaking, hookah-smoking Caterpillar "departs considerably from Carroll's," notes Hancher in *The Tenniel Illustrations to the "Alice" Books,* "but it still shows a dependence upon it" (31). In his revision of this design, Tenniel maintains Carroll's concept of the Caterpillar with human attributes, but Tenniel renders the creature's anatomy with naturalism.

Carroll regrettably creates anatomical confusion in his Caterpillar, which has the eyes, nose, mouth, and hand of a human (see fig. 38A). In contrast, Tenniel maintains the naturalism of the Caterpillar while still personifying the creature: positioned in silhouette (as opposed to a frontal view in the original), the creature's many appendages imply a human mouth and nose through which the Caterpillar speaks (see fig. 38B).[65] Carroll's hookah resembles a peace pipe, but

Figure 38. A (*left*): "Caterpillar on a Mushroom." Illustration by Lewis Carroll for his *Alice's Adventures Under Ground,* 1864; B (*opposite*): "Caterpillar on a Mushroom." Illustration by John Tenniel for Lewis Carroll's *Alice's Adventures in Wonderland,* 1865.

Tenniel improves the smoking device, which now looks as if it comes straight from the British Raj with its clearly defined water jar, bowl, gasket, and elaborate hose. Moreover, Tenniel shows the Caterpillar in the process of inhaling smoke from the hookah's hose, and smoke realistically billows out of the Caterpillar's mouth-like appendage.

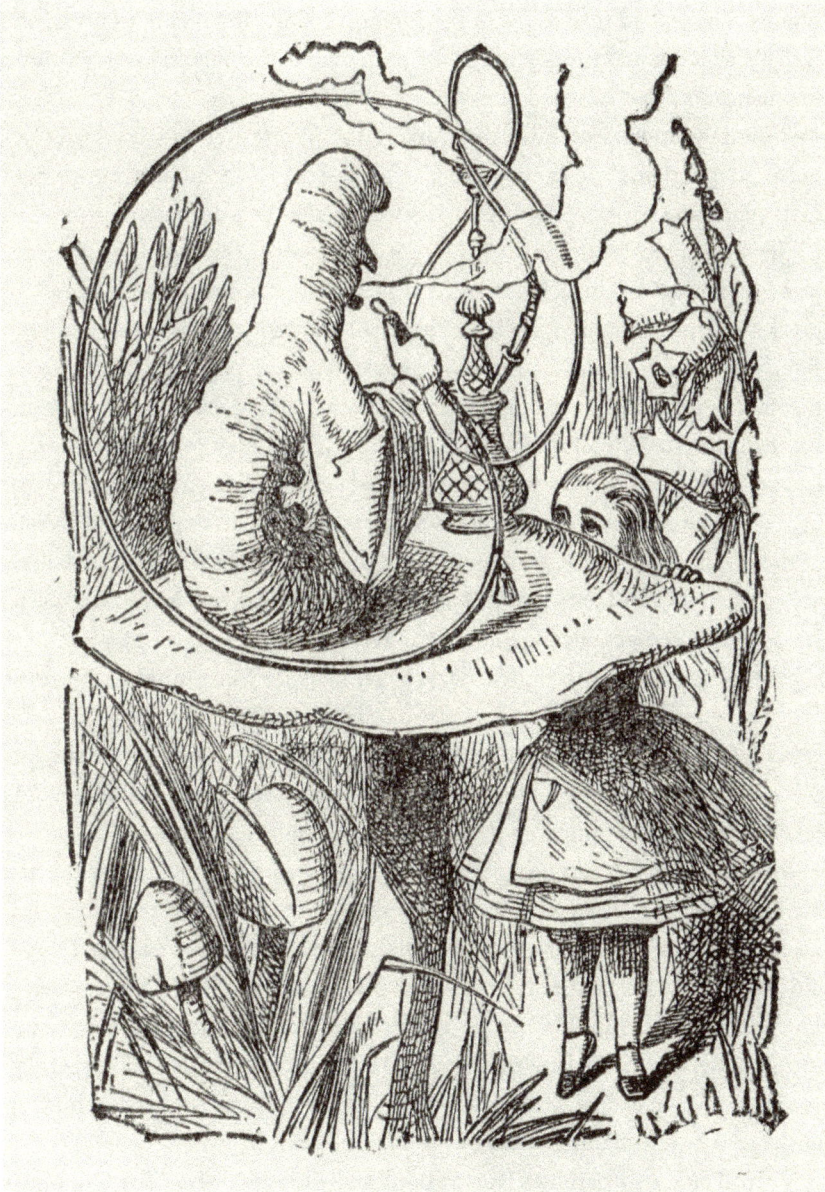

Alice and the talking Caterpillar are the focal point of both illustrations, but the setting is more striking in Tenniel's picture than in Carroll's as is the arrangement of the characters in relation to the mushroom. For his design, Carroll draws some sparse vegetation surrounding a crudely drawn mushroom, but Tenniel enhances the original in making the setting of Wonderland a believable fantasy world. Bell-shaped flowers frame Alice as she peeps over the top of an accurately rendered mushroom with a spongy gilled cap and a long stalk; two smaller egg-shaped toadstools in the foreground, waving blades of grass, and realistic shading make this setting look as lifelike as the natural history studies of mushrooms that Beatrix Potter drew in the 1890s.

Tenniel's drawing of Alice outgrowing the White Rabbit's house reveals both a "dependence" on the original Carroll design and a marked improvement in its rendering of domestic interiors as well as elements of the grotesque.[66] In *Under Ground*, for example, the White Rabbit's house is simply a rectangular box (see fig. 39A). Alice's elbow rubs against a door not pictured. Alice's foot presses against the top right-hand corner of the page. A single-line frame to signify an interior space was an unsophisticated choice for a Victorian audience that favored realistic representation in illustration. Tenniel builds the walls of a room in an actual Victorian dwelling and shows Alice attempting to free herself by extending her arm out a skillfully rendered curtained casement window (see fig. 39B). What we regrettably lose in claustrophobia and exaggerated growth in the original caricature, we gain in naturalism. Tenniel makes it look believable that a real child grows so impossibly large that she can outgrow a house. Dressed as a respectable Victorian girl, Tenniel's Alice wears a pinafore over a knee-length dress with puffed sleeves. While Alice has a nondescript dress and wears a blank expression in Carroll's depiction, Tenniel gives Alice a decided pout that expresses her exasperation in changing size every time she eats and drinks. In these ways, "Tenniel altered Carroll's drawing considerably," as Hancher notes, and improved it, "but he did not ignore it" (31).

Adding details to suit popular taste, Tenniel at times drew from Victorian life and his own *Punch* cartoons as Hancher elaborates in *The Tenniel Illustrations to the "Alice" Books*. The figure of Alice makes her debut in an 1864 Tenniel illustration of a girl garlanding a British Lion (Hancher 23). The Crystal Palace from the Great Exhibition of 1851 appears in the background of the croquet scene, showing Wonderland to look eerily like Victorian England. Tenniel also carries representational realism into the "Father William" sequence, showing once again how Tenniel sustains but refashions Carroll's vision.

Carroll famously parodies Robert Southey's didactic poem "The Old Man's

Figure 39. A (*above*): "Alice Outgrowing the White Rabbit's House." Illustration by Lewis Carroll for his *Alice's Adventures Under Ground*, 1864; B (*below*): "Alice Outgrowing the White Rabbit's House." Illustration by John Tenniel for Lewis Carroll's *Alice's Adventures in Wonderland*, 1865.

Comforts and How He Gained Them" (1799), a Victorian Sunday School favorite about a pious man who remains faithful to God and reaps the benefits of piety in his old age. Carroll's four cartoonish illustrations in *Under Ground* are simple line drawings that match the tone of Carroll's humorous parody of Southey's poem. In the drawings, the old man stands on his head, performs a back somersault, and balances an eel on his nose. The wardrobe of Father William and the young man is basic, and the settings are sparse to nonexistent. Carroll includes a few essential props in his four pictures, such as a chair and a laden table. But Tenniel adds naturalistic details to frame—not overwhelm—the figures: haystacks (resembling those in Tenniel's "Mr. Punch and his Family" from *Punch*, July-December 1856) surround a full-bodied but spindly-legged Father William, whose form approaches the grotesque. A modest Victorian home is the setting for Tenniel's Father William's back somersault, and an accurately rendered eel balances on Father William's nose. Father William wears low-heeled buckled pumps, breeches, hose, a patterned waistcoat, and an overcoat that falls down when he stands on his head to expose a huge belly. In these ways, Tenniel makes Carroll's original figures larger and more lifelike, as Barnard does with Phiz's Dickensian characters. Nonetheless, in the posture, rotundity, and wide grin of Tenniel's Father William and the positioning of Father William and the inquiring youth, we see the imprint of Carroll's original humorous drawings.

Tenniel also excelled in drawing Carroll's *Wonderland* and *Looking-Glass* characters who function as social caricatures, such as jurors and legal and political figures (for example, Benjamin Disraeli makes his appearance in Tenniel's *Looking-Glass* illustration as the man in the white paper hat in Alice's railway carriage); a world leader (for instance, the White Queen resembles Tenniel's own caricatures of Pope Pius IX from *Punch*); and working-class types (for example, cook, carpenter, and footman), often targeted as fodder for comedy centuries before *Alice*.[67] Of particular interest in the revision of the original illustrations are Tenniel's drawings of two characters—the White Rabbit, Esquire, and the Mock Turtle—who function as social caricatures of, respectively, the Victorian gentleman living in a time-obsessed industrial age, and bourgeois pretension.

Tenniel used his skill in anthropomorphization to turn the White Rabbit into a believable rabbit-human hybrid. Tenniel authenticated animal anatomy and added just enough clothing and a timepiece[68] to humanize Carroll's White Rabbit in constant fear of being late. "Belatedness, anxiety, physical props like the watch," notes Gillian Beer in "'*Alice*' in Time," "all bespeak the individual under the cosh of time-regulated society" (xxviii). As Beer points out, Carroll not only lived in a time-regulated society but also was intimately involved with time given his work as a logician and a mathematician. In order to make Carroll's inventive character a joke on the time-bound Victorian gentleman living in a society ruled by timetables, the character had to look like a rabbit and a dapper Victorian gentleman, but not fully like a rabbit or a human. As Rose Lovell-Smith argues in "The Animals of Wonderland," "The rabbit occupies a point between animal and human, simultaneously both these things and neither of them, an implication hardly made so firmly by Carroll's text" (384)—or, I would add, by Carroll's own pictures of the White Rabbit.

Carroll offers little physical description of the White Rabbit—for example, the White Rabbit has "pink eyes" (UG 1) and is "splendidly dressed, with a pair of white kid gloves in one hand, and a nosegay in the other" (13).[69] Of consequence, Carroll skews animal anatomy in his illustrations of the White Rabbit (see fig. 40A). The creature looks the size of a rabbit when positioned next to Alice, who in this illustration (UG 13) must crouch down on the ground to gaze upon the curious creature she follows down the rabbit hole. But the White Rabbit in this and other illustrations (for example, 33) lacks rabbitness: he has the ears of a donkey, the face and whiskers of a mouse, and a human hand. A full suit of rather nondescript clothing completely covers Carroll's White Rabbit's haunches and tail. He stands on his hind legs, as a human would, and socks and shoes adorn his paws, so no fluffy rabbit's tail or furry paw is visible to the viewer.

In contrast, Tenniel authenticates both the character's human and rabbit traits essential to the social caricature (see fig. 40B). The White Rabbit appears in a meadow—a rabbit habitat. It wears a waistcoat but no pants, revealing the creature's fluffy tail, haunches, and furry bottom paws. His front paws resemble human hands, and he walks upright as a human would. Tenniel's White Rabbit wears a fashionable waistcoat and carries a pocket-watch, details that grant him the look and worth of a real Victorian gentleman—indeed the White Rabbit's outfit resembles Mr. Brownlow's in Cruikshank's "Oliver Amazed" for *Oliver Twist* (see fig. 23A, ch. 2, 88). The timepiece symbolizes new technologies in Carroll's age that ruled industry and transportation: office workers and factory workers clocked in and out of work, railways ran on schedule according to timetables, and chronometers kept time at sea. The watch was concomitantly a mark of gentility and respectability and an essential accouterment for the gentleman part of the White Rabbit's status. Tenniel's rabbit also has the slight paunch of a middle-aged gentleman, carries his umbrella under his arm as if braced for rainy English weather, always appears in a hurry, and fears the consequences of his

Figure 40. A (*left*): "Alice and the White Rabbit." Illustration by Lewis Carroll for his *Alice's Adventures Under Ground*, 1864; B (*below*): "The White Rabbit, Esquire." Illustration by John Tenniel for Lewis Carroll's *Alice's Adventures in Wonderland*, 1865.

lateness: "'Oh! The Duchess, the Duchess! Oh! *Wo'n't* she be savage if I've kept her waiting!'" (*AA* 22). In contrast to Carroll's mouse-donkey hybrid, Tenniel's absentminded gentleman rabbit also looks imperious enough to take Alice for a servant girl—he calls her Mary Ann, a British euphemism for a maid—and orders her to fetch his gloves and fan, so he won't be too late.

A combination animal, the Mock Turtle relies upon anatomical precision to convey Carroll's joke on the bourgeois pretentiousness of the Victorians who made a form of "turtle soup," a rare delicacy, from veal, a much cheaper meat. When Alice asks the Queen of Hearts what a Mock Turtle is, the Queen replies, "'It's the thing Mock Turtle Soup is made from'" (*AA* 94). Carroll's humor relies on a convincing depiction of a turtle and a calf that Carroll cannot visualize. In *Under Ground*, Carroll's caricature of the Mock Turtle has an armadillo-like torso, a seal's head, and an eagle's talons.[70] Building upon Carroll's creative vision, Tenniel creates a believable hybrid animal with calf and turtle features. He brings to this combination animal "the conventional techniques of realism," notes Lovell-Smith, "such as the cross-hatching and fine lines used to suggest light, shade, and solidity of form in the Mock Turtle's shell and flippers" (391). Like a calf, Tenniel's Mock Turtle has a pronounced forehead and ears, small horns, hooves, and a switch on its tail. Like a turtle, it has a large heart-shaped shell covered with horny plates, a smooth bottom shell, and flippers. Tenniel's joining of believable bovine and reptilian features makes this joke on Victorian pretention complete. Nonetheless, Tenniel's illustrations of both characters are built upon Carroll's original imprint.

Tenniel's polishing and perfecting of Carroll's original designs and Barnard's and Mahoney's redeployment of Dickens's original illustrations by, respectively, Phiz and Cruikshank demonstrate a reengagement with the caricature tradition in a decade firmly associated with lifelike artistic representation and Royal Academy standards. Pre-Raphaelites and eminent Victorian narrative and genre painters became illustrators, making book illustrations that recall the beautifully bound books on display at the Great Exhibition of 1851 and prominently arranged on the circular tables of Victorian parlors. But within this new aesthetic of the Victorian illustrated book, the caricaturists' vision remains in view.

4

⟨⟨∽⟩⟩⟩

Caricature and Realism

Fin-de-Siècle Developments of the Victorian Illustrated Book

And if the disappointed author says to [his illustrator], "Why can't you draw
like Phiz?" he can fairly retort: "Why don't you write like Dickens?"

George Du Maurier, "The Illustrating of Books
from the Serious Artist's Point of View—1," 1890

At the fin de siècle, the Victorian illustrated book experienced what some critics
consider a decline and others call a third period of development. In *The Victorian Illustrated Book*, Richard Maxwell pronounces the passing popularity of the
genre: "An established form, a cultural institution sustained by artists, writers,
publishers, booksellers, and a large, eager audience, thrives for many decades,
then gradually disappears; time and circumstance have apparently killed it"
(418).[1] Likewise, Robert Meyrick, pleased by the inclusion of the Dalziels' engravings in the fine art section at "The Victorian Era Exhibition" (1897), reflects
in "'Spoils of the lumber-room'": "And yet, the craft [of illustration] that had just
been recognized as art was already under threat of extinction.... photographic
methods of reproduction had overtaken wood-engraving in British publishing"
(185).[2] In contrast, Arlene Jackson in *Illustration and the Novels of Thomas Hardy*
focuses her analysis on the fin de siècle, an oft-neglected period of illustration:
"The third period (1870–1895) has no particular artist to identify with, a fact in
itself significant, but is a continuation, with some differences, of the representational school of the 1860s" (12); Jackson continues, "The two earlier periods,
with their opposing styles of caricature and representationalism, have had their
proponents among art and literary historians[.] ... The end of the decade, however, did not signal the end of this 'golden age' of illustration" (12, 14).

This chapter examines the validity of both viewpoints. The illustrated book was not "killed," nor did it fade into "extinction." In the later decades of Victoria's reign, however, publishing trends and intertwining economic and aesthetic factors led to the decline of illustrated literature for mainstream newly released, large-circulation adult fiction produced in volume form in England.[3] George Du Maurier's anecdote about Phiz and Dickens in "The Illustrating of Books" presents two of the interlocking reasons for such a shift in the development of the illustrated book that this chapter examines: the changing nature of the novel and new directions in book illustration. However, the Victorian illustrated book thrived in several areas—certain serial formats, artists' books, children's literature, and the US market. In some of these forms of material culture, we witness a reengagement of the caricature tradition as well as a continuation of the representational school, also referred to as realism or naturalism. This chapter surveys late Victorian illustrated fiction marketed to different audiences according to social class, age, gender, and nation. It foregrounds two examples of fin-de-siècle illustration—one in England and the other in America, one in children's literature and the other in adult fiction—to demonstrate continuity in the arc of the illustrated book and a media frenzy of Pickwickian magnitude.

Beatrix Potter's *Peter Rabbit* (1902) and her successive children's tales demonstrate a commitment to naturalism, a trait that aligns her with John Everett Millais and the realistic school of illustration. A gifted naturalist, Potter, who knew Millais personally and received a compliment from him for her skill in observation, returned to her portfolio of natural history studies as models and inspiration for her children's book illustrations. Alternatively, Sixties artist George Du Maurier, savvy to the transatlantic development of the Victorian illustrated book, published his 1890s author-illustrated fiction in *Harper's New Monthly Magazine*, a major American periodical. In his best-known novel *Trilby* (*T*, 1894), Du Maurier engages theatricality and a persistent racialized stereotype of the Jew from *Oliver Twist* (*OT*, 1838)—aspects that show Du Maurier to be an inheritor of two illustrative styles: caricature and realism.

Why the Victorian Illustrated Book Waned as a Vehicle for Newly Released Wide-Circulation Publication in Volume Form

Not a single reason, but intertwining economic and aesthetic factors clarify why the demand for the Victorian illustrated book fell in the production of newly released, large-circulation adult fiction during the final decades of the nineteenth century in England. These include the decline of serial fiction, cost and quality considerations, a rise in literacy, the changing nature of the novel, new developments in illustration, and competition from other media.[4]

In the 1830s and 1840s, serialization, which spread payment over a long period of time, made literature affordable to those without the funds to buy a book or subscribe to a lending library. As the century progressed, however, consumers increasingly elected to pay a small annual fee to a major subscription library such as Mudie's or its competitor W. H. Smith & Son to borrow a book or a volume of a three-decker novel rather than purchase a novel in parts; with this system, multiple readers could borrow different volumes of a single title. By 1890, Mudie's Select Library (1725–1960) had 250,000 subscribers (Gerard 216).

The emerging free lending library provided Victorian readers with a way to access books other than purchasing a book or a serial in parts. The Public Libraries Act of 1850 was a crucial first step toward the creation of a public library system to offer opportunities for self-improvement to all social classes. This legislation gave local boroughs with a population of over 10,000 the right to levy a tax to finance a public library. Manchester opened the first public lending library in Britain in 1852, and Charles Dickens spoke at the inauguration.[5] However, the measure was imperfect because funds could be spent only on buildings, furnishings, and staff, not for the purchase of books, so libraries relied on philanthropic donations to build their collections. Important legislative amendments in 1855 and 1866 helped to rid restrictions on the establishment of libraries and the spending of library funds.

Some public libraries and subscription libraries took out periodical subscriptions, but demand for serials still decreased since people now had access to a serial through a free or subscription library and no longer had to purchase their own monthly installments. In addition, those readers who could easily afford to buy serials refrained from doing so because the overall quality of illustrated serials declined in the later decades of the nineteenth century. With mass production, texts and illustrations grew less expensive, lowering the cost of book production. However, with mass production came substandard printing practices and poorly manufactured materials.

By the late nineteenth century—as in the beginning of the century—the bound novel became the preferred form of publishing. Linda K. Hughes and Michael Lund in *The Victorian Serial* correlate the rise of volume publication and, in turn, the decline of serial fiction to the pace of life at the dawning of the twentieth century: whereas "Victorians valued slow, steady development in installments over time," epitomized by the serial unfolding over several years, readers at the fin de siècle favored "fast-forward visions of individual and communal life," more effectively served through volume publication (275). The goal of many late nineteenth-century novelists like Robert Louis Stevenson and Thomas Hardy was single-volume publication:

> in these years novelists and poets were conceiving of stories that jarred with the . . . slow, sure growth and development of serial literature; instead the appropriate form for such visions of personal and social stagnation was the single volume, an autonomous whole, in which all parts found their places in a unity of theme and effect. (Hughes and Lund 230)

Bound editions of works by late nineteenth-century authors that appeared serially with illustrations did not routinely include the illustrations that had accompanied these same works in their serial form. Hardy's illustrated fiction demonstrates this trend. When Smith, Elder and Co. brought out *The Hand of Ethelberta* in two volumes in 1876, the publisher included all of George Du Maurier's full-page engravings and pictorial capitals. In contrast, for the bound volume of *Tess of the d'Urbervilles* published in 1892, Harper & Brothers did not include the original *Tess* illustrations that appeared in *The Graphic*.[6] Hardy's fiction published in volume form without the original illustrations came to be considered his serious literary work.

Rising literacy rates and changes in the nature of the novel also influenced publishing practices and the production of illustrated literature. Victorian literacy rates are imprecise since the only criterion for literacy was the ability to sign a marriage register. Presumably, many who signed their name could read or write little else, and the figures do not reflect the numbers of older men and women who were illiterate. Nonetheless, a comparison of literacy figures from the first nationwide census published in 1840—a time when the illustrated book enjoyed enormous popularity—to the census figures of 1900—when newly released wide-circulation Victorian illustrated adult fiction was waning in England—reveals a marked increase in literacy. The 1840 census (based on data up until 20 June 1839) lists 67 percent of males and 51 percent of females as literate. By 1900—thirty years after passage of the Forster Act of 1870 (legislation that made education compulsory in England and Wales for children between the ages of five and thirteen)—97.2 percent of males and 96.8 percent of females in England and Wales were literate.[7]

With higher literacy rates, illustrations—once necessary to boost sales and to help illiterate or marginally literate readers follow a plot—were no longer vital to a publication's commercial success. At the fin de siècle, the illustrated magazine remained, but it catered to a less sophisticated audience, as Philip Allingham notes:

> rural and working class readers in Great Britain (and presumably immigrant English-as-Second-Language readers in America) found that the illustrated magazine supported their reading more than conventional books, cost far less than bound volumes, and offered better value in that, in addition to a serial instalment, the magazine would feature a plethora of other articles and illustrations, often of the "educational" or "improving" type. ("Why do Hardy's novels")

While pictures "supported" rural and working-class readers, more sophisticated readers still enjoyed pictures at the fin de siècle. There are two distinct types of readers, notes Du Maurier in "The Illustrating of Books": one "likes to have its book (even its newspaper!) full of little pictures" (1: 349), and the other "visualizes what he reads (at the moment of reading) with the mind's eye, unconsciously, perhaps, and without effort, but in a manner so satisfactory to himself that he wants the help of no picture; indeed, to him a picture would be a hindrance" (349).

In this climate, authors who were dually talented often did not illustrate their own fiction as William Makepeace Thackeray had done in the 1840s and 1850s. Robert Louis Stevenson was an amateur landscape painter, but his paintings never accompanied his fiction published during his lifetime. D. H. Lawrence and Samuel Butler were also talented writers who were artistically gifted, but they never published their own drawings to accompany their fiction. Henry James took art lessons, which impacted his style of writing, and recalls reading Dickens's illustrated novels; often quoted is James's conviction that *Oliver Twist* "seemed to me more Cruikshank's than Dickens's" (*A Small Boy and Others* 120). But James openly resisted book illustration and agreed only to a photographic frontispiece for the New York edition of his novels. Rudyard Kipling, the son of artist J. Lockwood Kipling, illustrated only his *Just So Stories* (1902) while his father illustrated two of his son's works, *The Jungle Book* (1894) and *Kim* (1901). When he became an author-illustrator in the 1890s, Du Maurier published his illustrated fiction in the US market, demonstrating border crossing in the evolution of the Victorian illustrated book. Hardy, who trained as an architect, was a capable draughtsman. He often created sketches to guide the illustrators of his serial novels, but Hardy only published his own illustrations for some of his poems as well as the maps he made for his Wessex novels and a treasure map for *Treasure Island* (1883).

Fin-de-siècle illustration proved incompatible with fiction for a host of reasons. In the words of Du Maurier, "if the disappointed author says to [his illustrator], 'Why can't you draw like Phiz?' he can fairly retort: 'Why don't you write like Dickens?'" ("The Illustrating of Books," 1: 353). But even before the novel's shift toward literary Modernism, some Victorians considered illustrations "improper intrusions" (Harvey 180) or "mere optical symbols or echoes" (James, *Golden Bowl* 333) and thus unnecessary. Good literary art, as James defines it in "The Art of Fiction," competes with representational illustration: "A novel is in its broadest definition a personal, a direct impression of life" (384); "It is here that [the author] competes with his brother the painter in *his* attempt to render the look of things, the look that conveys their meaning, to catch the color, the relief, the expression, the surface, the substance of the human spectacle" (390). John Harvey claims in *Victorian Novelists and Their Illustrators* that Du Maurier's late nineteenth-century "illustrations add nothing that the novel needs to have; they are simply respectable drawings of people who look just as the characters are described, posed as the scene requires: they are just such illustrations as the later 19th century tended to produce" (180).

Such "optical echoes" appear, for example, in Part First of *Trilby* where Du Maurier describes and draws individual busts and a group portrait of the "Three Musketeers of the Brush" ("*Les trois Angliches,*" *T* 162)—Talbot Wynne, or Taffy; Sandy, the Laird of Cockpen; and William Bagot called Little Billee (a character some believe is based on Sixties artist Fred Walker and others consider Du Maurier's self-portrait).[8] The opening scenes of *Trilby* are filled with well-executed renderings of Parisian landmarks that continue in the style of lifelike representation popular in the Sixties. In *Peter Ibbetson* (*PI*), many illustrations such as "*Le P'tit Anglais*" also "look just as the characters are described."

The Modern novel, informed by the theories of Sigmund Freud and Carl Jung, looks inward and explores the private self. Phiz's illustrations are compatible with Dickens's text because Phiz's pictures are given to storytelling, and Dickens's style is richly descriptive—full of eye. To Harvey, Phiz's illustrations for *The Old Curiosity Shop* have "merely sharpened our sense of Dickens's own creation. An author could have no justification for wishing away such illustrations as improper intrusions in his art, or as evasions of his own responsibility" (180). Many fin-de-siècle readers did "wish away" illustration, which became increasingly incompatible with the rise of literary Modernism. As Jane R. Cohen observes, "The later introspective stories of E. M. Forster and Virginia

Woolf with their psychological plots, stream-of-consciousness monologues, and symbolism, together with the increasingly egocentric and abstract prose of their successors, still seem to render illustration virtually inconceivable" (230). Maxwell likewise notes in his afterword to *The Victorian Illustrated Book*, "James Joyce did not have, or need, a Cruikshank" (395).[9]

Du Maurier's author-illustrated fiction of the 1890s demonstrates how realistic illustration jars with psychological themes with which Du Maurier himself experimented. *Peter Ibbetson* presents a concept called "dreaming true" (*PI* 201, 204); it is a form of mind traveling in which two lovers, the Duchess of Towers and Peter Ibbetson, dream themselves into each other's consciousness while they are asleep.[10] Mary, the Duchess of Towers, who teaches Ibbetson how to dream true, turns out to be his Parisian childhood love. Prison walls separate the two by day, but at night, in "a double dream, a dream common to us both" (*PI* 247), Peter and Mary visit their childhood selves.

Du Maurier pictures mind traveling by making the figures from the present time either more solid or more shadowy than the "dream people" (330) from the past. For example, in a drawing entitled "'Mother, Mother!'" (*PI* 214) set in a cherished garden in Passy, Peter Ibbetson, delineated in firm lines, kneels next to his mother, drawn in faint lines. Also rendered in faint lines and clothes of "a by-gone fashion" (212) are Ibbetson's childhood self, Gogo Pasquier, writing in his copy book; Mary Towers, then called Mimsey Seraskier, who "took no notice of me, nor did the others" (212); and Gogo's dog Médor, snoozing in the shade (214). In contrast, in "'*Maman M'a Donné Quat' Sous Pour M'en Aller à la Foire*'" (330), the tall, elegant, well-dressed figures of Peter and Mary look shadowy, but the "dream people" (330) from their childhood—Gogo, Mimsey, and the poulterer's son—appear solid and real (see fig. 41).

Peter and Mary, unnoticed by the "dream people," try in vain to stop the poulterer's son from falling off a high garden wall, an accident that cripples him for life. Ibbetson laments, "We cannot even touch these dream people without their melting away into thin air" (330)—but in this picture, rather, Peter and Mary look as if they will "melt away." The faint lines of the bottom half of their forms make Mary's full long skirt and Ibbetson's trousered legs almost dissolve into the surrounding winter streetscape. Neither combination of shadowy and firm figures successfully conveys the psychic mystery of a character living a dual life: one actual life and another achieved by projecting him or herself into a dream where "the things and people in my dream had the same roundness and relief as in life, and were life-size; one could move

Figure 41. *"Maman M'a Donné Quat' Sous Pour M'en Aller à la Foire."* Illustration by George Du Maurier for his "Peter Ibbetson" in *Harper's New Monthly Magazine*, October 1891. From Special Collections, Scribner Library, Skidmore College.

among them and behind them, and feel as if one could touch and clasp and embrace them if one dared" (217).

In addition to the growing incompatibility between late nineteenth-century illustration and literature, illustrations—once prized as a form of entertainment—followed a pattern of other Victorian commodities that decreased in value with mass production (for example, the writing desk).[11] As the illustrated book became more available and affordable for a rapidly growing middle-class readership,[12] it lost its novelty. Since the illustrated book no longer assured publishers excellent sales, many Victorian British publishers no longer agreed to cover the extra expense of illustrations even if a major novelist wanted to issue a work with illustrations. In this publishing climate, Du Maurier brought out his illustrated books in the thriving US market.

Some publishers took a fresher approach to the illustrated book and published works with photographic illustrations. The New York edition of James's works includes photographic frontispieces by Alvin Langdon Coburn, an important early twentieth-century American photographer known for his pictorialism. But, in general, the rise of photography and cinematography eclipsed the Victorian illustrated book. Although photography dates to Italy in 1515 where we find Leonardo da Vinci's description of an early optical device called a camera obscura, the genre came into its own shortly before Queen Victoria's ascension to the throne. In 1826, Nicéphore Niépce produced the first photograph using pewter plates, and in 1835, Niépce and L. J. M. Daguerre designed the process of daguerreotype photography. In England, William Henry Fox Talbot experimented with light to capture images on paper. In 1841, when first-generation caricaturists were commanding attention for their theatrical illustrations, Talbot patented his calotype process using negative and positive images. More photographic developments came in the 1840s and 1850s. David Brewster, Frederick Scott Archer, and Jules Duboscq demonstrated stereo daguerreotype at the Great Exhibition. A decade later in 1861, Thomas Sutton patented a camera with a single lens reflex plate, a design still commonly used nowadays. By the 1890s, photographs increasingly replaced hand-drawn illustrations in a range of popular publications—newspapers, magazines, and books.

Cinematography, the art of motion picture photography, arose at the end of the Victorian period and gained favor with consumers as the market for book illustration declined for wide-circulation publication of adult fiction in England. Building upon developments in photography, cinematography captured parts of Queen Victoria's Diamond Jubilee (1897). Robert Paul, who sold George Méliès a film camera at the start of his prolific filmmaking career, used a rotating camera head set on a tripod to create a panorama effect to preserve this historic occasion. A French illusionist and filmmaker, Méliès began shooting films in 1896 and improved cinematography through innovations in technique and narrative. Méliès created the prototype for early film studios and produced 513 films between 1896 and 1913 (ranging from one to forty minutes in length). These new art forms of cinematography and photography competed with book illustration, which some authors feared would date their work.

Surveying Forms of Fin-de-Siècle Illustrated Fiction

Amidst changing aesthetic tastes and advances in technology, the Victorian illustrated book did not die out at the end of the century; it evolved. Illustration remained in certain serial formats, although the relationship between author and illustrator was far less intimate than in the 1830s and 1840s. Illustrated material gained new markets—principally, in small-circulation artists' books, children's literature on both sides of the Atlantic, and adult fiction in the US. Installment publication, the form that launched Dickens's career, was still an easy, attractive way for a novice author to get published in England. For a publisher, parts publication was less of a financial risk than publishing in volumes and still guaranteed a writer a large middle-class readership. Stevenson published his debut novel serially in *Young Folks* in 1881; what we now know as *Treasure Island* first appeared under the title of *The Sea Cook* with one illustration. The work was popular, and it subsequently came out in book form in 1883 by an American publisher, Roberts Brothers of Boston, with four illustrations by Frank Merrill of *Little Women* fame.[13] Hardy's serial novels appeared with and without illustration, depending upon the journal in which he published. *Macmillan's Magazine*, which did not publish fiction with illustrations, brought out *The Woodlanders* from 1886–87. Had Hardy published *Tess of the d'Urbervilles* serially in *Macmillan's*, as he had hoped, it would not have been illustrated. Hardy published *Tess* in 1891 in a less prestigious periodical, *The Graphic*, which insisted on illustration as a publishing convention and censored portions of the novel deemed immoral for its middle-class readership.

Different from author and illustrator partnerships during the "Cruikshank-Phiz era" (Jackson 12), illustrators at the end of the nineteenth century commonly "received the completed manuscript of poetry, drama or fiction direct from the publisher," notes Kooistra in *The Artist as Critic*, "and produced the illustrations with little or no connection to the writer, who was sometimes surprised by the final product" (3). This was common practice, one that Du Maurier laments in "The Illustrating of Books": "What a fine thing it would be if author and artist could always meet in consultation over each separate design! But that seems impracticable" (2: 371). Whereas Dickens selected his book illustrators and worked with them in close collaboration, Hardy never met his principal *Tess* illustrator, Hubert von Herkomer, a Royal Academy painter. For serials published in *The Graphic*, it was not the serial's author but the magazine staff who supervised the illustration process.[14] There were four illustrators for *Tess*—Herkomer, E. Borough Johnson, Daniel A. Wehrschmidt, and J. Syddall. All four followed the representational school of illustration and produced illustrations with merit, although Wehrschmidt and Syddall have been considered "much inferior" to Johnson and Herkomer (Jackson 105). When fin-de-siècle illustrated serials appeared in book form, the illustrations were not typically included in the bound book, so readers today are often surprised to learn that *Tess of the d'Urbervilles* originally appeared in serial form with illustrations.

New markets arose for the illustrated book at the fin de siècle. The 1890s witnessed luxury books and periodicals that grew out of the Arts and Crafts and Art Nouveau movements. Much anticipated, in demand, and parodied by *Punch*, *The Yellow Book* (1894–97) was a short-lived publication under the artistic direction of Aubrey Beardsley and the literary editorship of Henry Harland, published by John Lane. *The Yellow Book* was distinct among its literary competitors with its yellow cloth binding (associated with aestheticism); exclusion of serials and advertisements; and insistence on high-quality essays, short stories, poems, and artwork. Moreover, the magazine presented art and literature on an equal plane. *The Yellow Book* published work by noted artists and authors, respectively, John Singer Sargent, Walter Sickert, Max Beerbohm, and Beardsley; Henry James, Sir Edmund Gosse, H. G. Wells, and William Butler Yeats. But the publication's distinct use of asymmetrically placed title pages to introduce artistic and literary contributions, generous white space, and distinctive typography made it an aesthetically valuable material object.

Aesthetics motivated William Morris to found the Kelmscott Press in 1891 in response to the poor quality of machine-made books.[15] Whereas three decades earlier, Dante Gabriel Rossetti worked with commercial publishers, binders, and printers to create books that were decorative works of art, Morris revived anachronistic printing techniques in what Walter Benjamin calls "the age of mechanical reproduction." Morris favored the technique of wood engraving even though photoengraving was in ascendance in book illustration. A champion of the Arts and Crafts movement, Morris carried his artistry into furniture and home decoration (including wallpaper, textiles, and stained glass) as well as bookmaking. He believed that the illustrated book "'gives us such endless pleasure and is so intimately connected with the other absolutely necessary art of imaginative literature that it must remain one of the very worthiest things towards the production of which reasonable man should strive'" (qtd. in Bland 19).[16]

As David Bland observes in *A History of Book Illustration*, "Everything in [Morris's] books had to be good—paper, ink, printing and binding" (275). Bland criticizes "the crowded appearance of the Kelmscott page, heavy type, heavy border and heavy cut all in the same plane" (275), but other critics see Morris's books as "beautiful. They were designed to be read slowly, to be appreciated, to be treasured" (Cody). Morris designed his typefaces, made his paper, and printed and bound his books by hand. Carefully crafted illustrated editions of Chaucer (famously illustrated by Edward Burne-Jones), the Romantic poets, and Morris's own writings are among the fifty titles Morris turned into expensive limited-edition volumes that "made an implicit statement about the ideal relationships which ought to exist between the reader, the text, and the author" as Cody argues in "Morris and the Kelmscott Press." What Morris strove to achieve was not financially viable, however. Jane R. Cohen concludes: "Even publishers who agree with William Morris that the illustrated book, because it combines so many arts and gives such pleasure, should 'remain one of the worthiest things towards the production of which reasonable man should strive' know that his view is more idealistic than economically realistic" (229).

Morris's venture gained a small following in other private presses, such as Charles Ricketts and Charles Shannon at the Vale Press, founded in 1894, and Lucien Pissarro at the Eragny Press, founded (in England) in 1895. These artistic approaches to bookmaking likewise proved too costly except for luxury editions for wealthy patrons. However, illustrated gift book editions of nineteenth-century novels that had originally appeared with and without illustrations also began to appear in the late nineteenth century. The works of Jane Austen and Elizabeth Gaskell illustrated by Hugh Thomson in the 1890s were in demand; "after *Cranford* appeared in 1891," notes Muir, "a 'Thomson' book became a feature of the Christmas market" (198). Although no longer referred to as "Christmas books" today, limited luxury editions with ample illustrations remain popular holiday items.

Illustration, which continued in serials and found a market in artists' books and gift books, established a true home in children's literature by the 1890s where it became "a venue for stylish artists. Children's book illustration was considered high art," as Linda Lear argues, "and children's books became part of Victorian fashion, like architecture and home décor" (*Beatrix* 33). For children's literature, age and gender were entering the nineteenth-century consciousness. There was a new understanding that a young child would want a book with far more pictures than words. Boys and girls would benefit from different types of reading material. Adventure tales would prepare Victorian boys for manhood, leading young male readers on journeys across the high seas to explore uncharted continents and unknown islands. Daniel Defoe's *Robinson Crusoe* (1719) was a major influence on Victorian boys' fiction, and books by Stevenson, R. M. Ballantyne, Captain Frederick Marryat, and G. E. Henty were nicknamed "Robinson Crusonades."[17] Likely, many girls secretly read their brothers' copies of *Treasure Island* and *King Solomon's Mines* (1885), the first in H. Rider Haggard's enormously popular Allan Quatermain series,[18] since girls' books—designed to prepare girls for their future roles as wives and mothers—were milder than boys' books and offered comparatively little fun or adventure.

Among the most popular Victorian tales for girls published in England are Charlotte Mary Yonge's *The Daisy Chain* (1856) and school stories by L. T. Meade, such as *A World of Girls* (1886), and, in the US market, Louisa May Alcott's *Little Women* (1868, 1869) and Susan Warner's *The Wide, Wide World* (1850). The tradition of books for both sexes did not disappear with the advent of gender-specific fiction. Animal tales, such as Anna Sewell's *Black Beauty* (1877) and Kipling's *The Jungle Book*, appealed to boys and girls. In this category of books for younger boys and girls we find Beatrix Potter's *The Tale of Peter Rabbit*, Kenneth Grahame's *The Wind in the Willows* (1908), and A. A. Milne's *Winnie-the-Pooh* (1926) and *The House at Pooh Corner* (1928), noteworthy for their illustrations by, respectively, Potter and Ernest Shepard.

From its crude beginning in chapbooks, children's book illustration underwent dynamic changes in the late eighteenth and nineteenth centuries. The advent of color printing in wood engraving in the mid-nineteenth century is associated with Edmund Evans, the pioneer of the picture book who elevated standards for children's book production and hired notable artists to illustrate children's books: Walter Crane, who was influenced by William Morris and the Arts and Crafts movement; Randolph Caldecott, whose legacy lives on in the Caldecott Medal awarded yearly to the best American children's picture book; and Kate Greenaway, whose popular designs found extensive life in children's clothing. Other publishing firms entered the market of color illustration in children's books, notably Routledge and Warne and Co., which became Potter's lifelong publisher. The nineteenth and early twentieth centuries produced memorable children's illustrators and author-illustrators—

in England, Edward Lear, John Tenniel, Kipling, Arthur Hughes, Crane, Caldecott, Greenaway, Potter, Arthur Rackham, Shepard, Edmund Dulac, and Kay Nielsen; and in the United States, Howard Pyle, N. C. Wyeth, Jessie Willcox Smith, E. W. Kemble, and W. W. Denslow. Some of these treasured authors wrote and illustrated tales that originated as stories for a specific child reader.[19]

The late century also witnessed a rise in the publication of illustrated adult literature in the US market. In the 1870s and 1880s, while the Victorian illustrated book was resisting book illustration for newly released wide-circulation adult fiction in volume form in England, American consumers were demanding illustrated periodicals, newspapers, encyclopedias, natural histories, architecture books, and adult and children's books.[20] Border crossing occurred in the evolution of the illustrated book well before Du Maurier published his 1890s fiction in American periodicals that, in turn, became illustrated books. Some American novels were illustrated in England before they were illustrated in America—*Evangeline* (1847) is a prime example of this trend. American publisher William D. Ticknor (later Ticknor, Reed, and Fields and then Ticknor and Fields) printed Henry Wadsworth Longfellow's long narrative poem *Evangeline* in 1847 without illustrations and published nineteen unillustrated versions between 1847 and 1865. In 1849, Longfellow's London publisher, David Bogue, printed an illustrated version of Longfellow's enormously popular epic poem about the expulsion of the Acadians with no less than forty-five wood engravings by Birket Foster (aided by Jane E. Benham). Routledge issued two editions of *Evangeline* with John Gilbert's illustrations in 1853 and 1856. In 1866, Ticknor and Fields marketed the first US illustrated edition of Longfellow's poem with pictures by F. O. C. Darley.

Uncle Tom's Cabin first appeared in 1851 as a forty-week serial in the American abolitionist periodical called *The National Era*. Jewett and Company made an unusual publishing move in 1850s America: the company published *Uncle Tom's Cabin* in book form in 1852 with six illustrations by Hammatt Billings, and, given the book's popularity, as a lavish illustrated edition with 117 illustrations by Billings in time for the Christmas market of 1852 (it is dated 1853, however). The first British edition, published by John Cassell in 1852, included twenty-seven illustrations by George Cruikshank. Moreover, as the demand for illustrated books grew in the US market, illustrated editions appeared of newly released illustrated fiction marketed for adult readers as well as of popular texts previously published without illustrations such as *Little Women*, which enjoyed enormous popularity on both sides of the Atlantic.[21]

Mark Twain published most of his major works via subscription publishing, a marketing system that anticipates publishing on demand today. Targeted at economically privileged patrons, subscription publication granted security to a publisher even before a firm printed and sold a book. Twain—like Dickens decades before him—wrote knowing his works would be illustrated and that pictures would be essential to the success of *The Adventures of Tom Sawyer* (1876) and its sequel, *Adventures of Huckleberry Finn* (1885), both subscription publications.[22] These two books each include decorative covers and frontispieces and well over a hundred headpieces, tailpieces, and marginal inset illustrations by, respectively, True Williams and E. W. Kemble, who drew readers to Twain's fiction.

Authors of books published by subscription, like authors whose works came out through serial publication, "sacrificed literary respectability for popular appeal and considerable profit" (David and Sapirstein, "Illustrators" 20); however, Twain embraced this form of publication and worked closely with publishers and editors as Dickens did with serial publishing—"choosing the most talented artists, directing their interpretations of text, selecting from the final prints, and at times removing material they deemed unfit for illustration" (21). "In many cases, Twain took illustrations into account as he wrote and edited his text," note Beverly David and Ray Sapirstein, "using them as counterpoint and accompaniment to his words, often allowing them to inform his general narrative strategy and to influence the amount of detail he felt necessary to include in his written descriptions" (22). For *Huck Finn*, Twain commissioned Kemble, a staff illustrator for *Life* (a comic weekly), and took full charge of the marketing and production of his work.

Among this array of illustrated material produced at the fin de siècle in the British and US markets, the work of two author-illustrators, Beatrix Potter and George Du Maurier, encourages us to look beyond periodicity in an examination of the Victorian illustrated book. Potter privately printed her first picture book for young children in England in 1901, the year of Queen Victoria's death, and went on to publish an entire series of children's tales that has never been out of print. In the 1890s, Du Maurier published three author-illustrated novels for an adult readership marketed by a US publisher; they became late Victorian blockbusters and resonated on both sides of the Atlantic. Although their work took dramatically different forms, both author-illustrators are inheritors of the school of realistic representation and, in Du Maurier's case, of two traditions: caricature and realism.

The Eye of a Naturalist—Beatrix Potter and Realistic Representation

In his landmark *Children's Books in England,* Harvey Darton singles out Beatrix Potter for producing the best illustrated children's books at the fin de siècle: "there is no better evidence for the new confidence which the creators of children's books had in their—relatively new—craft than the riches that accrued during the last years of the Victorian period and the first decade of the twentieth century. Beatrix Potter could almost stand for everyone" (326). In the field of illustrated Victorian children's books, Potter also "could almost stand" for the rich watercolor tradition of Randolph Caldecott, Walter Crane, and Kate Greenaway, a triumvirate of children's illustrators to which she is often compared.[23] Young Beatrix read illustrated books that were standards in the Victorian library and paid attention to contemporary graphic artists. She favored Caldecott and Crane over Greenaway.[24] Potter's father, Rupert Potter, collected Caldecott watercolors,[25] and Caldecott's blend of playfulness and naturalism informs Potter's animal illustrations; in particular, Caldecott's *A Frog He Would A-Wooing Go* (1883) finds expression in Potter's fishing frog character, Jeremy Fisher, from *The Tale of Mr. Jeremy Fisher* (1906). As a child, Beatrix read and enjoyed the nonsensical verse of Edward Lear and John Tenniel's illustrations of *Alice* and even made an attempt to illustrate Lear's "The Owl and the Pussy Cat" and the White Rabbit of *Wonderland* as well as Joel Chandler Harris's *Uncle Remus,* but she never published them.[26] However, if we look across illustrative styles in the arc of the Victorian illustrated book, Potter's artistic approach to illustration shows a reengagement with a style of lifelike artistic representation at times referred to as the Millais school.[27]

A comparison of John Everett Millais and Beatrix Potter may seem surprising: Millais was on the cusp of middle age when Beatrix was born; the older artist was Academy-trained and the younger largely self-taught; one exhibited at the Royal Academy shows, and the other made her mark in book illustration—a field "then as now . . . viewed as a stepchild among the arts" (Goodman 14).[28] Millais was the youngest pupil to be accepted at the prestigious Royal Academy—he was admitted at the age of eleven—while Potter at Millais's age took lessons from a Miss Cameron and earned a certificate from the Committee on the Council of Education in 1881.[29] A cofounder of the Pre-Raphaelite Brotherhood, Millais began an artistic movement that reformed British art in its aim for simplicity and truth to nature, and he has earned a secure place in art history as a successful painter and water colorist. Best-known as the author and illustrator of *Peter Rabbit*, Beatrix Potter is immortalized in the nursery—a place of childhood—that has overshadowed her accomplishments as a water-colorist and naturalist artist.

The lives and creative accomplishments of one of Victorian England's most successful society painters and a children's author-illustrator thirty-seven years his junior are interconnected, nonetheless. The Millais and Potter families often summered in Dalguise, Scotland, and Millais was a close friend of Potter's father. Rupert Potter, a businessman and lawyer, was an amateur painter and photographer, and he often assisted Millais by supplying him with photographs of subjects and landscape scenes that the artist used as an aide-memoire to complete his paintings when a model was not available or he had returned from a painting expedition. The Potters were dedicated to the arts, and with her father, who taught her photography, Beatrix frequently attended the exhibitions at the Royal Academy where Millais regularly exhibited.

In her journal entries from 1881–97, Potter mentions Millais in over forty-five entries; the only other individuals who occupied her thoughts to that extent are her father and her brother, Bertram. Some of the references are mundane— on 28 April 1883, Potter reports that she has visited four picture galleries and only likes best the pictures of children drawn by "Mr. Millais and perhaps Sir F. Leighton"; on 14 March 1884, Beatrix notes that she and her father visited Millais, who had been in bed for three days with neuralgia and a toothache (Linder, *JBP* 39, 71).[30] Other references reveal her wit, such as an earlier entry of 5 March 1883: "Papa asked Mr. Millais what he thought of the Rossetti pictures. He said they were all rubbish, that the people had goitres—that Rossetti never learnt drawing and could not draw. A funny accusation for one P.R.B. to make at another" (31).

Still other entries show Millais to be Potter's artistic mentor. On 6 March 1883, Potter comments, "Papa asked Mr. Millais about mixing the paints, and he very kindly said what I must get" (Linder, *JBP* 32). When she visited Millais's studio, he took an interest in Potter's artwork and included her in their discussions although at times he teased her. The fullest journal reference to Millais appears on 13 April 1896, the day of Millais's death. Potter recalls, "I shall always have a most affectionate remembrance of Sir John Millais. . . . He gave me the kindest encouragement with my drawings . . . but he really paid me a compliment for he said that 'plenty of people can *draw,* but you and my son John have observation'" (*JBP* 418).[31] Potter's biographer Linda Lear presents this compliment as "an encomium she privately cherished for the rest of her life" (*Beatrix* 45), for Millais here "made the distinction between those that could merely draw and those whose drawings had 'the divine spark of' observation" (96). To Lear, Potter's scientific illustrations have "such accuracy they could almost be photographs"; they possess "that spark, as well as a pure translucency that marks the influence of the Pre-Raphaelites both on Potter's pallet and use of light" (96). Potter admired the Pre-Raphaelites, who, in her estimation, had a "'somewhat niggling but absolutely genuine admiration for copying natural detail'" (qtd. in Hobbs 15).[32]

Potter particularly admired Millais's early style exemplified in *Ophelia* (1851–52), a canvas the Pre-Raphaelite artist painted out-of-doors and which earned him praise for his skill in drawing a beautiful, natural landscape. Millais took pains to paint and illustrate what he saw with accuracy, whether he was rendering an historical subject, an everyday landscape, or a portrait. For his famous portrait of John Ruskin in front of a waterfall in Glenfinlas, Scotland (1853–54), Millais captured every detail of the waterfall and rocky landscape, framing his subject with photographic realism (he completed the figure of Ruskin in his London studio, however). Potter likewise cherished pristine country scenery, and, as I have argued elsewhere,[33] she became a book author and illustrator after her unsuccessful attempt to become a naturalist artist.

Potter longed to enter "the grandiose world so genially dominated both at home and at the Academy by Millais" (57), notes Potter's biographer Margaret Lane. From childhood, Potter drew out-of-doors and filled her sketchbooks with drawings and watercolors of natural history specimens that she and her brother, Bertram, collected on their three-month family vacations in Scotland and the Lake District and later smuggled into the upper-floor nursery of their London home at No. 2 Bolton Gardens, West Brompton. Beatrix and Bertram snuck live and dead rabbits, mice, hedgehogs, owls, bats, and even a fox into the nursery. The live animals became pets, and some of the dead specimens proved invaluable to examine under a hand-lens or a microscope. From age eight, Beatrix dissected animals and plant samples, classified them, drew and painted them, and compared her drawings to the models on display at the Natural History Museum[34] from which they differ in one respect: Potter drew mushrooms in their woodland and grassy habitats just as they would appear in nature, a quality she carried into her book illustrations. Potter's portfolio of natural history studies was not well received in 1896 by the botanists and director at the Royal Botanical Gardens at Kew, and she directed her energies into illustrated children's tales.[35] In composing her book illustrations, Potter returned to "picture-letters" (*JBP* 250) that she sent to the children of Annie Carter Moore, her former governess, and her early natural history studies of animal and plant specimens.

Potter's still beloved series of twenty-three picture books shows her artistic skill, keen observation of nature, and talent for close-ups of one or two main figures, traits that distinguish the work of Sixties illustrators like Millais. Throughout her storybook series, relatively few illustrations include a group of characters, and many plates are close-ups of one animal character. Although she had difficulty drawing humans,[36] Potter was skilled in copying animals and nature with photographic accuracy. Potter placed her figures in well-executed landscapes—primarily the pond, the woodland, the garden, and the countryside; however, some of her stories are set in a middle-class Victorian home or a dollhouse, such as in *The Tale of Two Bad Mice* (1904), which she modeled after an actual dollhouse her publisher Norman Warne made for his niece Winifred Warne. Whereas Caldecott and Greenaway favored an idealized country setting, Potter, like Millais, showed an allegiance to identifiable geographical sites.[37] She set *The Tale of Mr. Jeremy Fisher* (1906) in Esthwaite Water and *The Tale of Squirrel Nutkin* (1903) in Derwentwater in the Lake District; the old owl's island where Squirrel Nutkin has his adventure and loses his tail is St. Herbert's Island of Derwentwater.

Potter excels as a naturalist in *Squirrel Nutkin* in the illustrations where Nutkin gathers pincushions from a briar bush and plays "ninepins" with fir cones and oak apples (36, 28). In both plates, Potter foregrounds figure over background although she includes in the woodland setting accurately rendered mushrooms, oak apples, fir cones, and rose hips—all subjects that Potter drew as a young artist. The shape of the upturned mushroom caps in the ninepins illustration as well as the brownish color and leggy stems of the fungus resemble a watercolor of a Cortinarius torvus mushroom that Potter completed in 1893 in Dunkeld in the Lake District.[38] A watercolor of a rose hip simply titled "Hips" executed at age twelve served as a model for an illustration of Nutkin as he "gathered robin's pincushions off a briar bush" (37). In both the rose hip study and the book illustration, Potter captures the orange-red hue of the fruit of the rose plant, the curling projections on each blossom's end, and the tear-like shape of the seed receptacle of the rose hip as well as the color and texture of the robin's pincushions, a red fibrous growth that forms on wild rose stems.[39]

The pictures of Squirrel Nutkin foremost recall Potter's studies of the British red squirrel, *Sciurus vulgaris*, which she drew from life and rendered with artistry and accuracy to the smallest detail. The illustration of Nutkin gathering pincushions (see fig. 42) shows the squirrel shifting its weight fully onto its back paws to free its forepaws to grip the pincushion. The squirrel's fluffy tail fans its back. The reddish-brown coat, red markings on its legs and arms, and the white

Figure 42. "Squirrel Nutkin Gathering Pincushions from a Briar Bush." Illustration by Beatrix Potter from her 'The Tale of Squirrel Nutkin' © Frederick Warne and Co., 1903, 2002. Reproduced by permission of Frederick Warne & Co. <www.peterrabbit.com>.

patch on its underside also reveal Potter's skill as a naturalist artist, expressed in an undated watercolor study entitled "Squirrels on a Log."[40]

For *The Tale of Mr. Jeremy Fisher*, Potter likewise called upon the many natural history studies she drew of water lilies with pronounced yellow centers, white petals, and spongy leaves.[41] Her drawings of Jeremy Fisher reveal detailed observations of a frog's webbed feet, bulging eyes, reptilian nose, and curving underside culled from her frog studies including "Sketches of Frogs," a pencil study of frogs drawn in various positions.[42] In one illustration of Jeremy Fisher swimming toward a water lily, the reader can anticipate a swift kick from Jeremy by the positioning of the frog's webbed feet under the water. The twenty-six illustrations for this book include close-ups of a beetle, a trout, and a water rat, as well as Jeremy the frog—all subjects that she drew from life. When her publisher questioned the authenticity of Jeremy's yellow-green coloring, Potter put her model in a jelly jar and brought it to Warne's London office to prove that her frog, like all her animals, was true to nature.[43]

Granted, Potter's children's book illustrations blend scientific observations with an element of fancy since most of her animals, including Jeremy Fisher, wear clothes. Potter admired the work of Tenniel as well as Caldecott, and her clothed animals resemble Tenniel's depiction of the White Rabbit for *Alice in Wonderland* in that clothes never obscure a character's animal characteristics. Potter never changed an animal's anatomy and criticized Kenneth Grahame because in Mr. Toad of *The Wind in the Willows* (1908), he created "'A mistake to fly in the face of nature—A frog may wear galoshes; but I don't hold with toads having beards or wigs!'" (qtd. in Linder, *A History* 175).[44] Peter Rabbit wears his trademark blue coat with shiny brass buttons and the shoes of a Victorian schoolboy. But his white underside, light brown fur, almond-shaped eyes, and fluffy white tail designate him a Belgian rabbit, modeled after Potter's own two pet Belgian rabbits, Peter and Benjamin.

Elements of nature also advance the moral of her stories. In *The Tale of Peter Rabbit*, Potter most famously uses a robin redbreast as a visual motif that recurs in *The Tale of Benjamin Bunny* (1904), *Peter Rabbit*'s sequel. The robin shows itself in Mr. McGregor's garden, a place where Peter's mother warns him not to venture. Each successive appearance in *Peter Rabbit* and *Benjamin Bunny* strengthens the bird's symbolic function as Peter's lapsed conscience. In commenting on Peter's character, the robin functions as a revealing detail in a Cruikshank or Phiz illustration. For example, Cruikshank's "Mr. Bumble and Mrs. Corney Taking Tea" from *Oliver Twist* introduces Paul Pry, an interfering busybody from an 1825 play called *Paul Pry* by John Poole; the figurine of Paul Pry on Mrs. Corney's mantel (not mentioned in the text) intimates Mr. Bumble's mercenary motive for marriage before Dickens reveals it. Potter incorporates an element of nature well known to English gardeners to serve a similar symbolic function.

The most famous of the robin's five appearances is the first (see fig. 43) where Peter Rabbit is gorging on radishes (20);[45] the robin redbreast is, as Margaret Lane notes, "boldly observant on the spade while Peter overeats himself of radishes" (71). The plate is noteworthy for its naturalism as well as its symbolism. A robin, which lays a blue egg the color of Peter's trademark jacket, is known to be active during the day, to frequent open farmland, and to have an acute sense of observation; this bird hunts by sight as well as hearing. From her study of birds in nature and dead birds that she found on her rambles,[46] Potter captured the traits and anatomy of the European robin with

Figure 43. "Peter Rabbit Eating Radishes." Illustration by Beatrix Potter from her 'The Tale of Peter Rabbit' © Frederick Warne and Co., 1902, 2002. Reproduced by permission of Frederick Warne & Co. <www.peterrabbit.com>.

its distinctive orange-red breast and face, whitish belly, brown upper parts, and black eye and bill. The background of the illustration is an English garden that Potter depicts with lifelike realism. There are leafy yellow-green lettuces, long and thin French beans, and tapering red radishes with large green leaves. Naughty Peter holds the conical taproot of an accurately rendered radish in each paw to facilitate continuous feasting. In this plate and throughout her storybook series, Potter illustrates with photographic accuracy and truth to nature, traits that recall Millais and the school of representational realism.

George Du Maurier—A Sixties Artist Reengaging Caricature and Realism in the US Periodical and Book Market

George Du Maurier made his reputation as a Sixties illustrator along with Millais, Dante Gabriel Rossetti, Holman Hunt, and Frederick Walker, among others. Du Maurier's illustrations demonstrate a commitment to naturalism and feeling, favor close-ups over panoramic views, and privilege figure over background. As an illustrator of his own novels that he published in the US market, however, Du Maurier was an inheritor of two illustrative traditions: realism and caricature.

In "The Illustrating of Books," Du Maurier reveals his dual artistic allegiances. On the one hand, he writes that Millais, Rossetti, and Hunt provide readers "extraordinary pleasure," and Tenniel's pictures for *Alice* are "simply perfect" (1: 351). In his letters, he frequently mentions Millais, admires Millais's work, and notes in a letter to his mother dated March 1863, that as an illustrator of *The Cornhill Magazine*, "I'm in devilish good company—Leighton and Millais" (D. Du Maurier 201). Like Millais, Du Maurier was a consummate illustrator of women and was known for capturing the pretentions of Victorian society and the intricacy of daily bourgeois life. On the other hand, Du Maurier also revered the early caricaturists of "the good old school" (1: 351) and championed the illustrated book when it was falling out of fashion as a form of adult entertainment in England. In "The Illustrating of Books," Du Maurier praises Thackeray as an author-illustrator, "who had a genuine gift of sketching," although he admits, "His drawing and execution do not come up to the standard of today, but we know what he meant his people to be like" (2: 371). Du Maurier also lauds the book illustrations and *Punch* drawings of John Leech, another caricaturist with whom he worked side by side at *Punch* and whose post as a cartoonist he eventually assumed;[47] in a rare 1895 interview with Robert H. Sherard published in *The Westminster Budget*, Du Maurier even calls Leech "'one of my intimates: my master'" (qtd. in Sherard 24).

In Du Maurier's bestseller *Trilby* (1894), the three English artists lend the eponymous Trilby O'Ferrall books to improve her mind written by Du Maurier's own favorite authors—Sir Walter Scott as well as Dickens and Thackeray whose books came out with caricature-style illustrations. At the end of the novel when Trilby is dying, Little Billee's mother, Mrs. Bagot, reads her *David Copperfield* (1850), illustrated by Phiz, "But the best of all was for Trilby to look over John Leech's *Pictures of Life and Character*, just out" (418). The original illustrators of Dickens are also foremost in Du Maurier's mind in his 1890 article "The Illustrating of Books":

Of course, the most delightful illustrations in the world are those one loved when one was young. . . . And, indeed, what does not the great Dickens himself owe to Cruikshank and Hablôt Browne, those two delightful etchers who understood and interpreted him so well!

Our recollections of Bill Sikes and Nancy, and Fagin, and Noah Claypole, and the Artful Dodger, of Pickwick and the Wellers, *père et fils*, Pecksniff, Mrs. Gamp and Mrs. Prig, Micawber, Mr. Dombey, Mr. Toots, and the rest, have become fixed, crystallised, and solidified into imperishable concrete by these little etchings in that endless gallery, printed on those ever-welcome pages of thick yellow paper, which one used to study with such passionate interest before reading the story, and after, and between. (1: 350)

Critics often cite this passage for its description of the Victorian reading experience: the Victorians "studied" illustrations before and after reading each part issue and between serial installments to refresh their memories. This excerpt is also psychologically revealing of Du Maurier's taste for illustration formed as a child: the original caricature-style illustrations for *Oliver Twist* and other Dickens's serials were etched in Du Maurier's mind. Du Maurier identifies himself with illustrators of "the new school, [who] are too much the slaves of the model" ("The Illustrating," 1: 351). But might he, albeit subconsciously, have modeled his Jewish villain Svengali after an image of Cruikshank's Fagin from *Oliver Twist* that was "fixed, crystallised, and solidified" in his mind since boyhood? In *Trilby* we see the imprint of the caricature tradition through Du Maurier's use of theatricality and a persistent racialized stereotype of the Jew.

In 1880, a decade before the publication of his best-known *Trilby*, George Du Maurier began his association with an American publisher, *Harper's*. He worked closely with *Harper's* London agents: first R. R. Bowker with whom he had a falling out after illustrating Hardy's *A Laodicean* (1881); then with James Ripley Osgood in 1886, publishing society scenes that recall his work for *Punch*. "Peter Ibbetson" (June–November 1891), "Trilby" (January–August 1894), and "The Martian" (October 1896–July 1897) appeared serially in *Harper's New Monthly Magazine* before they came out as bound editions; Harper & Brothers Publishers reprinted all his illustrations. Akin to illustrated books published in the heyday of the Victorian illustrated book in England, Du Maurier's novels in serial and volume form are chock-full of vignettes and full-page engravings—86 illustrations for *Peter Ibbetson*, 120 for *Trilby*, and 48 for *The Martian*. That one so well established in the British publishing scene elected to bring out his illustrated fiction with an American publishing house speaks to Du Maurier's keen awareness that the future of the illustrated book that he so eloquently supported lay across the Atlantic. The popularity of his illustrated fiction, in turn, demonstrates a transnational development in the evolution of the Victorian illustrated book.

For his three author-illustrated novels, Du Maurier created a fictional formula that combines veiled recollections of his Parisian boyhood, a wistfulness for the past, and psychic phenomena in vogue in the latter half of the nineteenth century—telepathic dreaming, mesmerism, automatic writing, and reincarnation.[48] *Trilby* quickly became a bestseller and is credited for impacting the publishing of "sellers" (as publishers called bestsellers then).[49] It tells about a menacing Jewish musical genius named Svengali, who hypnotized late nineteenth-century readers along with Trilby O'Ferrall; a French-Irish laundress and an artist's model, Trilby, under Svengali's control, becomes an opera virtuoso. *Trilby* boosted sales of *Harper's* and sold close to 300,000 copies during the first year of its publication (Kelly, *George Du Maurier* 87). Du Maurier admits his amazement that *Trilby* resonated with readers in America and England: "'So "Peter Ibbetson" was sent over to America, and accepted at once. Then "Trilby" followed, and the "boom" came—a "boom" which surprised me immensely, for I never took myself *au sérieux* as a novelist'" (qtd. in Sherard 24). "'Indeed this "boom" rather distresses me,'" Du Maurier confides further to Sherard, "'when I reflect that Thackeray never had a "boom." And I hold that a "boom" means nothing as a sign of literary excellence, nothing but money'" (24). But a "boom" in this case did signal literary excellence to many of Du Maurier's contemporaries like Henry James, who notes in an 1897 article published in *Harper's New Monthly Magazine*: "it was not till the first instalment of *Trilby* appeared that we really sat up" (603).

With the publication of *Trilby*, manufacturers and consumers "sat up," too. Du Maurier's novels created a consumer phenomenon called Trilby-mania. Galleries displayed prints from the book. Real and fictitious claims about the novel filled British and American newspapers. And Trilby, like Sherlock Holmes, attained the stature of a real person. Svengali Square, Little Billee Lake, and a town called Trilby popped up in Florida. Merchandizers capitalized on the scene where rising artist Little Billee draws Trilby's exquisite left foot on his Latin Quarter studio wall. A Chicago manufacturer marketed a high-heeled shoe named "the Trilby," and a New York caterer sold ice cream bars shaped to look like Trilby's left foot. There were many late nineteenth-century commercial ventures—Trilby sweets, games, puzzles, and even chowder and toothpaste. Parodies arose as early as 1895.[50] Quickly adapted for the Boston and

London stage, *Trilby* as a play also stimulated consumerism: demand grew for a Trilby hat, a type of narrow-brimmed fedora worn in the first stage production that men still wear today. The mania for all things *Trilby* died down after Du Maurier's death in 1896, although several feature films came out in the twentieth century—most famously in 1931 with John Barrymore as the consummately devilish Svengali, and in 1954 with Donald Wolfit as the evil hypnotist. These productions were named *Svengali* since "Svengali's persona as the evil Jewish hypnotist was sufficiently recognizable to be deemed a better box-office draw than the eponymous heroine of the novel" (Kerker).[51] The name Svengali is still synonymous with a manipulator, even to those who have never read the novel.

Some of Du Maurier's book illustrations for *Trilby* and his other two novels are pretty travel scenes and portraits in the Sixties style that critic John Harvey deems superfluous while other illustrations potentially undermine a psychological phenomenon like "dreaming true" (see fig. 41). But in his well-executed drawings, Du Maurier uses to effect theatrical elements (pose, props, gestures, lighting, et cetera) derived from his beloved caricaturists—Cruikshank, Phiz, Doyle, and his *Punch* colleague, Leech. In *Peter Ibbetson*, the eponymous hero assumes a melodramatic pose in "Weltschmertz": Ibbetson, now living in England following his mother's death, is sorely missing his former French life; he leans forward in his chair "with his head bowed over the black and yellow key-board of a venerable square piano-forte (on which he could not play), dropping the bitter tear of loneliness and *Weltschmertz* combined" (*PI* 120). The plate is a continuation of the Sixties style in that Ibbetson's sole figure commands the page, but the pose and the stage lighting reengage the caricature tradition. Ibbetson's entire figure is illuminated with a spotlight effect. His hands fully cover his face to hide his tears, but his sadness and weariness expressively carry into his body language, particularly his "bowed" head and hunched shoulders.

Equally dramatic is the plate entitled "'Bastard! Parricide!,'" illustrating a confrontation between Peter and his Uncle Ibbetson just as the eponymous protagonist finds out that his mother was once his uncle's mistress and that his uncle is likely his father. In contents and composition, this plate evokes Cruikshank's "Oliver Plucks Up a Spirit" for *Oliver Twist*. In these two plates, Cruikshank and Du Maurier, respectively, draw a son defending his dead mother's honor. Cruikshank captures large-fisted young Oliver about to deliver another blow to his tormentor, Noah Claypole. Likewise, Du Maurier foreshadows Peter killing his Uncle Ibbetson with the long stick that he holds high above his head. In both plates, the aggressors are really the victims of their tormentors and act in self-defense.

Theatrical elements also appear in Du Maurier's lesser-known third novel, *The Martian*.[52] The protagonist, Barty Josselin, becomes a world-renowned writer when an extraterrestrial named Martia inhabits his body during sleep, inspires him to write great books, and brings him renown. Barty is the recipient of automatic writing, a phenomenon in which a second personality is believed to transmit messages to the writer when he or she is in a hypnotic trance or asleep. Du Maurier never attempts to draw Martia until she reincarnates herself as Josselin's daughter Marty. However, the author-illustrator hints at Martia's presence in one well-executed, full-page illustration that sets a theatrical stage and leads the viewer's eye beyond the picture plane. "Martia, I Have Done My Best" (see fig. 44) captures handsome Barty Josselin, who has an aquiline nose, piercing light eyes, and a tall, graceful build. Looking out his open window at nightfall, Josselin is reaching his outstretched arms imploringly into the night sky. Of course, we do not see the extraterrestrial—she is offstage. But Josselin's compelling body language—an intent gaze, outstretched arms, and bent knee—intimates that Josselin is speaking to Martia, who comes to him in his sleep and prompts his astronomical writing. Martia thus hovers provocatively in the night sky beyond the picture plane but within the viewer's imagination.

The final plate of *The Martian* entitled "Marty" also employs theatrical staging. Martia, now reincarnated as Barty Josselin and Leah Gibson's daughter Marty, lies dying on an outdoor chaise. Du Maurier draws Marty and Leah as beautiful, majestic women, his specialty as an artist. Both dark-haired Leah and light-haired Marty are beautifully dressed and coiffed. Marty stretches out on a divan in a posture that accentuates her long limbs and slender form, while tall Leah bends over her dying daughter and tenderly holds her hand. Josselin, handsomely dressed in a tux and top hat, sits on the edge of the chaise and leans toward Marty at an angle that also magnifies his height. In this illustration, Barty's and Leah's eyes steadily fix upon Marty, forming a triangular configuration, while Barty's friend, Robert Maurice, positioned at the far right of the illustration, gazes in the opposite direction beyond the picture plane. Marty holds her hands close to her chest as if in prayer. Her eyes have a distant look, suggesting she is not long for this world. This illustration captures a moment before the deaths of Marty, Barty, and Leah that dramatically occur simultaneously. Marty wakes "from a gentle doze" (*M* 457), raises her head, and calls to her parents, "'Barty—Leah—come to me, come!'" (*M* 457). All three characters in this intense triangle of affection are simply "'no more'" (457), and so the novel ends.

Figure 44. "Martia, I Have Done My Best." Illustration by George Du Maurier for his "The Martian" in *Harper's New Monthly Magazine*, April 1897. From Special Collections, Scribner Library, Skidmore College.

Trilby is even more theatrical than *The Martian*. Like many serials illustrated by Cruikshank and Phiz, *Trilby* was easily adapted to the nineteenth-century stage in part owing to its most dramatic character, Svengali. C. C. Hoyar Miller refers to Beerbohm Tree's stage adaptation as the "complete embodiment of the pictures and descriptions in the book . . . it was fantastic, weird and comical in turns, and rose to great heights of tragic intensity" (154). Du Maurier draws Svengali playing the piano with intense passion in "A Voice He Didn't Understand" (*T* 63) and wielding a conductor's baton in "Au Clair de la Lune" (318), thus commanding Trilby to sing. Whether Svengali is reaching for piano keys in "A Voice He Didn't Understand," inspecting Trilby's throat in "'Himmel! The Roof of Your Mouth'" (73), playing a musical instrument in "The Flexible Flageolet" (31), or simply folding his arms in "All as it Used to Be" (133), Svengali possesses an intensity that recalls the villains of melodrama.

Svengali's hypnotic powers emerge to theatrical effect in a full-page engraving entitled "'*Et Maintenant Dors, Ma Mignonne!*'" (*T* 395) (see fig. 45A). Svengali in this plate is in the process of mesmerizing tone-deaf, tuneless Trilby O'Ferrall; the virtuoso performs in all the great European cities, but wakes with no recollection of her success as a singer. This illustration includes three figures—Marta, Svengali's aunt, who looks after Trilby and here places the diva's crown on her head; Trilby herself, dressed up as the opera diva called La Svengali; and Svengali, kneeling before Trilby, inducing a trance. Trilby is a majestic female in the fashion of *Peter Ibbetson*'s Mary, Duchess of Towers (see fig. 41) and *The Martian*'s Leah Gibson. In "'*Et Maintenant Dors, Ma Mignonne!*,'" Du Maurier captures Trilby's regal beauty and sensuality that entrances the three English painters. Her long neck and straight posture intimate her height even though she is seated. Trilby's attractive facial features are arresting even in her mesmeric state. Her shapely form appears visible through her low-cut, fitted gown with frills that accentuate her ample bosom and folds that reveal her rounded posterior and shapely thighs. But the caricatured figure of Svengali, bookended by the figure of his caricatured elderly aunt with the same prominent Semitic nose, dominates the illustrative stage. Svengali's demonic eyes and dark hair mark him a demon while his pointed left ear accentuates his resemblance to a devil.

Du Maurier's convincing depiction of hypnosis is crucial to the plot. Light emanating from Svengali's moving hands gives concrete form to a pseudoscience that fascinated Victorian audiences as much as it did Du Maurier, who first encountered it in Malines in 1859. Hypnotism is also called mesmerism after German physician Franz Mesmer. In the late eighteenth century, Mesmer theorized about animal magnetism from which hypnotism is derived. Mesmerism attracted attention in England in the early 1800s and engendered a craze called "mesmeric mania" in the 1840s. Though not a new phenomenon when Du Maurier published *Trilby*, hypnotism still fascinated the Victorian public. Some Victorians championed mesmerism as a magical cure-all while others feared that the person under hypnosis would lose all self-control. The Laird expresses the latter view when he warns Trilby that Svengali used hypnotism to cure the neuralgia in her eyes: "'He mesmerized you; . . . They get you into their power, and just make you do any blessed thing they please—lie, murder, steal—anything! and kill yourself into the bargain when they've done with you!'" (*T* 75). Trilby's motionless face and figure in this plate give concrete form to the mesmerist's ability to "just make you do any blessed thing they please.'"

Du Maurier also compellingly recalls qualities of Dickens's and Cruikshank's Fagin and incorporates them into his illustrations of Svengali. In Part First, Du Maurier describes Svengali as a character "of Jewish aspect, well-featured but sinister" (*T* 11) with "bold, brilliant black eyes, with long heavy lids" and "a beard of burnt-up black which grew almost from his under eyelids" (12). Over the course of the novel, Du Maurier calls Svengali a "demon," "an incubus," a "black spider-cat," and a "magician" (136, 137, 108, 452); likewise, he draws Svengali in a manner that accentuates his dark and diabolical nature. Pictured for the first time in "The 'Rosemonde' of Schubert" (21), Svengali leers at Trilby, who gazes beyond him to *les trois Angliches* (Taffy, Sandy, and Little Billee), not pictured. Playing a stirring rendition of this Schubert piece, Svengali "flashed a pair of languishing black eyes at [Trilby] with intent to kill" (20). In this plate, Du Maurier dramatically lights up Svengali's killer eyes and hooked nose that appears even longer and larger in profile.

In making Svengali a Jew and a devil, Du Maurier is reengaging a racialized depiction of the Jew prominent in *Oliver Twist*. Cruikshank's depiction recalls the medieval conception of the wandering Jew, excluded from Christian nation-states, that also appears in cartoons by Isaac Cruikshank and Thomas Rowlandson. Edgar Rosenberg in *From Shylock to Svengali* and, more recently, Milton Kerker in "Svengali, Another Byword in the Lexicon of Jewish Villainy" and Joseph Bristow in "'Dirty Pleasure': Trilby's Filth" examine the villainous Jew—a type that extends from Shakespeare's Jewish moneylender in *The Merchant of Venice* to Dickens's "receiver of stolen goods" (*OT*, Oxf. 1982 xxv) to Du Maurier's evil hypnotist.[53] Rosenberg aligns the look of Cruikshank's Fagin and Du Maurier's Svengali, noting, "Detail for detail the two Jews run equally true to type" (234).[54] Du Maurier's biographer Richard Kelly likewise draws a

Figure 45. A (*above*): "'*Et Maintenant Dors, Ma Mignonne!*'" Illustration by George Du Maurier for his "Trilby" in *Harper's New Monthly Magazine*, July 1894. From Special Collections, Scribner Library, Skidmore College; B (*opposite*): "The Jew and Morris Bolter Begin to Understand Each Other." Illustration by George Cruikshank for Charles Dickens's "Oliver Twist" in *Bentley's Miscellany*, November 1838. From the Norman M. Fox Collection, Scribner Library, Skidmore College.

connection between the demonic qualities of Fagin and Svengali as well as their physical appearance: "In *Oliver Twist*, for example, Fagin is suggested to have Satanic powers, and Cruikshank's illustration of [Fagin] bears a close resemblance to Du Maurier's drawing of Svengali" (117). Since Cruikshank's drawing came before Du Maurier's, and Du Maurier was a fan of both Dickens and Cruikshank, it seems more accurate to say that Du Maurier's Svengali bears a close resemblance to Cruikshank's Fagin. Moreover, as critics have often noted, Dickens and Cruikshank's Fagin prescribes to conventions of the archetypal "stage Jew," noted not only for strangeness and ugliness, but also deceitfulness, demonism, smarminess, and greed, qualities that reappear in Svengali's characterization.[55]

In "Oliver Introduced to the Respectable Old Gentleman," Cruikshank's
Fagin holds a toasting fork that resembles a devil's pitchfork. Fagin's leering grin
alone could easily kill unsuspecting Oliver in Svengali-like fashion. In making
Trilby his musical trill, Svengali does eventually "kill" (*T* 20) La Svengali. The
baton that Svengali uses to command Trilby to sing functions much like a devil's
pitchfork. Svengali has "big yellow teeth baring themselves in a mongrel canine
snarl" as well as "insolent black eyes" (136). Whereas Dickens describes Fagin as
a "loathsome reptile" (*OT*, Oxf. 1982 116), Du Maurier calls Svengali a pedigree-

less mongrel—animal associations that devalue these physically "repulsive" types. While Fagin's "villainous-looking and repulsive face was obscured by a quantity of matted red hair" (50), Svengali's "thick, heavy, languid, lustreless black hair fell down behind his ears on to his shoulders, in that musicianlike way that is so offensive to the normal Englishman" (*T* 11–12). Their hair color differs—Fagin has flaming hair, a color associated with the devil, and Svengali has a dark shock of hair—but both Jews have unkempt manes and looks that are "offensive to the normal Englishman." Du Maurier does not call Svengali "the Jew" as Dickens calls Fagin, but he refers to Svengali's disturbing Hebrew qualities that separate him from a refined Englishman. For example, Svengali speaks French with a "Hebrew-German accent . . . uttered in his hoarse, rasping, nasal, throaty rook's caw" (136).

In addition to his yellow teeth and snarly mouth, Svengali "is depicted as the hook-nosed Mephistophelian Jew-demon, a caricature already familiar from that of Fagin and others and one that continues to this day" (Kerker).[56] Interestingly, neither author makes direct mention of the length of his villain's nose. Dickens does comment on Noah Claypole's "small red nose" (*OT*, Oxf. 1982 36), an indirect clue to the length of Fagin's nose in "The Jew and Morris Bolter Begin to Understand Each Other" (see fig. 45B). This scene takes place at the Three Cripples pub where Fagin meets Noah Claypole, now in London under the name of Morris Bolter. Dickens narrates: "The Jew followed up this remark by striking the side of his nose with his right forefinger,—a gesture which Noah attempted to imitate, though not with complete success, in consequence of his own nose not being large enough for the purpose" (*OT*, Oxf. 1982 271). In the accompanying plate, Noah's nose is too small to accommodate this Victorian gesture to signal to another person that he or she is in the know. But Cruikshank in this and other plates makes much of Fagin's pointy Semitic nose, which is more than "large enough for the purpose" of striking with his long, bony right forefinger.[57] The racialized caricature of the hook-nosed villainous Jew that Du Maurier carries into *Trilby* in plates such as "'Et Maintenant Dors, Ma Mignonne!'" (see fig. 45A) thus comes as much from Cruikshank as it does from Dickens. Du Maurier does not describe Svengali's nose, but he draws Svengali's imposing nose in a manner that recalls Fagin's nose—it is long enough to signal in Fagin-like fashion that he, too, is in the know of Jewish villainy.

Of all the Svengali illustrations, "An Incubus" (*T* 137) (see fig. 46) is the most darkly comic. The title comes from a quote where Trilby perceives Svengali is "a dread, powerful demon, who . . . oppressed and weighed on her like an

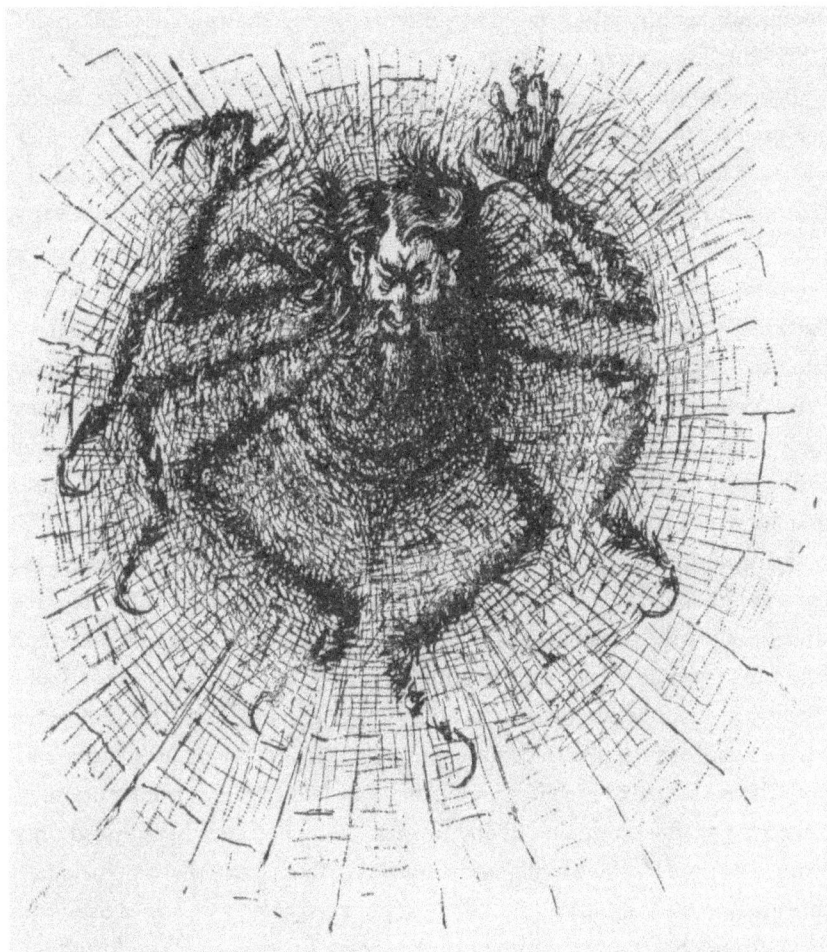

Figure 46. "An Incubus." Illustration by George Du Maurier for his "Trilby" in *Harper's New Monthly Magazine*, March 1894. From Special Collections, Scribner Library, Skidmore College.

incubus" (136–37). In this small but powerful vignette, Du Maurier draws Svengali as the embodiment of Trilby's fear: he is part human, part arachnid, and part demon. Svengali has a human head, but a spider's body. Blackness, a color long associated with darkness and witchcraft, extends from his spidery legs to his "killer" eyes, pronounced nose, and thick wild hair, here fashioned to suggest a devil's horns. An incubus preys upon women in the night. Gazing directly at the viewer, Svengali the male demon looks as if he can simultaneously hypnotize the viewer as well as Trilby, who falls under his sexual and musical control. Kelly calls this a nightmare cartoon: Du Maurier is "working within the nineteenth-century visual tradition epitomized in the drawings of Cruikshank" (155)[58] and arguably of Thackeray.

If we view this illustration as a manifestation of Trilby's fear of the musical genius, it recalls "Becky's Second Appearance in the 'Character of Clytemnestra'" (see fig. 14, ch. 2, 69), which we can read as a projection of Jos Sedley's dreaded fear of manipulative Becky Sharp in *Vanity Fair* (*VF*, 1848). Becky first binds Jos's hands in a web of green silk for a purse she is making before she fishes for him and presumably hooks him late in the novel. In "An Incubus," Svengali looks as if he can lure Trilby into a hypnotic web and deliver her a fate worse than that of Fagin's boys, who thieve for their master, or even of Jos Sedley, who is destined to be "'prey to woman'" (*VF* Oxf. 36). Trilby becomes La Svengali, an extension of Svengali, who even linguistically subsumes her. Trilby loses her own identity as she sings solely for Svengali's profit and dies a premature death.[59]

Svengali, too, dies, but his power extends beyond the grave through the power of photography.[60] Du Maurier draws a photograph of Svengali "looking straight out of the picture, straight at you" (*T* 430). This "splendid photograph by a Viennese photographer, and a most speaking likeness" (430) that Trilby receives just before her death forms the subject of a plate entitled "Out of the Mysterious East" (432). With near photographic accuracy, Du Maurier captures the essence of Svengali in this still tableau. Svengali's hands are motionless but raised as if to command Trilby to sing. Trilby becomes hypnotized once again, this time by the photographic portrait, which embodies the racialized caricature of the Jew. Although Trilby has not been able to sing since Svengali's death from a heart attack brought on by seeing *les trois Angliches* during one of La Svengali's performances, suddenly, "staring intently at the portrait, . . . her eyes dilated, and quite a strange light in them" (432). As Trilby begins to sing Chopin's "Impromptu in A Flat" (433), her eyes remain fixed on Svengali's photograph. Trilby's outstanding musical performance astounds the three artists and Mrs. Bagot. However, as soon as Trilby finishes the song, she folds her hands over her chest, utters three words in a faint voice—"'*Svengali*. . . . *Svengali*. . . . *Svengali!* . . . '" (435)—and dies. The photograph of the incubus is as potent as Svengali's person and mesmerizes Trilby to sing to her death.

In fin-de-siècle illustration in areas as diverse as Du Maurier's mesmerizing blockbusters and Beatrix Potter's enduring children's tales, we see fluidity and continuity between schools of illustration in the evolution of the Victorian illustrated book. Even as economic and aesthetic factors led to a marked decrease in newly released, large-circulation illustrated adult fiction published in Britain in volume form, the achievements of these author-illustrators invite us to think of the fin de siècle neither as a period of decline nor simply as an extension of the Sixties school of representational realism. Potter draws the landscapes and animals that populate her children's tales with near photographic accuracy, recalling the art of Millais. Du Maurier, an illustrator of the Millais school, reengages the caricature style associated with Cruikshank and continues the Sixties representational style of illustration. Du Maurier's theatrical presentation of Svengali also perpetuates a persistent stereotype of a minority group that gets a much-needed makeover in a graphic novel adaptation of *Oliver Twist* when Will Eisner remediates the Jewish villain in *Fagin the Jew* (2003).

CRCRO

Conclusion

The Victorian Graphic Classics—
Heir of the Victorian Illustrated Book

> In respect of illustration the modern novel has a withered limb,
> and while with many novelists it might just as well be withered, since
> they have no need of it, one cannot say who might have used it
> with the strength, suppleness, and sensitivity of a hand.
>
> John R. Harvey, *Victorian Novelists and Their Illustrators*, 1971

John Harvey concludes *Victorian Novelists and Their Illustrators* by raising the possibility that some modern novels might have benefited from "the strength, suppleness, and sensitivity of [an illustrator's] hand" (181). These sensitive hands may well belong to today's graphic novelists and artists who have revived a style of composing through two arts, a way of reading a book with pictures, and a canon of great books. The term "graphic classics" describes an intersection of the traditional canon of western literature and the graphic novel. Graphic novel adaptations have reduced the length of nineteenth-century novels and refashioned them into a prescient textual-visual, hyper-modern form that brings new audiences to authors including Charles Dickens, Lewis Carroll, the Brontës, Jane Austen, and most recently Anthony Trollope.

This chapter argues that the graphic classics is a late-stage evolution of the Victorian illustrated book, giving the genre new expression for our time.[1] This modern form of material culture is an heir of the Victorian illustrated book. The graphic classics is not the only form of word and picture storytelling that "makes it possible to think about Victorian illustrated books from a new perspective: to situate them, as it were, in a new canon" (419), as Richard Maxwell proposes in his afterword to *The Victorian Illustrated Book*.[2] But the Victorian illustrated book and the graphic novel, including the graphic classics, share marked similarities in how they are composed and how we read them; both genres have developed from related word and image traditions and have interwoven origins.

To the Victorians, reading was visual and verbal. The term "reader-viewer" readily applies to the audience of the graphic novel and the Victorian illustrated book. The graphic novel is essentially a lengthy, high-end comic book printed on quality paper and bound with a spine to make it appear like a novel. It is also cinematic in nature—made up of sequential panels (also called frames) with black-and-white and color graphics that incorporate word balloons, thought bubbles, captions, a variety of fonts and hand lettering, motion lines (also called speed lines), and sound effects (onomatopoeic words).[3] The eye moves over each panel to gather meaning, rather than move straight across to read the lines of text from the top of the page to the bottom as in reading a book composed all of words.[4] Nonetheless, as Stephen Tabachnick notes, "graphic novels offer a reading experience in which, as in traditional reading, the reader controls the speed of perception and can linger or look backward at will" ("Graphic Novel" 2).[5] George Du Maurier's oft-cited description of reading the Victorian illustrated book thus applies to reading the graphic novel; today's reader-viewer can study the graphics "with such passionate interest before reading the story, and after, and between" as Du Maurier suggests in "The Illustrating of Books" (1: 350).

Parallels also lie in the composing processes and the essential role pictures play in both hybrid art forms.[6] To recall Harvey's description of the relationship between author and illustrator in *Victorian Novelists and Their Illustrators*: "The novelist wrote in collaboration with an artist he had worked with often before; he wrote knowing he must have illustrations, and designed them at the same time that he was writing his monthly part—sometimes before" (180).[7] Leading authors of graphic novels such as Alan Moore and Neil Gaiman likewise work closely with artists, including pencillers, inkers, colorists, and letterers,[8] and write their texts, called scripts, knowing—even more than Dickens did—that pictures will play a quintessential role in their stories.[9] The script of a graphic novel cannot stand on its own as an unillustrated edition of a Dickens novel can. Author-illustrators also populate both genres; following in the footsteps of Lewis Carroll and William Makepeace Thackeray are, among others, Jeff Lemire, Stan Sakai, and Will Eisner, who popularized the term "graphic novel" to promote *A Contract with God, and Other Tenement Stories* (1978).[10]

The recognized father of modern comics, Rodolphe Töpffer, is an heir of the established father of graphic satire and caricature, William Hogarth.[11] The British Hogarth influenced the Swiss Töpffer, creator of picture stories like *Histoire de M. Jabot* (1833) that "featured the first interdependent combination of words and pictures seen in Europe" (McCloud 17).[12] Scott McCloud, Stephen Tabachnick, and other comics scholars align the birth of modern comics with Töpffer, who, like George Cruikshank and other caricaturists, was influenced by eighteenth-century British satirical artists who presented work in a sequence—principally Hogarth, William Rowlandson, and James Gillray.[13] Installments in monthly and weekly publications and daily and weekly comics—serial forms of publication—respectively, ushered in the Victorian illustrated book and the graphic novel. As Simon Grennan observes in "Perhaps I'll Draw and You Complete the Story . . .": "although we usually think of the comic-strip as a short-form medium, it parallels the historic development of the novel in becoming a long form through serialisation" (55).

The comic book is a "desultory form of publication" (*P*, Oxf. xxxiv), to recall Dickens's estimation of serialization, the publishing format in which he launched his professional career as a novelist. Indeed, many graphic novels are comic book series compiled to be read as a single-volume book.[14] Some authors and artists find the term "graphic novel" a pretentious marketing tool to ease the humble genre's entrance into libraries, bookstores, and the Academy. Frequently quoted is Gaiman's response to an editor of a literary page of a major newspaper who complimented him for being a graphic novelist, *not* a comic book writer; Gaiman reports in an article published in the *Los Angeles Times*: "'And I suddenly felt like someone who had been informed that she wasn't a hooker, that in fact she was a lady of the evening'" (qtd. in Erickson).

Regardless of what we call someone like Gaiman, his comment points to the marginality that the graphic novelist shares with the Victorian book illustrator. George Du Maurier admits in "The Illustrating of Books" that the illustrator of books and periodicals "must not hope for any very high place in the hierarchy of art. The great prizes are not for him!" (2: 374). Du Maurier's estimation of the illustrator's stature parallels Steven Weiner's assessment of the comic book artist: "few professionals saw the field as a real career. Comic books were the lowest rung of the cultural ladder; the pay was poor, the production shoddy" (3).[15] The idea that the field of comics is not a "real career" for professional artists echoes the worry that Dickens, according to William Harrison Ainsworth, was making a "grave mistake in writing fiction in this popular form, the loose-covered serial" (A. N. Wilson 19)—although history tells us otherwise.

"While film and theater have long ago established their credentials," as Eisner contends in *Graphic Storytelling and Visual Narrative*, "comics still struggle for acceptance, and the art form, after more than ninety years of popular use, is still regarded as a problematic literary vehicle" (3).[16] McCloud wrote *Understanding Comics* (1993) with the aim of "Setting the Record Straight" (the title of his first chapter), and he recognizes that to many readers, comic books are "crude, poorly-drawn, semiliterate, cheap, disposable kiddie fare" (3).

"The history of graphic novel adaptation is itself bedevilled by the idea that comics can introduce children to literature," notes Grennan ("Perhaps I'll Draw" 55). The impulse to adapt classics into graphic novels grows out of a comic book industry development that Albert Kanter initiated in 1941 with his Classics Illustrated comic book series. Kanter founded his series (originally called Classical Comics) as a gateway to the great books; he repackaged the classics in comic book form to appeal to young, reluctant readers. There are 169 titles in the series that ran from 1941–71 and had a huge fan base—2 to 4 million copies sold each month.[17] Classic story adaptation, a trademark of the comic book industry, paved the way for the current trend of adapting nineteenth-century novels into graphic novel format for a grown-up readership.

DC Comics began to target an audience of adult readers (many of whom were avid comic book readers from childhood) by publishing graphic novels about superheroes with mature content and high-quality visuals, notably Alan Moore's *Watchmen* (1986), with artwork by Dave Gibbons, and Frank Miller's *Batman: The Dark Knight Returns* (1986), with artwork by Klaus Janson. Art Spiegelman's author-illustrated, Pulitzer–Prize-winning graphic novel *Maus: A Survivor's Tale* (1986), a full-length story of the Holocaust, "permanently altered" the "graphic novel landscape" (Weiner 35). Suddenly there was a vast adult non-comics-reading public clamoring to read serious, in-depth graphic novels even though "its predecessor, the comic book, was the victim of a serious bad rap" (Van Ness 8).

With the 2015 graphic novel adaptation of Trollope's *John Caldigate* (*JC*, 1879) and recent manga-style adaptations of Austen's *Pride and Prejudice* (1813) and *Emma* (1816) by Udon Entertainment in 2014 and 2015, respectively, the popularity of the graphic classics shows no signs of abating. This chapter surveys graphic novel adaptation of nineteenth-century novels that originally appeared without illustrations or with few illustrations, the area of graphic classics most flourishing to date. Selected adaptations reveal how, in developing historical and psychological elements and topics improper for a Victorian middle-class readership, the graphic classics genre is rekindling the Victorian conception of illustration as revelatory—shedding light upon the text.[18] This chapter features graphic novel adaptations of two Victorian works that originally came out with illustrations—*Oliver Twist* (*OT*, 1838) and *Alice's Adventures in Wonderland* (*AA*, 1865)—to demonstrate how the graphic classics returns to and repurposes designs by those who first imagined these characters and scenes.

Many of Dickens's richly visual novels illustrated first by the caricaturists and then refashioned by Sixties artists are now reenvisioned by graphic novelists and artists. Graphic classics adaptations of Dickens's works surpass that of any other Victorian author. To date, there are graphic classics versions of *A Christmas Carol* (1843), *David Copperfield* (1850), *Oliver Twist*, *Great Expectations* (1861), and *A Tale of Two Cities* (1859). No title is more adapted than *Oliver Twist*. Although Carroll's *Through the Looking-Glass* (1872) has caught the graphic novelist's eye, there are more exciting adaptations of *Alice in Wonderland*. In graphic novel adaptations of *Oliver Twist* and *Alice in Wonderland*, we find reengagement with the schools of caricature and realism and the imprint of the original Victorian illustrators. Graphic novelists and artists revisit iconic illustrations and themes in the source texts, such as Cruikshank's caricature of the starving workhouse children in "Oliver Asking for More" and Alice's unstoppable growth motif drawn by Carroll in the caricature tradition for *Alice's Adventures Under Ground* (*UG*, 1864) and refined by John Tenniel for *Alice in Wonderland*. Most central to this chapter is *Fagin the Jew* (2003) in which Will Eisner intentionally revises Dickens and Cruikshank's persistent religious and ethnic stereotype of the Jew in *Oliver Twist*.

The Nineteenth-Century Graphic Canon

Graphic novel adaptations of nineteenth-century novels by publishers including Classical Comics, Marvel Comics, DC Comics, Dark Horse, Papercutz (an inheritor of Classics Illustrated), Barron's, Dynamite, and Campfire have brought new readers to works by canonical nineteenth-century authors. Russ Kick devotes an entire volume of *The Graphic Canon*, a three-volume anthology, to works published throughout the long nineteenth century.[19] Although Kick commissioned talented artists to adapt classics from the western canon ranging from the Bible and *The Odyssey* to *The Stranger* to show "a good deal of what comic art and illustration are capable of" (2: xii), his privileging of nineteenth-century literature for graphic novel adaptation is not surprising since literature from this period is richly descriptive and invites visualization. In "Steam Punk and the Visualization of the Victorian," Christine Ferguson notes that "by consistently calling on readers to see, look, and observe the scene being painted before them, canonical realist writers metaphorically aligned their novels with visual texts" (201).

Jane Austen's fiction has been ripe for graphic novel adaptation given her growing fan base, sparked in large part by film adaptations of her novels that have generated a multi-million dollar industry. In addition to graphic novel adaptations, there are kiddie-lit versions, supernatural variations, sequels and prequels, and consumer products ranging from high-end jewelry to dolls, magnets, even Band-Aids.[20] Marvel Comics launched the Marvel Illustrated imprint, which includes a line of graphic novel adaptations of Austen's works. First in the Marvel line came *Pride and Prejudice* in 2009, followed by *Sense and Sensibility* (1811) in 2011, *Emma* in 2012, and *Northanger Abbey* (1818) later in 2012.[21] Nancy Butler, a two-time RITA award winner[22] who adapted all four titles for Marvel, explains in her introduction to *Pride and Prejudice* that graphic artist Hugo Petrus "had a nice feel for historical eras"; for each of the five issues of *Pride and Prejudice* (later bound as one volume),[23] Petrus "would take my rough plot outlines and dash off loose gesture drawings before he sat down to do the pencil art. That way I could vet the artwork and make sure there was enough room in each panel for the oh-so-necessary Austen dialogue. It worked like a charm" (n. pag.).[24] In the Butler-Petrus collaboration, we see fluidity in the creation of a graphic novel that recalls how Victorian authors and illustrators worked closely and cooperatively to bring forth monthly installments of a serial novel.

Pride and Prejudice has the most graphic novel adaptations of all of Austen's novels.[25] Differences emerge among the text and graphics of the Marvel, Campfire, and Udon Entertainment adaptations; for example, Udon's *Pride and Prejudice*, scripted by Stacy King with art by Po-Tse, stylizes Regency dress to match *shōjo* manga romance style.[26] All three scriptwriters begin their adaptations by recalling one of the most well-known opening lines in all of English literature: "It is a truth universally acknowledged, that a single man in possession of a good fortune must be in want of a wife" (Austen 1). Austen is really saying the opposite: a dependent woman is in need of a man of fortune. Elizabeth Bennet, the novel's protagonist, and her four sisters must marry since Longbourn, the family estate, is entailed to Mr. Collins, their cousin. Elizabeth is not in need of a foolish husband, however, and she rightly rejects Mr. Collins's proposal of marriage.

In the Marvel version of *Pride and Prejudice*, artist Hugo Petrus includes details that visualize Mr. Collins's impossibility as a suitor. When Collins pompously proposes to Elizabeth and lists specific reasons for his offer of marriage, the

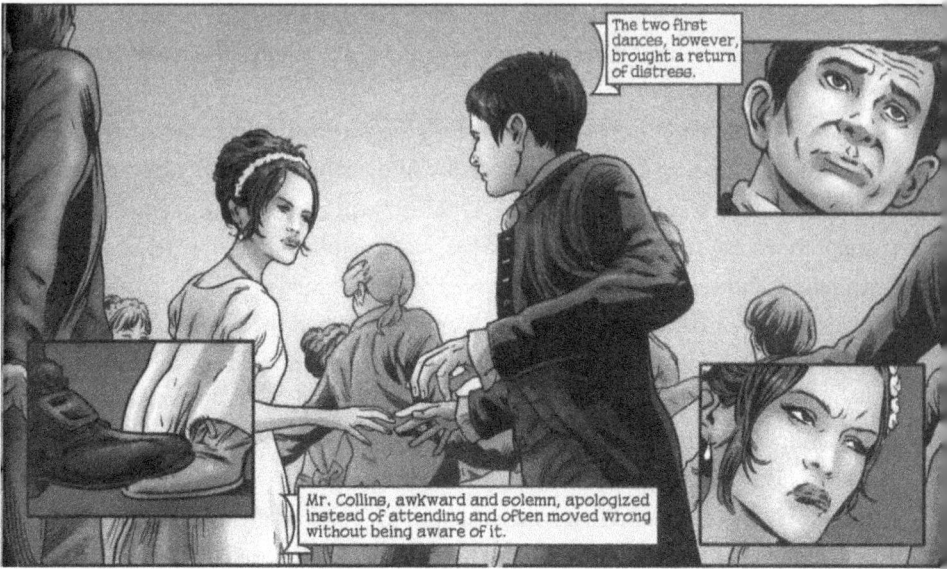

Figure 47. "Mr. Collins Dancing Poorly with Elizabeth." Artwork by Hugo Petrus for Nancy Butler's adaptation of *Pride and Prejudice*, 2010. © MARVEL.

graphics work additively with the text. Petrus pictures Collins holding up first one, then two fingers to designate each reason why he believes it is time for him to marry and Elizabeth Bennet is his choice. We can almost visualize silly Mr. Collins holding up a third finger to indicate the most important reason why he is proposing: "it is the particular advice and recommendation of the noble lady whom I have the honor of calling patroness" (Butler n. pag.).[27] Also noteworthy are three small inset panels within the frame of Elizabeth and Mr. Collins dancing—showing, respectively, Collins's large foot stepping on Elizabeth's dainty one, Elizabeth's look of displeasure, and Collins's clueless expression (see fig. 47). The caption inserted at the bottom of the panel reads: "Mr. Collins, awkward and solemn, apologized instead of attending and often moved wrong without being aware of it" (Butler n. pag.). In the left inset panel, Petrus zeroes in on Mr. Collins's large-buckled brown boot stepping firmly on Elizabeth's delicate slipper, magnifying his poor dancing skills. Unhappiness registers on Elizabeth's face both in the full panel and in the bottom right inset close-up of her face. Collins, in an inset panel in the top right of the page, looks completely puzzled that Elizabeth is not delighted to be his dance partner.

Reader-viewers are not surprised by her reaction. A ball was the prime time that a man and woman in Regency England could be together with a semblance of privacy since each dance lasted a half an hour, and decorum allowed a couple two dances. Stiff-limbed Mr. Collins dances without grace. Moreover, a man's skill on the dance floor was important to courting and an indicator of his sexual skill. Collins fails dismally in this regard, as the visual details in the frame and its three inset panels independently and cumulatively reveal.

The Campfire adaptation of *Pride and Prejudice* scripted by Laurence Sach and illustrated by Rajesh Nagulakonda teases out issues of social class snobbery of consequence to the marriage plot of Elizabeth Bennet and a desirable man of fortune, Mr. Darcy. Class tensions fly when Elizabeth defies Lady Catherine de Bourgh's threat never to enter into an engagement with Mr. Darcy (see fig. 48). Nagulakonda divides the full page into two vertical panels, one wide and the other narrow. Recalling the predilection of Sixties artists to focus on one or two figures, Nagulakonda uses close-ups of Elizabeth Bennet and Lady Catherine in both panels to intensify Lady Catherine's arrogance and Elizabeth's challenge to her conceit. In the larger panel, Lady Catherine de Bourgh (Mr. Collins's wealthy patroness) is positioned in three-quarter view, looking down her nose at Elizabeth. Lady Catherine wears an imperious looking hat while Elizabeth, out-of-doors without a hat, must angle her head upward to meet Lady Catherine's gaze.

Numerous close-ups of Elizabeth's and Lady Catherine's faces fill the narrow vertical panel, which takes the form of a verbal duel. In a word balloon on the top of the page, Lady Catherine declares: "Miss Bennet, I am shocked and astonished. I expected to find a more reasonable young woman" (Sach 97). In the next close-up, Lady Catherine adds insultingly in another word balloon, "Are the shades of Pemberley to be thus polluted?" (97); this line is a clever allusion to the penultimate paragraph of the source text where Lady Catherine condescends to visit Pemberley despite that "pollution" (Austen 476). As the language grows more heated, so do the faces of Lady Catherine and Elizabeth, who gazes downward at her social better, a gesture that challenges Lady Catherine's authority. Text and image work interdependently as Elizabeth's complexion flushes red, signaling anger, and she daringly declares to Lady Catherine: "I believe the world, in general, has too much sense to join in the scorn you speak of" (Sach 97).[28] Although the Campfire adaptation concludes in a two-page panel of a double wedding, Jane to Mr. Bingley and Elizabeth to Mr. Darcy, a small panel positioned below this happy wedding scene shows a defeated Lady Catherine entering the grounds of Pemberley. Joyous smiles and wedding bells in the top panel illustrate the limits of social class snobbery and celebrate romance.[29]

Charlotte Brontë's *Jane Eyre* and Emily Brontë's *Wuthering Heights* (*WH*),

Figure 48. "Lady Catherine and Elizabeth Bennet in a Verbal Duel." Artwork by Rajesh Nagulakonda for Laurence Sach's adaptation of *Pride and Prejudice*, 2013. © Campfire 2014.

both published in 1847 without illustrations, appear in graphic novel formats by Barron's Graphic Classics and Classical Comics. Given Barron's emphasis on young and reluctant readers, this series, not surprisingly, modernizes and abridges the Brontë sisters' works to make them more student-friendly.[30] The 2009 Barron's adaptation of *Wuthering Heights*, retold by Jim Pipe and illustrated by Nick Spender, waters down Emily Brontë's metaphorical language, although it does include a few of the most memorable lines, such as Catherine's famous declaration, "I *am* Heathcliff—he's always, always on my mind" (Pipe 17). Both Brontë novels in the Classical Comics Original Text version are longer than the Barron's adaptations and include much more of the original dialogue written by Emily and Charlotte Brontë, respectively.[31] Scriptwriters Amy Corzine and Seán Michael Wilson interpret the source texts, using flashbacks and dreams to bring a visual dimension to the psychological and supernatural dimensions of, respectively, *Jane Eyre* and *Wuthering Heights*, both illustrated by John Burns.

The Classical Comics Original Text adaptation of *Jane Eyre* uses text and graphics interdependently to illustrate Charlotte Brontë's compelling interest in psychic phenomena that gained force in reaction to the rise of empiricism, skepticism, and scientism in the nineteenth century that challenged religious truths (Dickerson 773–74).[32] Dreams for Charlotte Brontë serve both as presentiments and glimpses into the unconscious. Jane famously foresees the burning of Thornfield Hall in her prophetic dreams in chapter 25 of the source text of *Jane Eyre*, even though she is currently unaware that the arsonist is Rochester's mysterious mad wife locked in the attic. This dream occurs just before the scene where Jane wakes to find "a woman, tall and large, with thick dark hair" and a "savage face," ripping Jane's veil and trampling upon it (C. Brontë 242). Most scenes in the Corzine graphic novel adaptation are in color, which designates the present, but the backgrounds and figures in the dream sequence are bluish-gray, which indicates a dream state.

The first frame of this two-panel dream sequence (see fig. 49) shows Jane's dream in a thought bubble looming over her head as she sleeps, so we simultaneously see Jane sleeping and dreaming. In the dream, Jane stands in front of Rochester (who is positioned behind a brick wall) and holds a baby swaddled in blankets. In the adjacent panel (comprised entirely of her dream), Rochester's mansion, Thornfield Hall, is in ruins; adhering to the source text, Jane drops the baby, and they both tumble down a hill. A gutter, a necessary aspect of graphic storytelling, creates a sense of timing in between these two sequential panels to signal Jane is moving deeper into her dream. A caption that cuts across and connects the two panels reads: "The hurry of preparation for the bridal day,

Figure 49. "Jane Eyre's Prophetic Dream." Artwork by John M. Burns for Amy Corzine's *Jane Eyre: The Graphic Novel*, 2008. © Classical Comics Ltd.

and the anticipation of the great change made me feverish. One night, when Mr. Rochester was absent from home, my anxious excitement continued in dreams" (Corzine 80). Jane's dreams are a manifestation of her "anxious excitement," but the wailing child also foretells the destruction of Jane's psyche. The baby in the second panel of the dream sequence, its mouth open as if to cry, arguably symbolizes Jane's former self that she fears losing when she becomes Mrs. Rochester.[33] The head of the baby approaches the gutter while the figure of Rochester on a horse rides into the moonlit night. Using dreaming and alternating color palettes, Burns also foreshadows Bertha's burning of Thornfield Hall, which Jane foresees.

The most striking scene in the Classical Comics Original Text adaptation of *Wuthering Heights* also involves a psychic twist. Mr. Lockwood, the novel's first narrator, journeys from the neighboring Thrushcross Grange to pay a call upon his landlord, the inhospitable Heathcliff, living at Wuthering Heights. Forced to spend the night at Wuthering Heights due to harrowing weather, Lockwood finds himself in the childhood bedroom of Catherine Earnshaw, Heathcliff's soulmate who marries Edgar Linton, former owner of the Grange. This scene is as notable for its presentation of Catherine's subversive writing in the margins of her Bible as it is for the supernatural return of Catherine Earnshaw Linton. Catherine's ghost wakes Lockwood from a dream following his discovery of Catherine's scribbles on the windowsill of her room and in the margins of her Bible, placements that underscore her marginal place in a gendered world.

The entire sequence unfolds in twenty-three panels in this adaptation. Wilson and Burns show Lockwood falling asleep after discovering "Catherine Earnshaw, varied to Catherine Heathcliff, and again to Catherine Linton" on the windowsill (S. M. Wilson, *WH* 17). In the next panel (see fig. 50), the words "CATHERINE CATHERINE CATHERINE" appear in a swirling pattern "vivid as spectres" (18) in a midnight blue light, surrounding Lockwood and waking him from his dream. Three panels later, Lockwood begins to peruse Catherine's Bible, which contains disconnected sentences and entire diary entries in the margins. Wilson and Burns use a montage effect, so the reader-viewer can see Catherine's writing within the pages of the Bible, which Emily Brontë describes as "faded hieroglyphics" (*WH* 38). Catherine's writing is not "faded" in this interpretation, but it is in a different font, creating a collage effect. The following panels are flashbacks depicting what Catherine writes in the margins of her Bible, such as how she and Heathcliff defy the tyrannical old servant Joseph when he preaches a three-hour sermon in the cold garret of Wuthering Heights.

Sound effects work additively in the next sequence where Lockwood falls into another dream. The "fire" of Catherine's spirit returns as a specter and repeatedly cries to be let back into the house: "Let me in! Let me in! . . . I'm come home . . . Let me in!" (S. M. Wilson 20–21). Onomatopoeic words "tap tap tap" and "SMASH," inserted directly into the panels, bring vivid sounds to this dream vision. Lockwood, unable to release the casement window, smashes the glass to seize the tapping branch, which turns into the "fingers of a little ice-cold hand!" (20). Catherine's "ice-cold hand" becomes covered with blood in the following frames when Lockwood, as the source text dictates, "pulled its wrist on to the broken pane, and rubbed it to and fro till the blood ran down and soaked the bed-clothes: still it wailed, 'Let me in!' and maintained its tenacious gripe" (*WH* 42). Akin to the prophetic dream sequence of *Jane Eyre*, swirling letters, flashbacks, dreams, and authentic dialogue work interdependently to make this supernatural visitation as real as the red blood that drips down Catherine's icy cold hand in a chilling scene that haunts Heathcliff and the entire novel.

Adaptations of Dickens's *A Christmas Carol* (*CC*) even more dramatically

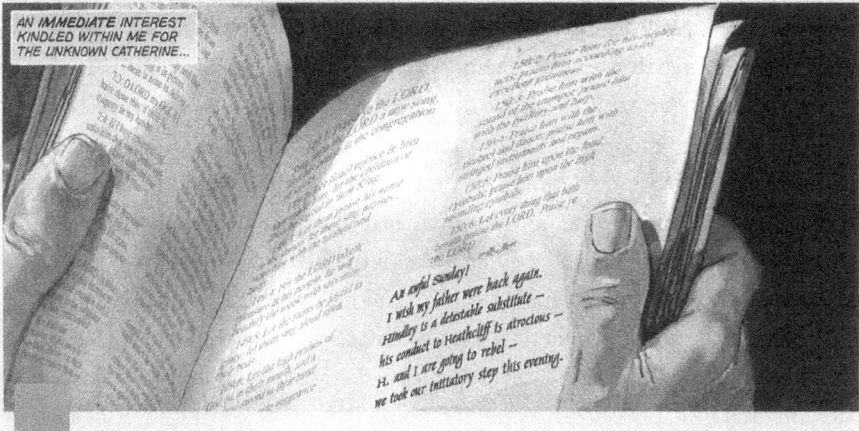

Figure 50. "Catherine Earnshaw's Bible." Artwork by John M. Burns for Seán Michael Wilson's *Wuthering Heights: The Graphic Novel*, 2011. © Classical Comics Ltd.

use swirling letters, onomatopoeic words, and sound effects to enhance the supernatural element of Scrooge's ghostly visitations.[34] The Classical Comics Original Text version of *A Christmas Carol* (nominated by the *Sunday Times* as one of the top best graphic novels of 2008) expands the visual dimension of Dickens's pure text, which originally appeared with eight illustrations by caricaturist John Leech. This version adapted by Seán Michael Wilson and illustrated by Mike Collins uses a combination of close-ups, long shots, and full-page panels to give chilling resonance to Jacob Marley's famous line drawn from the source text: "'I wear the chain I forged in life, . . . I made it link by link, and yard by yard'" (Dickens, CC 30). Whereas Leech draws the ghost of Scrooge's former partner, Jacob Marley, wearing a substantial chain in the original illustration, Collins in "Marley's Ghost" (see fig. 51) expands the white chain that drapes over and over him and literally rises out of the page and surrounds Marley's figure, rendered in an eerie blue that gives off a supernatural glow. Sound effects—particularly the double repetition of "CLANK" in this panel and other onomatopoeic words such as "RATTLE," "CHINK," "OOOOHH-HHH!" and "OOAARGH!" (S. M. Wilson, CC 35)—work interdependently with the graphics to illustrate the length and weight of Marley's fetters. The intensity of Marley's sufferings awakens greedy Scrooge to stop saying "Humbug," embrace the visits of three spirits, and change his fate.

There are numerous adaptations of fin-de-siècle novels that originally appeared without illustrations. In "The Graphic Novel and the Age of Transition," Tabachnick surveys, for example, adaptations of Oscar Wilde's *The Picture of Dorian Gray* (1891), Robert Louis Stevenson's *Dr. Jekyll and Mr. Hyde* (1886), and H. G. Wells's *The Time Machine* (1895). The 2008 Marvel Illustrated adaptation of *Dorian Gray*, scripted by Roy Thomas with artwork by Sebastian Fiumara, does not even attempt to translate the novel's lengthy philosophical passages, but in adapting Wilde to this new medium, Fiumara expands the scenes with Sybil Vane, the actress who initially captivates Dorian with her performance of *Romeo and Juliet*. While the Marvel adaptation of *Dorian Gray* does not develop the novel's homosexual subtext, another 2009 adaptation by Graphic Classics, scripted by Alex Burrows with artwork by Lisa K. Weber, develops Lord Henry's influence over Dorian through the graphic medium, such as in the frames where Lord Henry Wotton and Dorian stand next to a statue of a male nude in Basil Hallward's garden where they first meet. In one panel, Dorian sits on the base of the nude and leans on his arm as he gazes enthrallingly at the aristocrat, who seduces Dorian with his hedonistic view of life. The caption reads enticingly, "Lord Henry's languid voice slowly unfolded

Figure 51. "Marley's Ghost." Script by Seán Michael Wilson, pencils by Mike Collins, inks by David Roach, and colors by James Offredi for *A Christmas Carol: The Graphic Novel*, 2008. © Classical Comics Ltd.

life's mysteries to Dorian" (9). Lord Henry's body language is even more important than the words he speaks in a word balloon—"So remember, the only thing worth pursuing in life is beauty and a fulfillment of the senses!" (9). Lord Henry leans into his cane and extends his right arm and leg toward Dorian, whose eyes lock with his. This plate visualizes how Lord Henry has instantly captivated Dorian Gray, who, under the influence of his decadent friend, will explore every vice and destroy himself and others in the process.

A related development to the nineteenth-century graphic classics is the popular Neo-Victorian graphic novel, which draws heavily upon literary and historical characters from fin-de-siècle novels. There are three principal types of the Neo-Victorian graphic novel. In one type, an adaptor builds a new storyline from characters of Victorian novels, such as in the Eisner-award winning *The League of Extraordinary Gentlemen* (1999), written by Alan Moore and illustrated by Kevin O'Neill. Alternately, Neo-Victorian adaptations inspired by Victorian history include the heavily footnoted yet fictional *From Hell* (1991) about the origins of Jack the Ripper, written by Alan Moore and illustrated by Eddie Campbell, and *Gotham by Gaslight* (1989), a DC Comics adaptation written by Brian Augustyn and illustrated by Mike Mignola that merges Jack the Ripper with Batman. Neo-Victorian graphic novels in a third category bring contemporary superheroes face to face with characters from nineteenth-century novels; DC Comics published two prime examples in 2011—*Batman: Through the Looking Glass*, written by Bruce Jones with artwork by Sam Kieth, and *Batman: Noël*, adapted and illustrated by Lee Bermejo.

More than any other Neo-Victorian graphic novel, *The League of Extraordinary Gentlemen*, first published as a six-issue comic series in 1999, "fuses almost every late-Victorian literary character that students have ever heard of into a monstrously inclusive plot" (Ferguson 204). In this novel set in 1898, Victorian characters become "superheroes" fighting injustice. The league includes Robert Louis Stevenson's divided man, the respected Dr. Henry Jekyll and the infamous Edward Hyde; Bram Stoker's Mina Harker from *Dracula* (1897), who joins with her fiancé to bring down Count Dracula; Jules Verne's Captain Nemo, the mysterious antihero from *Twenty Thousand Leagues Under the Sea* (1870), who is motivated to fight the evils of British imperialism; Griffin, the scientist from H. G. Wells's science-fiction novella *The Invisible Man* (1897), who develops a body to absorb (rather than reflect) light to appear invisible; and H. Rider Haggard's Allan Quatermain, a big-game hunter from *King Solomon's Mines* (1885), who remains sensitive to the native Africans in the midst of Britain's "civilizing influence." *The League* thus allows reader-viewers to experience intertextuality—not between a canonical work and its graphic novel adaption as in editions of *Oliver Twist* or *Jane Eyre*, but among fin-de-siècle works joined in a fictional context.

The cover of the first issue of *The League of Extraordinary Gentlemen* illustrates the dark side of the late British Empire in arranging fin-de-siècle fictional characters as Victorian superheroes against a backdrop of portraits, paintings, and sculptures. A headless but elegant ancient statue, a skull, and a painting of a skeleton lying on its back symbolize the duality of the late Victorian era—a time that was elegant and alive, yet simultaneously deadly and deadened as these images show. Among framed portraits of respectable gentlemen on the wall hang, for example, a picture of a native, likely from one of Britain's colonial holdings, and a painting of an elephant in chains in an exotic setting; these graphics visualize the ugliness of the imperialistic British Empire at century's end that Captain Nemo fights against. Hyde, whose hideous face appears behind that of Dr. Jekyll, highlights simultaneously how darkness lies within members of the League of Extraordinary Gentlemen as well as in the Empire that the league's members vow to protect.

Batman: Noël combines aspects of Bob Kane and Bill Finger's renowned American superhero and Gotham City from DC Comics with elements of Dickens's *A Christmas Carol* and Victorian London. In his dedication, author-illustrator Lee Bermejo aptly writes, "With respect, to Charles Dickens." Moreover, the letterer, Todd Klein maintains an authenticity to Dickens's classic by bringing "a turn-of-the-century Victorian twist to the proceedings with his sharp, succinct chiseled fonts" (Jim Lee qtd. in Bermejo n. pag.). Bermejo casts Batman in the role of Ebenezer Scrooge, but the character looks like the Dark Knight rather than the Dickensian Scrooge. Bermejo favors dark variations of the caped crusader's costume, but includes the most distinctive elements of Batman imagery—the cowl (covering most of the face) with its distinguishing bat-like ears, the stylized bat emblem across the chest of the bat suit, the cape, the utility belt, and the gauntlet-style gloves. Bob Cratchit works for Scrooge/Batman in this adaptation and has a very ill son appropriately named Tim after Tiny Tim and Tim Drake (the third Robin). With a contemporary comic book twist, the three ghosts who visit Batman/Scrooge are also comic book legends—Catwoman, the Ghost of Christmas Past; Superman, the Ghost of Christmas Present; and the Joker, the Ghost of Christmas Future. Bermejo notes in a commentary that he cast Batman as Scrooge to "emphasize the change from the lighthearted Batman of the past to the darker, violent vigilante of today. This of course mirrored the narrative structure of A CHRISTMAS CAROL as well" (Bermejo n. pag.).

Change is possible even for the most unlikely vigilante, who, in this graphic novel, gets a second chance just as Scrooge does. Batman/Scrooge brings down the Joker, saves Cratchit from dabbling in crime by giving him "A raise, benefits, P.T.O, 401(k), the works" (Bermejo n. pag.), and brings Christmas cheer to Tim Cratchit and "Old friends, business associates, pretty much anyone whose life he'd previously made miserable" (n. pag.). Bermejo's dialogue cleverly updates Dickens's work for readers of the twenty-first century, although the pictures confirm that Scrooge still rewards Cratchit with a prize turkey as in the source text.

Bermejo alternates long shots with close-ups to create a stunning cinematic effect enhanced by boldly lettered sound effects that leap off the pages along with Batman/Scrooge. As DC Comics copublisher and renowned comic book artist Jim Lee notes in the foreword, "Lee [Bermejo]'s neo Gothic work operates on the surface level to entice and please while painting a darker, more disturbing world just underneath that very same scintillating surface" (Bermejo n. pag.). Scrooge's tomb in a chilly, gray-toned graveyard (see fig. 52) displays Batman's secret identity as the caped crusader: "Here lies a bat. He died boring predictable and nobody loved him!" (n. pag.). The sky looks bleak, the trees are bare, and snow covers the ground. Bermejo draws a black-and-gray toned costumed Batman/Scrooge literally climbing out of the grave, clawing the ground, and pushing aside snow and rubble as he vows, "Sometimes it takes dyin' . . . . . . to teach a fella how ta LIVE" (n. pag.). In this plate, Batman's determination to escape death extends from the angle of his pointed bat ears to his exposed chiseled jaw and gritted teeth. With one of his massive muscled arms, Batman/Scrooge seemingly pulls himself up from the grave. With the other arm and gloved hand, he reaches toward the reader-viewer and beyond the picture plane—a gesture that signals the dark vigilante will shed his underworld darkness and once again become the more lighthearted caped crusader of early Batman comics, saving the Cratchits in the process.

Although this graphic mash-up might offend the sensibilities of Victorian purists, some graphic classics adopt a literary tone, such as the 2015 adaptation of *John Caldigate*, commissioned by Cardiff University and KU Leuven (a Belgian University) to celebrate the bicentennial of Anthony Trollope's birth. Trollope was a prolific and popular Victorian author whose novels capture clerical life, the politics of the middle-class Victorian drawing room, and the political arena. *John Caldigate*, a lesser-known Trollope novel, has been adapted as

Figure 52. "Nobody Loved Him." Illustration by Lee Bermejo for his *Batman: Noël*, 2011. © DC Comics.

Dispossession (2015), translated as *Courir deux lièvres* for the French version (To run two hares).[35] Scriptwriter and graphic artist Simon Grennan transformed a lengthy novel of over 500 pages with no illustrations into a 94-page graphic novel with 576 separate color images; not surprisingly, the adaptation is subtitled *A Novel of Few Words*.

Originally published in *Blackwood's Magazine* from April 1878 to June 1879, *John Caldigate* follows the life of a seemingly unpromising Cambridge graduate. The eponymous hero chooses between "the ties of land, entail and good stewardship and the appeal of risk and speculation" (xv), notes R. C.

Terry in the introduction to the 1995 Folio Society edition commissioned with sixteen illustrations by Francis Mosley.[36] Caldigate dispossesses himself of his title and the prospect of an inherited estate at Folking to pay off his gambling debts; receiving ready money by selling his entail to his father, Caldigate heads to Australia on a ship called the *Goldfinder*, promptly finds gold, and subsequently returns to England a rich man. Reuniting with his father, Caldigate marries a genteel English woman, Hester Bolton, and lives happily ever after until his Australian past rears its head in the form of a bigamy charge leveled by Euphemia Smith, the widowed adventuress Caldigate meets on his voyage.

Mrs. Smith who "had seen better days . . . was now going out to the colony, probably—so the old lady said who was the informant—in search of a second husband" (Trollope, *JC* 32). In "Performing the Voyage Out," Janet C. Meyers suggests that Mrs. Euphemia Smith magnifies "the single middle-class woman's precarious liminality in relation to home and colony" (131). Caldigate lives with Euphemia Smith in the mining town of Ahalala but never marries her; perhaps owing to the pressures of Mudie's Lending Library or his own morals,[37] Trollope never tells the reader they have been living together until Mrs. Smith returns to England and makes a legal claim on Caldigate, now married to Hester. Jailed for bigamy, Caldigate earns a royal pardon when the postage stamp and postmark on a letter that he allegedly sends to a Mrs. John Caldigate (Euphemia Smith) turns out to be a forgery. As Eileen Cleere observes in *Avuncularism*, "blackmail replaces bigamy in the novel's economy of crimes" (201).

In "Perhaps I'll Draw and You Complete the Story . . . ," Grennan explains how he adapted Trollope's novel for a twenty–first-century readership. "Little is ever described in detail," notes Grennan; "Rather, Trollope is both accurate and equivocal. 'Perhaps,' he writes, or 'it was said of.' He provides readers with various points of view, never strictly his own, and we make our own sense of them" (55). Grennan gives graphic expression to Trollope's "equivocal" style through what he describes as "visual techniques of unambiguous ambiguity that I developed in my set of rules for drawing the book" (Interview with Grennan). Using a consistent six-panel format, Grennan places the characters at various distances from the reader-viewer and in different types of tableaux, and from these positions the reader-viewer can see all the dimensions of the novel and complete the story.[38]

Building upon an historical dimension intimated in *John Caldigate*, Grennan innovatively develops Aboriginal and Chinese presences in the Australian gold rush an element that Trollope only hints at. For the scenes set in the mining towns of New South Wales, Grennan depicts the Aborigines both clothed and naked. The Australian natives dominate these frames that include 700 words of Wiradjuri, an Aboriginal language also not included in the original novel. The presence of the Chinese and Aborigines in Australia would not have been widely known to Trollope's contemporary readers, but Grennan depends upon today's readers to be knowledgeable about this period of Australia's history.[39] Conversely, notes Grennan, "Trollope's first readers had knowledge and experience unavailable to us in the 21st century, on which he relied. The meaning of Smith's straw hat and Dick's yellow trousers (Ned's in *Dispossession*) are the most obvious examples" (Interview with Grennan). To Trollope's Victorian reader-viewers, clothes and hats spoke to social class and propriety.

Upon his return to England, Dick Shand, Caldigate's first mining partner, has reformed his ways—he is no longer a gambler or an alcoholic—but he still has bush manners and wears roughly made yellow trousers "of strong material, and in good order, made of that colour for colonial use" (Trollope, *JC* 381). Trollope dwells on the yellow trousers, which he correlates with Shand's equally glaring conduct: "His yellow trousers and the manners which accompanied them were not generally acceptable in merchants' offices and suchlike places" (495). The yellow pants—the same color of sturdy cloth worn by Australian convicts (Meyers 141)—mark Dick (aka Ned) as an outsider in his homeland. Grennan uses a more brilliant color palette for the prodigal son's pants than for the clothes of the other English gentlemen and employs the yellow trousers as a motif foreshadowing Shand's return voyage to Australia at the close of the novel. Caldigate loans his former partner (who helps to exonerate him) the capital to return to Queensland and establish himself as a junior partner of a sugar plantation.

To Trollope's first readers, the description of Mrs. Euphemia Smith's straw hat—part of a "Dolly Varden" style of dress visualized by Phiz in the illustrations for Dickens's historical novel *Barnaby Rudge* (1841)—independently would have signaled that although the widow is attempting to act innocent, she is anything but that. Phiz drew this popular Dickensian character, known for her flirtatiousness and flashy dress as much as for her disingenuousness, on a series of separate plates to accompany the novel. Dolly Varden also found her way onto canvas most famously in an 1842 oil painting entitled *Dolly Varden* by William Powell Frith where Dolly sports a straw hat with red ribbons and a rich red cape, details that Grennan consciously recalls for Mrs. Smith's wardrobe in *Dispossession*.

Trollope first points out Mrs. Smith, who shares Caldigate and Shand's second-class accommodations on board ship, via a reference to her straw hat. In the source text, Shand says to Caldigate, "'Have you observed that woman in the brown straw hat?'" (*JC* 31); Caldigate replies, "'She struck me as talking better than her gown, if you know what I mean'" (32). Trollope's Victorian readers would have known exactly what Trollope means—that Mrs. Smith is a consummate actress, and she is acting above her second-class berth, believing she would be better suited in first class. Grennan consistently pictures Mrs. Smith in a ribbonless straw hat, but tilted in the manner of the Phiz and Frith depictions; we see her in this hat on the voyage out, in the diggings in Australia, and on her return to England to press bigamy charges. Only in the two panels where she gets into a fistfight with Caldigate at Ahalala does her trademark hat tumble to the ground (Grennan, *D* 52).

Of particular interest, too, is Grennan's decision to depict Mrs. Smith sailing back to Australia as the final wordless panel of the graphic novel, whereas the source text ends with the sentencing of Mrs. Smith to three years of hard labor for forgery (see fig. 53). Critic Janet Meyers reads this verdict as a defeat of the imperial project's aim to make new identities available to emigrant women through colonization: "By making literal Mrs. Smith's superfluous position in relation to the nation through her marginalization within the confines of a prison, Trollope implies that emigration, like transportation, had failed to stabilize the empire or to reform convicts or settlers" (142). Meyers also laments the defeat of Mrs. Smith as a character, noting Dick Shand can find "success in the colony as a partner on a sugar estate. For Euphemia Smith no such recuperation is possible, either in Britain or in Australia" (141).

Grennan takes a more optimistic approach to Mrs. Smith's fate. Grennan explains:

> Trollope also hints at respect for Mrs. Smith, in that, although she is described as degraded, vulgar and criminal by the end of the book, he makes no mention of the fate of the remainder of the £20K that Caldigate has given to her, Crinkett, Smith and Adamson. She is imprisoned with hard labour for fraud for three years, but the money awaits her/their release. She will exit prison a rich woman. So I sought to make Mrs. Smith's position even more equivocal in *Dispossession*, plausibly having a jury acquit her of the envelope forgery as she continues to protest that she and Caldigate were married. The reader of *Dispossession*, as *John Caldigate*, never knows the truth of the matter. (Interview with Grennan)

Figure 53. The final panel from *Dispossession*. Illustration by Simon Grennan for his *Dispossession*, 2015. London: Jonathan Cape, p. 100.

The final wordless panel of a slyly smiling Mrs. Smith on board a ship—still wearing her faux innocent straw hat and red dress, but now draped in a fur wrap to indicate her presumed wealth—successfully translates Trollope's equivocation. Mrs. Smith may suffer, as Trollope suggests in her reaction to her prison sentence in the source text, but there is no evidence that she will not ultimately come out victorious as Grennan elects to show her in the last plate.

Critical and popular interest in this adaptation of *John Caldigate* even before its publication makes it intriguing to imagine graphic classics of more of Trollope's forty-seven novels. John Everett Millais's illustrations for Trollope's works may prove as influential to graphic novel adaptations as the original illustrations of *Oliver Twist* and *Alice in Wonderland* already have.

Oliver Twist and the Graphic Novel's Reengagement with and Revision of a Persistent Caricature of Fagin the Jew

Will Eisner contends in his introduction that *Fagin the Jew* (*FTJ*) "is not an adaptation of *Oliver Twist*! It is the story of Fagin the Jew" (*FTJ* 4). However, this graphic novel is a reimagining of *Oliver Twist* in which Fagin is the lead character. With the mission of humanizing a Jewish stereotype, Eisner gives Fagin a sympathetic past; parents, Abraham and Rachael; and a first name, Moses—names all drawn from the Old Testament. The first half of *Fagin the Jew* envisions the life of Dickens's Fagin before the novel begins, and the second half adapts *Oliver Twist* from Fagin's perspective.

"Upon examining the illustrations of the original editions of *Oliver Twist*," recalls Eisner in his introduction to the graphic novel,

> I found unquestionable examples of visual defamation in classic literature. The memory of their awful use by the Nazis in World War II, one hundred years later, added evidence to the persistence of evil stereotypes. Combating that became an obsessive pursuit, and I realized that I had no choice but to undertake a truer portrait of Fagin by telling his life story in the only way I could. (*FTJ* 4)

Eisner offers a sympathetic "portrait" of Fagin's life story. To Brian Bendis, a recognized comic book writer in his own right,

> Will took his complicated feelings about race and caricature and applied them directly to his feelings about Judaism and how Jews have been reflected in the media for hundreds of years, by sinking his teeth directly into the classic *Oliver Twist* and one of the most famous Jewish stereotype characters in all of fiction . . . Fagin." (2)

Two experiences influenced Eisner's commitment to raise awareness of how still-existing religious prejudice against the Jewish people historically turned Jews into a stereotype that Dickens propagates in his novel.[40] Eisner grew uncomfortable with his own racist caricature of an African-American, Ebony, an amusing counterfoil to the Spirit in his syndicated comic *The Spirit* created in 1940 at a time when comics had many racial stereotypes akin to Eisner's. Further, during World War II, Eisner, who was Jewish, confronted horrific anti-Semitism firsthand.

Eisner frames the graphic novel as a conversation between Moses Fagin and his creator, Charles Dickens, set on the night before Fagin is to hang. The opening full-page panel depicts Dickens and Moses Fagin, who sits in a corner of his prison cell and pleads with Dickens to present a more compassionate portrayal of him. Fagin says in a word balloon (in a font that approximates handwritten, capital letters that carries throughout the entire script): "Tarry a bit, Mister Dickens, while ol' Fagin here tells you, Sir, what I really was and how it all came to be!!" (*FTJ* 5). Moses is now a bearded old man who looks tired and worn out. Dickens's face is not visible, and Dickens does not speak in this scene. Eisner never shows Dickens's face in this panel or the closing panels that frame the graphic novel and also take place in Fagin's prison cell. In these final scenes, Fagin defies his creator: "I've asked you here to confront a man you wrongfully portrayed! One who will soon be swinging lifeless in that yard! . . . Doomed to wear for eternity that warped and evil image!" (112). Eisner, speaking through Fagin, also challenges Dickens's anti-Semitic portrayal of Jews in the final panel (before the epilogue): "A Jew is not Fagin any more than a gentile is Sikes" (114). Dickens, with his back to the reader-viewer, replies somewhat sympathetically as he exits the prison cell: "Goodbye, old Fagin . . . er, oh, in my later books I'll treat your race more evenly!" (114). This line likely refers to Dickens's kinder treatment of the Jewish "race" in his characterization of Mr. Riah, a benevolent Jewish moneylender, in his last completed novel, *Our Mutual Friend* (1865).

Eisner notes in the appendix that even though Dickens insisted he was not anti-Semitic, there exists ample evidence of anti-Jewish remarks and epithets in Dickens's letters and conversations (123). Jewish civil rights activists wrote to Dickens in the 1850s, asking him to present a fairer representation of the Jews. Eliza Davis, wife of a Jewish banker in London, wrote a letter of complaint to Dickens, asking him to eliminate this ethnic profiling for *Oliver Twist's* republication in an 1867 edition. Davis, according to critic Jeet Heer, upbraided Dickens because the author does not identify his Christian villains by their religion, and "to identify Fagin constantly as a Jew was to conflate him with all Jews" (*FTJ* 131). Davis and Dickens engaged in spirited communication through the post, and Davis apparently influenced Dickens, who eliminated most of the references to Fagin as a "Jew" for the 1867 edition. To Eisner, Dickens's revision "was too late, for the earlier and well-distributed editions still in use today contain the original text that uses 'Jew' to refer to Fagin" (*FTJ* 124). Hence, Eisner wrote and illustrated *Fagin the Jew*.

Eisner openly declares his aim to remediate an offensive literary and visual anti-Semitic stereotype in a book whose popularity endures:

It has always troubled me that Fagin "the Jew" never got fair treatment, and I challenge Charles Dickens and his illustrator, George Cruikshank, for their description and delineation of Fagin as a classic stereotypical Jew. I believe this depiction was based on ill-considered evidence, imitation, and popular ignorance." (*FTJ* 124)

Dickens in many ways perpetuated a stereotype that grew out of "centuries of Christian mythmaking, while reflecting ideas that still permeated British society at that time," notes Heer (131), but Dickens gave this racialized stereotype lasting life. Dickens introduces Fagin as "a very old shriveled Jew, whose villainous-looking and repulsive face was obscured by a quantity of matted red hair. He was dressed in a greasy flannel gown, with his throat bare" (*OT*, Oxf. 1982 50). Dickens does not reveal any particulars about Fagin's past and simply names him "a receiver of stolen goods" (xxv) in his 1841 preface to the third edition of *Oliver Twist*.

As I have argued elsewhere, Dickens initially makes Fagin a nurturing character, a quality that would be reassuring to his middle-class readers[41]—for example, Fagin provides Oliver with food and shelter. But over the course of the novel, Fagin's disturbing qualities far outnumber any good deed he does. Fagin's character in Dickens's source text grows dark when he colludes with Monks, Oliver's twisted half brother; in time, the "merry old gentleman" (*OT*, Oxf. 1982 53)—itself a reference to the devil[42]—becomes simply "the Jew."[43] "If we accept Dickens's description of Fagin as 'the Jew,'" notes Heer,

> then what conclusions can we draw from reading *Oliver Twist*? The Jew is filthy, the Jew is a criminal, the Jew is a corruptor of children, the Jew values money more than human relations, the Jew is linked with poison, the Jew is a Judas-like betrayer, the Jew is an animal, the Jew is a murderer, the Jew is the Devil. In sum, a large part of what makes Fagin's character so oppressively unforgettable is that he combines in one package centuries of loathsome anti-Semitic stereotypes. (130)

Through the character of Fagin, this anti-Semitic "package" endures.

In *Fagin the Jew*, Eisner imagines a compelling personal history to change this perception of Fagin as an animalistic, dirty, betraying, greedy thief who corrupts children. Eisner elucidates Fagin's past and why he must turn to crime in order to survive. We meet Moses Fagin as a child, an immigrant from Bohemia, who arrives in nineteenth-century England with his parents, Abraham and Rachael, during the second wave of Jewish immigration. Moses's father believes

"England is a tolerant country" (*FTJ* 10), but anti-Semites cruelly murder him. Rachael Fagin dies soon after. Moses finds a kindly benefactor in Eleazor Salomon, who takes orphan Moses into his home as a houseboy and then finds him a job to clean a school for poor Jewish children opened by a Jewish philanthropist named Emmanuel Lopez. Losing his job due to a misunderstanding involving Lopez's daughter Rebecca, Moses Fagin, who is polite and hardworking, finds himself on the streets. Wrongfully accused of a crime, Fagin is deported to Australia, where Dickens sends many undesirables in his fiction, including Abel Magwitch of *Great Expectations* (1861) and the Artful Dodger of *Oliver Twist.*

Eisner takes not only Dickens but also George Cruikshank to task, noting how

> Cartoonists certainly understand how easy it is to rely on a common image in the visual language to portray a character, but like the mistakes of illustrators before him, Cruikshank's misuse of a necessary staple in portraying Fagin, one that was so common to contemporary publications, is a contribution to further reprehensible stereotyping of Jews by bigots throughout history. (*FTJ* app. 124)

Cruikshank draws upon the accepted visual stereotype of the Jew established by cartoonists before him, evident in Thomas Rowlandson's etching "A Jew Broker" (1789). Cruikshank makes Fagin look like a Sephardic Jew, the first group of Jews to immigrate to England seeking refuge from the Spanish inquisition, as opposed to an Ashkenazic Jew of the second wave of emigration from Germany and Eastern European countries in the 1800s. "The popular illustrations of Jews," notes Eisner, "including Cruikshank's, were based on the appearance of the Sephardim, whose features, when they arrived, were sharper, with dark hair and complexions, the result of their four-hundred-year sojourn among the Latin and Mediterranean peoples" (app. 125).[44]

Eisner remediates Cruikshank's "greasy flannel-gowned" Fagin, whose pronounced nose repulsively extends to his top lip, and makes him an Ashkenazic Jew with a pleasing appearance. Young Moses Fagin has a small nose, sensitive eyes, and a well-developed physique (see fig. 54). Cleaning the school for Jewish children, Fagin wears fitted pants that cling to his muscular thighs; his rolled-up shirtsleeves show off his biceps. Eisner's Moses Fagin is also attractive to women, including wealthy Rebecca Lopez, whose father owns the school he cleans. When Moses forgets his class status and kisses Rebecca, Emmanuel Lopez throws him out, and Fagin finds himself back begging in the London streets and then sent to Australia. Even after a ten-year stint at an Australian

Figure 54. "Fagin at the School," 2003. Artwork by Will Eisner for his *Fagin the Jew*, 2013. Image © Will Eisner Studios, Inc.

penal colony, Fagin, who returns to London, has a round face and kindly, sparkling eyes; as Heer notes, "This is a sharp contrast to the original drawings of Fagin done by George Cruikshank, who depicted a hook-nosed, sinister Fagin every bit as ugly as the one Dickens described in prose" (132).

The cover of *Fagin the Jew* shows Fagin smiling broadly as he walks down a London street, holding the hand of Artful Dodger and another of his steady boys. Eisner also draws a broad-smiling, twinkly-eyed Fagin dancing jollily with his young pickpockets, who sing, "We'll all be rich as royalty 'cause we're all in Fagin's family" (*FTJ* 83). Nonetheless, Eisner acknowledges that Fagin has a brutal side: Fagin may refer to the pickpockets as "my boys" and his "family," but the boys "required a bit of discipline" (*FTJ* 52); panels show Fagin kicking and throwing the boys around, although he justifies his actions: "Still, I kept myself and my boys from the bitter refuge of workhouses" (52).

Although Eisner changes some of the details of *Oliver Twist*, Fagin's invented history seamlessly intersects with the source text. In a flashback midway through the graphic novel, Fagin, now well established in the criminal element of London, recalls how Oliver "joined my 'family' as usual, recruited by one of my steady boys" (*FTJ* 53). Fagin learns of Oliver's origins from Noah Claypole, the charity boy who makes Oliver miserable at Mr. Sowerberry's and whom Fagin later employs as his snitch. Fagin in this adaptation tries to persuade Sikes not to murder Nancy, crying out, "Stop Sikes! Have mercy! Nancy is a loyal girl!" (96), but Sikes kills Nancy with a chair in front of Fagin and Bull's-eye. Oliver does briefly visit Fagin in the source text, and Eisner expands this scene: when Oliver seeks out Fagin in the condemned cell, the two characters piece together Oliver's history, rendered through flashbacks (103–05). In these scenes in Eisner's version, we discover that Fagin possesses the locket that lies at the bottom of the Thames in the source text. Fagin, while chanting the sacred Jewish prayer, the *Shema*, kindly tells Oliver where to find the proof of his parentage—"I give you a future boy!" (108).

A closeness between Oliver and Fagin resonates in Eisner's adaptation through an interdependent combination of graphics and words. For example, in the panel where Oliver enters Fagin's prison cell (see fig. 55), the caption, written from Fagin's viewpoint, evokes sympathy: "I lay in my cell, exhausted from writhing and flailing against my sorry fate[.] . . . Aided by his influential new benefactor and patron Mr. Brownlow, Oliver was allowed to visit me here. His visit added to my comfort and helped me endure the agony of an undeserved fate" (*FTJ* 103). The cell is as barren as Cruikshank depicts it in "Fagin in

Figure 55. "Fagin in the Condemned Cell with Oliver," 2003. Artwork by Will Eisner for his *Fagin the Jew*, 2013. Image © Will Eisner Studios, Inc.

the Condemned Cell" (see fig. 16, ch. 2, 75; fig. 36A, ch. 3, 135). Fagin sits not on a cot or a bench, as James Mahoney imagines this scene for the Household Edition of Dickens (1871; see fig. 36B, ch. 3, 135), but on a cold stone floor. Whereas Mahoney's illustration of this same scene follows Cruikshank's theatrical staging and recalls Cruikshank's hook-nosed, Sephardic-looking Fagin (whose appearance evokes that of the Elizabethan stage Jew and eighteenth-century cartoons), Eisner's Fagin is not Semitic looking or crazed as he contemplates death by hanging.

Despite his incarceration in the many panels showing his visit with his "dear, dear boy" (FTJ 103), Moses lights up with pleasure that nearly restores his jollity. Moses hugs Oliver. He clasps his hands as if seeing Oliver has answered a prayer and kindly offers to assist him: "So tell me, how can I help you?!" (103). Wearing tattered clothes that hang on his now shrunken form, Fagin plays the role of the Good Samaritan and looks nearly as fair as blond-haired Oliver Twist. Although Eisner remediates Fagin's stereotypical appearance from the text and illustrations of the source text, he reengages some of the theatrical staging of the caricature tradition within the original illustrations of *Oliver Twist*. For example, in one full-page panel, Oliver, moved by Fagin's plight, sheds big tears while Fagin desperately clings to him, burying his face against Oliver's chest to hide his own weeping; an accompanying caption narrates the scene melodramatically from Fagin's point of view: "We clung together, I as a drowning man who holds onto a floating log, and Oliver as a mourner unable yet to separate from an attachment, the memory of which will forever remain with him" (FTJ 109). In the panels that follow, large thought bubbles dramatically emanate from Fagin's mind to show Moses imagining Oliver's happy future—finding the locket proving his parentage, being adopted by the childless Mr. Brownlow, and walking with his new "father" in the tranquil countryside.

Eisner adds an epilogue that creates an even more staged ending to Fagin's tale. We meet a grown-up Oliver Twist Brownlow, now a barrister, married to Adele, the granddaughter of Rebecca Lopez, who truly loved Fagin when he was an innocent youth cleaning her father's school for Jewish children. Rebecca always maintained Fagin's goodness because Moses returned stolen property that Sikes robbed from Fagin's onetime benefactor, the wealthy Jewish merchant Eleazor Salomon.[45] We learn Fagin might have had a respectable life if the kindly bachelor Eleazor Salomon, who wanted to adopt Fagin as his heir, had actually found Moses Fagin before Moses was transported to Australia. In the style of the realistic school of illustration, Eisner ends the tale with a close-up of a broadly smiling Fagin holding a locket that once belonged to Salomon;

the locket contains Fagin's portrait as a young man. This panel offers filial clo-
sure for Fagin through a material object that stands as a testimony to the love
Salomon felt for young Moses Fagin whom he thought of "as his son" (*FTJ* 120).
In this final twist, *Fagin the Jew* thus daringly aligns orphaned Moses Fagin with
the eponymous orphan Oliver Twist, who is successfully adopted by his own
"Eleazor Salomon," the kindly bachelor Mr. Brownlow.[46]

Despite Eisner's efforts to revise the character of Fagin, graphic novel adaptations of *Oliver Twist* that came out after *Fagin the Jew*, such as by Campfire and
Papercutz, essentially reuse the anti-Semitic stereotype of Fagin as imagined by
Cruikshank and carried by Du Maurier into his depiction of Svengali—particularly Fagin's dark eyebrows and pronounced nose. Campfire's 2011 adaptation
of *Oliver Twist*, written by Dan Johnson with illustrations by Rajesh Nagulakonda,[47] is only eight-four pages, so it omits much of the plot,[48] but this version develops the major themes and characterization in Dickens's source text.
Nagulakonda gives Fagin not red but black hair, thick black eyebrows, and a
large Semitic nose that extends beyond his mouth toward his sneering grin and
jutting chin (for example, Johnson 34, 67, 74). Nagulakonda also recalls the
caricature school in his theatrical posing of Fagin throughout this graphic novel
including his excessively large and long nose and his long finger that he points
at Oliver and at his own nose (for example, 34, 74).

Although Campfire does not include a version of the iconic "Fagin in the
Condemned Cell," it does, for example, recall Cruikshank's illustration of
"Monks and the Jew," a plate that shows Fagin and Monks leering at Oliver
through a window in the Maylie's country home where Oliver finds refuge after
the failed burglary attempt at this very house (in the source text, Sikes leaves
Oliver in a ditch, believing he is dead). In the original Cruikshank illustration, a
hook-nosed, black-hatted Fagin stands next to an equally sinister-looking black-
hatted Monks. Both peer in to see Oliver dozing over his books in a "cottage-
room, with a lattice window" (*OT*, Oxf. 1982 216). Cruikshank captures a moment between sleep and waking where Oliver perceives "the hideous old man"
and screams for help, "'The Jew! The Jew!'" (217). In Campfire's adaptation,
this scene extends over four panels (Johnson 60). Oliver is first studying and
then falling asleep. An ominous thought bubble showing Oliver's dream, an
exquisite stage effect, depicts Monks and Fagin, again pointing his very long
finger and nose at Oliver. The next frame closely resembles Cruikshank's original design: Oliver awakes to see an ominous looking Monks and Fagin (who
is now hatless) similarly positioned outside Oliver's window.[49] Nagulakonda
draws Oliver's eyes partially open (they are closed in Cruikshank's illustration),

suggesting Oliver actually sees Fagin and Monks. The two vanish from the scene in the next panel, leading Oliver in the fourth panel of the sequence to scream for help. Johnson echoes the Dickensian dialogue in the second and third frames where the sight of Fagin "sent the blood tingling to his heart, and took away his voice and power to move" even though "It was but an instant— a glance, a flash, before his eyes—and they were gone" (60).[50] In staging the scene over four panels, Johnson and Nagulakonda present this instant both as a terrible dream and a real visitation by the sinister Fagin and Monks, engaging the two commonly held interpretations of the Cruikshank illustration of this same scene.

The 2012 Papercutz adaptation of *Oliver Twist*, written by Loïc Dauvillier and illustrated by Olivier Deloye, is the longest and most complete retelling of these *Oliver Twist* graphic classics at 238 pages.[51] Deloye makes Fagin a caricature of a Semitic Jew. Fagin's enormous sausage-shaped nose—often reddened, hooked, and swollen (for example, Dauvillier 98)—dominates Papercutz's rendition of "Fagin in the Condemned Cell" (237). The illustration is recognizable to the viewer familiar with the original although this version loses nearly all of the psychological intensity of Cruikshank's illustration owing to the ridiculousness of Fagin's sausage nose. Also gone are the shackles and the biting of the hand, but Deloye recalls the intense fear in the eyes of Fagin, who sits alone in his empty cell.

The panel has no word balloons or captions. Deloye includes the cot and the barred window from the Cruikshank original, although he reverses the placement of the cot (in this version it is on the same side as the window). As in Eisner's drawing, Deloye's Fagin sits on the floor of the barren cell. The walls in the Papercutz version are bare—gone are the sheriff's notices from Cruikshank's design. Deloye includes a detail that recalls James Mahoney's version for the Household Edition (see fig. 36B, ch. 3, 135); not initials, but the names of two previous inmates on death row are scratched into the prison wall. This detail foreshadows Fagin's fate, anticipated in the next three frames: a guard gestures to Fagin to leave his cell; an angry crowd yells at Fagin ("Hang Him!" "Child-Killer!" "Thief!" "Murderer!"); and the hangman commands Fagin to climb up the scaffold ("This Way, You!" [Dauvillier 127]).

Campfire and Papercutz also dramatically reengage Cruikshank's iconic staging of the starvation of the workhouse children in "Oliver Asking for More" (see fig. 8, ch. 2, 57). Johnson and Nagulakonda exacerbate Dickens's attack on the parish workhouse system. In the source text, the branch workhouse run by Mrs. Mann seems relatively innocuous—Oliver even asks if Mrs. Mann will come with him when he moves to the parish workhouse. In Campfire's adaptation, Mrs. Mann calls the orphans "brats" (Johnson 6) and threatens them: "And the next time you complain about being hungry, I'll lock you all in the coal cellar!" (6).[52] Taunts follow Oliver to the parish workhouse where the board reminds orphan Oliver to "say your prayers every night, and pray for the people who feed you and take care of you" (8)—ironic words since no one cares for Oliver or feeds him very much.

Through eight sequential panels, we witness Oliver's starvation at the workhouse; the drawing of lots to see who must ask for more gruel; Oliver's famous request, "Please, sir. I want some more" (Johnson 9);[53] and the parish board's response to "that troublemaker" (10). Like Mahoney (see fig. 35B, ch. 3, 133), Nagulakonda reverses the orientation of the original Cruikshank illustration (see fig. 35A, ch. 3, 133) by placing the backdrop of starving workhouse children to Oliver's left. Close-ups of the malnourished orphans also fill two horizontal frames positioned above the three-panel sequence in which Oliver asks for more and is beaten by the large, pot-bellied master of the workhouse, who is wielding the very spoon he uses to ladle the meager gruel. Nagulakonda intensifies Oliver's suffering by the hands of the corrupt workhouse system in depicting the cook's violent reaction to Oliver's polite request for "more" (see fig. 56). Motion lines in the third of the three-panel sequence dramatize the force of the master's impending blow, knocking Oliver's bowl, which bleeds off the page. The master has glaring white teeth, poised as if to eat Oliver Twist, and coarse diction ("What? Why you little—" [Johnson 9]). Oliver in the third panel of the sequence is posed dramatically on his knees; he closes his eyes in fear and raises his hands in a protective gesture to ward off the impending blows.

The 2012 Papercutz adaptation[54] also revisits "Oliver Asking for More," but in this adaptation, Oliver has a more authoritative voice, of consequence since the eponymous character is undeveloped in Dickens's source text. The scene unfolds over thirty panels. There is no drawing of lots, but Oliver utters his famous request to the master, who in this version is eating a hearty meal at a table with the other parish officials. The master throws Oliver into a dark cell. In three subsequent consecutive panels, Dauvillier and Deloye augment Oliver's character when he cries, "Open Up! I want out!"; "I didn't do anything!"; "Open up!" (Dauvillier 22). Cries and exclamation marks intensify Oliver's justified outburst against the cruel parish authorities, but the letters in each of the three word balloons get progressively smaller. Diminishing font size is a convention of graphic novel format to decrease forcefulness, in this case of Oliver's power. But Oliver's brief protest prepares the reader for a subsequent

Figure 56. "Oliver Asking for More." Artwork by Rajesh Nagulakonda for Dan Johnson's adaptation of *Oliver Twist*, 2011. © Campfire 2014.

scene in the source text where "Oliver Plucks up a Spirit" to defend his dead mother's honor.[55]

Whereas Eisner's adaptation targets the persistent stereotype of Fagin, the other two adaptations dramatize sensational and sordid elements of the source text not illustrated by Cruikshank. Johnson and Nagulakonda develop Nancy's character as a battered woman in the Campfire adaptation. In the source text, Sikes threatens, controls, and kills Nancy, traits that we associate with a male batterer. In this adaptation, Sikes also beats her. Nancy confides to Oliver: "I have promised that you will be quiet and silent. If you are not, you will not only harm yourself, you will harm me too. See here! This is what I have done for you already! Remember this, and don't let me suffer more for you just now" (Johnson 38). The graphics show Nancy lowering her cloak to reveal three prominent cuts and part of a fourth on her upper arm. Nancy's expressive eyes register pain and fear that Sikes will soon strike her again.[56]

Johnson and Nagulakonda's depiction of Sikes as a batterer brings to the foreground Dickens's advocacy for abused women in *Oliver Twist*, written long before this taboo topic came to be recognized as a social problem demanding redress. Prostitution was on the rise in Victorian England, and in the mid 1840s, Dickens assisted Angela Burdett-Coutts in setting up a home for the redemption of fallen women called Urania Cottage, a safe house for those who wanted a fresh start. This graphic novel adaptation makes vivid Dickens's subtext of protest against domestic abuse well over a century before this term or "battered woman's syndrome" entered our language.

Nagulakonda also develops the underlying sensuality of the source text in the scene where Sikes confronts Nancy for her alleged betrayal and murders her. In the source text, Sikes pulls back the bed curtains and wakens Nancy, who is "half-dressed" and exhibits "an expression of pleasure at his return" (*OT*, Oxf. 1982 302). Dickens distracts the reader from this glint of arousal with Nancy's murder that swiftly follows. In this adaptation, however, we see a sensual-looking Nancy with a coy smile on her face as she awakes and realizes, "Bill . . . it is you—" (Johnson 75). Nancy looks as if she is expecting sex, but Sikes is there to kill her; true to Dickens's text, Sikes responds to Nancy brusquely, "Get up!" (75). The command appears in a jagged-edged word balloon, a visual effect that intensifies his rage. In the next two panels, Sikes threatens and then throttles Nancy as she attempts to speak the exact words from the source text—"I have been true to you. Upon my guilty soul I have" (75). Cruikshank does not provide an illustration of Nancy's murder, and Dickens gives just enough detail to make the murder theatrical; this was one of the scenes that Dickens often chose for his dramatic readings. Whereas Mahoney drew the aftermath of the murder scene for the Household Edition of Dickens (see fig. 37, ch. 3, 138), Nagulakonda shows the murder itself. A close-up panel of Sikes throttling Nancy and another of a smoking gun in Sikes's hand (he shoots her in this adaptation) convincingly mark him a "murderer," as Dickens calls Sikes right after Bill Sikes kills Nancy (*OT*, Oxf. 1982, 303).[57]

In the Papercutz adaptation of *Oliver Twist*, Dauvillier and Deloye present Nancy's murder in a sequence that covers more than three full pages of the graphic novel. All the panels are darkly lit, creating a menacing tone for the moment when Sikes takes his lover's life. Word balloons are at a minimum in this sequence of panels, and the few words that do appear are mainly vocalizations of screaming and beating: "AAAAAAAAAAAAAHHHH" (Dauvillier 212), and "WHAM" (213) and "NO! BILL! NO!" (213). These sound effects function additively to the graphics, providing a soundtrack of horror. Mimicking the savagery in Dickens's characterization of Bill Sikes (for example, Sikes "growled out these words" [OT, Oxf. 1982 76]), Deloye carries such beastiality into Sikes's glaring white teeth, jutting chin, and clenched fist, gripping a weapon ready to strike Nancy down (Sikes assaults Nancy with a pistol in the source text). Three adjacent vertical panels are staged to theatrical effect (Dauvillier 213). Sikes in one frame seizes a piece of wood, raises it high above his head in the second, and then in the third frame clubs Nancy, who exudes terror through her facial expression, body posture, and scream.

Even more dramatic is the page that follows the murder. This page is comprised of four wordless, stacked horizontal panels (see fig. 57). In the first panel, Bull's-eye cowers as he sniffs at a pool of bright red blood on the floor; this is Nancy's blood, and the eyes of Bull's-eye register fear. The next panel focuses on Sikes's shoes and trouser legs covered with Nancy's blood. Sikes is standing in a pool of bright red blood that also spatters the wall of the room. These details realize Dickens's description of "the body—mere flesh and blood, no more—but such flesh, and so much blood!" (OT, Oxf. 1982 304). All four horizontal panels graphically show "so much blood!" In the third panel, Sikes's bloody hand holds the gory murder weapon. The bottom panel chillingly closes in on Nancy's bloodied hand clasping a now bloodied handkerchief with Rose Maylie's name written upon it in cursive.

The white handkerchief alludes to a key scene in Oliver Twist: Rose, described as Nancy's "sister-woman" in an initial heading for chapter 40,[58] offers to help Nancy escape to safety, but Nancy requests only a token from Rose, her white handkerchief. In Dickens's source text, a martyred Nancy

> staggered and fell: nearly blinded with the blood that rained down from a deep gash in her forehead; but raising herself, with difficulty, on her knees, drew from her bosom a white handkerchief—Rose Maylie's own—and holding it up, in her folded hands, as high towards Heaven as her feeble strength would allow, breathed one prayer for mercy to her Maker. (OT, Oxf. 1982 303)

Using a montage effect, Deloye embeds the words "Rose Maylie"; elegantly embroidered on the white handkerchief, Rose's name makes palpable the "sister-woman" connection and Nancy's true nature. The close-up of Nancy's bloodied

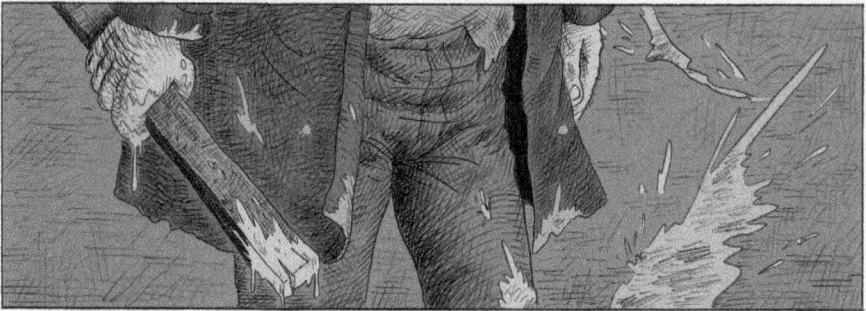

Figure 57. "Nancy's Murder." Artwork by Olivier Deloye for Loïc Dauvillier's adaptation of *Oliver Twist*, 2012. © Papercutz.

hand, a visual synecdoche for the bloodied corpse, paints the horror of "mere flesh and blood, no more" (304) that we imagine in our mind's eye from the source text. Deloye fixes our eyes on the blood-spattered white handkerchief, a symbol of Nancy's original innocence that is perverted by a life on the streets with Fagin and Sikes.

In these graphic novel adaptations of *Oliver Twist*, we see an engagement with the theatrical aspects of the caricature school of illustration as well as the designs of many of the original illustrations, but none of these adaptations is merely reiterative. The panels devoted to the murder of Nancy, a scene too indelicate for the sensibilities of a Victorian middle-class readership, shed light upon Sikes's brutality and Nancy's saintliness that Mahoney hints at in depicting the murder's aftermath (see fig. 37, ch. 3, 138). All three graphic novel adaptations bring to the foreground the indelible mark of the caricaturist in the presentation of Fagin, the villainous Jew that Nagulakonda and Deloye perpetuate and Eisner remediates. Eisner's adaptation quintessentially demonstrates how crucial the original illustrations are to *Oliver Twist*. More than the other adaptors, Eisner set out to revise Fagin's racialized physical appearance established by Cruikshank as well as his devious character created by Dickens.

Graphic *Alice* and the Reengagement of Two Schools of Illustration: Caricature and Realism

Lewis Carroll's *Alice's Adventures in Wonderland* has captured the attention of sequential artists more than any other Victorian illustrated book. Mark Burstein in *Alice in Comicland* aligns Carroll and the *Alice* books with the comic book tradition since Carroll "was very much alive during the time of the development of proto-comics, and can himself be considered a progenitor" (9). Carroll's juvenilia *The Rectory Umbrella* (a family magazine dating to about 1850) includes a cartoon entitled "The Scanty Meal"; in it, Carroll uses a staple of the graphic novel format, a word balloon with a long tail, to satirize *The Scanty Meal* (1847), a painting by the distinguished Victorian equine artist J. F. Herring.[59] To Craig Yoe, editor of *Alice in Comicland*,

> Carroll had Alice think one of the greatest defenses of comic books/
> graphic novels before the form was even fully realized. Alice sits on the
> bank and ponders, "What is the use of a book without pictures or con-
> versations?" Absolutely nothing! And comics go beyond even the appeal
> and power of a profusely illustrated book like *Alice in Wonderland*. (17)

In addition to the many film versions, photo shoots, and merchandise surrounding *Alice,* comic book parodies of *Alice* appear as early as Jack Davis's adaptation of *Alice's Adventures in Wonderland* for *MAD Magazine* in 1954 and continue most recently into a host of *Alice* erotica and *Alice* spin-offs. Zenescope's 2012 adaptation of *Alice in Wonderland* for the Grimm Fairy Tales series follows Alice, now a grown up sex magnet, as she returns to Wonderland. *Hatter M.: The Looking Glass Wars* trilogy, launched in 2010 by Automatic Pictures Publishing, reinterprets Carroll's classic from the vantage point of the enigmatic Mad Hatter. Yoe favors the free, fanciful, and outlandish adaptations of Alice over the "'straight'" (20) versions. But the faithful graphic novel adaptations by Dynamite and Campfire Classics reveal how graphic artists have built upon Carroll's original caricatures that Tenniel redrew with realism, translating the Victorian illustrated book into a fresh hybrid textual-visual medium for a new generation of reader-viewers.

Dynamite first issued *The Complete Alice in Wonderland* serially as four separate comic books published from 2009 to 2010 and then printed it as one book, following publication of the fourth installment. The first two issues adapt *Wonderland,* and the latter two adapt its sequel, *Through the Looking-Glass.* A feature entitled "Creating Wonderland" in the first issue offers insight into the collaborative partnership of scriptwriters Leah Moore and John Reppion and graphic artist Érica Awano as well as the importance of the original text and illustrations to the adaptation process. Moore and Reppion advise Awano to incorporate details in the panel where Alice falls down the rabbit hole to "prefigure the rest of the story" (n. pag.). A comparison of the sketch and finished version of this particular panel reveals how Awano has added a portrait of the Cheshire Cat, the Caterpillar, playing cards, red roses, and other props that hint at Alice's adventures to come. Moore and Reppion also direct Awano to Tenniel's landmark illustrations for "further reference or inspiration" and to the 1907 illustrations of Arthur Rackham to draw upon the "darkness of his drawings" and their "sense of menace" (n. pag.).[60] Moore and Reppion include many of the famous lines from *Alice,* such as "I'm opening out like the largest telescope that ever was! Good-bye feet!" (n. pag.), although they regrettably delete Carroll's famous credo, "'what is the use of a book . . . without pictures or conversations?'" (*AA* 11). Moore and Reppion recommend a palette to the colorist that is "very old fashioned looking" to make the panels resemble "hand tinted Victorian photographs" (n. pag.) and capture the feel of the era.

In contrast, Campfire's 2010 graphic novel adaptation of *Alice in Wonderland,* scripted by Lewis Helfand with graphics by Rajesh Nagulakonda, uses vivid colors that make Alice's adventures look bright and contemporary rather than Victorian but includes Carroll's famous credo about pictures and conversations ("What is the use of a book without pictures or conversation?" [Helfand 5]). Nagulakonda's graphics are more caricature-like than Awano's realistic illustrations and less successful in capturing Carroll's social caricatures of the White Rabbit (a Victorian gentleman/rabbit) and the Mock Turtle (a hybrid calf/turtle), both of which Tenniel expertly rendered for *Wonderland*. Nonetheless, the Dynamite and Campfire Classics adaptations recall and refashion illustrations that Tenniel drew or redrew from Carroll's designs in both small and significant ways and use graphic novel format to animate Alice's adventures and her bodily transformations.

Awano and Nagulakonda both follow Tenniel's conception of the playing cards as costumed figures in granting them human heads above their playing card bodies, making possible the Red Queen's threat to behead them. Although Alice is blonde in both adaptations, and Awano slightly changes Alice's hairstyle (giving her bangs), Alice in both graphic novel adaptations wears a blue pinafore dress and white stockings, a fashion that Tenniel trademarked. Both versions recall specific illustrations designed by Carroll and redrawn by Tenniel, such as Alice outgrowing the White Rabbit's house. Awano also expertly carries forward the pantomimic aspects of Tenniel's illustrations, such as of the Fish-Footman delivering an oversized letter to the Frog-Footman; Awano's creatures possess human-looking bodies and large heads and look as if they are wearing animal masks such as in a pantomime, much as Tenniel imagined them.

To those familiar with Tenniel's illustrations of Alice outgrowing the White Rabbit's house, Awano's illustrations are a redeployment of the iconic scene by Tenniel, who refashioned Carroll's designs with naturalism for a Sixties readership. Whereas Tenniel uses three plates to illustrate the growth scene up to the point where Alice kicks the lizard up the chimney in *Wonderland*, and Carroll uses five illustrations to show the same sequence in *Under Ground*, the Dynamite team allocates twenty-five panels—a mix of panoramas and close-ups—to present this same series of events. The sound effects add an aural dimension to Alice's uncontrollable growth, which becomes not only volatile but also noisy.

Frame by frame, the growth scene in the Dynamite adaptation unfolds before our eyes. Alice enters the White Rabbit's house, finds a bottle, and swiftly drinks its contents; a motion line and the words "GLUG GLUG" convey movement and sound, respectively, and illustrate the speed with which Alice is drinking. In the very next panel, Alice hits her head; a sound effect, "BUMP," and a speech balloon with the word "OUCH!" (n. pag.) bring loud noises into the picture plane to magnify the effects of Alice's change in size. As we turn the page, the panels proportionately increase in height to accommodate Alice, who is in the process of outgrowing the White Rabbit's house. Whereas Carroll best captures the claustrophobia of the scene, Tenniel expertly transforms Carroll's simple rectangular box into an authentic Victorian domestic interior house with casement windows (see figs. 39A and 39B, ch. 3, 145). The graphic novel medium allows for an expansion of this iconic scene into three segmented panels, calling attention to the expansiveness of Alice's form (see fig. 58): the left panel shows Alice's left foot on the grate of the fireplace, the center panel features her head and right leg in an uncomfortably twisted position, and the right panel focuses on her left arm and part of her torso as well as some toppled over furniture.

Sound effects in these three panels and surrounding ones (for example, "BOOOF," "CRASSH," and "CRASSH SMASH"), all in vivid colors and bolded capital letters inserted directly into the frames, magnify the enormity of Alice's size, the disruption she is causing to the White Rabbit's house, and the discomfort Alice is experiencing due to her uncontrollable growth. Nonetheless, Awano carries on Tenniel's style of representational realism and uses these top three vertical panels of a five-panel page to create a country house that includes furniture and a chandelier that Alice is in the process of knocking over. The positioning of Alice is nearly identical to that of the Tenniel plate (see fig. 39B, ch. 3, 145), but Awano's room is larger, which minimizes the menacing aspect of the scene since Alice still has room to grow. Still, Alice keeps on growing and growing, until, in the following panels, she reaches one hand out the window and one foot up the chimney.

In the two smaller panels on the page positioned below the frames of Alice outgrowing the house, Awano shifts our focus from Alice to the disgruntled homeowner, the White Rabbit. Tenniel more believably captured Carroll's social caricature of the Victorian gentleman/rabbit perpetually afraid of lateness than Awano does: Awano's rabbit wears a nondescript vest whereas Tenniel's rabbit has a fashionable waistcoat, umbrella, and pocket watch—details that authenticate the character's human traits (see fig. 40B, ch. 3, 148). However, Awano's White Rabbit looks angry enough to burn down his own house to rid himself of Alice (as the source text dictates) although he first decides to send Bill the Lizard down his chimney (Bill is subsequently kicked out by Alice's enormous foot). In contrast, Tenniel's White Rabbit looks terrified of Alice's large hand that descends from the window of his house, and Carroll's White Rabbit looks like a mouse with donkey ears dressed in a suit (see fig. 40A, ch.

Figure 58. "Alice Outgrowing the White Rabbit's House." Artwork by Érica Awano for Leah Moore and John Reppion's *The Complete Alice in Wonderland*, 2009. *The Complete Alice in Wonderland* ™ and © 2014 Dynamite Characters, LLC. Image used with permission courtesy of Dynamite Entertainment. www.dynamite.com. All Rights Reserved.

3, 148). Moreover, throughout the sequential frames appear colored sound effects that are onomatopoeic words to vocalize the disruption Alice's growth is causing to the White Rabbit's house. This graphic novel adaptation keeps Alice in a noisy state of perpetual growth until she discovers some tasty little cakes and changes size again, shrinking smaller than the Caterpillar sitting atop a mushroom.

A major device available to the graphic artist is the opportunity to change the size, shape, and layout of panels to influence the reader-viewer's speed of reading. On the first hand, for the Campfire adaptation, Nagulakonda creatively varies panel angles, curves frames, and creates the illusion that panels are tumbling into each other to make the growth sequence of *Wonderland* fast-paced and dynamic. Close-ups of Alice finding the bottle in the White Rabbit's house and sipping from it seemingly tumble into successive panels of Alice outgrowing the house, sticking first her hand out the window and then her foot up the chimney, sending Bill the Lizard flying out the chimney in a close-up panel with a blaring sound effect, "AAAIIEE!" (Helfand 21). The technique of overlapping panels speeds up the processes of reading and viewing and gives the illusion that Alice's bodily transformations are happening very quickly. On the other hand, three of the panels in this sixteen-panel sequence reengage the same iconic Tenniel illustration of Alice outgrowing the White Rabbit's house (see fig. 39B, ch. 3, 145), although Alice's orientation is reversed. These three panels seemingly suspend time by returning the reader-viewer's gaze to Alice's discomfort, the impossibility of her situation, and her futile efforts to free herself.[61] The Campfire *Alice* also cleverly devises a collage technique to animate the growth series, demonstrating how the graphic novel can approximate time-lapse photography. Superimposed images of Alice, each smaller than the one above it or larger than the one below it, simulate the processes of shrinking and growing, respectively. Alice is changing size in front of our very eyes.

Whereas Tenniel depicts Alice discovering the bottle whose paper label reads "'DRINK ME'" (*AA* 16), Nagulakonda animates this same scene by superimposing images of Alice in four sizes, each successively smaller than the previous one (Helfand 9). The first three Alice figures are in faint lines and pale colors. However, the fourth and smallest Alice figure appears in solid lines and bright colors to indicate her present shrunken size. The shift in color palette illuminates the small size Alice has now become.

Much as in the "DRINK ME" scene, in the "EAT ME" scene (Helfand 10), Nagulakonda gives the illusion of rapid fire change, in this case of growth, by superimposing three increasingly larger figures of Alice onto the first image (see fig. 59). Faint lines and pale colors depict Alice as she first bites the cake marked "EAT ME" and famously declares (echoing the source text, *AA* 20): "Curiouser and curiouser! Now I'm opening out like the largest telescope that ever was!" (Helfand 10). In the largest image, Alice, who is now more than nine feet high, appears in solid lines and bright colors that signal she has completed her

Figure 59. "Curiouser and Curiouser!" Artwork by Rajesh Nagulakonda for Lewis Helfand's adaptation of *Alice in Wonderland*, 2010. © Campfire 2014.

transformation, at least for now. Helfand and Nagulakonda also increase the height of the panels, which seem to grow larger to accommodate Alice's now tele-scopic height.

Growing blends seamlessly into the following dramatic scene where Alice cries great tears, shrinks once again, and nearly drowns in a pool of her own tears (Helfand 11). Alice is contemplating her identity in two interconnected thought bubbles—"Let me think: was I the same when I got up this morn-ing?" and "But if I'm not the same, the next question is, who in the world am I?" (11)—when the panel angle shifts to a long shot, showing just how tiny Alice has become.[62] The final panel on this page is a close-up of Alice falling into the pool of her own tears, a scene that Tenniel and Carroll rendered. However, in the graphic novel format, the words "SPLASH!" in a wavy font mimic the color and sound of the brightly colored blue water noisily splash-ing outside the frame into the outside gutter. Nagulakonda animates the rush of water, Alice's long flying locks, and the terror on her face. There is no clo-sure to this dramatic moment—the figure of drowning Alice bleeds into the gutter—and the drama continues as the reader-viewer turns the page to find Alice attempting to swim in the water, declaring in a word balloon: "I wish I hadn't cried so much! I shall be punished for it now, I suppose, by being drowned in my own tears!" (12).

One of the most disquieting bodily distortions in *Under Ground* and *Won-derland* occurs when Alice, upon eating one side of a mushroom, shrinks so rapidly that "she felt a violent blow underneath her chin: it had struck her foot!" (*AA* 53). Carroll drew this eerie scene in *Alice's Adventures Un-der Ground* as did Rackham in his 1907 edition of *Alice in Wonderland*; in contrast, Tenniel did not delineate it or the frightening scene where Alice's "immense length of neck . . . seemed to rise like a stalk" (*UG* 62) above the treetops, both of which Awano and Nagulakonda illustrate. Tenniel "rejected [these] two unpleasant possibilities" (Morris 191). Might both distortions have been perceived as too disturbing for an 1860's middle-class readership that valued aesthetic appeal? Awano may have been following Rackham's in-terpretation of this scene, since the scriptwriters directed her to his illustra-tions, but the scene's inclusion in the Dynamite and Campfire adaptations shows an engagement with and redeployment of Carroll's author-illustrated *Under Ground*.

Those familiar with Carroll's drawing of Alice's large head balancing pre-cariously on her disproportionately small feet and hands will recognize the imprint of Carroll's caricature (see fig. 60B) within Awano's graphics (see

Figure 60. A (*above*): "She Felt a Violent Blow on Her Chin." Artwork by Érica Awano for Leah Moore and John Reppion's *The Complete Alice in Wonderland*, 2009. *The Complete Alice in Wonderland* ™ and © 2014 Dynamite Characters, LLC. Image used with permission courtesy of Dynamite Entertainment. www.dynamite.com. All Rights Reserved; B (*left*): "She Felt a Violent Blow on Her Chin." Illustration by Lewis Carroll for his *Alice's Adventures Under Ground*, 1864.

fig. 60A). However, Carroll's single illustration powerfully grows into three panels that animate the distortion, frame by frame. In the first panel, a tiny Alice attempts to wrap her arms around the large, round mushroom to break off a part of it from each side; the Caterpillar tells Alice that eating one side of the mushroom will make her grow taller, and eating the other side will make her shorter. The sound effect "CHOK" appears directly where each of Alice's hands is breaking off a piece of the mushroom, so the reader-viewer hears her action. In the second frame, Alice is loudly eating the piece of the mushroom—"MUNCH MUNCH" is inserted in large bold letters—that makes her shrink. The third panel, which resembles Carroll's original (see fig. 60B), is a more aesthetically pleasing rendition of this same disturbing scene, more along the lines that Tenniel might have achieved had he illustrated this scene. Awano makes Alice's facial features pretty and gives fullness to Alice's hair that curls on the ground. Carroll's Alice, in contrast, looks dreamy and complacent in his *Under Ground* illustrations, as if she is accepting of her gruesome distortion.

Alice's wide eyes and alarmed expression in Awano's depiction match the source text where Carroll indicates that Alice "was a good deal frightened by this very sudden change" (*UG* 62). "Good gracious!" (Moore and Reppion n. pag.)—Alice exclaims in a word balloon positioned against the gray-blue sky. Alice looks as if she knows she must act quickly because, according to the source text, "There was hardly room to open her mouth, with her chin pressing against her foot, but she did it at last, and managed to bite off a little bit of the top of the mushroom" (*UG* 62). At this point, Alice's neck elongates uncontrollably, and an eagle takes her for a serpent. In graphic novel format, a scene that Carroll depicts in two small pictures in his handwritten *Under Ground* becomes a terrifying twelve-panel sequence across a two-page spread (Moore and Reppion n. pag.). Alice's long neck and head reach above the treetops, much as Carroll attempts (*UG* 62–63), but Awano's illustration, which improves upon the original, approaches the transformation from a variety of angles. Close-ups, long shots, and one aerial view show the extent of Alice's extremely strange bodily distortion.

Graphic *Alice*—in recalling designs from Carroll and Tenniel—is an inheritor of the schools of caricature and realism, refashioned once again in a new medium. Growing, shrinking, twisting, turning, and vocalizing her discontent, a dynamic Alice transforms before our eyes in the graphic classics, bringing new readers to Carroll's enduring tale.

☙❧

The Victorian illustrated book bridges aesthetic periods and connects two derided genres, the serial and the comic book. This resilient genre thus moves beyond Queen Victoria's time to find new expression for our time. The graphic classics returns to, reuses, modifies, and in some cases remediates characters and iconic scenes and also foregrounds historical and psychological elements indelicate for a Victorian readership. In adaptations of *Alice, Oliver Twist,* and other nineteenth-century novels, panels of different shapes and sizes, sound effects, motion lines, superimposed figures, panoramic views, and new approaches to iconic illustrations demonstrate the graphic novel's ability to reshape a nineteenth-century classic into a form that engages twenty-first century readers with words and images on multiple levels. The graphic classics refashions the style and creative vision of an author or illustrator into a prescient hybrid form that recalls the revelatory dimension of the Victorian definition of illustration and resituates the nineteenth-century novel for a new age. Peeling back these layers of illustration reveals the still powerful original imprint of the Victorian caricaturist and realist.

Notes

Introduction: The Arc of the Victorian Illustrated Book

1. Madame Merle presents her meditation on identity to Isabel Archer in ch. 19 of James's *The Portrait of a Lady*. The following passage posits that the self has a "shell" of material "things." Pondering where the self begins and ends, Madame Merle declares:

> you must take the shell into account. By the shell I mean the whole envelope of circumstances. There is no such thing as an isolated man or woman; we are each of us made up of a cluster of appurtenances. What do you call one's self? . . . It overflows into everything that belongs to us—and then it flows back again. I know that a large part of myself is in the dresses I choose to wear. I have a great respect for *things*! (181)

2. See Deborah Cohen's chapter on "Home as a Stage: Personality and Possessions" in *Household Gods: The British and Their Possessions*, 122–44.

3. Kooistra includes a parenthetical reference to Thad Logan's *The Victorian Parlour: A Cultural Study* that, in turn, quotes from a period source by Lucy Orrinsmith, who describes the Victorian parlor as follows: "On a circular table (of course with pillar and claws) are placed books—too often selected for their bindings alone—arranged like the spokes of a wheel" (2). The table I imagine has claw feet as a nod to Orrinsmith's description.

4. In *Drawn from Memory*, Shepard includes one line drawing entitled "Spend the afternoon in the drawing-room" featuring Shepard and his brother reading in the drawing room in front of the fire with books on the carpet between them. In *North and South*, the reference to the Hale family's books appears in ch. 10, "Wrought Iron and Gold," 72, and the reference to the Thornton family's books in ch. 15, "Masters and Men," 103.

5. The Household Edition of Dickens includes John Forster's biography *The Life of Charles Dickens* in addition to the complete works. I recommend Allingham and Louttit's "The Illustrators of the Household Edition of the *Works of Charles Dickens* (22 vols., 1871–79)" in <http://www.victorianweb.org/art/illustration/barnard/household.html>, accessed 8 Oct. 2014. For the American Household Edition, Harper and Brothers replaced some British artists with American illustrators; for example, Thomas Nast illustrated *The Pickwick Papers*.

6. Arlene Jackson calls attention to the Victorian illustrated book's third, oft-neglected period in *Illustration and the Novels of Thomas Hardy*. Richard Maxwell discusses the decline

of the genre in his afterword to *The Victorian Illustrated Book*, but also considers ways in which the genre crossed borders into advertising, the art book, the art press, and modernist objects, 385–419.

7. Paul Goldman and Simon Cooke's *Reading Victorian Illustration, 1855–1875* also follows the format of an essay collection, focusing on this one productive period of the Victorian illustrated book.

8. Even the most recent edition on the Victorian illustrated book, Paul Goldman and Simon Cooke's *Reading Victorian Illustration, 1855–1875*, shows scholars actively recalling these early assessments.

9. Philip Allingham separates Leech from the other caricaturists in his commentary on "Ignorance and Want" and notes that Leech's whimsical style, "although it may be described as caricature verging at times on cartoon, was more rigorously realistic and less emblematic than Browne's," <http://www.victorianweb.org/art/illustration/carol/6.html>, accessed 8 Nov. 2014.

10. Lisa Surridge and Mary Elizabeth Leighton are in the process of co-authoring a book on Victorian illustrated serial fiction from 1859–75.

11. Navasky and Maidment focus on the comic print, and their works inform my re-valuation, especially if we consider that by the late eighteenth century in England, the term "caricature" had broadened to include book illustration as well as strictly visual forms of print culture.

12. To answer this question, Harvey suggests that *Pickwick* made "the comic fancy a reality one could laugh at" (8) and also raises the eighteenth-century tradition of graphic satire and caricature, which I discuss in ch. 1.

13. This term appears variously in criticism. Throughout this book, I follow A. N. Wilson in *The Victorians*, who writes this as two words and italicizes *Pickwick*; notes Wilson, "*Pickwick* mania seized first Britain, then abroad" (19). To confuse this terminology further, Wilson also writes the phrase as two words without italicization later in this same discussion.

14. Critics of the illustrated book including John Harvey, Richard Maxwell, Paul Goldman, Simon Cooke, Robert Patten, and Jane R. Cohen have likewise argued for *Pickwick's* importance to the genre.

15. There are many variations of Trilby-mania. Throughout this book, I follow Richard Kelly, author of the biography *George Du Maurier*, who hyphenates the two words and does not italicize the title of the novel; Kelly advances, "The enormous popularity of the book and the play led to what was called Trilby-mania" (121).

16. This term "graphic classics" is also the name of Barron's series of graphic novels. Another major publisher of this genre has a similar name, Classical Comics.

17. There are several interpretations of this sculpture that resides in the Vatican.

18. Lessing's eighteenth-century terminology illuminates how we read illustrations in the Victorian illustrated book where in some cases, the author and illustrator jointly determined which moments to delineate through illustration. Such is the case in George Eliot and Frederick Leighton's collaboration for *Romola*, published serially in *The Cornhill* (1862–63). Goldman devotes a section of "Defining Illustration Studies" to the chosen moment of illustration, 25–27.

19. See Julie Gardham's article "The Mirror of the World" for University of Glasgow,

Special Collections. Along with her examination of Caxton's *Mirror*, Gardham includes some of the primitive woodcuts that English craftsman made for the 1481 edition.

20. Fashionable illuminated addresses were also used to mark major occasions like Queen Victoria's Golden and Diamond Jubilees in, respectively, 1887 and 1897.

21. In *Charles Dickens and His Publishers*, Robert Patten notes five types of piecemeal publishing in place by 1740: "fascicle issue, cheap part reprints, newspapers and magazines, instalment fiction, and series" (46).

Chapter 1. *The Pickwick Papers* and the Rise of the Serial

1. There was no installment of *Pickwick* in June 1837 because Dickens was distraught over the death of his beloved sister-in-law, Mary Scott Hogarth. Part 15, issued in July 1837, includes an "Address" by the author, explaining how a "sad bereavement" prevented timely publication of part 15. Some critics list the serial as running from March 1836 to October 1837. Part 1 of Pickwick was published in April 1836; however, the eight-page ad announcing works published by Chapman and Hall is dated "March, 1836," so one might assume that part 1 is a March issue. The final double number, which contains parts 19 and 20, was published in November 1837, and page 1 of the Advertiser is correctly dated 1 Nov. 1837. However, the date "October 30, 1837" appears in an "Address" by the publisher included in the November issue; this may be the source of the misstatement that the final double number was issued in October 1837. I am grateful to Charles Parkhurst of Charles Parkhurst Rare Books for verifying and explaining these details about *Pickwick* that have perplexed many Dickens scholars.

2. I recommend *Picturing Scotland Through the Waverley Novels* to those interested in Scott's contribution to the Victorian illustrated book. Hill provocatively challenges claims by critics including Richard Maxwell that Scott resisted illustration for his novels and included them when financial problems made book illustration a commercial incentive.

3. See Maxwell's chapter "Walter Scott, Historical Fiction, and the Genesis of the Victorian Illustrated Book" in *The Victorian Illustrated Book*, 1–51. John Harvey asserts in *Victorian Novelists and Their Illustrators* that in general "the traditional novel had little place for pictures" (8) and that Sir Walter Scott's work was not illustrated except for a vignette or a frontispiece.

4. Richard Maxwell likewise notes in "Walter Scott, Historical Fiction, and the Genesis of the Victorian Illustrated Book": "During the late Middle Ages, 'illustration' meant spiritual or intellectual illumination. By the end of the sixteenth century the same word [illustration] often denoted the action of making something clear, typically by providing an explanatory and confirming example; to illustrate was to use one text to shed light on another" (1).

5. Thackeray uses the term "illuminate" to describe his illustrations for *Vanity Fair*, noting in his "Before the Curtain" preface that the serial is "brilliantly illuminated with the Author's own candles" (Oxf. 2).

6. These works are entitled *The Second Tour of Doctor Syntax, in Search of Consolation: A Poem*, published in 1820, and *The Third Tour of Doctor Syntax, in Search of a Wife: A Poem*, published in 1821.

7. Jane Austen mentions Dr. Syntax in a letter to her beloved sister, Cassandra Austen,

dated March 2–3, 1814; the full quote included in Gillian Dow and Katie Halsey's "Jane Austen's Reading: The Chawton Years" reads: "I have seen nobody in London yet with such a long chin as Dr Syntax, nor Anybody quite so large as Gogmagoglicus" (n. pag.).

8. Another example of Syntax, whose pointed chin surpasses his nose, is "Doctor Syntax in a Court of Justice" also for *The Second Tour of Doctor Syntax*, 176.

9. Likewise, in one of Syntax's adventures from *The Third Tour of Doctor Syntax* called "Doctor Syntax Pursued by a Bull," Combe comments on Rowlandson's drawing of the frightened long-chinned figure in his trademark black suit scurrying up a tree to escape a mad bull, his hat falling off in the process.

10. In *Life in London*, Egan also implores his illustrators to exude "Hogarthian energy": "May thou also, Bob and George, *grapple* with an *Hogarthian* energy in displaying *tout à la mode* the sublime and *finished* part of the creation . . . what must always be a welcome visitor at every residence, and likewise an admired portrait over all the chimney-pieces in the kingdom, a PERFECT GENTLEMAN" (12).

11. Later in that same chapter, Egan calls attention to the authenticity of another crowded Robert and George Cruikshank plate entitled "Bow Street. Tom & Jerry's Sensibility Awakened at the Pathetic Tale of the Elegant Cyprian, the Feeling Coachman, and the Generous Magistrate": "The plate is an accurate representation of the Public Office, Bow Street: and the portrait of *Coachy*, is a fine specimen of the talents of the artist in his *personification* of CHARACTER. The countenance of the prisoners, as standing in the felon's box with irons on their legs, are also depicted with felicity of expression" (186).

12. Charles Dickens married Catherine Hogarth on 2 Apr. 1836.

13. According to the 1891 Victorian "London Census" transcription, a "jobmaster" hired out carriages, drivers, and horses. For more information, see <http://www.census1891.com/occupations-j.php>, accessed 16 Oct. 2016.

14. Biographers and critics from our time and Dickens's recognize that *Pickwick's* triumph was at least in part accidental. James Kinsley, editor of the 1986 Oxford edition and clearly a *Pickwick* fan, admits, "it started off almost by accident, with no serious design or goal, and gradually took on significance" (x). Robert Patten uses the term "accident" to describe Chapman and Hall's lucky decision to promote serial publication: "Dickens and his publishers discovered the potential of serial publication virtually by accident" (*CDP* 46). Kinsley also suggests the role chance played when "Dickens was discovered (and discovered himself) to be writing a novel" (*P*, Oxf. ix). Hereafter, the Oxford edition of Pickwick will be cited in the text parenthetically as "Oxf." followed by a page number.

15. For more discussion of these publication figures, see Patten, *CDP*, 65.

16. Dickens did not have "to invent a new comic climax every six pages," as Patten observes in *CDP* (65).

17. By 1740, this affordable format was well established for a host of popular hack publications, such as lurid weeklies about Old Bailey trials and trashy romances. Serials appeared in monthly parts and as a regular feature of a weekly or monthly magazine. Dickens—who made his career as a serial writer—participated in both forms of serialization. For example, *Pickwick* appeared in parts, but subsequent Dickens novels came out serially in *Bentley's Miscellany* at the cost of two shillings and sixpence and in Dickens's own two-penny weekly magazines, *Household Words* and *All the Year Round*.

18. Dickens used this expression in the preface to the 1869 Charles Dickens edition of *David Copperfield*; the line reads, "like many fond parents, I have in my heart of hearts a favourite child. And his name is DAVID COPPERFIELD." See "*David Copperfield* by Charles Dickens Prefaces, (1850 and 1869)."

19. As illustration became lucrative, caricaturists like George Cruikshank, Hablot Knight Browne, and John Leech found competition from Royal Academy painters including John Everett Millais, Dante Gabriel Rossetti, and Marcus Stone, who distinguished the illustrated book during its prime, as I explore in ch. 3.

20. For more on *Pickwick* and social class, see A. N. Wilson, *The Victorians*, 19–21.

21. Like *Sketches by Boz*, *Pickwick* proved formative for Dickens in its prison scenes that the author later developed in *David Copperfield* (1850) and *Little Dorrit* (1857).

22. This phrase is the title of Walter Houghton's 1963 book, *The Victorian Frame of Mind*.

23. The club members travel by coach and so provide an authentic record of coaching inns and journeys by coach relevant to historians of transportation today.

24. Likewise, Dickens's installments of *Nicholas Nickleby* became a vehicle for Post Office reform when copies of Henry Cole's postal reform play entitled "A Report of an Imaginary Scene at Windsor Castle Respecting the Uniform Penny Postage" were bound into part 13 (April 1839) of *Nickleby*, the best-selling novel of 1839.

25. A Philpot is an earthenware Staffordshire jug bearing the face or figure of a well-known person or character.

26. In *The Victorians*, 19, A. N. Wilson compares Weller to Sancho Panza, Don Quixote's loyal servant who acts as his squire.

27. Joe the "fat boy," a character with no other name, suffers from what today we call narcolepsy.

28. See Michael Hollington, *The Reception of Charles Dickens in Europe*, vol. 1, xxxv–xliii, for a complete list of translations of Dickens's works published between 1837–2013.

29. The Royal Doulton website lists the dates of manufacture for each *Pickwick* figurine and character jug. See <http://www.seawaychina.com/Pickwick-Papers-Royal-Doulton-Seriesware.aspx>, accessed 15 Oct. 2016.

30. Meisel includes this instruction from the script of Stirling's play and discusses the other two *Pickwick* adaptations in *Realizations*, 252.

31. "The first thirty-five years of the nineteenth century introduced more radical changes in book production than the preceding 350," as Patten observes (*CDP* 55).

32. In *Charles Dickens and His Publishers*, Patten similarly notes: "It is interesting to speculate what would have been the appearance of Dickens's work twenty years earlier, when woodblock and copperplate were the only processes perfected. There is no question that the mechanical advances and limitations in block-making significantly affected the shape of his serial fiction" (58–59).

33. For more detailed information on developments in printing that impacted production of illustrated books including stereotyping and photographic processes, I recommend Patten's *Charles Dickens and His Publishers*, 56–58.

34. Richard Hoe's rotary press made paper production even faster, permitting 20,000 impressions per hour by the year 1858; see Banham, "The Industrialization of the Book 1800-1970," 277.

35. Cruikshank's enormously popular *The Bottle* (1847) and *The Drunkard's Children* (1848) were reproduced with glyphography, which Richard Vogler describes as "a cheap form of graphic reproduction inferior to etchings" (159). This mode of reproduction allowed the publisher to sell all eight plates of *The Bottle* for only one shilling.

36. To Benjamin, only an "authentic" and "autonomous" work of art possessed an "aura," a term that captures a unique artwork's original function ("its original use value" [224]) and the life of its creator. However, *Pickwick* and other popular illustrated serials recall a time when authors and artists were intimately involved in the creation of works over a 1 ½- to 2-year period that arguably have a type of "aura," despite their reproducibility.

37. George P. Landow uses "created" and "invented" to describe the mass audience that *Pickwick* engendered in "Social and Economic Forces Influencing *Pickwick*'s Mass Readership" in *The Victorian Web*, <http://www.victorianweb.org/authors/dickens/pickwick/patten.pw2.html>, accessed 18 Sept. 2014. Likewise, A. N. Wilson notes in *The Victorians*, "*Pickwick* revealed (and perhaps in some senses created) the existence of a new public" (19).

38. For a full account of population changes, see Sally Mitchell, *Daily Life in Victorian England*, 13.

39. In *Daily Life in Victorian England*, 13, Mitchell states that in 1901, 80% of English people lived in cities. Richard Soloway in "Population and Demographics," 617, estimates that 75% lived in and around large cities in the industrial north at this time.

40. In *The English Common Reader*, 172, Altick suggests that this figure is based on the number of men and women ages sixteen to twenty-five who could sign the marriage register. Likely, the many "illiterate" adults are not reflected in this figure.

41. I am using the term "self-improvement," not "self-help"—a phrase aligned with Samuel Smiles, who used it in an 1845 speech and published a book entitled *Self-Help* in 1855.

42. Much to my chagrin, I have discovered that Victorian publishers often stopped an unsuccessful serial mid-track to recoup their losses.

43. *Bentley's Miscellany* (1837–40) demonstrates this trend. The first editor, Dickens, used *Bentley's* to showcase his own fiction. Initially, a feature entitled "Songs of the Month" preceded the *Oliver Twist* installments in 1837. By January 1838, *Oliver Twist* became first bill and remained so throughout 1838. *Bentley's* billed *Jack Sheppard* (1839) first for the final four months of *Twist*'s serial publication. Not surprisingly, at the conclusion of *Jack Sheppard*, *Bentley's*, under Ainsworth's editorship in 1839, repeated the same formula of promoting the editor's own work and starting a new serial alongside an older, successful one; *Guy Fawkes*, another Ainsworth and Cruikshank collaboration, had first billing in the final months that the wildly popular *Jack Sheppard* concluded. Ainsworth—who began his career as a three-volume novelist with *Rookwood* (1834) and ironically advised Dickens against serial publication—earned great popularity as a serial novelist; he also collaborated with Cruikshank for *The Miser's Daughter* (1842) and *Windsor Castle* (1843).

44. I recommend Eliot's full chapter in *The Cambridge Companion to the Victorian Novel*, edited by Deirdre David.

45. This figure comes from 1844, seven years after *Pickwick* concluded. Coffee stalls in 1842 typically sold baked potatoes, ham sandwiches, and bread and butter for 2 pence, or 1/6th of a shilling. For one penny, or 1/12th of a shilling, a working-class family could purchase a stale 4-lb. loaf of bread to feed the entire family; however, a fresh loaf the same

size could cost as much as 8 ½ pence in the 1840s or 2/3rds of a shilling; see Bentley, *The Victorian Scene*, 102.

46. In *Daily Life in Victorian England*, 36–37, Mitchell estimates that skilled workers like shipbuilders and steelmakers could earn £100 to £200 a year, a wage similar to middle-class bank clerks, teachers, senior clerks, civil servants, and small business owners, who typically earned £150 to £200 a year.

47. *Pickwick* mania arose during a decade of reforms including a reduction of the Stamp Tax in 1836 and inauguration of the Penny Post in 1840. With the lower Stamp Tax, a newspaper cost one penny to send through the post. Beginning on 10 Jan. 1840, all prepaid mail weighing up to ½ ounce could travel nationwide for only one penny. With these measures, reading material became more widely available.

48. Michael Steig in "Dickens, Hablôt Browne, and the Tradition of English Caricature" begins his article by comparing Dickens to Hogarth and suggests that "Dickens at times found Hogarth a useful touchstone" (219–20).

49. The stroller rants at his wife and child, manically telling Hutley that he fears they will retaliate upon him for starving them to fund his addiction to drink.

50. Philip Allingham's "The Discovery of Jingle in the Fleet," <http://www.victorianweb.org/art/illustration/phiz/pickwick/34.html>, accessed 7 July 2013, and ch. 2 from Michael Steig's *Dickens and Phiz* inform my analysis.

51. Dickens was testing out ideas he developed in his more mature fiction: emigration for rehabilitation factors heavily in *David Copperfield* (1850); Pickwick's incarceration for refusal to pay the corrupt lawyers of Mrs. Bardell (who sues him for a breach of promise) comes full force in his condemnation of the Chancery Court in *Bleak House* (1853).

52. The pairing of the grandfather and young girl is a visual anticipation of Little Nell's relationship with her degenerate grandfather in *The Old Curiosity Shop* (1841). A few small discrepancies between Dickens's text and Phiz's image include, for example, Jingle's position near the fireplace, not by the wall, and the woman watering the plants who looks gaunt, but not "haggard" as the text states.

53. Philip Allingham suggests that the barking dog vignette "parallels the granddaughter who fruitlessly tries to rouse her grandfather to an awareness of her and their surroundings" ("Discovery"). See <http://www.victorianweb.org/art/illustration/phiz/pickwick/34.html>, accessed 7 July 2013.

54. Philip Allingham goes on to note that the use of farce is not surprising since Dickens was writing several farces about mistaken identities at the time he was composing *Pickwick*: "*The Strange Gentleman* (performed at London's St. James's Theatre on 29 September 1836), whose plot involves mistaken identities at an inn in the north of England, and *Is She His Wife? Or, Something Singular*, again at the St. James's ([Dickens] and his wife, accompanied by his sister-in-law, Mary, attended a performance on 6 March 1837)."

55. Another plate depicting Pickwick in a compromising situation with a lady is Phiz's "Mrs. Bardell Faints in Mr. Pickwick's Arms" (Aug. 1836). Pickwick's landlady, the Widow Bardell, faints in front of witnesses. Dickens and Phiz theatrically stage her response to an alleged marriage proposal that Pickwick never actually makes (the widow misconstrues an innocent question to be a nuptial proposal). Mrs. Bardell leans into Pickwick's chubby arms and portly stomach while little Tommy Bardell ferociously kicks Pickwick in the

shin. Philip Allingham's *The Victorian Web* entry (accessed 18 Sept. 2014) entitled "Mrs. Bardell faints in Mr. Pickwick's arms" informs my analysis.

56. Harvey also makes this point on jollity and fatness, noting Mr. Pickwick "is the hero of the book because it is supposed to be especially funny to see a plump, prosperous, elderly man in *contretemps* where all his dignity is lost" (9).

57. Jane R. Cohen includes Seymour's image of a thin Mr. Pickwick in *Charles Dickens and His Original Illustrators,* 44.

58. Jane R. Cohen suggests that Seymour did not have to use Chapman's fat friend as a model; rather, he "simply selected from his earlier work one of his stock elderly Cockneys, suitably altered him, and the 'immortal' Pickwick, as Dickens called him, was created" (44).

59. Jane R. Cohen includes pictures by Seymour, Buss, and Browne to show how little Pickwick changes across these illustrators; see *Charles Dickens and His Original Illustrators,* 44.

60. When this serial appeared, postage, paid by the recipient, was high, except in major towns like London, which had a Twopenny Post prior to the nationwide Penny Post in 1840.

61. What Pickwick tells the ladies anticipates his comic misadventure: "'I should be very happy to afford you any amusement, . . . but I haven't done such a thing these thirty years'" (*P*, Oxf. 370).

Chapter 2. Caricature: A Theatrical Development

1. In *Reading Victorian Illustration, 1855–1875,* Paul Goldman calls caricature "a vignette style, playful in line, comic even when the text was not comic and, above all, theatrical, whimsical and decorative. Gestures were grandiose, facial expressions generalized, printing was usually light and there was little psychological depth or true interaction with text" (Goldman and Cooke 28). In *Caricature,* E. H. Gombrich and E. Kris playfully dub caricature the "Cinderella" of graphic art, but they qualify, "if the comic artist has the great advantage of being readily understood by his contemporary public"—as George Cruikshank, Hablot Knight Browne, and Robert Seymour were—"he pays for it by being more difficult of appreciation for the generations to come" (3–4).

2. Jonathan Hill goes into detail on the three Eastlake paintings and the two Wilkie paintings (including *Rent Day* [1807]) translated into these stage productions in "Cruikshank, Ainsworth, and Tableau Illustration," 440–41.

3. In *Daily Life in Victorian England,* 227–28, Sally Mitchell observes that in the later 1830s, more members of the middle class began to attend the theater.

4. *Oliver Twist* came out in *Bentley's Miscellany* from February 1837 until April 1839. There were three months that it did not appear—June 1837, October 1837, and September 1838—and the final issue was a double number. *Jack Sheppard* ran in *Bentley's* from January 1839 to February 1840.

5. These terms come from John Ruskin's *Sesame and Lilies,* 17.

6. *Oliver Twist* is Newgate-like in its sympathetic treatment of prostitutes and thieves in Fagin's criminal den. A real-life Jewish criminal named Ikey Solomon, a notorious receiver of stolen goods, is a likely model for Fagin. However, Dickens does not glamorize a life of crime as Ainsworth does in *Jack Sheppard* or *Rookwood,* which romanticizes highwayman

Dick Turpin. *Twist*'s perversion of the middle-class home and its inclusion of hidden identities, kidnapping, and murder align *Twist* with sensation fiction, a popular novel form that thrilled and shocked its Victorian audiences with the above subject matter as well as adultery, bigamy, illegitimacy, and madness. See Mirella Billi, "Dickens as Sensation Novelist," where she calls Dickens "the father of sensation fiction" (178).

7. Newgate or Old Bailey novels were popular from the 1820s to the 1840s.

8. The real Jack Sheppard sustained notoriety well after his death because of *The Newgate Calendar*, a monthly publication that began in the mid-eighteenth century to report Newgate Prison executions of notorious criminals. The *Calendar* appeared in various forms including a standard five-volume edition published in 1774 and a popular four-volume collection published in 1824–28. *The Newgate Calendar*—one of three top books found in a typical early Victorian middle-class home, along with the Bible and *Pilgrim's Progress*—sermonized against the life of crime that Newgate fiction glamorized.

9. When Sheppard was hanged at Tyburn in 1724, an estimated 200,000 were in attendance (a third of London's population at the time). Ainsworth patterns his fictional hero after the real-life Sheppard, but embellishes his romantic and criminal exploits. Some critics feared that Ainsworth, in transforming a thief into a dashing fictional hero, might induce readers to emulate Sheppard's drinking, womanizing, and thieving. The original audience recognized the influence of Hogarth's *Industry and Idleness* (1747) on both Ainsworth's novel and Cruikshank's accompanying illustrations (Meisel 268).

10. *Twist* also has elements of realism since Dickens aimed to "draw a knot of such associates in crime as really do exist; to paint them in all their deformity, in all their wretchedness . . . to shew them as they really are, . . . which would be a service to society," as he notes in his 1841 preface to the third edition (*OT*, Oxf. 1982 xxvi). *Oliver Twist* might best be seen as a combination novel, as Archibald argues: "*Oliver Twist* defies categorization. It is and is not a Newgate novel. It is and is not sensation fiction. It is and is not realism. . . . it is a hybrid of or bridge between these genres" ("'Of All the Horrors'" 53).

11. J. Pattie and J. Turner produced *Oliver Twiss*, by "Poz" in 1838; it came out in penny parts with Dickensian characters humorously renamed—Mr. Bumble is Fumble, and Mr. Sowerberry is Merrberry. "Poz" also wrote a *Pickwick* imitation entitled *Posthumous Papers of the Wonderful Discovery Club*, also published in 1838.

12. See Meisel, *Realizations*, 255–57, for detailed discussion of these adaptations.

13. The commercialization that *Jack Sheppard* stimulated was not surpassed until the publication of George Du Maurier's *Trilby* (1894).

14. The most successful adaptation of *Jack Sheppard* staged at the Adelphi Theatre by John Baldwin Buckstone—a production that earned the endorsement of both illustrator and author (Meisel 271)—is a testimony to the importance of Cruikshank's illustrations.

15. Thackeray anticipates a claim Cruikshank himself made thirty years later in "The Artist and the Author." Newgate fiction is known for poor prose as well as an exciting plot. In the introduction to *Rookwood*, Ainsworth humbly declares the inferiority of his "slight sketches" to the "admirable" renderings of this "inimitable artist": "It were needless to say a word in commendation of the admirable designs by GEORGE CRUIKSHANK which accompany this edition. They will speak (and eloquently) for themselves. But I may be

allowed to express the gratification I feel at the graphic manner in which my own slight sketches have been worked out by this inimitable artist" (xxviii).

16. "There are no less than ten of Jack's feats so described by Mr Cruikshank" (57), Thackeray adds. The verb "described" suggests the stroke of the artist, not the author, delineated Sheppard for its original readership.

17. Sheppard met Edgeworth Bess at Haynes Tavern and quickly grew addicted to her affections and drink; stealing supplemented his meager wages as a carpenter's apprentice, skills that made him an escape artist extraordinaire.

18. Jack files off his fetters in under an hour, then saws through two iron bars, and after the file breaks, uses a gimlet to pierce an oaken beam nine inches in thickness.

19. Ainsworth changes the facts in *Jack Sheppard*. Lyon and another criminal named Poll Maggott visited Sheppard at Newgate and distracted the guards, and the two criminal associates dressed Sheppard in women's clothing and led him to safety. In contrast, in Ainsworth's fiction, a different criminal, Sheppard's partner Joseph "Blueskin" Blake, disguises himself as an old man and smuggles in escape tools—a file, giblets, a chisel, and a piercer.

20. Richard Vogler calls "Oliver Asking for More" "the most famous illustration ever done to accompany a novel. The concept of an orphaned child asking for more when forced to live on a legally fixed diet insufficient to sustain life somehow caught the fancy of Englishmen of all classes, and the theme of 'asking for more' was used repeatedly in later decades of the last [nineteenth] century in *Punch* cartoons" (149). The theme of "asking for more," parodied in *Punch*, has resonated in political cartoons on topics as diverse as Watergate to soliciting donations for starving African children.

21. Parish records confirm that children died from malnourishment and suffered greatly from dysentery and ringworm.

22. *Dombey and Son* came out in monthly parts between October 1846 and April 1848.

23. Cruikshank caricatures the facial features of the old couple. For example, the old lady has decidedly masculine features that jar with the bow on her nightcap; her unladylike jaw drops open so wide that it nearly swallows her chin.

24. Thackeray calls this character the Marquis of Farintosh in the text, but the description of this suitor matches the drawing entitled "The Marquis 'en Montagnard.'" There is no direct mention of the "Marquis 'en Montagnard'" in the text, and the use of the quotation marks in the title of the illustration suggests it is a nickname for this particular suitor.

25. Dickens describes the setting at great length, noting tea preparations, Mrs. Corney's romping cats, wine bottles, and the round table where Corney and Bumble sit—all details which Cruikshank accurately renders.

26. A shipwreck scene based on Clarkson Stanfield's *The Abandoned* (1856) tellingly appears to the right of the mantle above a portrait of the betrayed husband.

27. Thackeray places *The Good Samaritan* painting in the backdrop of illustrations for *Vanity Fair* (1848) and *Pendennis* (1850) and features it as a pictorial capital for ch. 2, vol. II of *The Virginians* (1859).

28. Meisel discusses how the novel's theatricality converges in the character of Becky Sharp in *Realizations*, 330. His analysis of *Vanity Fair* and *tableau vivant*, 332–37, informs this discussion.

29. Charades was a favorite Victorian parlor game and is still played at parties today. Participants in the Victorian age acted out words in a phrase well known to the audience. Speaking was against the rules, but clues were allowed, and the players could divide words into syllables. Many Victorian novels include charade scenes, most famously *Jane Eyre* (1847) and *Vanity Fair*.

30. See, for example, Deborah A. Thomas's "Thackeray, Capital Punishment, and the Demise of Jos Sedley," where she argues that the public execution of François Benjamin Courvoisier impacted Thackeray's treatment of Jos Sedley's demise; to Thackeray, "executions, if they occur, should take place away from public view" (9).

31. John Sutherland raises the names of Becky's solicitors and other evidence to convict and clear Becky of murder in his essay, "Does Becky Kill Jos?" in *Is Heathcliff a Murderer?*

32. John Buchanan-Brown elaborates this point in *The Book Illustrations of George Cruikshank*, 43–44. Cruikshank also uses lighting most skillfully in Ainsworth's *The Miser's Daughter* (1842) in "Abel Beechcroft Discovering the Body of the Miser in the Cellar." The final plate in *The Drunkard's Children* (1848) depicting the drunkard's daughter—now a prostitute and "gin mad" in the process of committing suicide—has led critics to compare Cruikshank to Rembrandt.

33. In *George Cruikshank's Life, Times, and Art*, vol. 2, 87, Patten, for example, notes Cruikshank simply did not heed Dickens's caution that the artist could not capture this chase scene.

34. In *George Cruikshank's Life, Times, and Art*, vol. 2, Patten claims, "The whole plate is bravura pictorial narration, fully in accord with Dickens's vivid prose yet independent and supplementary, a similar story told by different means" (87–88).

35. Likewise, Patten states in *George Cruikshank's Life, Times, and Art*, "It is arguably the most celebrated etching Cruikshank ever made and among the most famous book illustrations of all time" (2: 88–89). He adds, "What makes the illustration so immeasurably powerful is not only the physiognomy of the figure but also its evocation of Fagin's psychic terror" (91).

36. Those invested in Sixties illustration often make the claim that the caricaturists were not capable of showing psychological depth; see, for example, Paul Goldman's "Defining Illustration Studies," 28.

37. See ch. 4 where I discuss in more depth the anti-Semitic depiction of Fagin and reference the work of Deborah Heller, Susan Meyer, and Lauriat Lane.

38. To create the plate, Cruikshank posed in front of the mirror, crouching and gnawing at his knuckles and tossing his hair about; in doing so, Cruikshank transformed himself into a desperate Fagin, and that is what he drew. For a fuller account of Cruikshank's creation of this plate, see Patten, *George Cruikshank's Life, Times, and Art*, 2: 91.

39. In ch. 51, Dickens devotes only the final paragraph to Fagin's imminent hanging and the spectacle of Victorian execution:

> Day was dawning when they again emerged. A great multitude had already assembled; the windows were filled with people, smoking and playing cards to beguile the time; the crowd were pushing, quarrelling, and joking. Everything told of life and

animation, but one dark cluster of objects in the very centre of all—the black stage, the cross-beam, the rope, and all the hideous apparatus of death. (*OT*, Oxf. 1982 347)

Fagin's hanging occurs offstage, although the rowdy populace anticipates it with "a peal of joy" (340).

40. Plates like "Fagin in the Condemned Cell" brought Cruikshank critical acclaim. Charles Baudelaire believed Cruikshank's strength as an artist lay in his mastery of the grotesque. John Ruskin recognizes in *Modern Painters* that Cruikshank's "tragic power, though rarely developed, and warped by habits of caricature, is, in reality, as great as his grotesque power" (*Elements* 341). Ruskin ranks Cruikshank foremost among etchers and compares him to Rembrandt, Albrecht Dürer, and William Hogarth.

41. Tenniel's illustrations made *Alice's Adventures in Wonderland* a success, and they are still reproduced today in editions like *The Annotated Alice*, edited by Martin Gardner; references to the text of *Alice in Wonderland* come from *The Annotated Alice* and are cited parenthetically in the text as *AA* followed by the page number. Translated into more than seventy languages and never out of print, *Alice in Wonderland* has become a cultural icon, sparking collectible commodities—for example, clothing, games, bed linens, porcelain figurines and plates—as well as films, graphic novels, and stage adaptations (as early as 1876 in London).

42. Although little known today, Surtees was a popular nineteenth-century author and an avid sportsman and hunter, activities which provided him with plenty of material for his series. Surtees did write two society novels, *"Ask Mama"* (1858) and *"Plain or Ringlets?"* (1860).

43. Surtees, a country gentleman with his own pack of hounds, began his books as a series of loosely related adventures published in the *New Sporting Magazine* between 1831–34, which led to serial publication of *Handley Cross*, published in that magazine between 1838–39. The novel version, illustrated by John Leech and published in 1854, has merited critical attention.

44. This same stereotype appears in William Mulready's 1840 design for the first prepaid envelope accompanying the Penny Post as well as numerous political cartoons about the first and second Opium Wars between England and China in, respectively, 1839–42 and 1856–60.

45. In *The Dickens Picture-Book*, Hammerton more generally states of Cruikshank: "He could not draw a pleasing female figure" (4). In my article "Cruikshank's Illustrative Wrinkle in *Oliver Twist*'s Misrepresentation of Class" in *Book Illustrated*, I analyze the consequences to Dickens's text of Cruikshank's inability to draw an attractive woman.

46. See Kathleen Tillotson's introduction to the Clarendon Press edition of *Oliver Twist*, xxxvi; Tillotson suggests that Dickens would have likely criticized Cruikshank for his portrayal of Nancy had the author conceived of the women as a pair sooner.

47. Thackeray had supporters like Charlotte Brontë, who called Thackeray a "wizard of a draughtsman" (qtd. in Richard Dunn's essay "Out of the Picture?" in *The Brontës in the World of the Arts*, 40). Du Maurier also praises Thackeray in "The Illustrating of Books," 2: 371. For criticism of Thackeray, see, for example, Graham Everitt, *The Illustrated Book*, and Donald Hannah, "The Author's Own Candles."

48. Harvey hands Thackeray a backward compliment, noting that the artist "consistently

succeeds" in small designs like pictorial capitals. In "Thackeray's Pictorial Capitals," 136–37, Joan Stevens applauds the pictorial capitals for previewing a chapter or commenting on the narrator.

49. Many critics gloss over Carroll's illustrations to promote subsequent illustrators of *Alice*. See, for example, *The Tenniel Illustrations to the "Alice" Books* where Michael Hancher refers to faults in Carroll's "naïve" (32) drawings. Richard Kelly also criticizes Carroll's illustrations in "'If You Don't Know What a Gryphon Is.'"

50. Browne worked consistently into the 1850s whereas Cruikshank found his employment drying up by the end of the 1840s. Nonetheless, Phiz, like Cruikshank, could not "make the transition to the new kind of illustration" (Steig, *Dickens and Phiz* 11).

51. As Meisel notes in *Realizations*, "That there were conventions for the representation of character and emotion or the embodiment of a situation in the nineteenth century we know from old movies and the crude relics that survive even today as mock melodrama" (5).

52. In *Charles Dickens and His Original Illustrators*, Jane R. Cohen points to how Robert Seymour, "the experienced artist, whose name had originally been considered the only real asset to the project, was now playing second fiddle to an obscure writer supposedly hired to concoct a story around the plates" (46).

53. A. N. Wilson concurs in *The Victorians*: "Seymour's suicide was prompted by his own mental illness, not Dickens's success" (18).

54. Indeed, Patten devotes a full chapter to "The Artist and the Author" in vol. 2 of *George Cruikshank's Life, Times, and Art*.

55. Ainsworth insisted Cruikshank never actually wrote a line in either book and called Cruikshank's claim of authorship an "'absurd pretension'" trumped up "'in his dotage'" (qtd. in Patten, *George Cruikshank's Life, Times, and Art* 2: 485). John Buchanan-Brown advances in *The Book Illustrations of George Cruikshank* that Cruikshank's claim for origination of Ainsworth's *The Tower of London* and *The Miser's Daughter* was "better substantiated" than for *Oliver Twist* (27). Harvey sympathizes: "Cruikshank's desire to usurp his novelists is well-known as an aberrant nuisance, and I have wanted to show that, far from being simply a function of his conceit and eccentricity, this desire is understandable and deserving of sympathy. Everyone said he was the new Hogarth, and he must surely have felt he had the right to be not less than an equal in any collaboration" (34). Moreover, Jane R. Cohen believes that "The allegations of the Seymours, like those of Cruikshank, are not without some basis" (50).

Chapter 3. Realism, Victorian Material Culture, and the Enduring Caricature Tradition

1. Brian Maidment lists works by early caricaturists that commanded a market throughout the nineteenth century in *Comedy, Caricature and the Social Order, 1820–50*, 7–14.

2. ABE Books sells many of these late nineteenth-century reprinted publications.

3. Carroll based the character of Alice on his favorite child friend, Alice Liddell. Underneath this photograph is a drawing of Alice made by Carroll. The British Library discovered it in 1977 when cleaning the *Under Ground* manuscript.

4. Gleeson White in *English Illustration, 'The Sixties': 1855-70* views the Sixties as a period

of fifteen years. In *Illustrators of the Eighteen Sixties*, Forrest Reid notes the Sixties is "a move-ment rather than a decade" (1) and recognizes that fine work came out before 1855 and after 1870. Goldman and Cooke suggest in *Reading Victorian Illustration, 1855–1875*, 1, that the term Sixties "inaccurately" labels this style of illustration that preceded and succeeded that productive decade.

5. In *Reading Victorian Illustration, 1855–1875*, Goldman and Cooke say about the Sixties: "the primary aesthetic is one of 'poetic naturalism,' a means of representing deep feeling which was still rooted in observation of the 'real' world" (1).

6. A painting hung in the drawing room of a fashionable home or in a Royal Academy exhi-bition, but an illustrated periodical entered circulating libraries, the family parlor, and servants' quarters. Frances Sarzano adds in *Sir John Tenniel*: "In the 'sixties' many painters experimented with book-illustration, while others made it a bread-and-butter occupation" (11).

7. Queen Victoria opened the first ever World's Fair on 1 May 1851, visited it more than forty times, and exhibited many of her own treasures there. Dubbed Prince Albert's brain-child, the Great Exhibition was a monumental international exposition of culture, technol-ogy, and industry with a humanitarian vision. Prince Albert advanced: "'THE EXHIBI-TION of 1851 is to give us a true test and a living picture of the point of development at which the whole of mankind has arrived in this great task, and a new starting point from which all nations will be able to direct their future exertions'" (*ODIC* 1: 4).

8. The 990,000 square foot building that Sir Joseph Paxton designed used more large sheets of affordable, strong glass than ever before and did not require interior lighting. Writ-ing for *Punch* under a pseudonym on 13 July 1850, Douglas Jerrold referred to the building as a "palace of very crystal," and the phrase "Crystal Palace," in turn, appeared in *Punch* on 2 Nov. 1850. Noteworthy among the wondrous exhibits are the Great Diamond of Runjeet Singh, known as the "Koh-i-Noor" or Mountain of Light; a pair of exquisite cut-glass chandeliers eight feet in height made by a Birmingham manufacturer; and an elab-orately carved wooden cradle made of Turkey boxwood to symbolize the union of two Royal lineages, the Royal Houses of England and Saxe-Coburg and Gotha, Prince Albert's homeland.

9. There was a British side of the building and a side devoted to foreign nations and colonial holdings in Asia, Africa, America, and Australasia.

10. Parenthetical text citations are cited as *ODIC*, followed by volume and page, hereafter in the text and notes. Whereas in the eighteenth century, France was foremost in book illus-tration, in the nineteenth century, an increasingly industrialized Britain gained prominence in illustration and book production. There were national exhibitions of commerce before 1851, such as the French Industrial Exhibition of 1844; some argue the Great Exhibition was the British response to this impressive French achievement.

11. In his introduction to section 3, class 17, in the *ODIC*, Robert Ellis posits that the manufacture of books and papers, "ministering not to the personal or domestic wants of mankind, so much as to their intellectual requirements . . . is coextensive with the diffusion of knowledge" (2: 536). Ellis's phrase draws from a popular self-education movement, "The Society for the Diffusion of Useful Knowledge," which promoted inexpensive publications for the increasingly literate lower and middle classes not privy to a formal education. Shar-ing Prince Albert's humanitarian goals for the exhibition, Ellis contends:

morally and intellectually considered, the present Class relates to a species of industry exercising indirectly a more extensive influence over social economy than any of those into which this Exhibition has been subdivided. Books, it has been said, carry the productions of the human mind over the whole world, and may be truly called the raw materials of every kind of science and art, and of all social improvement. (2: 536)

12. See, for example, *The Pictorial Bible* published by John Kitto in London in 1855. It includes about 200 illustrations—initials, tailpieces, maps, and vignettes, <http://archive.org/stream/pictorialbible02kitt#page/no/mode/2up>, accessed 17 July 2013.

13. Prior to Bulaq, there was a short-lived press during the French expedition in Egypt that ended with France's withdrawal from Egypt. Entry 248 does not appear with the other items in "Paper, Printing, and Bookbinding" but at the end of vol. 3 under "Egypt," 1410. See Peter Colvin's "Muhammad Ali Pasha," 251.

14. Although the Arts and Crafts movement (1860–1910) is closely aligned with William Morris and the fin de siècle, this initiative began with the Pre-Raphaelites, particularly Rossetti, who took pride in the art of the book and who joined with Morris (as well as Edward Burne-Jones, Philip Webb, and others) in the creation of Morris's business entitled Morris, Marshall, Faulkner & Co (1861–75), which they dubbed "the Firm."

15. White notes that *The Art Journal* aimed to bring "fine art to the homes of the great British public through the medium of wood-engravings in a way not attempted previously" (14). There was also "an illustrated chronicle of the Great Exhibition, which was afterwards merged in a *Magazine of Art*" (14).

16. A shopkeeper might use pages of a book to wrap edible and non-edible items, and periodicals also found extended life as curlpapers for women's hairdos and pie tin liners in Victorian kitchens. Defacing a book by cutting out an illustration for framing—an all too common habit that collector-authors Gleeson White and Forrest Reid practiced—seems a more minor offense than using pages of a book to wrap up fish and chips.

17. In *Mary Barton*, Mr. Carson takes down the "little used" Bible to find the words of Luke 23:34; "They know not what they do," the phrasing which Gaskell includes in her novel, forms part of the line that reads in the Bible, "'Father, forgive them; for they know not what they do.'" Carson's action marks a profound change in the nature of the entitled mill owner who initially blames an innocent man for murder (Jem Wilson) and ultimately forgives his son's actual murderer (John Barton).

18. Reading in the nineteenth century was also viewing. Lewis Carroll memorably calls attention to the importance of pictures in a famous line from *Alice in Wonderland*: "'and what is the use of a book,' thought Alice, 'without pictures or conversations?'" (*AA* 11); this and all quotes from *Alice* come from *The Annotated Alice*, a version of *Alice's Adventures in Wonderland* edited and annotated by Martin Gardner, hereafter cited parenthetically in the text as *AA* followed by a page number. *Jane Eyre* (1847) opens with Jane ensconced in the window seat in Gateshead, pouring over pictures in Bewick's *History of British Birds* (1797, 1804) in which "Each picture told a story" (6). Maggie Tulliver, criticized for reading *The Political History of the Devil* (1726) by Daniel Defoe in *The Mill on the Floss* (1860), seems more fascinated with the image of "Ducking a Witch" than the

book's contents. For further discussion of C. Brontë's and Eliot's child readers, see my book *Images of the Woman Reader*, ch. 2 and ch. 3.

19. The unfortunate process of "extracting" (11) quality illustrations from periodicals, as Forrest Reid calls it, arose when magazine illustration came to be seen as art worth collecting. Reid, too, was a collector with a conscience when it came to "rare" magazines: "to mutilate a volume of *The Cornhill* or *Good Words* is an act of vandalism, to say nothing of the really rare magazines" (11). Gleeson White calls this process "print-splitting" and explains how to extract prints from inexpensive publications and frame them. White likewise cautions: "hesitate before cutting up a fine book, and be not hasty in mutilating a volume of *Once a Week* or the *Shilling Magazine*" (7).

20. In this opening notice, the publisher expresses a "'desire to render an act of justice to the eminent artists . . . by exhibiting, with the aid of the finest printing, the real quality of those illustrations, as Works of Art'" (qtd. in Reid 11–12).

21. Regrettably, Reid does not disclose the source of this quotation.

22. Although Walter Benjamin argues in "The Work of Art in the Age of Mechanical Reproduction" that in the process of duplication, an original art work loses its aura, "Rossetti finds a way to imbue his poetic objects with the kind of aura that neither craft nor commercial manufacture—and his books participate in aspects of both—is supposed to allow" (Helsinger 185).

23. For more discussion of this spelling change, Rossetti substituting an "e" for the "i" in "Elfin," see Stephanie Pina's "Pre-Raphaelite Sisterhood."

24. I recommend Simon Cooke's *Victorian Web* entry on "Dante Gabriel Rossetti as an Illustrator," <http://www.victorianweb.org/art/illustration/dgr/cooke.html>, accessed 7 Oct. 2014.

25. Paul Goldman, who likewise foregrounds William Allingham's *The Music Master* in "Defining Illustration Studies," underscores that "Rossetti's single drawing for 'The Maids of Elfen-Mere' was to prove immensely influential on all the other artists working in illustration at the time and not only on other Pre-Raphaelites" (27). Rossetti, however, pulled out the illustration from his own copy and wrote to his mother of the "offending" drawing: "'there are some illustrations by Hughes, one by Millais, and one which used to be by me till it became the exclusive work of Dalziel, who cut it'" (qtd. in Reid 33).

26. Forrest Reid likewise observes: "without reading a line of the text we should know that we are looking at the inhabitants of two worlds—that the boy belongs to this earth, while the Maids are only visitors here" (35). Reid regrettably does not indicate the source for this quote.

27. Laurence Housman used D. G. Rossetti's 1860s drawings to guide his illustrations for an 1893 edition of *Goblin Market* published just before Christina Rossetti's death. C. Rossetti asked Housman to look at D. G. Rossetti's frontispiece to ascertain how the goblins should look; while Housman earned praise for recalling D. G. Rossetti's initial designs, Christina found them lacking.

28. D. G. Rossetti also designed illustrations for sister Christina's *The Prince's Progress* (1866). In *Christina Rossetti and Illustration*, Lorraine Kooistra describes how publishers marketed *Goblin Market* for public consumption.

29. Between 1861 and 1871, Rossetti also designed bindings for Algernon Charles Swin-

burne's *Atalanta in Calydon* (1865) and *Songs Before Sunrise* (1871), his brother William Michael's translation of Dante's *Inferno* (1865), his sister Maria's commentary on Dante (1871), and his own book of poetry entitled *Poems* (1870).

30. Illustrators of *Goblin Market* often emphasize sin and sexuality versus virtue, sexuality or innocence in their depictions of, respectively, Laura and Lizzie facing temptation. In *Christina Rossetti and Illustration*, Kooistra includes the cheery, child friendly illustrations of Ellen Raskin for a 1970 Dutton version as well as, at the other extreme, the sensual plates of Kinuko Craft for a 1973 edition published by *Playboy*.

31. Kooistra's separate readings of these two Rossetti images (69–74) are persuasive, but she curiously does not comment on their contiguous placement in the book D. G. Rossetti designed.

32. Laura's facial features and form recall those of Fanny Cornforth, Rossetti's first model for his painting *Found* (1848–unfinished) about a fallen woman.

33. Rossetti includes details from the gilt frames he crafted for his own paintings to frame the sleeping sisters in the privacy of their boudoir. Kooistra suggests, alternately, that we are peeping into their boudoir via an open window.

34. Tennyson's *Poems*, issued by Edward Moxon in 1857, divides the 54 plates among two groups of illustrators—24 to established painters including Daniel Maclise, William Mulready, and Clarkson Stanfield; 30 to the Pre-Raphaelites with 18 to Millais, 7 to Holman Hunt, and 5 to Rossetti. Tennyson took little interest in Moxon's "picture gallery," a reprinting of poems originally published without illustrations. Reid observes, "If the public wanted them they should have them, but the pictures that mattered [to Tennyson] were those his own art evoked" (43).

35. Judith Fisher similarly divides the nineteenth century into two periods of illustration in "Image Versus Text":

> from 1800 to mid-century, Isaac and George Cruikshank and Phiz and Thackeray drew on Hogarth's allusive and allegorical representation and on the great caricaturists James Gillray and Thomas Rowlandson to create "speaking" pictures. From the 1850s on, primarily through John Everett Millais's illustrations of Trollope's novels ... a style deriving from English genre painting emerged that increasingly subordinated the image to the text. (60)

36. Du Maurier's French father had hoped his son would follow him into a career in science, but art was George's passion. In 1856, Du Maurier trained in Charles Gleyre's Parisian atelier alongside James McNeil Whistler and E. J. Poynter. Du Maurier pursued further training at the Antwerp Academy in Belgium, but while studying there, he lost vision in his left eye and returned to London in 1860 and launched a career as an illustrator. Reid includes Whistler, Poynter, and Du Maurier in *Illustrators of the Eighteen Sixties* (1928).

37. Henry James remarks in *Du Maurier and London Society*, "*Punch*, for the last fifteen years, has been, artistically speaking, George du Maurier" (5). To Reid, "It was the novelist in him [Du Maurier], of course, that appealed to Henry James" (176). James, a fierce critic of the illustrated book, praised Du Maurier's book illustrations in an 1897 review of Du Maurier's illustrated fiction for *Harper's New Monthly Magazine*. See also Philip Allingham's

"George Du Maurier: Illustrator and Novelist" for *The Victorian Web*, <http://www.victorianweb.org/art/illustration/dumaurier/pva95.html>, accessed 15 Oct. 2016.

38. In addition to his work for *Punch* and *Once a Week*, Du Maurier produced illustrations for *The Leisure Hour, Good Words*, and *The Cornhill Magazine*.

39. Cynthia promised to marry Mr. Preston when, at the age of sixteen, he gave her £20, so she could buy a party dress.

40. Another excellent equine illustration in *The History of Henry Esmond* is "Parting," showing Henry leaving Castlewood to attend college at Cambridge. In *Wives and Daughters*, Lady Harriet sits sidesaddle on an elegant white horse in "Lady Harriet Asks One or Two Questions."

41. Bathsheba marries Troy (who loves Fanny Robin, who dies giving birth to Troy's child) and reluctantly agrees to marry Boldwood when she believes Troy to be dead. Troy, who is alive, returns and is murdered by Boldwood, who descends into madness, leaving Bathsheba to marry Gabriel Oak, who loves her all along. We are meant to believe Bathsheba and Troy are meeting illicitly in the woods. Even the title titillates since at this point in the narrative, readers are not yet privy to Bathsheba's secret marriage to Troy.

42. Jane R. Cohen notes: "Stone, who had no ties to the Hogarth-Cruikshank-Browne tradition, would not revert to their outmoded styles, which suited the author's desire for novelty in his work" (204).

43. "Like the best illustrations of such earlier visual commentators as John Leech, George Cruikshank, and Phiz (Hablot Knight Browne)," notes Philip Allingham, "this woodcut by Marcus Stone prepares the reader for a significant event in the narrative and compels the reader to be more attentive to nuances of the text that shed light on the characters' motivations, attitudes, and relationships" ("Working Class").

44. In "'Reading the Pictures, Visualizing the Text,'" Philip Allingham favors Fred Barnard over Phiz and advances: "Barnard has given us Dickens's characters as they step forth from the pages and into our minds: three-dimensional, substantial, active, and insistently real in settings not crowded with the symbolic details that were Phiz's landmark" (175). In the following sentence, Allingham highlights differences in technique and training between the two schools of illustration: "These 'New Men of the Sixties,' *in contrast to* the leading illustrators of the previous generation, were formally trained rather than self-taught" (162; my emphasis).

45. The caricaturists had to meet tight monthly deadlines—the novels were being illustrated as they were being written—but Barnard had Dickens's entire novel and Phiz's illustrations at his disposal before he began to illustrate. Although Barnard was robbed of Dickens's creative counsel, he was a close friend of Phiz, who provided Barnard indirect access to Dickens's original ideas. See Allingham and Louttit's "The Illustrators of the Household Edition of the *Works of Charles Dickens* (22 vols., 1871–79)."

46. Gleeson White, one of the caricaturists' harshest critics, recognizes illustrations by Barnard and other Sixties artists essentially "re-embody characters already stereotyped, for the most part, by the earlier plates of the original editions" (138). White adds in *English Illustration* that the Household Edition was a "bold enterprise: that it did not wholly fail is greatly to its credit" (138). White argues that many who praise the original illustrations of Dickens regard them with a nostalgic "halo of memory and romance," but the sketches in

White's opinion cannot compare to "the beauty of truth, the knowledge born of academic accomplishment, or literal imitation of nature" evident in the Household Edition that were simply "beyond [the caricaturists'] sympathy" (139).

47. Barnard collaborated with Luke Fildes and E. G. Dalziel for the illustrations for *The Mystery of Edwin Drood* (1870) published along with reprinted pieces and other stories in 1879 as volume 20 of the Household Edition series.

48. The Household Edition includes Forster's *The Life of Charles Dickens* in addition to Dickens's complete works. For more information on the Household Edition, I recommend Allingham and Louttit's "The Illustrators of the Household Edition of the *Works of Charles Dickens* (22 vols., 1871–79)."

49. This is a Victorian term for a large overcoat similar to a frock coat.

50. David's positioning and clothing resemble those in Phiz's "Somebody Turns Up," only here David looks warily at Heep. In "He Caught the Hand in His, And We Stood in that Connection, Looking at Each Other," Barnard eliminates all background detail to foreground the two figures. The reader-viewer readily sees Phiz's indelible imprint of a "red-sun" eyed, stubble-headed, clammy-handed Heep underpinning Barnard's realistically rendered depiction of "writhing" Uriah (*DC*, Norton 204).

51. Buss's painting *Dickens's Dream* (ca. 1875) came out after Barnard illustrated this novel.

52. A pronounced nose defines Fagin in Mahoney's plates for other scenes in *Oliver Twist*, such as where Fagin conspires with Monks in "'Fagin!' Whispered a Voice Close to His Ear."

53. Philip Allingham suggests that the "deliberately out-of-focus tiles and blurred background may indicate the influence of early photography as the illustrator employs a selective focus on the fugitive [Sikes]" in "Illustrations by James Mahoney" on *The Victorian Web*, accessed 17 Oct. 2016.

54. Another realistic urban backdrop appears in Mahoney's reinterpretation of "The Meeting" now entitled "When She Was About the Same Distance in Advance as She Had Been Before, He Slipped Quietly Down."

55. Dickens conceived of Nancy and Rose as Oliver's twin defenders; "Two Sister-Women" was the first descriptive headline for ch. 40. See Tillotson's introduction to the 1966 Clarendon Press *Oliver Twist*, xxxvi.

56. This detail is contradictory to the text since Dickens notes that Sikes held the murder weapon soaked in blood and hair in a fire he kindled "till it broke, and then piled it on the coals to burn away, and smoulder into ashes" (*OT*, Oxf. 1982 304).

57. Rose Lovell-Smith argues that Tenniel's skill with drawing animals aids our reading of Carroll's text in her article "The Animals of Wonderland." For example, "through his animal drawings, Tenniel offers a visual angle on the text of *Alice in Wonderland* that evokes the life sciences, natural history, and Darwinian ideas about evolution, closely related by Tenniel to Alice's size changes, and to how these affect the animals she meets" (385).

58. For example, Michael Hancher in *The Tenniel Illustrations to the "Alice" Books* applauds Carroll "for more powerfully evoking fetal claustrophobia" (31) than Tenniel in his *Wonderland* rendition of this same scene of Alice outgrowing the White Rabbit's house.

59. In his biography of Tenniel, Sarzano states: "he was untaught, except for a few les-

sons at the Academy Schools, which he quitted in dissatisfaction" (9), but he later notes on page 10 that Tenniel and several other artists went to Munich on a British government commission to study fresco technique. Tenniel attended anatomy lectures and studied sculpture on display at the British Museum and prints of costume and armor in its reading room.

60. For more discussion of the impact of Tenniel's monocularism on his artistry, see Morris's *Artist of Wonderland*, 2–3.

61. In *Illustrators of the Eighteen Sixties*, Reid praises Tenniel's contributions, "which have made the designs for the two *Alices* famous" (27); however, Reid places Tenniel in a group with John Gilbert and Birket Foster and calls all three artists "precursors" of the Sixties "since they were working before that date and remained uninfluenced either by the Pre-Raphaelites or the school of naturalistic artists that succeeded them" (20). Likewise, in *English Illustration, 'The Sixties': 1855–70*, White calls *Alice* "An epoch-making book of this season" and adds "*Alice in Wonderland* (Macmillan), with Tenniel's forty-two immortal designs, needs only bare mention, for who does not know it immediately?" (127).

62. Hancher suggests that the version Carroll showed Tenniel was not the same exact book he gave to Alice Liddell since Carroll did not finish his pictures until 13 Sept. 1864. Carroll gave Tenniel a copy to look at between 25 January and 5 April 1864, at which point Tenniel agreed to draw the pictures (27). In *Artist of Wonderland*, Morris states that Tenniel asked to see Carroll's manuscript (139).

63. For more information on pantomime in the Victorian era, see Morris, *Artist of Wonderland*, 156–62; Morris includes many playing card pantomimes of the period, such as *Harlequin Jack of All Trades* (1825) and the *Punch* article entitled "Our Courts of Law" (1849).

64. *Looking-Glass* (1872) carries forward these aspects of pantomime, although Carroll did not provide designs from which Tenniel could build. Hence, I center my discussion on *Wonderland*.

65. Kelly criticizes Carroll's anatomical confusion in the Caterpillar illustration in "'If You Don't Know What a Gryphon Is.'"

66. Foremost, Wonderland is a strange world where characters change size and shape: a baby turns into a pig, the Cheshire Cat dissolves into a grin, and Alice's body undergoes profound distortions.

67. Morris devotes a chapter to "Alice and Social Caricature" in *Artist of Wonderland*, 206–22. Morris does not believe the Lion and the Unicorn are portraits of, respectively, Gladstone and Disraeli. She argues, however, that Carroll was a fan of Gladstone and suspicious of the Pope. Although her chapter informs my discussion, Morris does not discuss the White Rabbit or the Mock Turtle in her work on social caricature in *Alice*, the two characters central to my analysis.

68. Alice is not startled that the rabbit can talk, or that he is talking to himself and muttering, "'Oh dear! Oh dear! I shall be too late!'" (*AA* 11), but she is astonished that the rabbit owns a watch and can tell time.

69. For *Wonderland*, Carroll changes the nosegay to a fan (*AA* 22).

70. Engen similarly describes Carroll's Mock Turtle as an "armour-plated, seal-faced turtle" (80).

Chapter 4. Caricature and Realism: Fin-de-Siècle Developments of the Victorian Illustrated Book

1. Maxwell qualifies in the next sentence in *The Victorian Illustrated Book*: "For some reason, however, it will not stay dead . . . and became a crucial starting point for symbolist, surrealist, postsurrealist, and eventually postmodern practices among artists, writers, and a range of other enterprising biblio-savants" (418–19). These later developments of the Victorian illustrated book grew out of the niche market of illustrated books aimed at collectors and an educated elite, dating to the genre's decline in the publication of mainstream fiction.

2. For "The Victorian Era Exhibition" at Earl's Court in 1897, the Dalziel Brothers earned the Diploma for a Silver Medal for engravings after John Tenniel's *Through the Looking-Glass*, plates from *Dalziels' Bible Gallery*, and select proofs from Millais's illustrations for *The Parables of Our Lord and Saviour Jesus Christ*.

3. Jane R. Cohen shapes the Victorian illustrated book to fit the arc of Dickens's publishing career, aligning the rise of the genre with Dickens's *The Pickwick Papers* (1836–37). I challenge the simple rise and fall organizational pattern that Cohen uses to describe the trajectory of the illustrated book in *Charles Dickens and His Original Illustrators*.

4. In her final chapter of *Charles Dickens and His Original Illustrators*, Jane R. Cohen likewise advances: "the technical, economic, sociological, and aesthetic conditions that fostered its rise also accelerated its degeneration" (229). Some of her insights inform this section although I take issue with her use of the term "degeneration," which connotes deterioration and eclipses late nineteenth-century developments in the evolution of the Victorian illustrated book.

5. See David Ward's "First Library of the People Marks 150 Busy Years" for a discussion of the opening of the Manchester Public Library.

6. For analysis of the reasons why publishers dropped illustrations for volume publication of Hardy's novels, I recommend Philip Allingham's "Why do Hardy's novels often have illustrations in periodical but not book form?" from *The Victorian Web*, <http://www.victorianweb.org/authors/hardy/pva151.html>, accessed 18 Oct. 2014.

7. For the 1840 statistics, see Richard Altick, *The English Common Reader*, 169–72. For the 1900 figures, see G. R. Porter, *The Progress of the Nation*, 147.

8. In *George Du Maurier*, Richard Kelly posits that "Little Billee is like Du Maurier in several respects" (113) and goes on to discuss the similarities the author shares with his fictional creation.

9. Joyce's *Ulysses* (1922) was, however, published in 1935 by the Limited Editions Club with illustrations by Matisse (J. R. Cohen 230), following in the tradition of artists' books.

10. Ibbetson returns in dreams to his early life in Passy, a Parisian suburb, especially when he is incarcerated in a home for the criminally insane after killing his devious uncle in a mad rage. The first half of *The Martian* is heavily autobiographical and suitable for realistic illustration. The English-French Barty Josselin, a thinly veiled depiction of Du Maurier, studies art in Antwerp, loses sight in one eye, fears total blindness, becomes an illustrator of Du Maurier's stature, and even becomes friends with the Du Maurier's real life artist friends, Edward Poynter and Holman Hunt.

11. See ch. 3 of my book *Posting It: The Victorian Revolution in Letter Writing* for discussion of how commodities like writing desks were classed and gendered items and fell out of fashion when made commercially following the Great Exhibition of 1851.

12. As industrial mechanization increasingly took over book production, the cost of paper decreased, and the paper tax was repealed in 1861.

13. Two years later in 1885, Cassell and Company brought out an illustrated edition of *Treasure Island* in England with a combination of plates by a French illustrator named Georges Roux, a few of Merrill's illustrations, and Stevenson's own treasure map. An advertisement for the just released *King Solomon's Mines* (1885) by H. Rider Haggard appears within this edition, further aligning these two adventure tales for boys. *Treasure Island's* most famous illustrator is N. C. Wyeth, who produced color illustrations for a 1911 American edition published by Scribner's, which includes the treasure map that Stevenson drew.

14. See Judith Fisher, "Image Versus Text," note 1, 85. She aligns the magazine's control over authors and artists with the shift from monthly publication to weekly publication in periodicals like *The Graphic* as well as the piecemeal production of illustrations used by such magazines.

15. Whereas D. G. Rossetti considered himself foremost a poet and artist who dabbled in book illustration and design, Morris regarded himself foremost a decorator, although he was also a poet, novelist, and translator; see Bland, 275.

16. Regrettably, Bland does not include the source for this quotation.

17. Nonetheless, these adventure tales for boys maintain morals and a commitment to King, God, and Empire.

18. This was an age where the exotic African setting Haggard had experienced personally was still unexplored; to Darton, Haggard "gave English boys a better idea of the potential wonders of the Empire than could be had from any school-task" (297).

19. Kipling wrote and illustrated *Just So Stories* (1902) to amuse his children and their friends. Potter wrote and illustrated *Peter Rabbit* (1902) and other stories in the series (which began as illustrated letters) for the children of her former governess, Annie Carter Moore. Carroll first told the story of *Alice in Wonderland* and then wrote it down for his favorite child friend, Alice Liddell. Stevenson found his inspiration in his stepson, Lloyd Osbourne, and J. M. Barrie discovered his muse for *Peter Pan in Kensington Gardens* (1906) in the sons of his close friends, Arthur and Sylvia Llewelyn Davies (daughter of George Du Maurier). Although initially a play, the book version of *Peter Pan* included the now famous illustrations of Arthur Rackham. Milne, immortalizing his son Christopher Robin, gained fame for *Winnie-the-Pooh* (1926), memorably illustrated by Ernest H. Shepard. See John Vaughn's "Victorian Children in Their Picture Books," 620, and Susan E. Meyer's *A Treasury of the Great Children's Book Illustrators*. Meyer distinguishes these illustrators, "all born in the nineteenth century . . . [who] delivered to the nursery the first children's publications as we know them today, charming books of wonder designed simply to entertain" (9).

20. The American illustrated book follows a later chronology than the Victorian illustrated book. Reading matter in colonial America primarily came from England. With the exception of the publication of *The Bay Psalm Book*, printed in Cambridge, MA, in 1640, small publishing firms mainly arose in America in the eighteenth century. The books produced by such firms are, in Muir's view, "crude and lacking in either inspiration or technical ability"

(250). Even Alexander Anderson, who set the standards for American wood engraving with his 1795 publication of *The Looking-Glass for the Mind*, "was mainly a copyist of other men's work and seldom designed his own cuts" (Muir 251); Anderson copied woodcuts by famed British illustrator Thomas Bewick. With no international copyright in place, American publishers often created bootleg copies of popular British works, and this practice, which continued throughout the nineteenth century, infuriated Dickens, who complained about the inferior quality of these pirated editions and his loss in sales for works copyrighted in Britain only. To avoid literary bootlegging, Herman Melville arranged for near-simultaneous British and American publication of his books including *Moby-Dick* (1851).

21. May Alcott, Louisa May Alcott's sister, contributed four poorly executed illustrations for the first publication that were quickly withdrawn. Reviewers called May Alcott's illustrations "'pretty awful'" and commented on "'a want of anatomical knowledge'" (qtd. in Stern 87, 81). Despite *Little Women*'s rocky illustrative start, illustration became increasingly important to the commercial success of *Little Women* into the twentieth century. Frank T. Merrill provided over 200 black-and-white illustrations for a highly regarded 1880 quarto edition, the first to print "Little Women" (part 1, 1868) and "Good Wives" (part 2, 1869) in one edition. In 1915, Jessie Willcox Smith produced color plates that capture Alcott's vision of American domesticity and a girl's growth into a little woman. For discussion of *Little Women*, see, for example, a review by David A. Randall and John T. Winterich titled "One Hundred Good Novels" in Madeleine Stern's *Critical Essays on Louisa May Alcott*, 87, and an anonymous review entitled "Review of *Little Women*, part I, 1868," also included in Stern's collection, 81. For analysis of Merrill's and Smith's illustrations, see my book *Images of the Woman Reader in Victorian British and American Fiction*, 157–61.

22. Mark Twain's books feature child characters, but are richly sophisticated in social criticism and humor. Twain's later books marketed by Harper and Brothers contain a frontispiece and roughly one dozen illustrations.

23. To Elaine Showalter in *A Literature of Their Own*, Potter and Greenaway fit into the third generation of feminine novelists, many of whom became sensation writers, publishers, and editors as well as children's writers (20). Susan E. Meyer compares Potter to Greenaway, noting, "Each of them accomplished an independence of spirit through her writing and art, liberated from her oppressive Victorian milieu by exercising her rich imagination" (*Treasury* 127). Meyer regrettably does not give the source for this Potter quotation or for those included in note 24 and note 25.

24. Potter said of Greenaway: "'Kate Greenaway's pictures are very charming, but compared with Caldecott she could not draw'" (qtd. in Meyer, *Treasury* 130). Anne Hobbs in *Beatrix Potter's Art* notes that Potter was critical of Greenaway's drawings but approved of her designs (see p. 12) and points to how Potter "studied pages designed by others—Crane, Caldecott, the medieval illuminators—and made up her own dummies, cleverly using italics or white space for dramatic effect" (17).

25. "'I did try to copy Caldecott,'" Potter admits, "'but I agree I did not achieve much resemblance'" (qtd. in Meyer, *Treasury* 129).

26. For a list of illustrations that Potter created for other stories, see Hobbs and Whalley's *Beatrix Potter: The V&A Collection*, 106–09. Also, Hobbs briefly describes some of Potter's early efforts in *Beatrix Potter's Art*, 13.

27. To Jackson in *Illustration and the Novels of Thomas Hardy*: "the Millais era (1855–70) refers to the representational style of illustration given to Trollope's works" (12).

28. See my essay "Beatrix Potter: Naturalist Artist" for discussion of how Potter seemingly turned to the field of illustration because of the many opportunities for women artists to illustrate, in particular, books targeted for women and children with themes of motherhood, childhood, romance, and fantasy.

29. Potter studied with Miss Cameron from age twelve to age seventeen.

30. On 6 March 1883, Potter mentions that Millais is using "Papa's velveteen for a background and has torn it" (Linder, *JBP* 32), and we also learn the velvet comes from one of Beatrix Potter's mother's gowns.

31. In "Natural History: A Scientist's Eye," Linda Lear, one of Potter's biographers, likens Potter to a different eminent Victorian artist and critic closely associated with Millais: "Like the artist and critic John Ruskin, Potter understood that the only way to know something was to draw it. First the hand-lens, then the camera, and finally the microscope taught Potter how to 'see'" ("Natural History" 455).

32. Hobbs regrettably does not include her source.

33. For more discussion, see my essay "Beatrix Potter: Naturalist Artist" where I demonstrate how many of Potter's specialized nature studies reappear as illustrative details in the *Peter Rabbit* series.

34. With her governesses, Potter visited the South Kensington Museum (now the Victoria and Albert Museum) and the British Museum: Natural History (now the Natural History Museum).

35. Potter brought her portfolio of over 250 drawings and watercolors of mushrooms and fungi to the botanists at the Royal Botanical Gardens of Kew, but the director, William Thiselton-Dyer, dismissed her work. Potter was a woman and considered too young (she was thirty at the time); worse, her drawings illustrated theories based on her own scientific experiments (for example, showing lichens to be dual organisms of fungi and algae) in advance of commonly held theories of the time. Potter's rejection at Kew led her to search for other avenues to publish her watercolors. Illustration in the 1890s was an expanding field open to women (particularly of texts for women and children). Potter's extensive nature studies of fungi, flowers, animals, and water life inform her work as a children's book illustrator as I explore in my essay "Beatrix Potter: Naturalist Artist."

36. Potter's drawings of humans are inferior to her skillful renderings of fauna, flora, and animals, as I have discussed in "Natural Companions: Text and Illustration in the Work of Beatrix Potter." Potter's illustrations of animal characters in lake, woodland, and garden settings provide natural history lessons for child readers.

37. In *Beatrix Potter's Gardening Life*, Marta McDowell lists gardens around London, the Lake District, Scotland, and Wales that feature in Beatrix Potter's books.

38. Linder and Linder include this watercolor in *The Art of Beatrix Potter*, 144; it appears in the section entitled "Microscopic Work and Drawings of Fungi."

39. Linder and Linder reprint "Hips" in the section named "Early Work" in *The Art of Beatrix Potter*, 18.

40. "Squirrels on a Log" and several squirrel studies appear in Linder and Linder's *The Art of Beatrix Potter* in a section entitled "Animal Studies," 154–55.

41. See Hobbs and Whalley's *Beatrix Potter: The V&A Collection* for a detailed study entitled "Waterlilies: a close-up view of leaves and flowers amongst reeds," appearing opposite 33.

42. "Sketches of Frogs" is reproduced in Linder's *A History of the Writings of Beatrix Potter*, 178. It is among the many natural history studies that Potter recalled for her book illustrations.

43. This oft-cited anecdote appears, for example, in Linder's *A History of the Writings of Beatrix Potter*, 178.

44. Linder unfortunately does not indicate the source of Potter's quote.

45. The robin moves all about Mr. McGregor's garden and witnesses Peter gorging on radishes, 21; searching for parsley to cure his stomachache, 23; losing "one of his shoes among the cabbages, and the other shoe amongst the potatoes" (29); becoming "out of breath and trembling with fright" (42) after losing his jacket (and narrowly escaping Mr. McGregor by jumping out a window, knocking over three plants in the process); and losing all his clothes and shoes to "a scare-crow to frighten the blackbirds" (53).

46. Potter demonstrates a clear understanding of bird anatomy—feathers, bill, and underside—in her 1902 "Studies of a Dead Thrush 'Picked up in the snow'" in the section entitled "Animal Studies" in Linder and Linder's *The Art of Beatrix Potter*, 178.

47. According to Henry James, Du Maurier most admired Millais, Walker, and Leech, in that order; see James's 1897 article "George Du Maurier" in *Harper's New Monthly Magazine*, 600.

48. I have previously argued that Du Maurier used psychic phenomena in his fiction as a vehicle to achieve his unrealized aspirations. See my essay "Turning Life into Literature: The Romantic Fiction of George Du Maurier" in *The CEA Critic*.

49. For more discussion of *Trilby* and the bestseller system of publishing, see Edward L. Purcell's "Trilby and Trilby-Mania. The Beginning of the Best Seller System," published in *The Journal of Popular Culture*.

50. *Thrilby* features a mesmerist who hypnotizes tables and chairs, and *Biltry* burlesgues Du Maurier's illustrations as well as the text.

51. *Svengali* is also the name of Richard Walton Tully's silent 1922 and talking 1931 film versions of *Trilby*. See Richard Kelly, *George Du Maurier*, 121–23, for a full discussion of Trilby-mania. *Ibbetson* also had a popular following—it became an opera in 1931 and, like *Trilby*, gave rise to a popular motion picture, featuring Gary Cooper as Peter Ibbetson. However, film versions of *Trilby* have continued into the later twentieth and twenty-first centuries. A loosely adapted remake called *Svengali* came out in 1983, turning the Trilby character into a pop star named Zoe, and a 2013 film, also called *Svengali*, transforms the eponymous protagonist into a go-getting manager of a Welsh rock band; neither adaptation has a Jewish villain, as Louise McDonald discusses in "Softening Svengali," 238–41.

52. In the 1880s and 1890s, automatic writing and mesmerism filled the pages of the *Journal of the Society for Psychical Research*. Du Maurier gives the topic a supernatural twist by allowing Martia to write through Josselin during his sleep; the plot grows even stranger when the martian reincarnates herself as Barty's daughter Marty.

53. Rosenberg makes an explicit connection between Cruikshank's drawing of Fagin and Du Maurier's Svengali in *From Shylock to Svengali* (235). Kerker begins his examination of

villainy derived from Jewishness by defining "shylock," "fagin," and "Svengali" as noted in the 2004 *Merriam-Webster's Collegiate Dictionary*; he concludes that "With Shylock, Fagin and Svengali, the images have so taken hold that Webster was able to incorporate them as common nouns into the English language" (Kerker). In "'Dirty Pleasure': Trilby's Filth," Joseph Bristow associates Svengali with Fagin: "In obvious ways, Svengali conforms to the loathsome habits of his equally maligned literary forebear, the sexually exploitative Fagin of Charles Dickens's *Oliver Twist*" (161).

54. Rosenberg offers a lengthy description of the resemblance between Fagin and Svengali that extends from their unkempt hair, beaked noses, bushy eyebrows, Hapsburg lips, and long and bony fingers. After this convincing comparison, he ironically adds, "all similarities disappear. No such creature as Fagin ever trod the boards of the Adelphi" (235).

55. Deborah Heller in a book chapter on "The Outcast as Villain and Victim" notes that "Fagin embodies many characteristics long associated with Jews in English literature, particularly dramatic literature: he is dishonest, thieving, treacherous, avaricious, and ultimately cowardly" (41); Susan Meyer echoes this critique but adds to this list effeminacy and obsequiousness in "Antisemitism and Social Critique in Dickens's 'Oliver Twist'" (239). Lauriat Lane pinpoints stage convention in "Dickens' Archetypal Jew," noting, "Fagin is, of course, more than 'the conventional stage-Jew.' But it is true that stage convention provided some of the raw materials from which Dickens fashioned his highly symbolic figure" (95).

56. Du Maurier did not give a pronounced nose to all Jewish people, nor are all his Jews villainous. In *Peter Ibbetson*, the antagonist Uncle Ibbetson has a taint of Jewish and African blood, but not a Semitic nose, and Jewish Leah Gibson, who Barty Josselin marries in *The Martian*, is a stunning, statuesque woman. But the drawings of Svengali have the kind of pronounced nose that characterizes Cruikshank's depiction of Fagin. Even if Du Maurier in part based Svengali on his Jewish friend Felix Moscheles from his days in Gleyre's atelier, he altered Moscheles's appearance and drew him with a hooked nose (Moscheles's friends, in contrast, found his prominent nose handsome). Laura Vorachek in "Mesmerists and Other Meddlers" posits that a Du Maurier cartoon entitled "Hypnotism—A Modern Parisian Romance" in *Punch's Almanack for 1890* might be an early model for Svengali. "While the doctor is not explicitly described as Jewish in the text," Vorachek notes, "he does have the same large nose that Du Maurier will later draw on Svengali" (208). Edmund Wilson observes in a chapter on "The Jews" in *A Piece of My Mind* that although he has not found any evidence that Du Maurier himself had Jewish blood, "in each of his three novels a rather unexpected Jewish theme plays a more or less important role" (103).

57. Fagin's prominent nose, which marks him as a Semitic Jew, even extends beyond his jutting chin in "Fagin in the Condemned Cell" (see fig. 16, ch. 2, 75).

58. In *George Du Maurier*, Kelly also suggests this illustration shows "the influence of Hieronymus Bosch in his nightmare cartoons depicting a two-headed monster, men smoking out of their own brain pans, and a black spider with a human head" (155).

59. To Kelly, "Svengali emerges as a mythic character, one that transcends individual personalities and stands even today as an embodiment of a controlling evil genius" (*George Du Maurier* 116–17). In the introduction to their 2016 essay collection, *George Du Maurier: Illustrator, Author, Critic Beyond Svengali*, 1, Simon Cooke and Paul Goldman advance that

Du Maurier's enigmatic character has eclipsed the multi-faceted career of this important nineteenth-century novelist, critic, and illustrator.

60. I recommend Garrett Stewart's "Reading Figures: The Legible Image of Victorian Textuality," which examines how the photograph of Svengali that Trilby receives after his death leads to her demise; his reading informs this discussion.

Conclusion: The Victorian Graphic Classics—Heir of the Victorian Illustrated Book

1. For *The Graphic Canon*, editor Russ Kick commissioned talented artists to adapt excerpts of classics from the western canon, ranging from the Bible and *The Odyssey* to *The Stranger* to show "a good deal of what comic art and illustration are capable of" (2: xii).

2. Maxwell suggests the following are twentieth-century incarnations of the illustrated book: art presses, artists' books, Joseph Cornell's boxes (that approximate illustration but move outside the space of the book), and other "modernist objects that recall the form of the book but are not exactly books in themselves" (395). Maxwell's interests lie in the "modernist/surrealist experiment in reconstructing the Victorian illustrated book" (411), such as art by Max Ernst, and post–World War II work of Edward Gorey, Tom Phillips, and Joseph Cornell. Maxwell draws parallels, for example, between a Cornell box and a chapter from Lewis Carroll's *Alice*.

3. "Sequential art," a term that Eisner popularized to define the medium of comics, is "A train of images deployed in sequence" (Eisner, *Comics* 6). Building upon Eisner's definition of "sequential art," Scott McCloud in *Understanding Comics* describes comics as "juxtaposed pictorial and other images in deliberate sequence" (9), a definition that reveals the interchangeability of the terms "comics" and "sequential art." To compound the difficulty of definition, McCloud suggests that Roldolpfe Töpffer, the father of "comics," was "neither artist nor writer—had created and mastered a form that was at once both and neither. A language all its own" (17).

4. "Reading in the pure literary sense was mugged on its way to the 21st century by the electronic media," notes Will Eisner in *Graphic Storytelling and Visual Narrative*, and electronic media "influenced and changed the way we read" (5). "'Those accustomed to scanning regular columns of type often have difficulty assimilating the haphazard captions in comics at the same time as jumping from image to image,'" as Paul Gravett recognizes (qtd. in Eisner, *Graphic* 4)

5. To Tabachnick, while viewing a film, one cannot linger over a passage or review it again, as one can in reading a book or a graphic novel. In "The Graphic Novel and the Age of Transition," Tabachnick adds: "unlike film or drama, the graphic novel can be seen as the attempt of the physical book to survive in an electronic age by combining the advantages of the traditional reading experience with those of the computer screen, which often provides visual objects alongside text" (2).

6. The graphic classics genre differs from illustrated editions of books that appeared without illustrations and had pictures later "grafted onto" them (Harvey 180). For example, the 1894 Peacock edition of Jane Austen's *Pride and Prejudice* illustrated by Hugh Thomson and

the 1943 Random House edition of Charlotte Brontë's *Jane Eyre* illustrated by Fritz Eichenberg appeared decades after the novels, both originally published without illustrations.

7. Harvey's use of the word "design" here is curious; it would be more accurate to say that the novelist often determined which scenes would benefit from illustration while writing the monthly parts.

8. More rare in the graphic novel field is the kind of enduring partnership that Dickens sustained with Hablot Knight Browne, who illustrated ten of Dickens's works over a span of fifteen years. English comic book artist Dave Gibbons memorably collaborated with Alan Moore for the twelve-issue series *Watchmen* and "For the Man Who Has Everything," a Superman story. In a 2014 interview with Hayley Campbell, Gaiman explains that the creative process with an artist "'is *very much* a collaboration. If we put it in terms of a movie, I would be the writer, the director and often in some ways the editor. And they get to be the cameraman and all the actors'" (qtd. in Campbell).

9. Some illustrators like Cruikshank were also etchers and engravers and other artist/illustrators like Rossetti relied on the Dalziel brothers to engrave their illustrations; likewise, some graphic artists like John Burns ink and color, others work only in pencil and rely on a colorist and inker, and some like Will Eisner create graphics and text.

10. Will Eisner popularized the term "graphic novel" to describe his semiautobiographical collection of four interrelated stories about immigrant life in New York City in the 1930s, particularly Jewish immigrants. Most critics consider *A Contract with God* (1978) the first modern graphic novel. Named after Eisner, the Eisner Awards, founded in 1998, go to adaptors, artists, letterers, inkers, and critics across a wide range of categories in the comics medium as well as to educators and academics who specialize in this field.

11. The history of comic books deserves separate, in-depth study. Most timelines of Western comic history include publications like France's *Le charivari* and England's *Punch* as well as artists like Switzerland's Rodolphe Töpffer and Germany's Wilhelm Busch. The contributions of Belgian artist Frans Masereel and American artist Lynd Ward—whose wordless novels, respectively, *Passionate Journey* (1919) and *God's Man* (1929) are composed entirely of sequential woodcuts—have escaped classification as comics, but the work of both artists demonstrates the potential of the comic book form. For the starting point of American comics, most critics designate the year 1896 and "The Yellow Kid," the main comic strip character in Richard Outcault's *Hogan's Alley*.

12. Scott McCloud, Stephen Tabachnick, and other comics' critics align the birth of modern comics with Töpffer. Like the first generation of caricaturist illustrators, Töpffer was influenced by the same British satirical artists who presented work in sequence—principally William Hogarth, who created successive visual panels like *The Rake's Progress* (ca. 1733–35) to narrate a moral story of the road to sin; Thomas Rowlandson, who designed illustrations to accompany William Combe's popular *Tours of Doctor Syntax* series (1812, 1820, 1821); and James Gillray, a political cartoonist famously known for *John Bull's Progress* (1793).

13. "The sophistication of the picture-story did grow" from its origins in cave painting and hieroglyphics (a trail Scott McCloud follows in *Understanding Comics*), "reaching great heights in the nimble hands of William Hogarth" (McCloud 16).

14. The graphic novel is often a compilation of a series of comic books published individually—sometimes as few as three or four issues or as many as twelve or more.

15. "For much of this century," McCloud likewise argues in *Understanding Comics*, "the word 'comics' has had such negative connotations that many of comics' most devoted practitioners have preferred to be known as 'illustrators,' 'commercial artists' or, at best, 'cartoonists'!" (18).

16. Likewise, in *Comics and Sequential Art*, Eisner notes, "for reasons having much to do with usage, subject matter and perceived audience, sequential art was for many decades generally ignored as a form worthy of scholarly discussion" (xi).

17. Russian-born immigrant Albert Lewis Kanter (1897–1973) began the Classical Comics/Classics Illustrated series in 1941 with an adaption of Alexandre Dumas's *The Three Musketeers* (1844), followed by comic book adaptations of works by, among others, Charles Dickens, Mark Twain, Daniel Defoe, Sir Walter Scott, Herman Melville, and William Shakespeare. The sales figures seem high by today's standards, but such figures were then commonplace for the most popular books and comics. This series never aimed to replace the classics or interpret them with sophistication, as we find in graphic novel adaptations today by, for example, Classical Comics. Classics Illustrated, dubbed "Classics Desecrated" (Gravett, *Graphic Novels* 185) by many educators, was published in 26 languages and sold in 36 countries. The series aimed for brevity—titles were reduced from 64 to 56 to 48 pages given rising paper costs while the price of the publication increased from 10 cents to 15 cents and eventually to 25 cents. Not surprisingly, the line's competitors, cheap paperback editions and Cliff's Notes (now CliffsNotes), led to its demise. Papercutz explicitly bills itself as a "modern reboot" of Kanter's Classics Illustrated.

18. For example, to describe how his own illustrations for *Vanity Fair* light up the text, Thackeray states in "Before the Curtain," the preface to *Vanity Fair*, that the serial is "brilliantly illuminated with the Author's own candles" (*VF*, Oxf. 2). Martin Meisel explains in *Realizations* that after the 1820s, the meaning of "illustration" shifted from verbal enrichment or annotation to pictorial re-creation and/or enhancement of a text (30, 54).

19. Vol. 2 features works published throughout the long nineteenth century on both sides of the Atlantic by, for example, Jane Austen and Mary Shelley at the beginning of the 1800s; the Brontë sisters, Walt Whitman, Charles Dickens, Herman Melville, and Lewis Carroll in the mid-1800s; and Mark Twain, Robert Louis Stevenson, and Oscar Wilde in the later decades through the fin de siècle.

20. Although Austen's novels originally appeared without illustrations, lavishly illustrated versions came out at the end of the nineteenth century with drawings by Hugh Thomson in 1894 and Henry and Charles Brock in 1898. Recalling Trilby-mania and *Pickwick* mania, Austen's novels have sparked a commercial boom with a host of products showing her image or name including T-shirts, note cards, mugs, book bags, specialty teas, finger puppets, and even a Jane Austen action figure. A line of Jane Austen inspired jewelry as well as cookbooks, coloring books, and Regency clothing (with some items named after various characters in *Pride and Prejudice*) are also available for purchase.

21. For *Northanger Abbey* and *Emma*, Janet Lee worked with Nancy Butler as the collaborating artist, and for *Sense and Sensibility*, Butler collaborated with Sonny Liew, one of the cover artists for the Marvel Illustrated *Pride and Prejudice*.

22. The Romance Writers of America sponsor the RITA Award, the highest mark of distinction in romance fiction.

23. Covers from the individual issues appear in the back of the book version of Marvel's graphic novel adaptations of Jane Austen's fiction.

24. For the *Pride and Prejudice* graphic novel installments, Elizabeth appears on all five covers designed by Sonny Liew and Dennis Calero, and Darcy appears on two of them.

25. Other *Pride and Prejudice* graphic novel adaptations include a simplified retelling edited by Hilary Burningham and published by Evans Brothers Ltd. in 2004; and an Eye Classics edition adapted by Ian Edginton, illustrated by Robert Deas, and published by SelfMadeHero in 2011. The first two titles in Udon's literary classics line are *Pride and Prejudice* and Victor Hugo's *Les Misérables* (1862). See Udon Entertainment's website at <http://www.udonentertainment.com/blog/tag/manga-classics/>.

26. The two-tone cover of the Udon *Pride and Prejudice* adaptation is pink and plum to appeal to a female demographic. A picture of Elizabeth Bennet dressed in pink graces the front of this hardback book; eight large pink roses frame Elizabeth, reading a book on a rose-colored fainting couch. The back cover shows Elizabeth Bennet in a different lacy, pink dress holding a rose to her heart. A dashing Mr. Darcy approaches Elizabeth from behind; he is wearing a fitted jacket and trousers that accentuate his shapely physique. Text on the back cover claims, "this bold new manga adaptation" will bring young adult readers "All of the joy, humor, and romance of Jane Austen's original story."

27. Interestingly, for the Campfire adaptation, Sach and Nagulakonda include a list of the names of the five Bennet daughters; one panel has Jane's name followed by a check mark, and the subsequent panel has Jane's check mark crossed off and Elizabeth's name checked to magnify how quickly "Mr. Collins had only to change from Jane to Elizabeth" (30).

28. Elizabeth wins this verbal duel, but she expresses worry in a thought bubble on the following page: "I am certain that Lady Catherine will now call on Mr. Darcy to obtain from him the promise that I have refused her. Will he be swayed by her?" (98).

29. Campfire's adaptation also enhances characterization. A prime example is the scene of Jane Bennet riding to Netherfield Park on horseback in the rain, an episode that has attracted past illustrators of *Pride and Prejudice*. In the source text, Mrs. Bennet denies Jane her request for a carriage since it likely will rain, and Jane will have to spend the night at Mr. Bingley's home, Netherfield Park. The source text indicates that Jane protests slightly, "'I had much rather go in the coach'" (Austen 40)—a line that Sach includes verbatim (20)—but Sach and Nagulakonda develop Jane's personality to convey a stronger protest. Nagulakonda shows annoyance on the faces of Jane and her horse as they trek through pelting streaks of rain in a verdant but puddled landscape. Sach adds a thought bubble that works interdependently with the graphic: "Oh Mama, you are impossible!" (21). With these five words, Jane sheds some of her cloying sweetness and expresses feelings that the modern reader can relate to.

30. Graphic Classics, as part of Barron's Educational Series, aims to "introduce many of the world's literary masterpieces to young readers. Elementary and secondary school teachers will value these books as a way to make great novels and plays accessible to their students—especially to those students who resist reading." See <https://www.goodreads.com/book/show/6226505-wuthering-heights>.

31. Classical Comics produces several versions of their graphic classics—Original Text, Quick Text American English, and Quick Text British English; however, the colored art-

work is the same for all three scripts. Original Text retains much of the classic's pure language, although the adapter truncates the text to fit into word balloons, thought bubbles, and captions. Quick Text, in contrast, updates the classic into modern American English or modern British English to make it a "fast-paced read" (F. Macdonald 144).

32. Franz Anton Mesmer discovered the technique named after him in 1779; mesmerism first entered England in the early 1800s and gained force in the 1840s when John Elliotson, founder of the London Phrenological Society, promoted interest in mesmerism via pamphlets and demonstrations. Telepathic dreaming, mesmerism, and clairvoyant communication gained popularity in the later nineteenth century as Freud explored free association through dreams, Gertrude Stein investigated automatic writing in William James's laboratory, and Henri Bergson explored memory in *Matière et mémoire* (1896). These psychic phenomena surface as literary strategies that Du Maurier uses in his late nineteenth-century fiction, as I explore in chapter 4 and my article "Turning Life into Literature," but are also anticipated in the work of the Brontë sisters.

33. See Margaret Homans's "Dreaming of Children: Literalisation in *Jane Eyre* and *Wuthering Heights*" included in the St. Martin's edition of *Jane Eyre*, edited by Heather Glen, 147–67.

34. There are several adaptations of *A Christmas Carol* (1843), originally illustrated by John Leech. The Classical Comics adaptation also makes palpable the poverty of Dickens's London through the chilling presentation of Ignorance and Want (S. M. Wilson 94).

35. In the Francophone world, graphic novels (called *bande dessinée*) assume the status of literature and reach a sophisticated adult audience; not surprisingly, this Trollope adaptation, written in English, was published in a French edition months before its British debut.

36. In an e-mail interview (8 July 2015), Francis Mosley explains the approach to illustrating Trollope as follows:

Well I try to look for scenes where there is an interesting landscape or interior (a nineteenth-century sorting office, for example) and give a sense of light (or dark) that is atmospheric in the hope of giving a reader a sense of being there. Having scenes in a gold mining camp in Australia is a gift compared to the many Trollope novels where just about all the action takes place in drawing rooms. There are only so many viewpoints in a room and only so many ways of arranging the furniture or decoration. That said, limitations can be the mother of invention, and "picturesque" scenes can have their own pitfalls. As a general rule I try to avoid the more dramatic episodes as they can come across as wooden or frozen in comparison to what the writing is describing, and there is also the additional danger of being in conflict with the reader's imagination.

37. For more discussion of Trollope's decision not to disclose freely that John Caldigate and Euphemia Smith are living in sin, see Diana Archibald's *Domesticity, Imperialism, and Emigration in the Victorian Novel*, 98–99.

38. Before *Dispossession* appeared in English, I obtained the French version and interviewed Grennan about his adaptation of *John Caldigate*.

39. See a recap of Grennan's presentation to the reading group of the Trollope Soci-

ety posted on 4 July 2014 in *The Trollope Jupiter*, <https://thetrollopejupiter.wordpress.com/2014/07/04/dispossession-a-graphic-novel/>.

40. Critics commonly associate Fagin's characterization with the notorious early nineteenth-century Jewish "receiver of stolen goods," Ikey (Isaac) Solomons; this connection makes the religious stereotype more disturbingly real. See the Oxford World's Classics 1999 edition of *Oliver Twist* with an introduction and notes by Stephen Gill, 467.

41. For an examination of Dickens's oscillation in his characterization of Fagin, see my essay "Cruikshank's Illustrative Wrinkle in *Oliver Twist*'s Misrepresentation of Class" in *Book Illustrated*, edited by C. Golden, 117–46.

42. For discussion of Fagin's devilish nickname, see the Oxford World's Classics 1999 edition of *Oliver Twist* with an introduction and notes by Stephen Gill, 467.

43. Dickens turns Fagin into a character who deserves to swing from the rope and leaves Fagin contemplating his own death, "To be hanged by the neck till he was dead" (*OT*, Oxf. 1982 343). Cruikshank, in turn, captures Fagin's crazed, demonic look in one of *Twist*'s best-known plates, "Fagin in the Condemned Cell" (see fig. 16, ch. 2, 75).

44. The visual depiction of the stereotypic Jew derives from eighteenth-century graphic satirists, notably William Hogarth and Thomas Rowlandson; Eisner demonstrates this resemblance in the appendix to *Fagin the Jew*.

45. It is curious that Eisner has the Jewish Adele convert to Christianity when marrying Oliver Twist Brownlow (*FTJ* 115).

46. The IDW adaptation of *Twist* scripted by Philippe Chanoinat and illustrated by David Cerquiera abridges a great deal of the classic, compromising the authenticity to the original, but it offers a sympathetic rendition of Fagin akin to Eisner's in *Fagin the Jew*. Nancy and Sikes are greatly eclipsed—Nancy does not risk her life to meet Mr. Brownlow and Rose Maylie on London Bridge, and Sikes does not murder Nancy. Monks is cut entirely from the novel. Worse, Chanoinat also invents plot details. Following the robbery of the Maylies' household, Oliver recuperates at Mr. Brownlow's home, not at the Maylies, and "The police arrested the whole gang" (52)—presumably meaning Sikes, Monks, and Fagin. Sikes (wanted for robbery, not murder in this adaptation) does not attempt to destroy his dog or run through the streets of Jacob's Island onto the roof of Fagin's den.

Nonetheless, this adaptation deserves mentioning because text and image interdependently develop Fagin's character in ways that challenge Dickens's source text. Chanoinat grants Fagin decency in the final pages and elevates his importance by concluding with Fagin's demise. Mr. Brownlow tells Oliver that "This Mr. Fagin, in a surge of generosity, totally exonerated you by explaining to the police what he and his friends had subjected you to. Which just shows that even the worst men have a piece of humanity left in them" (52). Fagin is not labeled derogatorily as the "Jew" but called "Mr. Fagin," a title of respect, and the word "surge" suggests an outpouring of good-heartedness. Cerquiera adds to this characterization in depicting a tearful, grateful Oliver visiting Fagin in jail; Fagin is also weeping, and the two are embracing (*OT*, Chanoinat 53), showing Fagin surely has a "surge" of "humanity left in" him.

47. Campfire explains that its graphic novels are aural and visual: "It is night-time in the forest. A campfire is crackling, and storytelling has begun" <http://www.campfire.co.in/about-us)>. Other nineteenth-century novels adapted by Campfire are Dickens's *A Christ-

mas Carol, Austen's *Pride and Prejudice*, Robert Louis Stevenson's *Dr. Jekyll and Mr. Hyde* (1886), Rudyard Kipling's *Kim* (1901), and H. G. Wells's *The Time Machine* (1895).

48. Not only its brevity, but the following features suggest the Campfire adaptation of *Oliver Twist* is suitable for the young adult reader: a page of pictorial introductions of all the characters, a section entitled "Bringing Dickens's Times to Life," and the use of an occasional footnote within one of the panels to explain a term, such as "charity boy" (Johnson 14).

49. There are small differences between the illustrations for the original serial and the graphic novel; for example, in the adaptation, Oliver's little table is directly below the window, which is curtained but not latticed.

50. The source text reads: "what was that, which sent the blood tingling to his heart, and deprived him of his voice, and of power to move!"; Dickens continues, "It was but an instant, a glance, a flash before his eyes; and they were gone. But they had recognised him, and he them" (*OT*, Oxf. 1982 217).

51. Papercutz markets this edition to middle-school readers to present Dickens's classic to a younger audience.

52. In the Campfire adaptation, Mrs. Mann says to Oliver in a private aside, "And watch your tongue, boy!" (Johnson 7), which undercuts her fake public farewell—"Oh, my dear sweet Oliver! Be good to Mr. Bumble, my lamb!" (7). Here, "lamb" is a false term of endearment, for Oliver is truly just a common "boy," a cog in the wheel of the workhouse system.

53. In Dickens's text, a comma follows "sir," not a period (*OT*, Oxf. 1982 10).

54. Papercutz keeps intact the novel's most famous phrase, "Please, sir, I want some more," and grants that critical scene thirty panels (Dauvillier 19–22). From the source text it includes the choosing of straws, Oliver asking politely for "more" when the lot falls to him, and the reaction of the fat cook, who, in this adaptation, throws Oliver into a cell and then calls for Mr. Bumble (reversing the order of this sequence in the source text). This version has a "Table of Contents" that lists all Dickens's original lengthy chapter titles. Dauvillier often dumbs down Dickensian dialogue, transforming Dickens's cutting satire of the parish rations of "one porringer, and no more—except on occasions of great public rejoicing" (*OT*, Oxf. 1982 9) to "We're sick of eating gruel! And there's not even enough of it!" (Dauvillier 19). Dauvillier's colloquial diction like "Yuck" and "Hey" and sound effects like "BAM" and "SLAM" alongside Deloye's cartoon-style graphics at times compromise the adaptation's faithfulness to the original, despite the famous request for more gruel.

55. Dickens devotes several paragraphs to Oliver's "roused" spirit and the resulting physical and emotional transformation that occurs: "His breast heaved; his attitude was erect; his eye bright and vivid; his whole person changed, as he stood glaring over the cowardly tormentor who now lay crouching at his feet" (*OT*, Oxf. 1982 36). Cruikshank shows a bright-eyed Oliver with erect posture and an enormous fist that gives concrete form to Oliver's "collecting his whole force into one heavy blow" (36), knocking blubbering Noah to the ground. Papercutz devotes over thirty panels to this scene (36–39) and includes motion lines and sound effects to show Oliver flying into a rage as he hits Noah for calling his mother a "trollop" (Dauvillier 36). Outcries and screams are part of Dickens's text, but Papercutz intensifies the aural dimension by adding "BAM" four times in the panel where Oliver pummels Noah and "EEEEEEEEEE" to magnify Charlotte's fright of Oliver's power

(37). The bolded sound effects reinforce how Oliver's "whole person changed" (*OT*, Oxf. 1982 36).

56. Nagulakonda shows far greater adeptness than Cruikshank in drawing women, making Nancy comely as Dickens describes her: "They wore a good deal of hair: . . . They were not exactly pretty, perhaps; but they had a great deal of colour in their faces; and looked quite stout and hearty" (*OT*, Oxf. 1982 57). Whereas Cruikshank's Nancy has a sly expression, slovenly appearance, and a prematurely old and common face (see fig. 22, ch. 2, 87), Nagulakonda's Nancy has attractive chestnut hair, expressive eyes, and a neat appearance. Indeed, Nagulakonda's fallen Nancy and genteel Rose Maylie look like "Two Sister-Women" (*OT*, Clarendon xxxvi).

57. Regrettably, in this adaptation Sikes shoots Nancy with the gun, rather than use it to strike her down (in the source text, Sikes decides not to shoot Nancy with the gun to avoid noise and detection). Campfire also drops out Rose Maylie's handkerchief, an important textual detail exquisitely illustrated in the Papercutz version.

58. For discussion of Dickens's term "Sister-Women" in the first descriptive chapter headline, see Kathleen Tillotson's introduction to the Clarendon edition of *Oliver Twist*, xxxvi.

59. In *The Scanty Meal*, three horses and two pigeons are eating a very small portion of food. John Tenniel also created sequential comics for *Punch*, including "Mr. Spoonbill's Experiences in the Art of Skating" (1855) (Burstein 10).

60. All the references to Moore and Reppion and Awano come from Dynamite's first issue of *Alice*.

61. Regrettably, Nagulakonda, like Awano, gives Alice room to keep growing. Carroll more than any of the successive illustrators intensifies Alice's claustrophobia in showing her to be literally pushing against the boundaries of a room suggested only by a rectangular box (see fig. 39A, ch. 3, 145).

62. Peacock feathers in this sequence, not mentioned in the text, provide a prop to measure how small Alice has become; the feathers appear to grow larger as Alice grows smaller and smaller and vocalizes her perplexity.

Bibliography

Ainsworth, William Harrison. *Jack Sheppard*. 1839. Ed. Edward Jacobs and Manuela Mourão. Peterborough, ON: Broadview, 2007. Print.

———. "Jack Sheppard." *Bentley's Miscellany*. Illus. George Cruikshank. Vols. 5–7. Jan. 1839–Feb. 1840. Print.

———. *The Miser's Daughter: A Tale*. 1842. Illus. George Cruikshank. London: Parry and Co., 1848. Print.

———. *Rookwood: A Romance*. Illus. George Cruikshank. London: John Macrone, 1836. Print.

———. *The Tower of London: A Historical Romance*. Illus. George Cruikshank. London: Richard Bentley, 1840. Print.

Alcott, Louisa May. *Little Women or Meg, Jo, Beth, and Amy*. 1868, 1869. Illus. Frank T. Merrill. Boston: Little, Brown, and Co., 1880. Print.

———. *Little Women or Meg, Jo, Beth, and Amy*. 1868, 1869. Illus. Jessie Willcox Smith. Boston: Little, Brown, and Co., 1922. Print.

Allingham, Philip V. "The Discovery of Jingle in the Fleet." *The Victorian Web*. George P. Landow, editor-in-chief and webmaster. Web. 7 July 2013. <http://www.victorianweb.org/art/illustration/phiz/pickwick/34.html>.

———. "George Du Maurier: Illustrator and Novelist." *The Victorian Web*. George P. Landow, editor-in-chief and webmaster. Web. 7 July 2013. <http://www.victorianweb.org/art/illustration/dumaurier/pva95.html>.

———. *Hardy's Illustrated Fiction, 1870–1900*. Saarbrücken, Ger.: Lambert Academic Publishing, 2011. Print.

———. "Ignorance and Want." *The Victorian Web*. George P. Landow, editor-in-chief and webmaster. Web. 8 Nov. 2014. <http://www.victorianweb.org/art/illustration/carol/6.html>.

———. "Illustrations by James Mahoney for Charles Dickens's Works." *The Victorian Web*. George P. Landow, editor-in-chief and webmaster. Web. 1 June 2015. <http://www.victorianweb.org/victorian/art/illustration/mahoney/74.html>.

———. "Mrs. Bardell faints in Mr. Pickwick's arms." *The Victorian Web*. George P. Landow, editor-in-chief and webmaster. Web. 18 Sept. 2014. <http://www.victorianweb.org/victorian/art/illustration/phiz/pickwick/13.html>.

———. "'Reading the Pictures, Visualizing the Text': Illustrations in Dickens from *Pickwick to the Household Edition, 1836 to 1870, Phiz to Fred Barnard." In *Reading Victorian Illustration, 1855–1875*. Ed. Paul Goldman and Simon Cooke. Surrey, UK: Ashgate Publishing Ltd., 2012. 159–78. Print.

———. "Sir Hubert Von Herkomer, R. A. (1849–1914)." *The Victorian Web*. George P. Landow, editor-in-chief and webmaster. Web. 27 Oct. 2014. <http://www.victorianweb.org/art/illustration/herkomer/bio.html>.

———. "Standing before the dressing-glass was a middle-aged lady in yellow curl-papers, busily engaged in brushing what ladies call their 'back hair.'" *The Victorian Web*. George P. Landow, editor-in-chief and webmaster. Web. 8 Oct. 2014. <http://www.victorianweb.org/art/illustration/phiz/pphe/23.html>.

———. "Why do Hardy's novels often have illustrations in periodical but not book form?" *The Victorian Web*. George P. Landow, editor-in-chief and webmaster. Web. 14 Oct. 2014. <http://www.victorianweb.org/authors/hardy/pva151.html>.

———. "Working Class and Upper-Middle Class Worlds Collide: Charlie Hexam and Bradley Headstone visit Mortimer Lightwood and Eugene Wrayburn in their chambers." *The Victorian Web*. George P. Landow, editor-in-chief and webmaster. Web. 12 Oct. 2014. <http://www.victorianweb.org/art/illustration/mstone/25.html>.

Allingham, Philip, and Chris Louttit. "The Illustrators of the Household Edition of the *Works of Charles Dickens* (22 vols., 1871–79)." *The Victorian Web*. George P. Landow, editor-in-chief and webmaster. Web. 8 Oct. 2014. <http://www.victorianweb.org/art/illustration/barnard/household.html>.

Allingham, William. *The Music Master*. 1855. New York: Arno Press, 1967. Print.

Altick, Richard. *The English Common Reader: A Social History of the Mass Reading Public, 1800–1900*. Chicago: U of Chicago P, 1957. Print.

Anonymous. Review of *The Pickwick Papers*. *Examiner* 15 (July 1837): 421–22. Print.

Archibald, Diana C. *Domesticity, Imperialism, and Emigration in the Victorian Novel*. Columbia, MO: U of Missouri P, 2002. Print.

———. "'Of All the Horrors . . . the Foulest and Most Cruel': Sensation and Dickens's *Oliver Twist*." In *Victorian Sensations: Essays on a Scandalous Genre*. Ed. Kimberly Harrison and Richard Fantina. Columbus, OH: Ohio State UP, 2006. 53–63. Print.

Austen, Jane. *Pride and Prejudice*. 1813. Pref. George Sainstsbury. Illus. Hugh Thomson. New York: Dover, 2005. Print.

Banham, Rob. "The Industrialization of the Book 1800–1970." In *A Companion to the History of the Book*. Ed. Simon Eliot and Jonathan Rose. London: Blackwell, 2007. 273–90. Print.

Barham, Richard Harris. *The Ingoldsby Legends, or Mirth and Marvels*. Illus. George Cruikshank, John Leech, and John Tenniel. London: Richard Bentley, 1855. Print.

———. *The Ingoldsby Legends, or Mirth and Marvels*. Illus. George Cruikshank, John Leech, and John Tenniel. London: Richard Bentley, 1864. Print.

Barker, Juliet R. V., ed. *The Brontës: A Life in Letters*. New York: Overlook P, 2002. Print.

———, ed. *The Brontës: Selected Poems*. London: J. M. Dent, 1993. Print.

Barker, Matthew Henry. *The Old Sailor's Jolly Boat, Laden with Tales, Yarns, Scraps, Fragments, etc., to Please All Hands*. 1844. Illus. George and Robert Cruikshank. London: Willoughby, n.d. Print.

Beckett, Gilbert à. "To Correspondents." *Figaro in London* 154 (Saturday, 15 Nov. 1834): 184. Print.

Beer, Gillian. "'*Alice*' in Time." *Modern Language Review* 106.4 (Oct. 2011): xxvii–xxxviii. Print.

Bender, Hy, ed. *The Sandman Companion.* New York: DC Comics, 1999. Print.

Bendis, Brian Michael. Fwd. to *Fagin the Jew.* 2003. By Will Eisner. Milwaukee: Dark Horse, 2013. 1–2. Print.

Benjamin, Walter. "The Work of Art in the Age of Mechanical Reproduction." 1936. In *Illuminations.* Ed. Hannah Arendt. Trans. Harry Zohn. New York: Schocken Books, 1969. 217–51. Print.

Bentley, Nicholas. *The Victorian Scene, 1837–1901.* London: Jarrold, 1968. Print.

Bentley's Miscellany. Vols. 1–14. London: Richard Bentley, 1837–43. Print.

Bermejo, Lee, adapt. *Batman: Noël.* Artwork by the author. Fwd. Jim Lee. New York: DC Comics, 2011. Print.

Bettley, James. *The Art of the Book: From Medieval Manuscript to Graphic Novel.* London: V&A Publications, 2001. Print.

Bewick, Thomas. *History of British Birds.* 1797, 1804. 2 vols. Newcastle: Edward Walker, 1804.

Billi, Mirella. "Dickens as Sensation Novelist." In *Dickens: The Craft of Fiction and the Challenges of Reading.* Ed. Rossana Bonadei, Clotilde de Stasio, Carlo Pagetti, and Alessandro Vescovi. Milan, It.: Unicopli, 2000. 176–84. Print.

Bland, David. *A History of Book Illustration: The Illuminated Manuscript and the Printed Book.* 1958. Berkeley and Los Angeles: U of California P, 1974. Print.

"Boz's Oliver Twist." *Spectator* 11 (24 Nov. 1838): 1114–16. Print.

Briggs, Asa. *Victorian Things.* Chicago: U of Chicago P, 1989. Print.

Bristow, Joseph. "'Dirty Pleasure': Trilby's Filth." In *Filth: Dirt, Disgust, and Modern Life.* Ed. William A. Cohen and Ryan Johnson. Minneapolis: U of Minnesota P, 2005. 155–81. Print.

Brontë, Anne. *The Tenant of Wildfell Hall.* 1848. Ed. Herbert Rosengarten. New York: Oxford UP, 2008. Print.

Brontë, Charlotte. *Jane Eyre.* 1847. Ed. Richard J. Dunn. 3rd ed. New York: Norton, 2001. Print.

Brontë, Emily. *Wuthering Heights.* 1847. Ed. Linda H. Peterson. Boston: St. Martin's, 1992. Print.

Buchanan-Brown, John. *The Book Illustrations of George Cruikshank.* London: David and Charles; Rutland, VT: Charles E. Tuttle Co., 1980. Print.

———. *Early Victorian Illustrated Books: Britain, France and Germany.* London: British Library Board, 2005. Print.

Burlingham, Cynthia. "Picturing Childhood: Illustrated Children's Books from University of California Collections, 1550–1990." Web. 10 July 2013. <https://web.archive.org/web/20130629053945/http://unitproj.library.ucla.edu/special/childhood/index.htm>.

Burne-Jones, Edward. "Essay on *The Newcomes.*" *Oxford and Cambridge Magazine* 1.1 (Jan. 1856): 50–61. Print.

Burrows, Alex, adapt. *The Picture of Dorian Gray.* By Oscar Wilde. Artwork Lisa K. Weber.

In *Graphic Classics: Oscar Wilde*. Ed. Tom Pomplun. Mount Horeb, WI: Graphic Classics (Eureka), 2009. 4-49. Print.

Burstein, Mark. Introd. to *Alice in Comicland*. Ed. Craig Yoe. San Diego: IDW Publishing, 2014. Print.

Buss, Robert. *Dickens's Dream*. ca. 1875. Charles Dickens Museum, London. Watercolor painting.

Butler, Nancy, adapt. *Pride and Prejudice*. By Jane Austen. Artwork Hugo Petrus. New York: Marvel, 2010. Print.

Campbell, Hayley. "Neil Gaiman on Collaboration." *Ideas Tap*, 7 Sept. 2014. Web. 3 Nov. 2014. <http://www.ideastap.com/IdeasMag/the-knowledge/the-art-of-neil-gaiman-on-collaboration>.

Carlyle, Thomas. *On Heroes, Hero-Worship, and the Heroic in History*. London: James Fraser, 1841. Print.

Carroll, Lewis. *Alice's Adventures Under Ground*. 1864. Illus. by the author. Introd. Martin Gardner. New York: Dover, 1965. Print.

———. *Alice's Adventures in Wonderland*. Illus. John Tenniel. London: Macmillan, 1866; New York: Knopf, 1984. Print.

———. *The Annotated Alice: Alice's Adventures in Wonderland* and *Through the Looking-Glass*. 1865, 1872. Ed. Martin Gardner. Illus. John Tenniel. New York: Norton, 2000. Print.

Cerrito, Joann, ed. *Nineteenth-Century Literature Criticism*. Vol. 37. Detroit, MI: Gale Research Group, 1993. Print.

Chanoinat, Phillippe, adapt. *Oliver Twist*. By Charles Dickens. Artwork David Cerquiera. San Diego, CA: IDW Publishing, 2009. Print.

Chesterton, G. K. *Charles Dickens*. New York: Dodd Mead and Co., 1906. Print.

Cleere, Eileen. *Avuncularism: Capitalism, Patriarchy, and Nineteenth-Century English Culture*. Stanford: Stanford UP, 2004. Print.

Cody, David. "Morris and the Kelmscott Press." Web. 25 March 2015. <http://www.victorianweb.org/authors/morris/kelmscott.html>.

Cohen, Deborah. *Household Gods: The British and Their Possessions*. New Haven: Yale UP, 2006. Print.

Cohen, Jane R. *Charles Dickens and His Original Illustrators*. Columbus, OH: Ohio State UP, 1980. Print.

Cohen, Morton N., ed. *The Letters of Lewis Carroll*. 2 vols. London: Macmillan and Co., Ltd., 1979. Print.

Collins, Philip, ed. *Dickens: The Critical Heritage*. London: Routledge and Kegan Paul, 1971. Print.

Colvin, Peter. "Muhammad Ali Pasha, the Great Exhibition of 1851, and the School of Oriental and African Studies Library." *Libraries & Culture* 33.3 (Orientalist Libraries and Orientalism) (Summer 1998): 249–59. Print.

Combe, William. *The Second Tour of Doctor Syntax, in Search of Consolation: A Poem*. Illus. Thomas Rowlandson. London: R. Ackermann, 1820. Print.

Cooke, Simon. "Arthur Hughes as Illustrator." *The Victorian Web*. George P. Landow, editor-in-chief and webmaster. Web. 23 Oct. 2014. <http://www.victorianweb.org/victorian/art/illustration/hughes/intro.html>.

———. "Dante Gabriel Rossetti as an Illustrator." *The Victorian Web*. George P. Landow, editor-in-chief and webmaster. Web. 7 Oct. 2014. <http://www.victorianweb.org/art/illustration/dgr/cooke.html>.

Cooke, Simon, and Paul Goldman, eds. *George Du Maurier: Illustrator, Author, Critic Beyond Svengali*. Ashgate: Surrey, UK and Burlington, VT, 2016. Print.

Corzine, Amy, adapt. *Jane Eyre: The Graphic Novel*. Original Text. By Charlotte Brontë. Artwork John M. Burns. Litchborough, UK: Classical Comics, Ltd., 2008. Print.

Coutts, Henry T. *Library Jokes and Jottings: A Collection of Stories Partly Wise but Mostly Otherwise*. London: Grafton and Co., 1914. Print.

Cruikshank, George. *The Artist and the Author: A Statement of Facts*. London: Hodgson and Co, 1872. Print.

———. *The Bottle. In Eight Plates*. London: David Bogue, 1847. Print

———. *The Drunkard's Children, A Sequel to The Bottle. In Eight Plates*. London: David Bogue, 1848. Print.

———. *Illustrations of Time*. London: Published by the Artist, 1827. Print.

———. *My Sketch Book*. London: Published for the Artist by Charles Tilt, 1834. Print.

———. *Points of Humour*. London: C. Baldwyn, 1823–24. Print.

Dalziel, George, and Edward Dalziel. *The Brothers Dalziel: A Record of Fifty Years Work in Conjunction with Many of the Most Distinguished Artists of the Period 1840–1890*. London: Methuen and Co., 1901. Print.

Darton, Harvey. *Children's Books in England*. 1982. 3rd ed. Rev. by Brian Alderson. New Castle, DE: Oak Knoll, 1999; London: British Library, 1999. Print.

The Database of Mid-Victorian Illustration at Cardiff University. Web. 19 Sept. 2014. <http://www.dmvi.cf.ac.uk/>.

Dauvillier, Loïc, adapt. *Oliver Twist*. By Charles Dickens. Artwork Olivier Deloye. New York: Papercutz, 2012. Print.

David, Beverly R., and Ray Sapirstein. "Illustrators and Illustrations in Mark Twain's First American Editions." In *The Adventures of Tom Sawyer*. By Mark Twain. Ed. Shelley Fisher Fishkin. New York: Oxford UP, 1996. 20–23. Print.

———. "Reading the Illustrations in Huckleberry Finn." In *Adventures of Huckleberry Finn*. By Mark Twain. Ed. Shelley Fisher Fishkin. New York: Oxford UP, 1996. 33–40. Print.

"*David Copperfield* by Charles Dickens Prefaces, (1850 and 1869)." Web. 21 Dec. 2014. <http://etc.usf.edu/lit2go/166/david-copperfield/2934/prefaces-1850-and-1869/>.

Dickens, Charles. *A Christmas Carol*. 1841. Introd. G. K. Chesterton. Boston: Charles E. Lauriat Co., n.d. Print.

———. *David Copperfield*. 1850. Ed. Jerome H. Buckley. Illus. Hablot Knight Browne. New York: Norton, 1990. Print.

———. *David Copperfield*. 1850. Illus. Fred Barnard. Household Edition. London: Chapman and Hall, 1872. Print.

———. *Dombey and Son*. 1848. Illus. Hablot Knight Browne. London: Chapman and Hall, 1905. Print.

———. *Dombey and Son*. 1848. World's Classics. Ed Alan Horsman. Oxford: Oxford UP, 1982. Print.

———. *Hard Times*. 1854. New York: Dover, 2001. Print.

———. *Little Dorrit*. 1857. Ed. Alan Horsman. New York: Oxford UP, 1982. Print.

———. *The Mystery of Edwin Drood*. Illus. Luke Fildes. London: Chapman and Hall, 1870. Print.

———. "Oliver Twist." *Bentley's Miscellany*. Illus. George Cruikshank. Vols. 1–5. Feb. 1837– Apr. 1839. Print.

———. *Oliver Twist*. 1838. Ed. Kathleen Tillotson. Illus. George Cruikshank. New York: Oxford UP, 1982. Print.

———. *Oliver Twist*. 1838. Ed. Kathleen Tillotson. Introd. and notes Stephen Gill. Illus. George Cruikshank. World's Classics. New York: Oxford UP, 1999. Print.

———. *Oliver Twist*. 1838. Ed. Kathleen Tillotson. Illus. George Cruikshank. Oxford: Clarendon Press, 1966. Print.

———. *Oliver Twist*. 1838. Illus. James Mahoney. Household Edition. London: Chapman and Hall, 1871. Print.

———. *Our Mutual Friend*. Illus. Marcus Stone. 2 vols. London: Chapman and Hall, 1865. Print.

———. *Our Mutual Friend*. 1865. Ed. Stephen Gill. London: Penguin, 1976. Print.

———. *The Pickwick Papers*. 1837. *The Works of Charles Dickens*. Vol. 7. New York and Boston: Books, Inc., n.d. Print.

———. *The Posthumous Papers of the Pickwick Club*. 1837. Ed. James Kinsley. Illus. Robert Seymour and Hablot Knight Browne. New York: Oxford UP, 1986. Print.

———. *The Posthumous Papers of the Pickwick Club*. Illus. Robert Seymour and Hablot Knight Browne. London: Chapman and Hall, 1837. Print.

———. *Sketches by Boz*. 1836. Ed. Dennis Walder. Illus. George Cruikshank. New York: Penguin, 1996. Print.

———. "To R. H. Horne." 8 Feb. 1840. In *Dickens: The Critical Heritage*. Ed. Philip Collins. London: Routledge and Kegan Paul, 1971. 45. Print.

Dickerson, Vanessa D. "Supernatural Fiction." In *Victorian Britain: An Encyclopedia*. Ed. Sally Mitchell. New York: Garland, 1988. 773–74. Print.

Dillard, R. H. W. Introd. to *Treasure Island*. By Robert Louis Stevenson. New York: Signet, 1998. vi–xv. Print.

"Dispossession: A Graphic Novel." *The Trollope Jupiter*, 4 July 2014. Web. 3 Nov. 2014. <http://thetrollopejupiter.wordpress.com/tag/john-caldigate/>.

Doll, Jen. "200 Years of Pride and Prejudice Book Design." *The Wire*, 25 January 2013. Web. 13 Nov. 2014. <http://www.thewire.com/entertainment/2013/01/pride-and-prejudice-200th-anniversary-covers/60978/>.

Dow, Gillian, and Katie Halsey. "Jane Austen's Reading: The Chawton Years." *Persuasions Online* 30.2 (Spring 2010). Web. 20 Dec. 2014. <http://www.jasna.org/persuasions/online/vol30no2/dow-halsey.html>.

Du Maurier, Daphne, ed. *The Young George Du Maurier: A Selection of His Letters, 1860–67*. Westport, CT: Greenwood Press, 1969. Print.

Du Maurier, George. "The Illustrating of Books from the Serious Artist's Point of View." *The Magazine of Art* (Aug.–Sept. 1890): 1: 349–53; 2: 371–75. Print.

———. "The Martian." *Harper's New Monthly Magazine*. Illus. by the author. Oct. 1896– July 1897. Print.

———. *The Martian*. Illus. by the author. New York: Harper and Brothers Publishers, 1897. Print.

———. "Peter Ibbetson." *Harper's New Monthly Magazine*. Illus. by the author. June–Nov. 1891. Print.

———. *Peter Ibbetson*. Illus. by the author. New York: Harper and Brothers Publishers, 1891. Print.

———. "Trilby." *Harper's New Monthly Magazine*. Illus. by the author. Jan.–Aug. 1894. Print.

———. *Trilby*. Illus. by the author. New York: Harper and Brothers Publishers, 1894. Print.

Dunn, Richard J. "Out of the Picture?: Branwell Brontë and Jane Eyre." In *The Brontës in the World of the Arts*. Ed. Sandra Hagan and Juliette Wells. London: Ashgate, 2008. 30–44. Print.

Egan, Pierce. *Life in London; or, The Day and Night Scenes of Jerry Hawthorn, Esq. and his elegant friend Corinthian Tom, accompanied by Bob Logic, The Oxonian, in their Rambles and Sprees through the Metropolis*. Illus. George and Robert Cruikshank. London: Sherwood, Neely and Jones, 1821. Print.

Egg, Augustus. *Past and Present, Nos. 1–3*. 1858. Tate Britain. Oil paint on canvas.

Eisner, Will. *Comics and Sequential Art: Principles and Practices from the Legendary Cartoonist*. New York: Norton, 2008. Print.

———. *A Contract with God, and Other Tenement Stories*. 1978. Artwork by the author. Reprint. New York: Norton, 2006.

———. *Fagin the Jew*. 2003. Introd., artwork, and app. by the author. Fwd. Brian Michael Bendis. Afterword Jeet Heer. 2003. Milwaukee: Dark Horse, 2013. Print.

———. *Graphic Storytelling and Visual Narrative*. Tamarac, FL: Poorhouse Press, 1996. Print.

Eliot, George. *The Mill on the Floss*. 1860. Ed. and introd. Gordon S. Haight. World's Classics. Oxford and New York: Oxford UP, 1981. Print.

Eliot, Simon. "The Business of Victorian Publishing." In *The Cambridge Companion to the Victorian Novel*. Ed. Deirdre David. Cambridge: Cambridge UP, 2001. 36–61. Print.

Eliot, Simon, and Jonathan Rose, eds. *A Companion to the History of the Book*. London: Blackwell, 2007. Print.

Engen, Rodney. *Sir John Tenniel: Alice's White Knight*. Aldershot, UK: Scolar Press, 1991. Print.

Erickson, Steve. "Dreamland: When Neil Gaiman Writes the Last Chapter of 'The Sandman' this Fall, the Greatest Epic in the History of Comic Books—Seven Years and 2,000 Pages—Will Come to a Close." 3 Sept. 1995. Web. 7 July 2015. <http://articles.latimes.com/1995-09-03/magazine/tm-41687_1_neil-gaiman/2>.

Everitt, Graham. *The Illustrated Book*. Cambridge, MA: Harvard UP, 1938. Print.

Feltes, N. N. *Modes of Production of Victorian Novels*. Chicago: Chicago UP, 1986. Print.

Ferguson, Christine. "Steam Punk and the Visualization of the Victorian: Teaching Alan Moore's *The League of Extraordinary Gentlemen* and *From Hell*." In *Teaching the Graphic Novel*. Ed. Stephen E. Tabachnick. New York: MLA, 2009. 200–07. Print.

Fisher, Judith L. "Image Versus Text in the Illustrated Novels of William Makepeace Thackeray." In *Victorian Literature and the Victorian Visual Imagination*. Ed. Carol T. Christ and John O. Jordan. Berkeley and Los Angeles: U of California P, 1995. 60–87. Print.

Flanders, Judith. *Inside the Victorian Home: A Portrait of Domestic Life in Victorian Britain.* New York: Norton, 2003. Print.

Forster, John. *The Life of Charles Dickens.* 1872–74. 3 vols. Philadelphia: J. B. Lippincott Co., 1882. Print.

Frye, Northrop, Sheridan Baker, and George Perkins. *The Harper Handbook to Literature.* New York: Harper and Row, 1985. Print.

Gardham, Julie. "The Mirror of the World." University of Glasgow, Special Collections. Web. 17 Aug. 2014. <http://special.lib.gla.ac.uk/exhibns/month/aug2005.html>.

Gaskell, Elizabeth. *The Life of Charlotte Brontë.* 1857. New York: Penguin, 1998. Print.

———. *Mary Barton.* 1848. Ed. Edgar Wright. New York: Oxford UP, 1998. Print.

———. *North and South.* 1855. Ed. Alan Shelston. New York: Norton, 2005. Print.

———. *Wives and Daughters.* 1866. 2 vols. Illus. George Du Maurier. London: Smith, Elder and Co., 1866. Reprint. London: British Library, 1966. Print.

Gerard, David E. "Subscription Libraries." *Encyclopedia of Library and Information Science.* Ed. Allen Kent, Harold Lancour, and Jay Elwood Daily. Vol. 29. New York: Marcel Dekker, 1980. Print.

Gibbons, Frank. *Batman: The Dark Knight Returns.* 1986. Artwork Klaus Johnson. New York: DC Comics, 1997.

Golden, Catherine J. "Beatrix Potter: Naturalist Artist." *Woman's Art Journal* (Spring/Summer 1990): 16–20. Print.

———, ed. *Book Illustrated: Text, Image, and Culture 1770–1930.* New Castle, DE: Oak Knoll, 2000. Print.

———. "Cruikshank's Illustrative Wrinkle in *Oliver Twist*'s Misrepresentation of Class." In *Book Illustrated: Text, Image, and Culture 1770–1930.* Ed. Catherine J. Golden. New Castle, DE: Oak Knoll, 2000. 117–46. Print.

———, ed. *Hannah M. Adler Collection.* Saratoga Springs, NY: Skidmore College, 1993.

———. *Images of the Woman Reader in Victorian British and American Fiction.* Gainesville: UP of Florida, 2003. Print.

———. "Natural Companions: Text and Illustration in the Work of Beatrix Potter." In *Beatrix Potter as Writer and Illustrator. Beatrix Potter Studies VIII* (1998): 50–68. Print.

———. *Posting It: The Victorian Revolution in Letter Writing.* Gainesville: UP of Florida, 2009. Print.

———. "Turning Life into Literature: The Romantic Fiction of George Du Maurier." *The CEA Critic* 58.1 (1995): 43–52. Print.

———. "The Victorian Illustrated Book: Authors Who Composed with Graphic Images and Words." Diss. University of Michigan, 1986. Print.

———. "'The Yellow Wall-Paper' and Joseph Henry Hatfield's Original Magazine Illustrations." *ANQ* 18.2 (Spring 2005): 53–63. Print.

Goldman, Paul. *Beyond Decoration: The Illustrations of John Everett Millais.* London: British Library; New Castle, DE: Oak Knoll, 2005. Print.

———. "Defining Illustration Studies: Towards a New Academic Discipline." In *Reading Victorian Illustration, 1855–1875: Spoils of the Lumber Room.* Ed. Paul Goldman and Simon Cooke. Surrey, UK: Ashgate Publishing Ltd., 2012. 13–32. Print.

———. *Victorian Illustration: The Pre-Raphaelites, the Idyllic School and the High Victorians.* Aldershot: Scolar Press, 1996. New ed. London: Lund Humphries, 2004. Print.

Goldman, Paul, and Simon Cooke, eds. *Reading Victorian Illustration, 1855–1875: Spoils of the Lumber Room.* Surrey, UK: Ashgate Publishing Ltd., 2012. Print.

Gombrich, E. H., and E. Kris. *Caricature.* London: Penguin Books Ltd., 1940. Print.

Goodman, Helen. "Women Illustrators of the Golden Age of American Illustration." *Woman's Art Journal* 8.1 (Spring/Summer 1987): 13–22. Print.

Gravett, Paul. "Classical Comics: Turning Classics into Comics." Web. 3 Nov. 2014. <http://www.paulgravett.com/index.php/articles/article/classical_comics>.

———. *Graphic Novels: Everything You Need to Know.* New York: HarperCollins, 2005. Print.

Great Exhibition of the Works of Industry of all Nations, 1851. Official Descriptive and Illustrated Catalogue. By Authority of the Royal Commission. In Three Volumes. London: Spicer Brothers, 1851. Print.

Grennan, Simon, adapt. *Courir deux lièvres: un roman de peu de mots. D'après John Caldigate.* By Anthony Trollope. Artwork by the adaptor. Paris: *Les Impressions Nouvelles,* 2015. Print.

———, adapt. *Dispossession: A Novel of Few Words. After John Caldigate* by Anthony Trollope. Artwork by the adaptor. London: Jonathan Cape, 2015. Print.

———. "Perhaps I'll Draw and You Complete the Story." *Times Higher Education* (16 Apr. 2015): 54–55. Print.

Guérin, Pierre Narcisse. *Clytemnestra.* 1817. *Musée des Beaux Arts.* Orléans, France. Oil on canvas.

Guliano, Eduard, ed. *Lewis Carroll: A Celebration.* New York: Crown Publishers, 1982. Print.

Haggard, H. Rider. *King Solomon's Mines.* 1885. New York: Dover, 1996. Print.

Hagstrum, Jean. *The Sister Arts: The Tradition of Literary Pictorialism and English Poetry from Dryden to Gray.* Chicago: U of Chicago P, 1958. Print.

Hammerton, J. A. *The Dickens Picture-Book: A Record of the Dickens Illustrations.* London: Educational Book Co. Ltd., 1910. Print.

Hancher, Michael. *The Tenniel Illustrations to the "Alice" Books.* Columbus, OH: Ohio State UP, 1985. Print.

Hannah, Donald. "The Author's Own Candles: The Significance of the Illustrations to *Vanity Fair.*" In *Renaissance and Modern Essays Presented to Vivian Sola Pinto in Celebration of His Seventieth Birthday.* Ed. George R. Hibbard. London: Routledge and Kegan Paul, 1966. 119–27. Print.

Hardy, Thomas. *Far from the Madding Crowd.* 1874. New York: Bantam, 1974. Print.

———. *The Hand of Ethelberta.* 1876. Ed. Tim Dolin. New York: Penguin, 1998. Print.

———. *A Laodicean.* 1891. Ed. John Schad. New York: Penguin, 1998. Print.

———. *Tess of the D'Urbervilles.* 1891. Ed. Scott Elledge. 3rd ed. New York: Norton, 1991. Print.

Hargreaves, Alice Liddell. "Alice's Recollections of Carrollian Days as Told to Her Son, Caryl Hargreaves." *The Cornhill Magazine* (July 1932): 1–12. Print.

Harris, Laurie Lanzen. *Nineteenth-Century Literature Criticism.* Vol. 3. Detroit, MI: Gale Research Co., 1983. Print.

Harris, Neil. "Pictorial Perils: The Rise of American Illustration." In *The American Illustrated*

Book in the Nineteenth Century. Ed. Gerald W. R. Ward. Charlottesville: UP of Virginia, 2002. 3–19. Print.

Harrison, Antony H., ed. *The Letters of Christina Rossetti*. Charlottesville: U of Virginia P, 1997. Print.

Harrison, Kimberly, and Richard Fantina, eds. *Victorian Sensations: Essays on a Scandalous Genre*. Columbus, OH: Ohio State UP, 2006. Print.

Harthan, Jonathan. *The History of the Illustrated Book: The Western Tradition*. London: Thames and Hudson, 1981. Print.

Harvey, John Robert. *Victorian Novelists and Their Illustrators*. New York: New York UP, 1971. Print.

Hastings, Chris. "Bigamy! Blackmail! Betrayal! A scorching new graphic novel by . . . celebrated Victorian novelist Anthony Trollope." *Daily Mail,* 5 July 2014. Web. 14 July 2015. <http://www.dailymail.co.uk/news/article-2681860/Bigamy-Blackmail-Betrayal-A-scorching-new-graphic-novel-celebrated-Victorian-novelist-Anthony-Trollope.html>.

Heer, Jeet. "Rewriting Dickens: Eisner's *Fagin the Jew*." In *Fagin the Jew*. By Will Eisner. Milwaukee: Dark Horse, 2013. 128–33. Print.

Helfand, Lewis, adapt. *Alice in Wonderland*. By Lewis Carroll. Artwork Rajesh Nagulakonda. Campfire. New Delhi, Ind.: Kalyani Navyug Media Pvt. Ltd., 2010. Print.

Heller, Deborah. "The Outcast as Villain and Victim: Jews in Dickens's *Oliver Twist* and *Our Mutual Friend*." In *Jewish Presences in English Literature*. Ed. Derek Cohen and Deborah Heller. Montreal: McGill-Queen's UP, 1990. 40–60. Print.

Helsinger, Elizabeth. "Rossetti and the Art of the Book." In *Book Illustrated: Text, Image, and Culture 1770–1930*. Ed. Catherine J. Golden. New Castle, DE: Oak Knoll, 2000. 147–93. Print.

Hicks, George Elgar. *The General Post Office, One Minute to Six*. 1860. Museum of London. Oil paint on canvas.

Hill, Jonathan E. "Cruikshank, Ainsworth, and Tableau Illustration." *Victorian Studies* 23.4 (Summer 1980): 429–59. Print.

Hill, Richard J. *Picturing Scotland Through the Waverley Novels: Walter Scott and the Origins of the Victorian Illustrated Book*. Burlington, VT: Ashgate, 2010. Print.

Hobbs, Anne Stevenson. *Beatrix Potter's Art*. London: Frederick Warne and Co., 1989. Print.

Hobbs, Anne Stevenson, and Joyce Irene Whalley. *Beatrix Potter: The V&A Collection*. London: The Victoria and Albert Museum and Frederick Warne and Co., 1985. Print.

Hodnett, Edward. *Five Centuries of English Book Illustration*. Aldershott, UK: Scolar Press, 1988. Print.

Hogarth, William. *The Rake's Progress*. ca. 1733–35. Eight paintings. Sir John Soames Museum, London. Oil on canvas.

Holme, Geoffrey. *British Book Illustration Yesterday and Today*. London: Studio Ltd., 1923. Print.

Hollington, Michael. *The Reception of Charles Dickens in Europe*. Vol. I. London: Bloomsbury, 2013. Print.

Homans, Margaret. "Dreaming of Children: Literalisation in *Jane Eyre* and *Wuthering Heights*." In *Jane Eyre: Contemporary Critical Essays*. Ed. Heather Glen. New York: St. Martin's Press, 1997. 147–67. Print.

Horace. "Art of Poetry." In *Horace for English Readers*. Transl. E. C. Wickham. Oxford: Oxford UP, 1903. 340–63. Print.

Houghton, Walter. *The Victorian Frame of Mind, 1830–1870*. New Haven: Yale UP, 1963. Print.

House, Madeline, and Graham Storey, eds. *Letters: Charles Dickens*. 10 vols. Oxford: Clarendon, 1965. Print.

Hughes, Kristine. *The Writer's Guide to Everyday Life in Regency and Victorian England from 1811–1901*. Cincinnati, Ohio: Writer's Digest Books, 1998. Print.

Hughes, Linda K., and Michael Lund. *The Victorian Serial*. Charlottesville: U of Virginia P, 1991. Print.

Interview with Charles Parkhurst, e-mail, 13 July 2016.

Interview with Francis Mosley, e-mail, 8 July 2015.

Interview with Simon Grennan, e-mail, 4 July 2015.

Jackson, Arlene M. *Illustration and the Novels of Thomas Hardy*. Totowa, NJ: Rowman and Littlefield, 1981. Print.

James, Henry. "The Art of Fiction." In *Partial Portraits*. 1888. London: Macmillan, 1899. 375–408. Print.

———. *Autobiography*. 1911. New York: Criterion Books, 1956. Print.

———. *Du Maurier and London Society*. London: Kessinger Publishing, 2004. Print.

———. "George Du Maurier." *Harper's New Monthly Magazine* 95 (Sept. 1897): 594–609. Print.

———. "George Du Maurier." *Harper's Weekly* 88 (14 Apr. 1894): 341–42. Print.

———. *The Golden Bowl*. 1904. New York: A. M. Kelley, 1971. Print.

———. *The Portrait of a Lady*. 1881. Ed. Jan Cohn. Boston: Houghton Mifflin, 2001. Print.

———. *A Small Boy and Others*. 1913. New York: Scribner, 1914. Print.

Johnson, Dan, adapt. *Oliver Twist*. By Charles Dickens. Artwork Rajesh Nagulakonda. Campfire. New Delhi, Ind.: Kalyani Navyug Media Pvt. Ltd., 2011. Print.

Jones, Bruce, adapt. *Batman: Through the Looking Glass*. Artwork Sam Keith. New York: DC Comics, 2011. Print.

Jones, William B., Jr. *Classics Illustrated: A Cultural History, With Illustrations*. Jefferson, NC: McFarland, 2002. Print.

Katz, Bill. *A History of Book Illustration: 29 Points of View*. Metuchen, NJ: Scarecrow Press, 1994. Print.

Kaufman, Richard Frederick. "The Relationship Between Text and Illustration in the Novels of Dickens, Thackeray, Trollope, and Hardy." Diss. New York University, 1979. Print.

Kelly, Richard. *George Du Maurier*. Boston: Twayne, 1983. Print.

———. "'If You Don't Know What a Gryphon Is': Text and Illustration in *Alice's Adventures in Wonderland*." In *Lewis Carroll: A Celebration*. Ed. Edward Guliano. New York: Crown Publishers, 1982. 62–74. Print.

Kerker, Milton. "Svengali, Another Byword in the Lexicon of Jewish Villainy." *Midstream: A Quarterly Jewish Review* (Nov./Dec. 2005): n. pag. Print. *Free Library*. 2005 Theodor Herzl Foundation. Web. 14 July 2015. <http://www.thefreelibrary.com/Svengali%2c+a nother+byword+in+the+Lexicon+of+Jewish+villainy.-a0139755626>.

Kick, Russ, ed. *The Graphic Canon, Vol. II: From "Kubla Khan" to the Brontë Sisters, to The Picture of Dorian Gray*. New York: Seven Stories Press, 2012. Print.

King, Andrew, and John Plunkett, eds. *Victorian Print Media: A Reader*. New York: Oxford UP, 2005. Print.

King, Stacy, adapt. *Pride and Prejudice*. By Jane Austen. Artwork Po-Tse. Manga Classics. Udon Entertainment in association with Morpheus Publishing Ltd. Richmond Hill, Ontario, Can.: Morpheus Publishing Ltd., 2014. Print.

Kinsley, James. Introd. to *The Posthumous Papers of the Pickwick Club*. Ed. James Kinsley. Illus. Robert Seymour and Hablot Knight Browne. New York: Oxford UP, 1986. vii–xv. Print.

Kooistra, Lorraine Janzen. *The Artist as Critic: Bitextuality in Fin-de-Siècle Illustrated Books*. Aldershot, UK: Scolar Press, 1995. Print.

———. *Christina Rossetti and Illustration: A Publishing History*. Athens: Ohio UP, 2002. Print.

———. *Poetry, Pictures, and Popular Publishing: The Illustrated Gift Book and Victorian Visual Culture, 1855–1875*. Athens: Ohio UP, 2011. Print.

Kunzle, David. *The History of the Comic Strip, Vol. II: The Nineteenth Century*. Berkeley and Los Angeles: U of California P, 1990. Print.

Landow, George P. "Social and Economic Forces Influencing *Pickwick's* Mass Readership." *The Victorian Web*. George P. Landow, editor-in-chief and webmaster. Web. 18 Sept. 2014. <http://www.victorianweb.org/authors/dickens/pickwick/patten.pw2.html>.

Lane, Lauriat, Jr. "Dickens' Archetypal Jew." *PMLA* 73.1 (March 1958): 94–100. Print.

Lane, Margaret. *The Magic Years of Beatrix Potter*. London: Frederick Warne and Co., 1978. Print.

Lear, Linda. *Beatrix Potter: A Life in Nature*. New York: St. Martin's Griffin, 2008. Print.

———. "Natural History: A Scientist's Eye." *Nature* 508 (24 Apr. 2014): 454–55. Print.

L'Estrange, A. G., ed. *The Life of Mary Russell Mitford*. Vol. 3. London: Richard Bentley, 1870. Print.

Leighton, Mary Elizabeth, and Lisa Surridge. "The Plot Thickens: Toward a Narratological Analysis of Illustrated Serial Fiction in the 1860s." *Victorian Studies* 51.1 (Autumn 2008): 65–101. Print.

Lessing, Gotthold Ephraim. *Laocoön*. 1766. London: G. Routledge and Sons, 1905. Print.

Linder, Leslie. *A History of the Writings of Beatrix Potter*. London: Frederick Warne and Co., 1979. Print.

———. *The Journal of Beatrix Potter from 1881–1897*. London: Frederick Warne and Co., Ltd., 1979. Print.

Linder, Leslie, and Enid Linder. *The Art of Beatrix Potter*. London: Frederick Warne and Co., 1985. Print.

Lister, T. H. "Dickens' 'Tales.'" *Edinburgh Review* 68.137 (Oct. 1838): 75–97. Included in *Nineteenth-Century Literature Criticism*. Ed. Laurie Lanzen Harris. New York: Gale Research Co., 1983. 138–40. Print.

Locker, Arthur. "Charles Dickens." *The Graphic* (18 June 1870): 687. Print.

Logan, Thad. *The Victorian Parlour: A Cultural Study*. Cambridge, UK: Cambridge UP, 2001. Print.

"London Census." Web. 22 Sept. 2014. <http://www.census1891.com/occupations-m.htm>.

Longfellow, Henry Wordsworth. *Evangeline*. 1847. Illus. F. O. C. Darley. Boston: Fields, Osgood, and Co., 1869. Print.

Lopes, Paul. *Demanding Respect: The Evolution of the American Comic Book*. Philadelphia: Temple UP, 2009. Print.

Lovell-Smith, Rose. "The Animals of Wonderland: Tenniel as Carroll's Reader." *Criticism* 45.4 (Fall 2003): 383–415. Print.

Macdonald, Fiona, adapt. *Jane Eyre*. By Charlotte Brontë. Artwork Penko Gelev. Hauppauge, NY: Barron's Educational Series, 2009. Print.

MacDonald, George. *At the Back of the North Wind*. Illus. Arthur Hughes. London: Strahan and Co., 1871. Print.

Maidment, Brian. *Comedy, Caricature and the Social Order, 1820–50*. Manchester, UK: Manchester UP, 2013. Print.

Masereel, Frans. *Passionate Journey: A Vision in Woodcuts*. 1919. New York: Dover, 2007. Print.

Maxwell, Richard. "Afterword: The Destruction, Rebirth, and Apotheosis of the Victorian Illustrated Book." In *The Victorian Illustrated Book*. Ed. Richard Maxwell. Charlottesville: UP of Virginia, 2002. 385–422. Print.

———, ed. *The Victorian Illustrated Book*. Charlottesville: UP of Virginia, 2002. Print.

———. "Walter Scott, Historical Fiction, and the Genesis of the Victorian Illustrated Book." In *The Victorian Illustrated Book*. Ed. Richard Maxwell. Charlottesville: UP of Virginia, 2002. 1–51. Print.

Mayhew, Henry. *London Labour and the London Poor*. 1851. London: Penguin, 1985. Print.

McCloud, Scott. *Understanding Comics: The Invisible Art*. New York: HarperCollins Publishers, 1993. Print.

McDonald, Louise. "Softening Svengali: Film Transformations of *Trilby* and Cultural Change." In *George Du Maurier: Illustrator, Author, Critic Beyond Svengali*. Ed. Simon Cooke and Paul Goldman. Surrey, UK and Burlington, VT: Ashgate Publishing Ltd., 2016. 231–41. Print.

McDowell, Marta. *Beatrix Potter's Gardening Life: The Plants and Places That Inspired the Classic Children's Tales*. Portland, OR: Timber Press, 2013. Print.

McFarland, Ronald E. *The Long Life of Evangeline: A History of the Longfellow Poem in Print, in Adaptation and in Popular Culture*. Jefferson, NC: McFarland and Co., 2010.

Meisel, Martin. *Realizations: Narrative, Pictorial, and Theatrical Arts in Nineteenth-Century England*. Princeton, NJ: Princeton UP, 1983. Print.

Meyer, Susan. "Antisemitism and Social Critique in Dickens's 'Oliver Twist.'" *Victorian Literature and Culture* 33.1 (2005): 239–52. Print.

Meyer, Susan E. *A Treasury of the Great Children's Book Illustrators*. New York: Harry N. Abrams, 1983. Print.

Meyers, Janet C. "Performing the Voyage Out: Emigration and the Class Dynamics of Displacement." *Victorian Literature and Culture* 29.1 (2001): 129–46. Print.

Meyrick, Robert. "'Spoils of the lumber-room': Early Collectors of Wood-Engraved Illustrations from 1860s Periodicals." In *Reading Victorian Illustration, 1855–1875: Spoils of the Lumber Room*. Ed. Paul Goldman and Simon Cooke. Surrey, UK: Ashgate Publishing Ltd., 2012. 179–99. Print.

Millais, John Everett, illus. *The Parables of Our Lord and Saviour Jesus Christ*. Engraved by the Brothers Dalziel. New York: Dover, 1975. Print.

Miller, C. C. Hoyar. *George Du Maurier and Others*. London: Cassell and Co., 1837. Print.

Mitchell, Sally. "Broadsides and Chapbooks." In *Victorian Britain: An Encyclopedia*. Ed. Sally Mitchell. New York: Garland, 1988. 94–95. Print.

———. *Daily Life in Victorian England*. Westport, CT: Greenwood, 1996. Print.

———, ed. *Victorian Britain: An Encyclopedia*. New York: Garland, 1988. Print.

Moore, Alan. *From Hell*. Artwork Eddie Campbell. Marietta, GA: Top Shelf Productions, 2004. Print.

———. *The League of Extraordinary Gentlemen*. 1999–2000. 2002–03. Artwork Kevin O'Neill. Compilation. New York: Vertigo, 2004. Print.

———. *Watchmen*. 1986. Artwork Dave Gibbons. New York: DC Comics, 2014. Print.

Moore, Leah, and John Reppion, adapts. *The Complete Alice in Wonderland*. By Lewis Carroll. Artwork Érica Awano. Runnemede, NJ: Dynamite Entertainment, 2009. Print.

Morris, Frankie. *Artist of Wonderland: The Life, Political Cartoons, and Illustrations of Tenniel*. Charlottesville: U of Virginia P, 2005. Print.

"Mr. Dickens's New Work—*Oliver Twist*." *The London and Paris Observer* 14 (1838): 758–61. Print.

Muir, Percy. *Victorian Illustrated Books*. 1971. Revised impression. London: Portman Books, 1985. Print.

Navasky, Victor S. *The Art of Controversy: Political Cartoons and Their Enduring Power*. New York: Alfred A. Knopf, 2014. Print.

"Oliver Twist." *Spectator* 11 (24 Nov. 1838): 1114–16. Print.

Orrinsmith, Lucy. *The Drawing-Room; Its Decorations and Furniture*. London: Macmillan, 1877. Print.

Ovenden, Graham, and John Davis, eds. *The Illustrators of Alice*. New York: St. Martin's Press, 1972. Print.

Patten, Robert L. *Charles Dickens and His Publishers*. Oxford: Oxford UP, 1978. Print.

———. *Charles Dickens and "Boz": The Birth of the Industrial-Age Author*. Cambridge: Cambridge UP, 2012. Print.

———, ed. *George Cruikshank: A Revaluation*. 1974. Princeton, NJ: Princeton UP, 1992. Print.

———. *George Cruikshank's Life, Times, and Art*. Vol. 2: 1835-1878. New Brunswick, NJ: Rutgers University Press, 1996. Print.

———. "Serial Illustration and Storytelling in *David Copperfield*." In *The Victorian Illustrated Book*. Ed. Richard Maxwell. Charlottesville: U of Virginia P, 2002. 91–128. Print.

Pease, Donald E., ed. *Revisionary Interventions into the Americanist Canon*. Durham, NC: Duke UP, 1994. Print.

Pennell, Joseph. *Modern Illustration*. London: Bell, 1895. Print.

Pina, Stephanie Graham. "Pre-Raphaelite Sisterhood." Web. 23 July 2015. <http://preraphaelitesisterhood.com/the-maids-of-elfin-mere/>.

Pipe, Jim, adapt. *Wuthering Heights*. By Emily Brontë. Artwork Nick Spender. Hauppauge, NY: Barron's Educational Series, 2009. Print.

Plato. "Phaedrus." *The Dialogues of Plato, vol. 1, translated into English with Analyses and Intro-*

ductions by B. Jowett, M.A. in Five Volumes. 3rd ed. rev. and corrected. Transl. Benjamin Jowett. London: Oxford UP, 1892. 391–490. Print.

Porter, G. R. The Progress of the Nation. London: John Murray, 1847. Print.

Potter, Beatrix. The Tale of Benjamin Bunny. 1904. Illus. by the author. London: Penguin, 1989. Print.

———. The Tale of Mr. Jeremy Fisher. 1906. Illus. by the author. London: Penguin, 1989. Print.

———. The Tale of Mrs. Tiggy-Winkle. 1905. Illus. by the author. London: Penguin, 1989. Print.

———. The Tale of Peter Rabbit. 1902. Illus. by the author. London: Penguin, 1989. Print.

———. The Tale of Squirrel Nutkin. 1903. Illus. by the author. London: Penguin, 1989. Print.

"The Posthumous Papers of the Pickwick Club, No. 2." The Satirist (1 May 1836): 138. Print.

Price, Leah. How to Do Things with Books in Victorian Britain. Princeton, NJ: Princeton UP, 2012. Print.

Prideaux, William Francis. A Bibliography of the Works of Robert Louis Stevenson. London: Frank Hollings, 1917. Print.

Purcell, Edward L. "Trilby and Trilby-Mania, The Beginning of the Best Seller System." The Journal of Popular Culture 11.1 (Summer 1977): 62–76. Print.

Reed, Sue W. "F. O. C. Darley's Outline Illustrations." In The American Illustrated Book in the Nineteenth Century. Ed. Gerald W. R. Ward. Charlottesville: UP of Virginia, 2002. 113–35. Print.

Reid, Forrest. Illustrators of the Eighteen Sixties: An Illustrated Survey of the Work of 58 British Artists. 1928. New York: Dover Publications, Inc., 1975. Print.

Review of Wonderland. London Review (29 Dec. 1866). Print.

Rigby, Elizabeth. Review of Vanity Fair: A Novel Without a Hero. The Quarterly Review (Dec. 1848): 153–62. Print.

Rosenberg, Edgar. From Shylock to Svengali: Jewish Stereotypes in English Fiction. Stanford: Stanford UP, 1960. Print.

Rossetti, Christina. Goblin Market and Other Poems. Illus. Dante Gabriel Rossetti. London: Macmillan, 1862. Print.

Ruskin, John. Art of Old England: Lectures Given in Oxford. 1884. New York: United States Book Co., 1889. Print.

———. The Elements of Drawing: In Three Letters to Beginners. London: Smith, Elder, and Co., 1857. Print.

———. Sesame and Lilies. 1865. New York: John B. Alden, Publisher, 1885. Print.

Sach, Laurence, adapt. Pride and Prejudice: The Graphic Novel. Original Text. By Jane Austen. Artwork Rajesh Nagulakonda. Campfire. New Delhi, Ind.: Kalyani Navyug Media Pvt. Ltd., 2013. Print.

Sarzano, Frances. Sir John Tenniel. New York: Pelligrini and Cudahy, n.d. Print.

Seymour, Robert. Sketches by Seymour. 5 vols. London: G. S. Tregear, 1835. Print.

Shepard, Ernest H. Drawn from Memory. London: Curtis Brown Ltd., 1957. Print.

Sherard, Robert. "The Author of 'Trilby.'" The Westminster Budget (13 Dec. 1895): 21–25. Print.

Showalter, Elaine. A Literature of Their Own. Princeton, NJ: Princeton UP, 1998. Print.

Siemens, Lloyd. "Annuals and Gift Books." In Victorian Britain: An Encyclopedia. Ed. Sally Mitchell. New York: Garland, 1988. 27. Print.

Simon, Leslie. "Archives of the Interior: Exhibitions of Domesticity in *The Pickwick Papers*." *Dickens Quarterly* 25.1 (March 2008): 23–36. Print.

Sitwell, Sacheverell. *Narrative Pictures: A Survey of English Genre and its Painters*. London: B. T. Batsford, 1937. Print.

Soloway, Richard A. "Population and Demographics." In *Victorian Britain: An Encyclopedia*. Ed. Sally Mitchell. New York: Garland, 1988. 617–18. Print.

Spiegelman, Art. *Maus I: A Survivor's Tale: My Father Bleeds History*. Artwork by the author. New York: Pantheon, 1986. Print.

Spilka, Mark. "On the Enrichment of Poor Monkeys by Myth and Dream; or, How Dickens Rousseauisticized and Pre-Freudianized Victorian Views of Childhood." In *Sexuality and Victorian Literature*. Ed. Don Richard Cox. Knoxville, TN: U of T Press, 1984. 161–79. Print.

Steig, Michael. *Dickens and Phiz*. Bloomington: Indiana UP, 1978. Print.

———. "Dickens, Hablôt Browne, and the Tradition of English Caricature." *Criticism* 11.3 (Summer 1969): 219–33. Print.

Stern, Madeleine, ed. *Critical Essays on Louisa May Alcott*. Boston: G. K. Hall, 1984. Print.

Stevens, Joan. "Thackeray's Pictorial Capitals." *Costerus* 2 (1974): 113–40. Print.

Stevenson, Robert Louis. *Treasure Island*. 1883. Introd. R. H. W. Dillard. New York: Signet, 1998. Print.

Stewart, Garrett. "Reading Figures: The Legible Image of Victorian Textuality." In *Victorian Literature and the Victorian Visual Imagination*. Ed. Carol T. Christ and John O. Jordan. Berkeley and Los Angeles: U of California P, 1995. 345–67. Print.

Stone, Harry. *Dickens' Working Notes for His Novels*. Chicago: Chicago UP, 1987. Print.

Stout, Janis P. "The Observant Eye, the Art of Illustration, and Willa Cather's *My Ántonia*." *Cather Studies*, Vol. 5. Web. 2 July 2013. <http://cather.unl.edu/cs005_stout.html>.

Surtees, Robert. *"Ask Mama"; or, The Richest Commoner in England*. Illus. John Leech. London: Bradbury and Evans, 1858. Print.

———. *Handley Cross; or, Mr. Jorrocks's Hunt*. Illus. John Leech. London: Bradbury and Evans, 1854. Print.

———. *"Plain or Ringlets?"* Illus. John Leech. London: Bradbury and Evans, 1860. Print.

Sutherland, John. "Does Becky Kill Jos?" In *Is Heathcliff a Murderer?: Puzzles in Nineteenth-Century Fiction*. New York: Oxford UP, 1996. 66–72. Print.

———. "Rochester's Celestial Telegram." In *Is Heathcliff a Murderer?: Puzzles in Nineteenth-Century Fiction*. New York: Oxford UP, 1996. 59–65. Print.

Tabachnick, Stephen E. "The Graphic Novel and the Age of Transition: A Survey and Analysis." *English Literature in Transition* 53.1 (2010): 3–28. Print.

———, ed. *Teaching the Graphic Novel*. New York: MLA, 2009. Print.

Taylor, Judy. *Beatrix Potter: Artist, Storyteller and Countrywoman*. London: Frederick Warne and Co., 1986. Print.

Tennyson, Alfred Lord. *Poems*. London: Moxon, 1857. Print.

Terry, R. C. Introd. to *John Caldigate*. By Anthony Trollope. London: Folio Society, 1995. xi–xviii. Print.

Thackeray, William Makepeace. *An Essay On the Genius of George Cruikshank*. London: Henry Hooper, 1840. Print.

———. *The History of Henry Esmond*. 1852. Illus. George Du Maurier. London: J. M. Dent and Co; New York: E. P. Dutton and Co., 1906. Print.

———. *The Newcomes, Memoirs of a Most Respectable Family*. Ed. A. Pendennis, Esq, pseud. Illus. Richard Doyle. 2 vols. London: Bradbury and Evans, 1854, 1855. Print.

———. *The Paris Sketch Book of Mr. M. A. Titmarsh*. 1840. Illus. by the author. New York: Charles Scribner's Sons, 1904. Print.

———. *The Rose and the Ring*. 1855. Illus. by the author. New York: Pierpont Morgan Library, 1947. Print.

———. *Vanity Fair: A Novel Without a Hero*. 1848. Illus. by the author. 3 vols. New York: Charles Scribner's Sons, 1903. Print.

———. *Vanity Fair: A Novel Without a Hero*. Ed. John Sutherland. Introd. John Sutherland. Illus. and pref. by the author. Oxford: Oxford UP, 1983. Print.

———. *The Virginians: A Tale of the Last Century*. Illus. by the author. 2 vols. London: Bradbury and Evans, 1858, 1859. Print.

Thomas, Deborah A. "Thackeray, Capital Punishment, and the Demise of Jos Sedley." *Victorian Literature and Culture* 33.1 (2005): 1–20. Print.

Thomas, Roy, adapt. *The Picture of Dorian Gray*. By Oscar Wilde. Artwork Sebastian Fiumara. New York: Marvel, 2008. Print.

Trollope, Anthony. *John Caldigate*. 1879. Introd. R. C. Terry. Illus. Francis Mosley. London: Folio Society, 1995. Print.

———. *Kept in the Dark*. 1882. Illus. John Everett Millais. New York: Dover, 1978. Print.

———. *Orley Farm*. 1862. Illus. John Everett Millais. New York: Dover, 1981. Print.

———. *Rachel Ray*. 1863. Illus. John Everett Millais. New York: Oxford UP, 2009. Print.

———. *The Small House at Allington*. 1864. Illus. John Everett Millais. New York: Penguin, 1991. Print.

Twain, Mark. *Adventures of Huckleberry Finn*. 1885. Ed. Shelley Fisher Fishkin. Illus. E. W. Kemble. New York: Oxford UP, 1996. Print.

———. *The Adventures of Tom Sawyer*. 1876. Ed. Shelley Fisher Fishkin. Illus. True Williams. New York: Oxford UP, 1996. Print.

Van Ghent, Dorothy. "On Pride and Prejudice." In *The English Novel, Form and Function*. New York: Holt Rinehart and Winston, 1953. 105–23. Print.

Van Ness, Sara J. *Watchmen as Literature: A Critical Study of the Graphic Novel*. Jefferson, NC: McFarland and Co., Inc., 2010. Print.

"Vanity Fair—A Novel Without a Hero." *The North American Review* 100.207 (Apr. 1865): 626. Print.

Varnum, Robin, and Christina Gibbons. *The Language of Comics: Word and Image*. Jackson: UP of Mississippi, 2007. Print.

Vaughn, John. "Victorian Children in Their Picture Books." In *A History of Book Illustration: 29 Points of View*. Ed. Bill Katz. Metuchen, NJ: Scarecrow Press, 1994. 618–25. Print.

Veblen, Thorstein. *The Theory of the Leisure Class: An Economic Study of Institutions*. 1899. New York: Macmillan, 2012. Web. 18 Dec. 2014. <http://books.google.com/books?id=2kAoAAAAYAAJ&printsec=frontcover&source=gbs_ge_summary_r&cad=0#v=onepage&q&f=false>.

Versaci, Rocco. *The Book Contains Graphic Language: Comics as Literature*. New York: Continuum, 2007. Print.

Victoria, Queen. "Diaries 1838–9." In *Dickens: The Critical Heritage*. Ed. Philip Collins. London: Routledge and Kegan Paul, 1971. 44. Print.

The Victorian Web. George P. Landow, editor-in-chief and webmaster. Web. 1 May 2012–9 Jan. 2015.

Vogler, Richard. *The Graphic Works of George Cruikshank*. New York: Dover Publications, 1979. Print.

Vorachek, Laura. "Mesmerists and Other Meddlers: Social Darwinism, Degeneration, and Eugenics in *Trilby*." *Victorian Literature and Culture* 37.1 (2009): 197–215. Print.

Ward, David. "First Library of the People Marks 150 Busy Years." *The Guardian*, 17 Sept. 2002. Web. 14 July 2015. <http://www.theguardian.com/uk/2002/sep/17/books.education>.

Ward, Gerald W. R., ed. *The American Illustrated Book in the Nineteenth Century*. Charlottesville: UP of Virginia, 2002. Print.

Ward, Lynd. *God's Man*. New York: Cape and Smith, 1929. Print.

Weatherwax, Annie. "Graphic Lit 'The Graphic Canon,' Edited by Russ Kick." *The New York Times*. Sunday Book Review. Web. 30 Nov. 2012. <http://www.nytimes.com/2012/12/02/books/review/the-graphic-canon-edited-by-russ-kick.html?_r=0>.

Weiner, Stephen. *Faster Than a Speeding Bullet: The Rise of the Graphic Novel*. Introd. Will Eisner. New York: Nantier Beall Minoustchine, 2003. Print.

Weitenkampf, Franz. *The Illustrated Book*. Boston: Harvard UP, 1938. Print.

White, Gleeson. *English Illustration, 'The Sixties': 1855–70*. 1897. Bath, UK: Kingsmead Reprints, 1970. Print.

Williams, Andy. "Advertising and Fiction in *The Pickwick Papers*." *Victorian Literature and Culture* 38 (2010): 319–35. Print.

Wilson, A. N. *The Victorians*. New York and London: Norton, 2003. Print.

Wilson, Edmund. *A Piece of My Mind*. New York: Farrar, Straus and Cudahy, 1956. Print.

Wilson, Seán Michael, adapt. *A Christmas Carol: The Graphic Novel*. Original Text. By Charles Dickens. Artwork Mike Collins. Birmingham, UK: Classical Comics, Ltd., 2008. Print.

———, adapt. *Wuthering Heights: The Graphic Novel*. Original Text. By Emily Brontë. Artwork John M. Burns. Litchborough, UK: Classical Comics, Ltd., 2011. Print.

Yoe, Craig, ed. *Alice in Comicland*. Introd. Mark Burstein. San Diego: IDW Publishing, 2014. Print.

Zemka, Sue. "The Death of Nancy 'Sikes,' 1838–1912." *Representations* 110.1 (Spring 2010): 29–57. Print.

Index

Page numbers in *italics* refer to illustrations.

Helsinger, Elizabeth, 7, 100, 102, 104, 250n22
Henty, G. E., 162
Herkomer, Hubert von, 160
Hicks, George Elgar: artist of contemporary life, 126;
    General Post Office, One Minute to Six, 126, 137
High Victorian era, 1–2
Hill, Jonathan, 51, 242n2
Hill, Richard, 20
History of Book Illustration, A (Bland), 4, 161,
    256nn15–16
History of the Comic Strip, Vol. II, The: The Nine-
    teenth Century (Kunzle), 5
History of the Illustrated Book, The: The Western
    Tradition (Harthan), 4
History of the Writings of Beatrix Potter (Linder), 170
Hobbs, Anne, 167, 257n26, 258n32, 259n41
Hogarth, Catherine, 28, 238n12
Hogarth, William: graphic satire and caricature, 15,
    40, 50, 66, 188, 266n44; heirs (Gillray, Rowland-
    son, Cruikshank), 15–16, 24–25, 246n40, 247n55,
    251n35; importance of, 5, 7–8, 15, 16, 24–25, 40,
    188, 241n48, 262nn12–13; Industry and Idleness,
    243n9; Marriage à la Mode, 15; influence on
    Ainsworth and Cruikshank, 243n9; The Rake's
    Progress, 15, 25, 262n12
Horace, 11–12
Houghton, Walter, 239n22
Household Edition of Dickens: Academy-trained
    artists, 3, 92, 121, 235n5, 252–53nn46, 253n47–
    48; Barnard as illustrator of David Copperfield,
    94, 124–31, 125, 129; Mahoney as illustrator of
    Oliver Twist, 53, 94, 131–39, 133, 135, 138, 216,
    218, 221; popularity of, 2; publication formats,
    2, 122
Household Gods (Cohen), 235n2
Housman, Laurence, 250n27
Hughes, Arthur, 104, 114, 163, 250n25
Hughes, Linda K., 152–53
Hunt, William Holman, 110, 114, 172, 251n34

IDW, 266n46
Illustrated Book, The (Weitenkampf), 4
Illustrated London News, The, 39, 122, 131–32
"Illustrating of Books from the Serious Artist's
    Point of View, I and II, The" (Du Maurier), 50,
    110, 112, 150, 154, 159, 172–73, 187, 188
illustration: author-illustrator, 6, 7, 9–10, 52, 154,
    162–63, 172, 187, 256n19; caricature-style, 2–4,
    9–10, 16, 35, 50–51, 88, 92, 93, 102, 242n1; defini-
    tions of, 21–22; fin-de-siècle developments,

150–51, 159–64, 235–36n6; history prior to 1830s,
    11–17; realism, 93–94, 111, 121–22
Illustrators of the Eighteen-Sixties (Reid), 4–5, 101,
    105, 116, 140, 247n4, 254n61
Industrial Revolution, 31–32, 36–37
Ingelow, Jean, 18, 111

Jack Sheppard (Ainsworth): bestseller, 53, 243n13;
    biography of Sheppard, 54, 243nn8–9, 244n17,
    244n19; Cruikshank's illustrations in, 52–55, 55,
    85; Newgate novel, 52–53, 243n7; Oliver Twist
    and, 52–53, 240n43, 242–43n6; serialization of,
    52, 242n4; theatrical adaptations, 2, 53, 243n14
Jackson, Arlene, 2, 111, 150, 159, 235–36n6, 258n27
James, Henry: "The Art of Fiction," 155; on Crui-
    kshank, 154; on Du Maurier, 116, 174, 251n37,
    259n47; photographic frontispieces and, 158; The
    Portrait of a Lady, 1; A Small Boy and Others, 91;
    view of book illustration, 154–55
Jane Eyre (C. Brontë): Eichenberg's illustrations,
    261n6; graphic novel adaptation, 195–96; source
    text, 15, 245n29, 249n18, 261n6
John Caldigate (Trollope): connection to
    Barnaby Rudge, 206–07; graphic novel adapta-
    tion (Dispossession), 189, 203–08; illustrations by
    Grennan, 205–08, 208; illustrations by Mosley,
    204–05; plot of, 204–06, 265n37
Johnson, Dan, 217–2, 267n48, 267n52
Johnson, E. Borough, 160

Kane, Bob, 202
Kanter, Albert Lewis: biography of, 189, 263n17;
    Classics Illustrated, 189. See also Classics Il-
    lustrated
Kaufman, Richard Frederick, 5–6
Kelly, Richard: on Carroll, 254n65; on Du Maurier,
    174, 179–80, 183–84, 236n15, 247n49, 255n8,
    259n51, 260nn58–59
Kelmscott Press, 14, 160–61
Kemble, E. W., 163, 164
Kerker, Milton, 175, 179, 182, 259n53
Kick, Russ, 190, 261n1
Kieth, Sam, 201
King, Stacy, 191
Kipling, Rudyard, 154, 162, 163, 256n19, 267n47
Knight, Charles, 37–38
Kooistra, Lorraine Janzen: The Artist as Critic, 159;
    Christina Rossetti and Illustration, 107, 250n28,
    251n30, 251n31, 251n33; Poetry, Pictures, and Popu-
    lar Publishing, 1, 17, 18, 235n3

Wilkie, David, 51

William IV (King of England), 95

Williams, True, 163, 164

Wilson, A. N., 30–31, 35, 38, 236n13, 239n20, 239n26, 240n37, 247n53

Wilson, Edmund, 260n56

Wilson, Seán Michael, 195–96, 197, 199

Wives and Daughters (Gaskell), 133, 216

woodblock, 36, 239n32

Woolf, Virginia, 155–56

Wordsworth, William, 18

"Work of Art in the Age of Mechanical Reproduction, The" (Benjamin), 18, 37, 160, 240n36, 250n22

writing desk: commodity culture, 158; in *David Copperfield*, 130; indications of class and gender, 265n11; mass production of, 158

Wuthering Heights (E. Brontë): Barron's adaptation of, 195, 264n30; Classical Comics adaptation of, 196–97, *198*; source text, 196–97, 265n33

Wyeth, N. C., 163, 256n13

xylographica, 14

Yellow Book, The, 160

Yoe, Craig, 224, 225

Yonge, Charlotte Mary, 162

Zemka, Sue, 53

CATHERINE J. GOLDEN, professor of English and the Tisch Chair in Arts and Letters at Skidmore College, is author of numerous books, including *Posting It: The Victorian Revolution in Letter Writing* and *Images of the Woman Reader in Victorian British and American Fiction*. She is also the editor or coeditor of five additional books on topics ranging from Charlotte Perkins Gilman to Victorian illustration, literature, and culture.